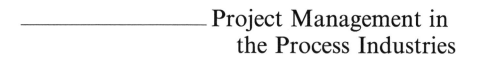

Project Management in
the Process Industries

Roy Whittaker has had over thirty years' experience as a project manager with extensive specialised knowledge of project management within the chemical industry.

Employed by ICI between 1955 and 1992, he has spent periods in maintenance, construction and the development of computer-aided design. But most of his time has been spent dealing with new capital investment in chemical plant and power stations as design engineer, project engineer, project manager and project group manager. He was responsible for some of ICI's largest projects in the UK and overseas. He has lectured widely including at Durham University Business School and as Honorary Visiting Fellow in Project Management at Cranfield University School of Management.

Roy Whittaker is currently an independent consultant in project management.

Project Management in the Process Industries

Roy Whittaker

JOHN WILEY & SONS
Chichester · New York · Brisbane · Toronto · Singapore

Other Wiley Editorial Offices

John Wiley & Sons, Inc., 605 Third Avenue,
New York, NY 10158–0012, USA

Jacaranda Wiley Ltd, 33 Park Road, Milton,
Queensland 4064, Australia

John Wiley & Sons (Canada) Ltd, 22 Worcester Road,
Rexdale, Ontario M9W 1L1, Canada

John Wiley & Sons (SEA) Pte Ltd, 37 Jalan Pemimpin #05-04,
Block B, Union Industrial Building, Singapore 2057

Library of Congress Cataloging-in-Publication Data

Whittaker, Roy.
    Project management in the process industries / Roy Whittaker.
        p.   cm.
    Includes bibliographical references and index.
    ISBN 0-471-96040-3
    1. Industrial project management.   2. Contracts.   I. Title.
HD69.P75W49   1995   95-9103
658.4′04–dc20   CIP

British Library Cataloguing in Publication Data

A catalogue record for this book is available from the British Library

ISBN 0-471-96040-3

Typeset in 10/12pt Times by Dobbie Typesetting Ltd, Tavistock, Devon
Printed and bound in Great Britain by Biddles Ltd, Guildford

This book is printed on acid-free paper responsibly manufactured from sustainable forestation, for
which at least two trees are planted for each one used for paper production.

Contents

Contents _____ vii

Foreword

The petrochemical industry, and to a lesser extent, the chemical industry as a whole, is the product of the years following the Second World War. The same period has seen the development of the role of the project manager. This book addresses the role of the employer's, or owner's, project manager in the process industries, the main components of which are taken to be the petrochemical, chemical, and oil-refining industries. Major projects in these industries are nowadays usually executed with the assistance of process plant contractors. This method of project execution is therefore assumed in this book, which contains much about the selection and employment of contractors, but less about the direct execution of design and construction than would have been the case had these functions been taken as being performed directly by the employer.

The book is primarily concerned with the direct contribution of the employer's project manager—with those activities which he performs himself or controls directly—rather than with the complete task facing his project team. It tries to avoid banausic detail and assumes familiarity with the basic techniques which a project manager will deploy, such as critical path scheduling and cost monitoring. Since it is concerned with the management of major projects, it assumes the presence in the project team of an engineering design manager as well as a construction manager, and therefore does not treat the subjects of design and construction in depth. It attempts to provide a sufficient description of various stages of the project without becoming, as it so easily could, overloaded with check-lists. The book is written from the point of view of the sophisticated employer who wishes to maintain some control of events and is ready to shoulder the responsibility which that entails. The employer is assumed to have previous experience of capital investment in the process industries and to understand, indeed, to have on occasion been directly responsible for, the engineering design and construction process.

Years ago, when new books on programming languages seemed to be published daily, it was said that the only qualification required of the author was to have written at least one program and to have a wife and a secretary to whom the book could be dedicated—the former for her patience and sympathetic understanding, the latter for her patient typing and re-typing of the manuscript. The illegibility of the latter seemed a matter of some pride for the author. This was in the days before word processors and, as George V might have said had he been alive today, we are all typists now. While new books on project management have never been so common as those on FORTRAN, a further effusion perhaps needs some justification. In defence of the present volume, the author can plead over thirty years' experience as a project manager and the observation that books on the subject have seldom been written by practising project managers. Few engineers and, it seems, even fewer project managers, commit their experience to paper at any length. Perhaps they have better things to do—who would write a book when they could manage a project? It is characteristic of engineers to value deeds above words.

One cannot spend a lifetime in industry, or one supposes in any other walk of life, without observing the same mistakes repeated at depressingly frequent intervals. While all need, and must be allowed, to make their own mistakes, ideally these would be new ones rather than mere repeats of past errors. However, a certain amount of re-invention of the wheel seems unavoidable. 'Si jeunesse savoit, si vieillesse pouvoit'—if the young knew, if the old could—as wrote Henri Estienne in the 16th Century. This follows perhaps as much from failure on the part of those with the knowledge to pass it on to their less-experienced colleagues as from the wilfulness of youth. More years ago than I care to remember, I spent seven years at university in engineering study and research without once being addressed by a practising engineer. Things have changed since then, but it is the memory of that particular omission that has led me, over the years, to try and contribute to the education and training of engineers and which is perhaps the fundamental trigger for this book.

As a project manager, I make no claim to be expert on anything, but to be a generalist—a jack of all trades. It helps if at some stage in a project manager's career he has been expert on something, if only to convince him that an expert does not always know everything, or occasionally even very much, about his subject—just more than anyone else available. Such value as this book has results from the author's experience of project management in the chemical industry and is offered in the hope that it will be of assistance to practising project managers. It is of course merely one man's view. In historical linguistics it is sometimes customary to precede a reconstructed word with an asterisk, to distinguish what is guessed, however plausibly, from what is known for certain. If this useful typographical convention were to be employed in this book— indeed, perhaps in most books on management subjects—the text would be littered with asterisks.

Naturally, over a lifetime's career, one incurs many debts towards friends and colleagues at all levels who have assisted one's efforts and contributed to

one's education. They are far too many to enumerate. In any case, as H. G. Wells put it, one hesitates between acknowledging one's obligations and implicating one's friends. They will know who they are and will, it is hoped, accept this general message of gratitude for their help and support over the years.

Chapter 1

Introduction

This book is concerned with the project management of process plant projects—the management of the design and construction of new process plants. It is written from the point of view of the process operating company (for simplicity, and despite the prolepsis this involves before contract award, referred to throughout as the 'employer') and is concerned primarily with major projects. Since inflation rapidly outdates any definition by monetary value, a major project is here taken to be one which requires upwards of about half a million man-hours of design or 2 million man-hours of construction. The book assumes the employment of engineering contractors to execute most of the work, since few operating companies now maintain the resources necessary to perform all this themselves. Some knowledge and experience on the part of the reader, if not of project management itself, at least of working in a project team and of project control techniques, is also assumed.

A major manufacturing company in the process industries requires constantly to renew its capital base. To such a company, capital investment is not merely an occasional necessity—to build a new office block when the existing one no longer provides satisfactory accommodation, or to construct a new fabrication yard every twenty years. To stay in business it needs to invest frequently in new plants and continuously to update and improve its existing facilities. The working life of a process plant probably averages less than twenty years, but the manufacturing company may make its investment decisions on a conservative assumption of around ten years. The capital investment process is thus not just an occasional venture, but an important and continuing part of the process manufacturer's business, and the management and technical resources devoted to development of the business in this way—research, marketing and economic studies, process development and design, engineering design and construction, commissioning—may well exceed those applied to existing operations.

The chemical industry has matured in little more than the working lifetime of some of those still engaged in it. Less than fifty years ago, it was enough simply to be able to operate some processes. As Dr Johnson might have remarked in the circumstances, they may not have operated well, but one was surprised to see them operate at all. The rare company that could synthesise ammonia, for example, had no difficulty in using it profitably. There was little competition either on a national or international level, the latter being restricted by the operation of cartels as well as by the difficulties and costs of transport. As the industry matured and competition intensified with the advent of new entrants—in heavy chemicals often subsidised by emerging states—price became important. It was no longer enough merely to be capable of making a product, manufacture had also to be efficient. The need to respond to much greater competition affected the design and construction of plants as well as their operation and, combined with ever-increasing sophistication and demands for higher standards of safety, prompted developments in the organisation of project execution and the concepts of project management.

Process plants may be defined as those which change bulk materials chemically or physically, or both. They contain a number of process equipment items which are supported in structures, linked by pipework and controlled by instrumentation. They require auxiliary mechanical and electrical equipment, including prime movers of various kinds, and they also involve civil engineering works such as foundations, buildings, access roads, water supply and drainage. Supporting facilities, for example, steam and power generation, feedstock and product storage, effluent treatment, are often extensive. Hazardous materials are frequently handled and safety is a prime consideration. Operation, which is more often than not continuous, needs to be reliable, and the plants convenient to maintain. Performance criteria, such as the output, quality, yield and production efficiency of products, the production of by-products and effluents, and the consumption of utilities, are usually closely specified.

In a project for the design and construction of a process plant, many types of activity are involved. These may include evaluation and development of processes, chemical engineering or process design, detailed engineering in civil, electrical, mechanical and control disciplines, metallurgical investigations, supply of plant and equipment, site investigation, construction, commissioning and testing. These activities comprise most of what may be called the execution phase of the project. Prior to this, there is often many years' work carried out by the process manufacturer in product and process research and development, market assessment, project analysis and evaluation, and the acquiring of the necessary finance. Production and sale of product, the ultimate purpose of the whole series of activities, follows the execution phase of the project.

This book deals with the execution phase of a process plant project and the problems of managing it. The project manager responsible for project execution may be involved in both the earlier and later stages but in a supporting role, and these stages will not be discussed other than in passing. The book is concerned with major projects and, since few process manufacturers today have the resources to execute these entirely by themselves, with the employment of process engineering contractors. The use of contractors does not affect the employer's project manager's ultimate responsibility, but does distance him from much of the day-to-day work and gives further emphasis to the importance of his contribution in the early stages of the project. In any major project, probably the most important part of the project manager's role is in setting it up correctly—securing satisfactory scope definition, an appropriate project team organisation, suitable contracts and so on—and this emphasis is naturally reinforced where the responsibility for performing major aspects of project execution are to be contracted to others. The book reflects this balance in its bias towards the initial aspects of project execution.

Project management has much in common with general management, but there are differences arising mainly from the discontinuous nature of projects. More often than the general manager, the project manager is faced with novel and transient problems. He cannot establish a method of working for his project which he can continually refine and improve over the years. He must decide how something should be organised and has usually to live with the results, for good or ill, for the duration of the project. Prior experience is thus more than usually desirable, since the opportunity to learn and apply the lessons to the current project, as opposed to the next, is restricted. On the other hand, the project manager is much less the prisoner of history. Each project gives at least something of a new start, untrammelled by the past. It is this need, and indeed the opportunity, continually to tackle fresh problems and to establish new, temporary organisations and methods of working that most distinguishes project from general management.

It is important also to distinguish between project management and project engineering, especially since for smaller projects the roles of project manager and project engineer are often combined. Major projects, with which we are concerned here, warrant a full-time project manager and, usually, several project engineers. Project management is then the direction and co-ordination of all the functions that are involved in the realisation of a process plant. Project engineering, which is discussed here only in passing, is the performance of part of the technical work of project execution, primarily design. The ambit of the job of the project engineer varies with the organisation concerned, but commonly includes the development of the layout and engineering line diagrams for the plant, together with supervision and co-ordination of the work of specialist design sections.

The work of a project manager is exposed to public scrutiny to an extent unusual at his level in the organisation. His objectives are defined in the documents authorising the expenditure on the project and these are widely known—much more widely than would be those of his colleagues in general management, even where such clear objectives existed. He takes the blame for failure and the credit for success, though his real contribution is, like that of any senior manager, often difficult to assess. Perhaps only the manager himself, and then only if he is both unusually perceptive and unusually honest, can really know his own value. After the battle of Tannenburg, the rumour grew that the victory was not that of the commander-in-chief, Hindenburg, but more properly belonged to his second-in-command, Ludendorff. Then it was said that the plan for the battle was the brain-child of the chief of staff Hoffman, to whom the real credit should be given. When this was put to Hindenburg, he replied to the effect that while responsibility for the victory might be difficult to assign, there would have been no doubt who would have been responsible had the battle been lost. However, the British have always admired a gallant failure—Waterloo is used as a metaphor for defeat, not victory—and have been as much concerned with style as with results—in the pantheon of national heroes, Scott is much more prominent than Shackleton. It would be misleading to suggest that in the UK a project manager will always be judged entirely on project performance.

In retrospect, decisions correctly made look either obvious or inevitable, usually both, where they can be identified at all. Incorrect decisions often appear, with hindsight, as the most appalling gaffes. As Samuel Goldwyn is alleged to have remarked 'With hindsight, I could have predicted that'. At the time of making the decision, the project manager may have been provided with a mass of contradictory data, most of it since discredited but all at the time of seemingly equal validity. Sometimes the need to make any decision at all will be unrecognised. It is a sound rule that the more important the decision, the more sparse and unreliable will be the data on which to base it. Perhaps the project manager's education is nearing completion when he correctly foresees a future problem, makes all the right dispositions to deal with it and still runs into trouble; or when he repeats a previously successful strategy only to see it fail. Projects are characterised by the presence of numerous variables, not all of which are evident and of which only a selection may be important at any instant. Success follows from identifying and controlling those variables which are important at the time. One is reminded of the economics professor, chided for setting the same examination questions each year so that the students would surely have both questions and answers memorised. He replied that this would not do them much good because, although the questions might remain the same, the answers changed continually.

An experienced employer's project manager should not be a mere functionary to do what he is told. He should have considerable independence to execute his project in the way he thinks best. He must identify the requirements and ensure that they are satisfied. He must make certain that the project is properly defined and costed, that all the implications are understood and the necessary resources to hand, and that execution does not begin until adequate definition of what is required is available. At the beginning, at least, he must not regard himself as being wholly in the clutch of circumstance; he must be a moulder of events. At the beginning he has more control than will be available at any later stage and he can lay the foundations for success or irretrievably damage the project's chances. The project manager cannot guarantee success by his actions, but he can ensure failure. And it should be said that project management can be a most rewarding activity. Like many other engineers, the project manager has the great satisfaction of seeing his efforts physically realised.

Chapter 2

Role and Organisation

2.1 THE ROLE OF THE PROJECT MANAGER

A process plant project is part of a business whose purpose is the manufacture and sale of product at a profit: so much is obvious. The project is partially separated from that business because by so doing, it is judged that more effective use of resources will be achieved. It is considered that, by having staff who specialise, to a greater or lesser extent, in project work, there are advantages to be gained which outweigh any disadvantages that may arise from the separation. It is necessary to guard against the latter: one of the first duties of the employer's project manager is to make sure that he does not lose sight of the requirements of the business he serves and for the benefit of which his project was conceived. But as well as being an executive of the business, he has a professional duty as a project manager. It is his responsibility to ensure that the forecasts of capital cost, programme and performance are sensible and that they are achieved. Success requires a clear and thoroughly understood basis for the project, defined in detail with accuracy and certainty. To ensure this, the project manager may sometimes have to step outside his own field and query, and perhaps refuse to accept as a basis for proceeding, the work of others.

A simplified illustration of the project life cycle is given in Figure 2.1. This splits the project, much more cleanly and definitely than would be the case in practice, into a number of overlapping stages. The conceptual stage varies widely from one project to another in both its nature and the period of time it occupies. It may represent many years of research and development, or merely an analysis of the market situation. Whatever its nature, it will usually call for

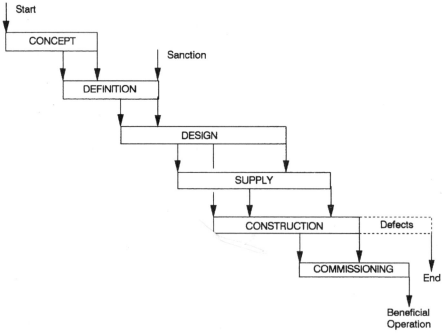

Figure 2.1 Main project stages

skills and experience different from those required of the project manager responsible for execution. The execution phase project manager should, of course, be involved in the conceptual stage, but when that involvement should best commence will depend on the nature of the particular project. It must be timed so that he can form a clear and full understanding of the business requirements and ensure that proper definition of the project is reached before sanction is given and engineering starts. The project manager's responsibility should continue until construction is complete and the defects, or guarantee, period ended. He may or may not be responsible for commissioning: either way, this is best carried out by a team formed primarily from the production staff who will be responsible for the operation of the new plant.

The employer's project manager's responsibilities for execution are outlined in Figure 2.2. Execution may be conveniently split into establishment—definition, strategy and contracts, carried out largely before the project is sanctioned, and engineering—the post-sanction work of design (including procurement), construction and commissioning. The project phases other than execution are, of course, equally important, in the sense that the links of a chain are of equal importance, but may be of more or less difficulty and hence less or more easily accomplished. In any particular project, the conceptual phase will include some or all of research, product development, process

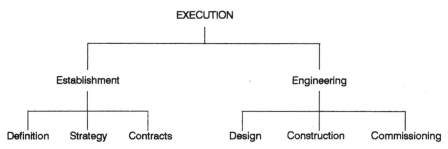

Figure 2.2   The project manager's responsibilities for execution

development, market research, investment analysis and financing. In a research-oriented project, discovering and proving the product may be the key to success and engineering the plant to manufacture it a much easier matter. This would usually be true of a pharmaceuticals plant, for example much more time and money would be spent on research and development than on the plant to manufacture the product. For a large-scale capital investment, however, project execution will often be the crucial stage. In phases other than execution, the project manager will make a contribution which will vary according to his experience and the particular circumstances of the project. In these other phases he will be a member of a team to which he brings his functional expertise—his skills of project execution including, for example, estimating, planning and project definition. Some organisations may extend the project manager's responsibility beyond execution but obviously, the wider his responsibility, the more general must his role become and the more difficult it must be for the organisation to find a manager with the required capabilities. The desirable level of generality of the role of a project manager is that he should be able to manage the efforts of his technical specialists without the need for intermediaries: he should be able to understand and appreciate what they have to do in the terms in which they do it, without requiring interpreters, and be able to contribute some informed judgement.

It is the need to establish, for every new project, what has to be done and how it should be accomplished which is the characteristic feature of project management, and which distinguishes it from the management of a continuing operation. For the employer's project manager, establishment may be more critical than the subsequent engineering stage. The crystallisation of the technical basis of the project, deciding how its execution will be organised, and enquiring for and awarding the necessary contracts, comprise the formative stages of the management of the project and are the foundation for all that follows. Mistakes at this stage are very difficult, and often impossible, to correct later without compromising the achievement of the project objectives. The vital importance of a sound footing for the project is not universally realised and not uncommonly the project manager has to fight hard to ensure it. Even when the project is properly established, engineering may still be fraught with difficulty, but here the employer's project manager's authority is less disputed and he has more assistance. His own project team plays a larger part, and the contractors appointed take much of the load.

The role of the project manager is considered in more detail below. Of course, it is possible to allocate the various parts of the role differently. Some organisations, for example, may appoint a project director as well as a project manager. Much depends on the availability of staff with the requisite skills, ability and experience. When major projects may have a life cycle of five years or more, it is difficult for any employer's organisation to develop staff experienced in all their aspects, and project roles may have to be tailored to suit the people available. Here it is assumed that an experienced and capable project manager is available, who works directly with the general manager of the sponsoring business without the intervention of a project director.

2.1.1 Conceptual Stage

It is not the project manager's job to decide whether the project should go ahead or, usually, to prepare and submit the project proposal for approval. He is, however, an important member of the team which the employer assembles to do the necessary investigation and analysis work and has several specific areas of responsibility where his judgements are final. In other areas, his contribution will depend on his experience and expertise relative to those of the other team members.

The project manager may play an important part in the selection of the process to be used, or in the development of an existing process. He is, of course, responsible for all estimates of capital cost and programme and, where required, will provide estimates of the costs of alternative proposals and practical advice to help guide research and development. If a joint venture company is to be formed to own and operate the plant, or if external finance is to be sought, he will play a part in these developments and will need to consider and plan for the way the organisation of the project will be affected.

2.1.2 Establishment

Project definition

For a major project, intended to be a revenue-producing investment rather than a technical development, the importance of good technical definition at the initial stage can hardly be overstated. The project manager must approach the question of technical definition of his project with a healthy scepticism. The extent to which he has been involved in developing the proposals will vary from one project to another, but his is the responsibility for accepting that the proposals can be engineered for a stated cost and in a stated time. He must be the judge of whether matters have progressed sufficiently far to support a capital cost estimate of the required accuracy, or to warrant letting contracts. Promoters of a new capital investment may let their enthusiasm outrun their judgement, and may view the technical staff as drags on progress who must be pushed as hard as possible. The project manager's task is to be realistic, whatever the pressure or the pervading euphoria. He must take the view, since others will certainly do so if things go wrong, that his is the sole responsibility for executing the project successfully, and that if the basis of the project is found to be unsound and disruptive changes prove necessary, this will be considered to be his fault alone. Yet, at the same time, he must not be so cautious as to deny his company a profitable opportunity.

The project manager must investigate and take into account all the external circumstances which will bear on project execution. These may include the location of the site and access to it, as well as the acceptability of the proposed site from an engineering point of view. He may need to investigate means of transporting large and heavy loads. He will need to establish the climatic and seismic conditions, and the available supplies of the required utilities and feedstocks. In a foreign country he must investigate the resources available locally for design, construction and fabrication and determine their costs. He must establish the customs duties and taxes likely to be payable, the regulations which have to be complied with and the technical and environmental standards that will apply. All of the results of these investigations will influence capital cost, some will affect programme, and some may have major effects on the off-plot facilities required by the project.

Strategy

The division between technical definition and execution strategy is not absolutely clear-cut, but the broad distinction is that technical definition establishes the scope and nature of the facilities to be designed and built, project execution strategy outlines how this is to be accomplished. The project manager's personal contribution to this stage is particularly important. He must decide how the project is to be organised and staffed, the division of the work into sections and how it is to be split between contracts, and the types of contract to be used. Special problems will need to be identified and allowed for, the need to recruit and train staff in an undeveloped country, for example, or the forced dependence on one particular supplier. Clearly, the major part of this work must be done before the project is sanctioned, although some of the more detailed aspects can be completed later.

The work directly connected with the award of the main contracts occupies a major part of the project manager's attention. Much of it is done before the project is approved, especially if contractors' bids are to form the basis of the sanction estimate. Preparation of the enquiry documents, assessment of bidders, evaluation of bids, and selection of contractors set the pattern for and establish many of the boundaries of the project. If done thoroughly and well, it is a major ingredient of success.

2.1.3 Engineering

Design and procurement

The project manager must manage the employer's own in-house design work and must, through his staff, monitor the performance of the contractors, applying corrective pressure as necessary. He must ensure that the work is performed to specification, cost and programme. He must manage the employer's input to the contractors' design processes and generally assist the contractors in the discharge of their obligations.

Construction

The employer's involvement in the construction of the plant can range from direct and complete responsibility to merely monitoring the work of a main contractor. Even where a main construction contractor is employed, the employer may retain overall control of, and responsibility for, the site. The project manager must, together with his construction manager, decide how the construction is to be carried out, place contracts as required, and direct and co-ordinate all the work.

Commissioning

The employer's commissioning team will usually be largely composed of production staff who will go on to run the plant on a permanent basis. If the new plant is to built on an existing works, the commissioning team may respond to the works manager rather than to the project manager. Some members of the team should have been seconded to the project for the design and construction phases.

2.1.4 Costs and Planning

As with all simplifications, the diagram in Figure 2.2 deals less than adequately with some features of the project manager's role. Capital costs and programme are aspects which run continuously through both the establishment and engineering phases.

Capital costs

The project manager has to produce a number of different estimates in the course of a project: preliminary estimates to guide research and development and decisions on the scope and size of the plant; the sanction estimate, much the most important of all, on the basis of which the project is approved; control estimates during the engineering of the project. He must monitor and control the capital costs throughout the course of the project. He may have to manage the cash flow, and may be constrained by foreign currency requirements.

Responsibility for the sanction estimate gives the project manager a great deal of control over the formative stages of the project. By properly reflecting the state of project definition in the contingency allowance, he should be able to ensure that any uncertainties are either resolved or fully understood and accepted.

Programme

The project manager must set, or at least agree to, the completion date for the project. He may set target and forecast dates, the first an optimistic objective, towards which the project team will work but which will be achieved only if there are no untoward events, the second a realistic expectation used for financial and commercial planning. He must decide what plans are to be developed, the techniques to be used, and must supervise their production. He must continuously monitor progress, ensuring that achievement is compared with plan and action taken to try to recover any delay.

2.2 PROJECT ORGANISATION

A large process manufacturing company will have many hundreds of capital projects in existence at any given time. All stages in the project life cycle will be represented. Some will be in research or development, some will be little more than a name on a list, others will have been given full authority to proceed into engineering. A large number—perhaps most—of these projects will be modifications, improvements or enlargements to existing plants. Many projects will be of modest size. Some will involve only a single engineering discipline, being concerned, say, only with civil work such as a new car park or road improvement, or with electrical work such as a new high voltage feeder. A large number of the projects that are initiated will never come to fruition, that is, they will never receive full sanction. Preliminary work will show that they are not viable, or market conditions will change, or some important assumptions will turn out to be false. Others will linger on for years with little work being done on them, waiting for the right market opportunity.

Thus, there is no *typical* project. Few involve the complete project life cycle—beginning in research, progressing through development, into design, procurement, construction and commissioning in a logical order. Major projects, in particular, seldom have much of a research and development component because few companies would wish to make a major investment in an untried process or product. If a large tonnage process is to be radically developed, modification of an existing plant, or the addition to it of a sidestream unit, are common ways to avoid too great a leap into the unknown. If the product is a new one, in all but the rarest of cases the market will have to be developed and the first plant to be built will be small. Major investment comes later, when a market for large tonnages has been developed, by which time the process will have been proven, perhaps in several smaller installations. Few projects follow the idealised path of the discovery of a new product, the invention of a manufacturing process and its development into production, all as a coherent set of events, and almost never on a large scale. If there is technical novelty at all in a large project, it will usually derive from the improved application of existing technology—a modification to process conditions, a new arrangement of the unit processes, or improvements to the detailed engineering.

Hardly any projects are so large, or so important, that they take such precedence over all other activities of the parent organisation that they may be considered in isolation, secure in the knowledge that no other considerations will be allowed to impinge. Projects such as that which the Lockheed Aircraft Corporation executed to build the giant C-5A military air transports, for which a whole new 11,000-man organisation was created, are rare indeed. In private industry this must be so: except in desperation, an established company should not be gambled on the success or failure of a single project. Almost all projects must be organised and executed as merely part, perhaps a very important part, of the total work of the initiating organisation. Most will not warrant the services of a full-time project manager, and fewer still those of a specially organised task force. The vast majority must be fitted into the continuing work of the employer and be undertaken according to current procedures.

To add to the difficulties of organisation, there appears to be no workable method of arranging an employer's projects in order of priority for resources. It is possible to set broad categories of capital investment work in priority order, for example as follows:

(1) Work concerned with the shut-down of operating plants
(2) Work concerned with the maintenance of operating plants
(3) Sanctioned projects
(4) Unsanctioned projects.

However, to try to set the priorities between two sanctioned projects promoted by different businesses is very difficult. Certainly, few business managers will voluntarily yield priority to another, and reference upwards to more senior levels in the organisation would be unwelcome and impracticable in all but the most important cases.

These considerations—that few projects correspond at all closely to the idealised project life cycle, that the organisation of most projects is influenced by the many others that a company will be simultaneously undertaking, and the difficulty of prioritising projects competing for resources—are seldom mentioned in discussions on project organisation and management. Together with the inevitably great variety in the projects undertaken by a large company, however, they are powerful determinants of what can be done, and how it may be accomplished, and lead to a variety of organisational solutions, at least at the detailed level. The project manager must operate in the real world, and must deal with what is possible, being frequently subject to externally imposed constraints on resources.

2.2.1 Task Force Organisation

The manager of a major project is usually allowed some freedom of action to organise the way it is executed. The idealised form of organisation is the task force, depicted in Figure 2.3. In this, all the resources necessary for the engineering of the project are separated from the rest of the organisation and

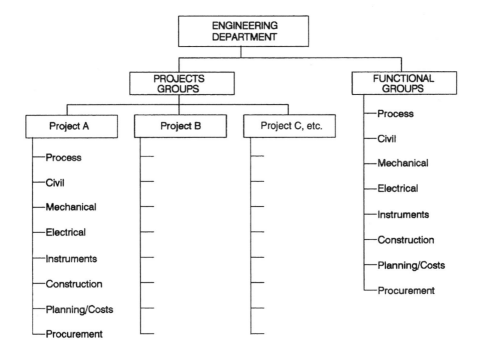

Figure 2.3 Task force organisation

put under the control of the project manager for the duration of the project. There are, of course, different ways in which task forces may be established. At one extreme, suitable for only the very largest projects of long duration, all staff working on the project may be wholly transferred to it, the project manager becoming responsible for all aspects of their employment including, for example, career development and rewards, as he is for any project engineers and other project staff who are under his permanent control. More frequently, functional engineers will merely be seconded to the task force so that the project manager controls only their day-to-day work, and they continue to respond for technical standards and career progression to their functional heads. In theory, a task force is a most desirable form of organisation, with a singleness of purpose and a clear command structure. Communication between members of the project team is facilitated and team working encouraged. An *esprit de corps* will readily develop. For several reasons, however, it is suitable only for the very largest projects which an organisation handles. If the project manager is to have complete control over his project team, he must be its most senior member, which is often not the case with smaller projects. Part-time project team members are also usual in small projects and are incompatible with use of a task force, especially if, as logic demands, all its members are to be relocated together. The task force has disadvantages for the remainder of the organisation, some members of which are likely to be upset by the establishment of a separate, seemingly élite, and highly visible organisation. The relocation of the task force will be disruptive (and will require the most ample provision of office space if it is to be other than a rare occurrence). There will be duplication and inefficient use of resources. There may even be a problem for task force members when the time comes for their reabsorption into the body of the department. It is clear that the difficulties surrounding the establishment of a task force will limit its use to the most important projects an organisation undertakes.

In general, however, it is not the major project which is most in need of the task force structure, which is merely a mechanism to give the project manager greater control over his team members and to ensure that his project gets their commitment and undivided attention. On major projects, this is hardly an issue. The size and importance of the project itself attracts a certain dedication; the fact that most, if not all, project team members are full time removes any competition for their services; the seniority and experience of the project manager gives him a great deal of power and influence as well as sapiential authority; the project manager may have much experience of working with many of his key team members and have long ago established effective working relationships with them. A thoroughgoing project task force organisation is thus neither so advantageous nor so necessary as might first be supposed.

A partial task force, in the sense that the project manager will arrange for key members of the project team to be relocated near him and under his day-to-day control for short periods, is more easily and more often utilised. In such an organisation, functional specialists would be brought together merely for the duration of their peak involvement in the project, while continuing to respond to their functional group. This gains many of the advantages of a task force organisation while avoiding some of the disadvantages.

Of course, in an owner's organisation using contractors for the detailed design and construction, the organisation shown in Figure 2.3 requires relatively small numbers in each function. The duties of the owner's engineers will be limited to the specification of what is wanted and the review, in whatever detail is deemed appropriate and is enshrined in the contract, of the contractor's work. There is, however, surprisingly little difference in the number of design engineers needed by the owner when a contractor is employed, compared with the requirement where the plant is to be designed in-house, though the need for more junior staff is very much reduced. The use of contractors undoubtedly leads to inefficiency in the use of resources, and few employers' project managers would dispute that an individual project could be executed more cheaply in-house were the resources available. Most employers will consider, however, that these extra costs are a good deal less than the savings accruing in the long term from avoiding the need to maintain a large permanent organisation for project execution.

2.2.2 Matrix Organisation

The more usual organisation adopted for projects is the so-called 'matrix' organisation shown in Figure 2.4. In this, the project manager manages a slice of a department which is otherwise organised on functional lines. The extent to which the permanent organisation can or should be functionalised depends on the nature of the work. In the petrochemical industry, mechanical engineering design can be conveniently divorced from projects and split into vessels, machines and piping, although even here, it is debatable whether projects and piping should be separated. With some other types of project, the advantages of separating project and mechanical engineering may be more questionable. Where one equipment item forms a very large part of the total project as in, for example, a boiler plant, the mechanical engineer with responsibility for that major item naturally has most of the work of project co-ordination, and the need for a separate project engineer is much reduced, if not eliminated.

In practice, the matrix organisation is more easily worked than might be supposed, because of the operation of unwritten rules. The project manager

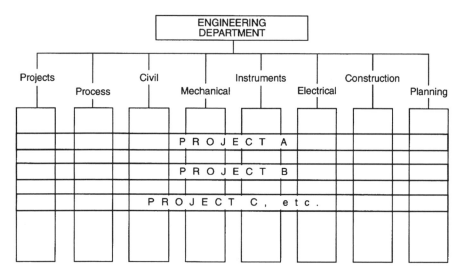

Figure 2.4 Matrix organisation

with twenty projects will not have to deal with twenty different engineers for each of the various engineering design functions. Both project managers and functional engineers will tend to specialise in particular technologies so that, where there is a history of continuous investment in a particular type of plant, they may have worked together for many years and have not only long-established and comfortable working relationships but common understanding of the technical problems and possibilities. In other cases, a functional engineer will, as far as possible, take functional responsibility for all of the projects of a given project manager, engendering effective working and minimising the pressures of competing interests.

There are benefits to be obtained from both functional and project organisations, and both are needed. The functional organisation exploits the fundamental idea of the division of labour to achieve better results in each activity than would be achieved without specialisation. In the process, the real objectives may be lost site of, barriers to effective working with others may be erected, and co-ordination may suffer. The project organisation applies a corrective by concentrating the efforts of its members, irrespective of discipline, on the task in hand, but does not develop the same functional expertise and, left to itself, has its own, different isolationist tendencies. There is often little, and need be no, communication between different project managers and different project teams. The combination of the project and functional organisations in a matrix can often provide the best of both worlds, but not without the application of a good deal of management skill and effort.

2.2.3 Project Organisation

Abstract arguments about the best form of organisation should not lose sight of the fact that all will count for nothing if individuals with the personal qualities required for the jobs are not available. Whilst it would not be right to proceed to the other extreme and merely design the organisation round the people available, their skills and experience must be taken into account. There is no doubt that organisational structures do affect people's behaviour. There are those who long for complete independence and will, if they can remotely justify it by reference to the organisation chart, defer to, or even communicate with, no one. The awkward individual will usually temper his behaviour towards the one who controls his job prospects.

A typical outline organisation chart for a major project is shown in Figure 2.5. Naturally, much will depend on the details of the particular project: the extent of the project manager's responsibility, the geographical dispersal of the different activities, the content of the project. Whether the functional sections remain responsible to their functional heads in a matrix organisation, or whether they are transferred to a task force makes little difference to the project organisation on paper: the difference is in the extent of the project manager's formal control of those working on the project. Those who must respond directly to the project manager are described below.

Chief process engineer

He will be responsible for the employer's contribution to the process technology. If the technology is to be provided by the employer, much of the

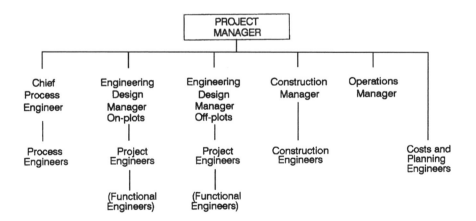

Figure 2.5 Project organisation

process design work will be done during the conceptual stage of the project, during which time the *chief process engineer* may respond directly to the business manager. During the execution stage, however, he should respond to the project manager for the production of the process package, leading a team charged with the development and production of flowsheets, heat and mass balances, and process, equipment and instrument data sheets. Jointly with the project engineers, he will produce the engineering line diagrams. Some of the detailed aspects of this work may be left to the contractor. If the latter provides the process technology, the employer's process engineers will merely check and comment on what is provided. In either case there will be a substantial workload involved in the various reviews required during the course of detailed design and, where the employer's own technology is involved, in clarifying intentions and answering queries.

Engineering design manager

The *engineering design manager* will be responsible for managing the employer's technical input to the design contractor, and for monitoring the contractor's work on a day-to-day basis to ensure that it complies with specification and with the contract. He will be resident in the contractor's office with a supporting team of project engineers and others as appropriate. Process and functional engineers will visit as necessary and required by him. Because he will be operating the contract, it is desirable, and may be contractually required, that the authority of the engineering design manager be specified in writing to the contractor. In common contractual terminology, he will be the engineer's representative, with specific delegated authority from the engineer (the project manager).

It is not unusual to employ separate design contractors for on-plot and off-plot, especially if the plant is to be built in a foreign country, where there may be advantages in using an indigenous contractor, with local knowledge, for the design of the off-plots. In such a case, more than one engineering design manager would be required. Each would have his team of project engineers and functional engineers, though the latter may well be common to both on-plot and off-plot.

Construction manager

A common division of responsibility in the UK, especially where construction on an existing site is concerned, is for the contractor to be responsible only for design and procurement, with the employer retaining control of construction, which he performs directly or more commonly, through the use of sub-contractors. In any case, on a site where existing operations are being carried on, the employer would wish to retain overall control. Thus the *construction manager's* role, and the size of his team, can vary considerably. Some construction input is desirable during the design process to advise on methods of construction and, if the design contractor is not to perform the construction, on the forms in which design information is to be made available.

Operations manager

Most employers will wish to inject their operating expertise into the design. Where the employer already operates the process which is to be used, a major part of his knowledge and experience of it will be held by his operating managers and engineers and the *operations manager* will channel their experience, as well as his own, into the project. In other cases, where the process is a new one to the employer, the operations manager may still provide general production know-how.

It is important that the operations manager is a full member of the project team responding to the project manager, and also that he has the confidence of the production function, can speak for it and can approve matters on its behalf. He must ensure that the full and final contribution of the production function is made during the design stage. If this is not done, it may be found that, as the plant takes shape on site, demands for changes are made which if allowed, will add to costs and seriously disrupt progress.

Planning and cost engineers

These functions are concerned with project control and must therefore respond directly to the project manager. There may be subordinate *planning and cost engineers* resident in the design and construction teams, and this would be especially necessary if these are located abroad.

Other considerations

If the plant is to be designed in the UK and built abroad, it will be necessary to appoint a senior engineer to be responsible for all activities in the country in question. As well as construction, these activities may include some part of the design, and there will be almost certainly be a considerable workload in liaising with the authorities on many matters from environmental permissions to the import of equipment and materials. If the employer already has operations in the country concerned, some help may be available from this source. It may well be that the responsibilities involved justify the appointment of a *deputy project manager*, who might combine this role with that of engineering design manager or construction manager.

What is certain is the need for the project manager to have confidence in his immediate subordinates. With activities proceeding at a number of locations, possibly thousands of miles apart, it is impossible for the project manager to exercise day-to-day supervision and he must rely on those responding to him to act as he would wish and to keep him informed of anything he needs to know. Detailed reporting is often impracticable, is always time-consuming and may be confidence-sapping. It is good practice for terms of reference to be produced for each of the key members of the project team. The major part of the benefit of this is derived from the process of developing and agreeing a common and clear understanding of roles at the beginning of the project and it may well be that, once agreed, the remits are never looked at again. Where the same team is executing a project similar to a previous one, remits will not be strictly necessary, but would then take very little time and effort to write. Remits should certainly be produced where there are novel aspects to the project: the more difficult and time consuming they are to develop, the greater their value. They might usefully be drafted by the person concerned and discussed and agreed with the project manager.

In organising his team and deciding the remits of team members, the employer's project manager should have regard for the way in which these things are done by the various contractors. The organisation of in-house design by the employer may be considerably different in detail from a contractor's design organisation. For example, for in-house design it is not uncommon for an employer's functional engineer to be totally responsible for his function— for procurement and cost control as well as for technical matters, whereas the contractor's functional engineer will usually have only a technical role. If the employer's functional engineers retain the same range of responsibilities when a contractor is employed as they would for in-house design, each of them must liaise, not only with the corresponding functional engineer in the contractor's organisation, but also with the contractor's procurement and cost control teams. This will greatly increase the communication load. More efficient working will be achieved by matching the job remits of the employer's engineers to those of the corresponding contractor's engineers, and making any other organisational changes that this necessitates.

It is not possible to consider the size of the project team required without knowledge of the details of the project. All that can be said here is that the extent of the work of project management varies very considerably with the degree of novelty of the non-technical aspects of the project, notably depending on the country in which the plant is to be built. A plant to be constructed on a new site in a developing country would probably require twice as much project management and project engineering effort in total as would a similar plant built on an existing UK site, as well as an increase in functional engineering.

2.3 LEADERSHIP AND TEAMWORK

The idea seemingly still persists in some quarters that leaders, if not exclusively born to the purple, may be developed only on the playing fields of a public school from where in happier times, equipped for their destiny, young men would sally forth to govern the colonies. Such romantic notions tend to obscure the mundane facts and to militate against the proper training of managers. Project management does not require the sort of leadership which can send men to their deaths with a smile on their lips and a song in their hearts. The project manager's leadership task is fortunately much simpler. He leads a team with high levels of education and training, who are capable and well motivated and who are doing work from which they derive a good deal of satisfaction (not to mention their income). It would be patronising to suggest that only with inspirational leadership will they do their job: rather, the position is that they will perform well if not obstructed. The project manager must merely ensure that each member of the team understands the nature of the project, his particular part in it, and the style and standard of performance that is required. After that, virtually all that is necessary is to ensure that work is co-ordinated, that contributions are treated with the respect they deserve, that good work is seen to be appreciated and credit given where it is due. The project manager, like any other manager, relies upon his team to do the vast majority of the work for which he is accountable. His job is to facilitate the team's work and to make it enjoyable, since to enjoy one's work is almost always to do it well. The leadership required really calls for little more than a certain amount of foresight, common sense, and the ability to empathise with others.

A project team is a temporary organisation of people, though not always as temporary as may be supposed from a single project. In an employer's organisation, a particular process or product line may call for fairly continuous capital investment and in such a case, it is likely that many members of a project team will have worked together continuously for some time, and on several projects, under the leadership of the project manager. They may have participated in the technical development leading to the new project and be well informed about it. In other cases, a project team may contain many staff who have not worked together before and who have no prior connection with the project. Before they can begin to make their full contribution, they will require to know, not only the scope, status and technical content of the project, but also how it is to be organised and what their own parts in it are to be. They will also need to understand what is less easily defined—the style of working required by the project manager.

Providing this initial information as quickly and efficiently as possible is a prime responsibility of the project manager, since it will bring forward the time when the new team begins to work effectively. Most projects will have a launch, or kick-off, meeting at which the salient points of the project—its scope and technical content and any unusual organisational or contractual features—are discussed. There will often be a design conference with the contractor to explain and agree the design basis. The co-ordination procedures, those internal to the employer as well as those relating to the contractor, will provide much of the administrative detail. If the project has no unusual feature, if the project team are experienced and have worked together before, and the contractor is not unfamiliar, this may be all that is required. In other cases, however, consideration should be given to a teamwork development exercise. This requires the key members of the project team to participate in some sort of shared experience: a conference of about a week's duration is common. Because relationships are more quickly forged under pressure, artificial situations, perhaps in the form of strenuous outdoor activities, are sometimes contrived. Others may question the acceptability of this and prefer a programme centred on the study of some important aspects of the project. The chief requirement of the exercise is that the team should work closely together on some common task, and it makes sense to combine this with performing useful work on, and communicating information about, the project.

It will not be necessary, may not even be possible, to say much about the style of management to be used. This will be communicated covertly as the new members observe and participate in discussions with the project manager. There is a wide variety of project management styles. Some project managers favour the kick and rush approach, in which everything is treated as urgent in the belief that the fastest way to get things done is to operate at a continuous crisis level. Others, like God, prefer to move in mysterious ways. Some require that no stone be left unturned, or even that every stone be turned several times, before any decision is made. Some may insist on arguing every problem to a conclusion, rather than merely to a decision, and expend much time and effort in ensuring that everybody knows why the decision they have collectively just arrived at is correct. Some project managers may feel a need to show their power by changing every proposal that comes before them, however insignificantly, or to demonstrate their abilities by always finding some previously undiscovered, even if irrelevant, aspect of any problem. The project team need to understand these foibles and work out how to respond to them. They need to know whether they are expected to act on their own initiative and refer upwards only when they think it necessary, or to consult with the project manager every step of the way. They need to understand how far their technical expertise and judgement will be trusted; whether their technical decisions are to be final, or merely advisory and subject to detailed checking and review. Until the answers to these and other similar questions are known and understood, team members will not operate at full efficiency. For his part, the project manager should realise that his actions will speak louder than his words and that his behaviour will influence that of his team, not always in the way he might believe, or would wish for.

A teamwork development exercise of the sort alluded to above can deal only with the key members of the project team and will tend to develop a core group in the larger project team. If carried too far, those members of the project team unavoidably excluded may feel slighted, and their resentment cancel out much of the benefit. It is also necessary to consider co-operation between employer's and contractor's staff. There may be a case for inviting the contractor's participation in a team-work development exercise. The project manager must certainly nurture co-operation with the contractor. Not all members of the employer's team will necessarily welcome the appointment of a contractor to execute the project: some may much prefer that the work be done in-house. In some cases, feelings of resentment are easily understood. An operating company may employ technical specialists to develop and maintain some unusual equipment which is especially important to its operations. The new project may be the culmination of years of development by such a specialist who now has to hand over the fruits of his efforts and watch while others with considerably less experience and competence take control. Little wonder if he then shows a tendency to let the contractor make mistakes that he can overtly correct, rather than to co-operate to forestall them. The project manager must ensure that his expert knows that his value is understood and appreciated without the need for such demonstrations.

It should go without saying that the project manager should work to raise and maintain the morale of his team. Two most important factors in this connection in process plant projects are the need to minimise change, which of course requires good initial definition, and the shielding of the team from outside interference. The extent to which continual change can demotivate the members of a project team is perhaps insufficiently appreciated. In design, work based on preliminary information which is expected to change will tend to proceed more slowly than usual because of the expectation that it will have to be done again. Having unexpectedly to perform re-work because of changed requirements will frustrate and annoy. On site, the reactions of a construction worker being told to dismantle and re-erect work for the third or fourth time—as was not uncommon on the large projects of the 1970s—can easily be imagined. As regards outside interference, in a manufacturer's organisation there will be many people interested in the project, some of whom may be able to exercise influence without any responsibility for the consequences, and who must be politely restrained.

2.4 MANAGEMENT OF INFORMATION FLOW

The project manager's role can, usefully, for the purposes of clarifying understanding, be separated into the management of the people involved, and management of the information flow. They are equally important. The information flow can be further subdivided into design information and control information. The first is the whole object of the design process: the specifications, drawings, orders and all the documentation which specifies what must be purchased and how the plant is to be constructed. The second is the information needed to monitor the progress and cost of what is being done.

The project manager needs constantly to have in mind the vast and complicated flow of design information that a major project engenders, and must always act in a way to try to minimise disruption. It is easy for the employer's staff, having no direct responsibility for the design, to forget the large numbers of people involved and just how tortuous, lengthy and slow are the information flows between them. The design organisation for a major project has something in common with a mass-production assembly line: it cannot easily or quickly deal with changes as could a small workshop. It is possible to treat as special only a small proportion of the data that is passed, and to do so requires inordinate effort and is not always successful.

It is also necessary to remember that the same staff who do the work must also, for the most part, produce the control information. They cannot do both at once. Sometimes the project manager will be quite prepared to sacrifice progress for the sake of control information: a fresh capital cost estimate will, for example, cause a notable interruption in progress but may be considered well worth it. But the project manager must beware of calling for information merely to increase his comfort level. Apart from wasting the time of others, it is all too easy for him to be swamped by excessive amounts of data. The only information that is really required is that which might prompt action. The rest is of the 'Well, I never' variety: much of this will be volunteered and the project manager must limit it as best he can. It may also be observed that when the data that is required cannot be elicited, the nearest approximation may be offered. Frequently, an aspect of a situation is measured and reported, not because there is good correlation between that aspect and the situation, but simply because none other is conveniently measurable. One is reminded of the man discovered one night on his knees under a lamp-post. When asked what he was doing, he replied that he had dropped his keys at the end of the street. 'But that is a hundred yards away, why are you looking here?' 'Because there's no light at the end of the street.'

What the project manager must do is to devote whatever time is necessary to deciding upon and commissioning exactly what control information he wants, to understand its implications thoroughly, and the sort of actions it might prompt him to take. The careful study of this selected information will be of much greater value than attempting to absorb all the masses of data which the project generates, most of which is the proper concern of others.

Chapter 3

Project Definition and Strategy

Project definition and strategy cannot be wholly separated from each other: there is interaction between them. Without good initial definition, those project strategies most likely to lead to a successful outcome are not possible. It is, however, convenient for discussion purposes to consider them separately, defining the terms as follows:

(1) *Project definition*—determining the scope and nature of the plant to be designed and constructed.
(2) *Project strategy*—establishing how the design and construction of the plant is to be accomplished.

This slightly arbitrary division encapsulates, in a simplified way, the early part of the role of the employer's project manager responsible for project execution: first he must define what is to be done, then how to do it.

3.1 PROJECT DEFINITION

If any one aspect of a project is arguably responsible for more project failures that any other, it is the lack of adequate definition, at the outset, of the project's scope and technical nature—the plant and equipment that are to be provided. It is not difficult to see why, if the project is inadequately or inaccurately defined when detailed engineering begins, this is likely to have serious effects. It will have a fundamental effect on the way the project is executed, since some form of multi-stage sanctioning process will be desirable and reimbursable contracts, difficult to administer and control, will be necessary. If the plant as built differs significantly from what was originally expected, it is obvious that the initial predictions of cost, time and performance are all likely to be seriously adrift. It is more difficult to see, given the obvious nature of this premiss, why poor initial project definition is so common.

Many of the spectacular project failures of recent years have been the consequences of inadequate technical definition at the time the projects were approved, sometimes compounded with other problems, and examples abound in all fields. The Sydney Opera House, sanctioned at A$6 million but eventually costing over A$100 million (and hence something of a record disaster in project management terms, whatever its merits as a building) was wildly over-spent primarily because of a ludicrously inadequate initial definition. Much of the UK nuclear power programme—Dungeness B, Hartlepool and Heysham A— averaged over 400% over-spent and about ten years late because of continual re-design during engineering. Concorde, costing more than four times the original official estimate—for all sorts of reasons, not all of them reflecting on project execution—was another development programme masquerading as a commercial project. In the boom years of the 1970s, hardly any major UK project achieved all its objectives of cost, time and performance.

Thus, recent history demonstrates frequent failure to understand how well a major project must be defined before sanction if it is to be successful. Inexperience on the part of those concerned, especially of the employer's project manager, would seem to be a major cause. Major projects are relatively infrequent and experience among employers of managing them is much less common than might be supposed. In the case of even the largest process manufacturer, few of his staff will have managed a major project, and the number who will have managed more than one will be small indeed. This is easy to understand when it is considered that an employer's project manager must usually accumulate many years' experience before he is entrusted with the management of a major project, that this might then occupy him for four or five years, and that afterwards there might be a considerable lapse of time before his next major project materialises, always supposing he is not moved or promoted.

Where inexperience in the project manager will be felt most grievously is in the stages which establish the project—definition and strategy. These stages do not provide continuous experience for the project manager, they occupy the first year or so of the project's life and then give way to other activities, so that even for the most experienced project manager, it may have been some time since he was last concerned with them. The project manager's direct contribution, as distinct from his work in managing the efforts of others, is much more important during these stages than during later project execution. Experience on other than large projects is of limited value to him. Small projects are much more tolerant of poor definition and change, so much so that they might almost be considered different in kind, rather than merely in size. General management has much less need of this establishing function, and hence provides experience of limited relevance to project management.

It is of fundamental importance that the employer's project manager accepts full responsibility for the technical definition of his project and does not proceed to sanction until he is satisfied with it. This may be more difficult than it sounds. Not all organisations excel at appointing project managers with clear remits. He may find himself in a position where the lines of responsibility and authority are blurred, where he is uncertain of the exact confines of his role, and is under pressure from managers more senior than himself to act in ways which he considers inimical to the interests of the project. He may be pressured to start execution too early before adequate information is available, or to agree to an arbitrary reduction in estimated costs, or to accept an unachievable programme, by those who will not subsequently regard themselves as responsible if project execution is unsuccessful. The project manager must set project objectives that, while offering real challenge, are nevertheless achievable. If he is to resist the pressures on him successfully, he must have confidence in his own judgement and have credibility with the business managers. This may be difficult for the experienced project manager and, for the inexperienced, barely possible. If all else fails, the project manager must ensure that the state of project definition is fully reflected in the estimates of time, capital cost and plant performance and that the sanctioning authority is made fully aware of the risks that are being taken. Admitting any inaccuracy or lack of confidence or unusual level of risk in a project proposal will adversely affect its chances of approval, so there will be understandable reluctance to do it. However, the project manager must not connive at the concealment of uncertainties in the interests of obtaining sanction.

In deciding the standard of definition the project requires and the technical risks that can be tolerated, the project manager must have regard to a number of factors, among them the state of the business and the commercial prospects for the particular project. Major projects have as their objectives the completion of major revenue-producing assets and, being concerned mainly with commodity products, rarely show predicted returns which would justify other than the standard accuracies and confidence levels that most companies expect in any project proposal. There is usually only a small tolerance—plus or minus 10%—on the capital cost estimate, a tight programme, and performance criteria which surpass the achievements of existing plants and include speedy progress to full output: difficult targets in any circumstances. The standard of definition required for success in these circumstances will usually require the expenditure of a significant proportion of the total design effort before sanction—up to a quarter of the total if there is no repeat element in the project. There may be considerable reluctance to spend the time and effort necessary to achieve the required definition. The cost of doing so will deter if the project seems unlikely to proceed; the time required will be grudged if the project is considered a winner. Only in hindsight can the pre-sanction stages of a project always be developed in an orderly and timely way, so that the information required at each stage is always to hand when needed. In real life, defining the scope of the project will often be the major critical path activity which is seen to be delaying the sanction proposal, and the availability of resources will frequently be a limiting factor.

Properly considered, the required accuracy of the capital cost estimate is perhaps the best guide to the level of project definition required. A tolerance of plus or minus 10% is usual. Such accuracy can only be achieved either by taking the design to the stage at which bulk materials—piping, electrics, instruments, and so on—can be reasonably quantified and prices obtained (whether this is done by the employer or by the contractors bidding for the job), or by comparison with recent similar plants. In either case, the estimating tolerance will be largely taken up by inaccuracies in the pricing. It will not cover many errors and omissions in the scope of the project, which must be allowed for in the contingency. Since there will almost certainly be limits on the contingency which can be included if the project is to be profitable, the accuracy with which the scope must be defined may be deduced. Thus, unless the estimate is able to rely significantly on costs obtained from recent similar plants, the process design must be complete, about a quarter of the detailed design accomplished, prices obtained for most of the main plant items, and the bulk equipment quantified and priced. There must be confidence in the process: what it does and how it does it. It is essential that the major process steps are capable, beyond any doubt, of being executed in the way that is proposed. The main equipment to be used must have been proven on the same or similar duties. The scope of the off-plot facilities must have been properly considered and defined. Quite small gaps or misunderstandings in the designers' knowledge at the time of sanction can have the most serious subsequent effects on costs and programme. It is a sound rule that few projects prove to have been as well defined as was thought at the time.

If, despite all the arguments against, the project manager finds himself committed to a project which is inadequately defined when contracts are let and detailed engineering begins, his options are severely limited. He must, of course, make certain that the implications and risks are fully understood by the business management. He must ensure that accurate estimates of cost, time and performance are produced as soon as possible and are formally considered by the sanctioning authority. He must tailor his contract strategy to allow for his lack of knowledge of what the project will require, developing reimbursable arrangements with his chosen contractors, whose operations he must manage in detail.

3.2 PROJECT STRATEGY

The strategy (perhaps rather too portentous a term, but one that has been widely adopted in business circles in the last decade or so) for a project is a coherent set of policies for project execution which will permit the business requirements to be satisfied. It must take into account all the major constraints on the project and will include, as a major part, how the main engineering contracts are to be organised. Being concerned only with project execution, the project strategy is based on the assumption that the business decision to invest has been taken or, more probably given the timing of events, accepted as a working hypothesis. It is therefore a subset of the overall business strategy which, among other things, has guided the actions leading to the investment decision.

The project strategy will define very broadly the main project activities that are to be undertaken, where and how they will be done, who is to do them and to what programme. It is not necessary, though it may be desirable, that the strategy be contained in a single document: in some companies this is termed the project execution plan. Much of the strategy will be expressed or implied in any Pre-Qualification Enquiry sent to potential bidders, and more in the Enquiry or Invitation to Bid itself. Elements of it will be in the Information Memorandum which, if project finance is being sought, will have to be provided to prospective financing institutions. Where the contracting arrangements are at all complicated, there should desirably be a contract strategy document describing the way in which the major contracts are to be organised and let. The degree of definition required before engineering starts has already been discussed. What must also be understood by members of the project team is the balance between time, cost and quality that is to be sought for the project. This is not to say that every part of the strategy is, or is capable of being, written down. Some of the more subtle aspects can perhaps only be communicated by example. In such cases the members of the team will take their cue from the project manager, sometimes being influenced more by how he behaves than by what he says.

A major project could hardly be executed without a strategy of some kind, even if it were not consciously formulated or assembled. Two considerations must guide the project manager. The first is that control over any project activity diminishes with time, as progress is made and decisions are taken. The project manager must exert his influence at the start. Later it may be impossible or excessively costly. This is true for the project as a whole as well as for individual parts of it and for individual functions. Though the resources engaged on any project increase sharply as progress is made, as does the information and data available to work on, so that the effort involved in project control becomes very much greater, this control is increasingly concerned with detail. It is at the initial stage that the employer's project manager exerts his main influence and lays the foundations for success—or perhaps irretrievably damages the project's chances. The project manager cannot guarantee success by his actions, but he can at least keep the possibility alive. Alternatively, he can ensure failure.

The second consideration is that major projects are not easily manoeuvrable—they are more akin to an ocean liner than a sailing dinghy—and success depends crucially on setting the correct course at the outset. Later, one may see the rocks but be unable to avoid them. It is not often possible in a project to adjust procedures following examination of a quarter's or a year's results, as would be done in a continuing operation. Major decisions must often be made on the basis of limited information and then lived with for the duration of the project. This emphasises the importance of these early policy decisions and puts a high premium on the project manager's previous experience.

Thus it is one of the first, and certainly one of the most important, tasks of the project manager to determine the project strategy. It is not, of course, something that is decided in an afternoon. It is gradually formulated over a period of months as the project crystallises, as various possibilities are explored, as various risks are identified and discussions held with various managers of the business, with members of the project team, with potential contractors and with others involved. By the time execution commences the strategy should be reasonably well developed and understood by the project team. Even after this, major disturbances may require it to be revised. If the project contains much that is new to the project manager and his team, development of the project strategy is likely to take much time and effort and indeed, because so much must be based on judgement and experience, may be overtaken by events in some areas before it is completed.

For the vast majority of projects which a large multi-national process company undertakes, much of the project execution strategy will be pre-determined. Of the hundreds or even thousands of projects which such a company undertakes in any given year, only a few will require a major new plant on a green-field site. The remainder will be smaller projects, modifications or additions to, or developments of, existing facilities and projects where the scope for different ways of proceeding will usually be limited and the projects will be executed in accordance with established procedures in a largely routine way. It is self-evident that the greater the novelty and the more degrees of freedom there are in the project, the greater the need for a considered strategy.

The development of a project strategy is a very iterative process, and much other project development will be going on at the same time. The strategy will initially be based on many assumptions, all of which will have to be confirmed, or abandoned, as a result of further work. Until detailed design starts, and even sometimes thereafter, the project strategy will continue to develop. It is not possible to provide an exhaustive list of all the factors which might have to be considered in the development of the strategy, but some of the factors of greatest importance and most likely to require consideration are outlined below.

3.2.1 Objectives

The first requirement is the formulation of clear project objectives by the business management. The project manager should have been involved with the business managers in this process. His input is necessary to provide preliminary information on what can be done, how long it will take, how much it will cost and so on. Of course, it is often not possible at this early stage to arrive at firm conclusions. Many assumptions will be made and much will depend on the correctness of these. The project manager must understand thoroughly the basis of the project objectives and the nature and extent of any uncertainties. He can then try, in the preliminary development of his strategy, to allow some flexibility where it appears most likely that it will be needed. The objectives lead on to the definition of the scope of the project as discussed above, and in both definition and strategy the project manager may sometimes have a message which is unpalatable to the business. If he believes that circumstances offer small chance of executing the project successfully, the project manager must make his voice heard, and whether he carries conviction may depend crucially on his personal credibility. He may find something on the lines of the *project difficulty score*, illustrated in Figure 3.1, validated against previous projects, a help in crystallising his thinking and convincing others. Developed for application to plastics plants projects in the UK, this can easily be adapted to suit other categories of chemical plant.

3.2.2 Business Requirements

For the owner, unlike the engineering contractor, the project is not an end in itself. Successful completion does not *per se* bring benefit to the employer. He has, in addition, to make and sell the product at a profit. So it is probable that a passable attempt at the right project would be more beneficial to the employer than perfect execution of the wrong one. Without suggesting that such extremes are likely, it is clear that the project manager must do all he can to ensure that the right project is chosen. He is the servant of the business and it is the business's interests which must guide his actions.

The project objectives must obviously include the nature of the product to be made and of the feedstocks to be used, the size of plant, where it is to be built and the time and cost targets. Views on the relative importance of cost, time and quality may be less clear. Not all business managers will admit that any one of these parameters is less than crucially important, or that the

FACTOR	RANGE	EXAMPLES
1. Process	1 - 10	Repeat = 1, Major capacity increase = 5, Radically new process = 10
2. Plant	1 - 5	Greenfield = 1, Brownfield = 2, Major modification = 5
3. Site	1 - 5	UK sites = 1 - 4, New overseas site in difficult country = 5
4. Number of Parties		Score 1 for each organisation involved
5. Expertise	1 - 5	Experience, in-house = 1, Marginal effort to oversee contractor = 5
6. State of Economy	1 - 10	Low inflation, slack =1, High inflation, over-heated = 10
7. Pressure on Costs		Score 1 for each 5% imposed cost reduction
8. Pre-Sanction Effort	1 - 10	Scope firm, estimate to 10% = 1, Undefined, estimate accuracy > 25% = 10

Total Score: 7 - 12 it's a cinch   13 - 20 reasonable
21 - 25 watch it   > 25 think again

Figure 3.1   Project difficulty score

wholehearted pursuit of one must inevitably call for some sacrifice in at least one of the others. Nevertheless, the project manager must make some sort of judgement about priorities and act accordingly, even if he has to pay lip-service to the view that absolutely nothing can be compromised. Whatever the view from outside, engineers know that the project process, indeed any engineering design, is one of continual compromise and that members of the project team daily trade off cost against time, time against quality and so on. It is the job of the project manager to ensure that there is consistent project behaviour in these matters which satisfies the business needs.

Over-optimism is one of the faults that the project manager will often find himself having to contend with. A business manager may envisage a project whose use of new technology will reduce costs, allow the plant to be built more quickly and to start up and reach full capacity without delay. Of course, one should strive to achieve all these things and as targets they are unexceptionable, but as forecasts they are unlikely to be reliable. As far as the project manager is concerned, the project objectives should be ones which he is reasonably confident of achieving, not mere aspirations. He should bear in mind the military maxim of 'Limited objectives, tight control', for major projects have something in common with military campaigns (without, it is to be hoped, the bloodshed!).

The nature and strength of the business can have a major influence on project strategy. If it is long established and solidly profitable (characteristics which increasingly seem to belong to a bygone age), the plant may be built to reflect this, designed to turn out good quality product consistently at high efficiency and with minimum down-time. A more speculative venture may require a plant in which the speed of getting into production is more important than longevity. If there is no certainty of the plant being required for more than a few years, it may be possible and appropriate to reflect this in some aspects of the plant design.

A joint venture project may be executed in quite different ways from one which is in single ownership. If joint ownership leads to the seeking of external finance for the project, there will be much extra preliminary work for the project manager to do and contractual arrangements will probably be affected. The joint venture partners may seek to perform some of the project activities themselves and to take on some of the contracts through associated companies. There will be different arrangements for approvals and reporting. The time required to establish the joint venture and agree responsibilities and methods of working is likely to add considerably to the project programme.

3.2.3 Technology

Some projects may require difficult decisions to be taken on the nature of the technology to be used. Such problems may centre on whether to use proven but obsolescent technology, or new and untried processes and techniques. The decisions may have repercussions on other matters such as the time allowed for design or construction, or for bringing the plant up to full output. The state of development of the technology and the extent of experience in its application are major factors influencing the project manager's estimates of design time and effort. With new technology, not only must more design effort be spent, but the work must proceed more slowly because there can be less overlapping of successive design activities—the results of many activities, needed as inputs to their following stages, cannot be so easily or so accurately guessed to allow preliminary work to start early.

Ownership of the technology may affect the way the project is executed. If the employer's own technology is to be used, contractual arrangements are likely to differ from cases where the contractor or a third party provides it. Whether and to what extent to repeat a plant design is another question which may be relevant—possibly balancing gain in reduced costs and time for the current project against a lost opportunity for design improvement which will affect all future plants of this nature.

3.2.4   External Influences

External influences on the project must be considered at an early stage. Economic aspects are the most important, none more so than the states of the economies of the relevant countries—where design, fabrication and construction are to be carried out. Almost by definition, large projects are found in cyclical industries since only commodity products can justify very large manufacturing plants. Large capital investments will be made simultaneously by many companies, all driven by the same economic factors. Counter-cyclical investment is more often talked about than made: most firms do not have the resources, even if they have the ambition, to invest during a trough and it will be a most fortunate project manager who has to manage a major project in times of recession. In times of rapid expansion the design, fabrication and construction industries will be overstretched—poor delivery times will be promised and these seldom achieved. Mistakes will multiply. Nevertheless, maximum pressure for early completion will be exerted by the managers of the business, mesmerised by visions of large profits. The project manager has to consider very carefully how he plans and manages a project in these circumstances—previous successful execution of a project in slack times is not an adequate preparation for the task—and this problem is referred to again in more detail in later chapters.

Other important and related economic aspects which must be considered are those of inflation, currency exchange rates, financing and taxation. Rates of inflation must be predicted and allowed for in the project estimates, but their effect can be more far-reaching if the project is faced with really high inflation. This could lead to quite different ways of execution, and terms and conditions of contracts would certainly be affected. Most major projects require worldwide purchasing and so are affected by exchange rates. Overseas projects are likely to have an even greater proportion of their total cost exposed to currency fluctuations and provision will have to be made for the management of these. The project may be sanctioned in the currency of the country in which the plant is to be built, adding another complication for those used to thinking in sterling. If external financing of the project is to be undertaken, the financing institutions will undoubtedly impose conditions on the project which will affect the types of contracts which can be negotiated and the liabilities which must be accepted. The project manager will also have to allow for the considerable time and effort which have to be devoted to the negotiation of the finance. An important influence on the contracting scheme for the project may be the tax regime of the host country—the imposition of withholding taxes, business taxes and the like.

The statutory requirements of the country in which the plant is to be built must obviously be complied with, and in the case of a plant to be built overseas, considerable investigation may be needed to find out what these requirements are and how they may be interpreted. Environmental regulations have been changing rapidly in recent years so that what was once acceptable may be so no longer. It is often a statutory requirement that the impact of the new installation on the environment is assessed. This may require site measurements over a substantial period of time to establish the undeveloped condition of the site before work is allowed to start. Import duties must be explored and these may be poorly defined in detail and may be affected by special treatment to which the project may be entitled under laws to encourage investment. There may be restrictions on the import of labour for construction, even though skilled local labour of the requisite quality is not available.

Geographical factors may affect the project in important ways. The project manager will be involved in site selection. Some engineering considerations—notably transport to the site of large and heavy equipment—may be of overriding importance and may rule out some proposed locations. Others, such as ground, seismic and climatic conditions will affect the costs and possibly the design and construction times. Provision may need to be made to supplement inadequate utilities' supplies. The arrangements for the supply of feedstock and the distribution of product will affect the amount of storage required on site.

Depending on the location of the site, there may be special steps which need to be taken to comply with the cultural and social values of the local people. These can range from the trivial—ensuring that the project number is divisible by three, or that site work starts on an auspicious day—to more important matters like the orientation of the plant to propitiate the local spirits. Generally, such matters are no great obstacle if one is aware of them in advance, but they can have serious consequences if, through ignorance, they are neglected. Labour costs may affect the degree of automation which is economic and appropriate. There is wide variation in the developments people find acceptable, not only as between different countries, but also in the same country. A car assembly plant keenly sought for Sunderland would be less enthusiastically received in Windsor. It is easier to place a plant among others of a similar nature where local people will be accustomed to the environmental intrusion made by the plant and to the work which it offers.

3.2.5 Resources

Clearly, the availability of the necessary resources to execute the project is a major influence on project strategy. The available numbers and expertise of the employer's own staff, those of potential design and construction contractors, as well as the capabilities of suppliers will all have to be considered. In the case of construction resources, it may be necessary to predict the forward construction workload in the region where the site is located and to make plans accordingly, or to persuade government to do so. Such plans may involve the recruitment and training of labour, or its import. The requirement for expatriate supervision and management must be assessed.

The project manager should be clear about the strengths and weaknesses of his position—of his own team, of the technology, and of contractors he might employ. His aim should be to combine the available resources into the strongest possible whole. Thus, some strengths of potential contractors will be more important to him than others. He must also take account of the systems and procedures available to him and to potential contractors.

All these matters will affect the contract strategy for the project and are discussed in more detail in later chapters. The division of the contracts between contractors and the terms of those contracts will be influenced greatly by the relative expertise and capability of the employer and of the potential contractors. There have been times when one particular aspect of project execution has assumed overwhelming importance. For example during the 1970s, construction performance in the UK reached such a low ebb as to dominate the execution of all large projects. More of this problem than was generally recognised at the time was the result of poor management and the lack of a properly developed project strategy. It should be obvious that construction can only be successful if the previous project stages have been completed satisfactorily.

The project manager must take account of the procurement situation expected at the time orders are to be placed. Delivery times will affect the programme, but views on the reliability of promises may also influence where orders are to placed. There is a need to be especially careful in cases where there is no available substitute—either for an equipment item or for a service. This can be the result not only of technical capabilities, but also of government or union restrictions. Any such situation where disturbance could be crippling needs to be given special consideration.

3.2.6 Experience

The recent experience of the employer—especially of the project manager himself—will be a major influence on the project strategy. To an extent, the project manager will be fighting the last war, that is, trying not to repeat past mistakes. It is important that, in drawing lessons from past experience, he does not confine attention to mistakes; successes can be equally instructive and he should also note those instances where failure was averted by chance. Nor should he think that repetition of a successful formula will necessarily suffice— different circumstances demand different responses and there are sometimes important unappreciated influences at work.

Experience is often undervalued. It is very easy to underestimate the requirements or effects of some novel aspect of a project. The experience of bidders should thus exert an important influence on how the project is to be executed. It will help to determine the employer's choice of contractor and of contract strategy. Construction experience may have a great deal of influence. The unhappy experience of the 1970s in the UK, for example, would have affected the strategy of every major UK project for the next few years.

3.2.7 Risk

In devising the project strategy, the employer's project manager is much concerned with the risks and uncertainties of project execution. Just as the project strategy is part of the overall business strategy, so the risks involved in project execution are part, sometimes a relatively minor part, of the total risks of the business venture. Project execution risks, if not the least of the employer's worries, are often dwarfed by the uncertainties of predicting the size of the market, the actions of competitors, future selling prices, costs of raw materials, variations in exchange rates and all the other vicissitudes that business is heir to. The employer's project manager is a contributor to the process of assessing and providing for the business risk. For managing the risks of project execution, he must take prime responsibility.

It is essential that the risks of project execution are thoroughly understood by both project and business management. It is desirable that the latter is a party to the risks which are to be incurred, but this is more difficult to achieve. Commonly, risk-taking is acceptable provided it comes off, not a logical position. Nevertheless, substantial uncertainty in the engineering of the project may sometimes be accepted. The advantages of new technology, for example, may be so great as to justify an adventurous approach. There may be no alternative to a site which presents significant difficulties in access or construction. Generally, however, the larger the project, the less the degree of risk that the employer will knowingly and voluntarily accept. In such projects, there is usually more than enough commercial risk to satisfy the most intrepid spirit, without compounding this with unnecessary uncertainty about plant cost, completion date and performance.

The process of authorising a project may require that the sanction proposal specifically identify any unusual risk. If it then transpires that no proposal identifying such a risk ever succeeds, all proposals submitted will be declared free of such uncertainties. The sanctioning authority may then complain about the excessively risk-averse nature of those managing the businesses. But in the inevitable situation where project proposals compete for limited capital resources, the business manager is forced to put forward the best case he can decently make. Optimism is, therefore, a normal feature of the average major process project proposal, partly because of the nature of the contest for approval, partly because only optimists would get involved in such an uncertain business. Of course, the sanctioning authority has seen it all before and will apply its own discounting factors to proposals presented. This game of bluff and counter-bluff must be avoided within the business team, at least. All members of the team will be committed to the project and will wish desperately for it to succeed. In the assessment of project prospects, however, of which the assessment of risks plays a significant part, it is necessary to strive for a certain detachment.

At its inception, a project may be the embodiment of a clear objective, or of no more than a vague aspiration. Whatever its provenance, it will be clouded with uncertainties which have to be dispelled or reduced before the project proposal is put forward for sanction. This requires a good deal of preliminary work by all the employer's staff concerned. The employer's project manager is responsible for ensuring that the risks of project execution are acceptable, that is, that there is an acceptable probability that the success criteria for time, cost and performance will be achieved. He does this primarily by ensuring satisfactory definition of all major aspects of project execution and by developing a sensible project strategy. Inadequate definition is probably the most frequent cause of project failure, so that this is an absolutely crucial area—for the employer's project manager one of the most important in the whole project. He may be faced with importunate demands from the business for an early start, a short execution period, a low capital cost. Seldom will a corresponding reduction in performance be conceded. Ill-considered surrender to these demands will burden the project with risks that are self-imposed, but for which no one but the employer's project manager will be held responsible. There may occasionally be projects where increased risks are considered acceptable and undertaken with the full knowledge and understanding of all parties, but the acceptance of greater risk is rare, and even more rarely remembered at the death. Project managers learn through experience, if they were not aware of it beforehand, that responsibility for any failure to meet project execution objectives is theirs and theirs alone.

Yet, of course, the employer's project manager must strike a balance between optimism and pessimism which is appropriate to the particular project, not only for the major decisions, but for many lesser matters as the project runs its course. He cannot be completely risk-averse. Technical development must be undertaken, capital costs must be reduced, project execution times must be trimmed if the competition is to be matched and, it is hoped, beaten. It is the employer's project manager's job to balance all the uncertainties in project execution; to weigh the advantages of new technology against the risks it involves; to seek cost reductions that can be delivered without adversely affecting plant performance; to minimise the project programme without jeopardising project execution; and to put forward the combination of characteristics that constitutes the optimum in all the circumstances. Difficult objectives encourage good performance, yet may also arouse unrealistic expectations. It may be appropriate to reconcile these conflicting considerations by the use of separate target and forecast; the first providing the difficult aim to stimulate performance, the second the expectation on which commercial plans are based.

Risks may usefully be classified into those which are controllable and those which are not. In the first category fall those which arise from, for example, incomplete design, or inadequate knowledge of the site, or lack of reliable equipment prices. The degree of risk from these may be reduced to an acceptable level by further effort. Even in this category there are risks which, while theoretically controllable, must nevertheless be incurred in full. An example might be the costs of transporting out-of-gauge loads to the site, where there may be no possibility of determining the costs with reasonable accuracy before sanction. Experience will sometimes enable much of the risk to be discounted. The engineer experienced in a particular activity may perceive it as much less risky than would one with no previous knowledge. The most economic way to arrange matters is for the party with the relevant skill and experience to take the risk and to control it.

Uncontrollable risks, for example, weather conditions which dominate North Sea offshore projects, or *force majeure* conditions generally, can sometimes be partially avoided or have their effects ameliorated. Some of their effects may be shared between employer and contractor, for example, the latter may be given an extension of time for circumstances outside his control, but must bear his own costs. There are two reasons why identifiable but uncontrollable risks are often better left with the employer. The first is that the contractor who has to assume the risks will charge a higher premium than the allowance an employer would make, not only because the premium will include a reward to the contractor for assuming the risk, but also because the contractor has a much smaller financial base over which to spread the risk and will therefore need to charge more for it. Secondly, the employer will pay the contractor's premium whether or not the risk eventuates.

Development of the project execution strategy must, at least for the major uncertainties, include a process for:

- Identifying possible risks
- Assessing their effects
- Devising ways of reducing them
- Allowing for any remainder

The identification of possible risks should emerge naturally during the development of the project strategy. To attempt here to list possible sources of risk would merely be to list all major aspects of a project, for any aspect may offer significant uncertainty in a particular case. Identification of a major uncontrollable risk is not a problem. Nor, for such a risk, is it difficult to secure agreement that proper consideration be given to its possible effects. Significantly novel aspects of a project are similarly plain to see. What can be more difficult for the project manager is to identify and take action about those risks which arise because of the way the project is to be executed, for example, too precipitate a start

Once the risks are identified, analysis of their possible effects follows. The methods used and the effort applied to this will vary with different circumstances. A single dominating risk, such as the North Sea weather, may be analysed in great detail. Much also depends on the data available. Poor data is seldom improved by extensive processing, but may be given a spurious validity thereby. Sensitivity analysis, probability analysis and Monte Carlo simulation may be employed in appropriate cases. In many instances however, where no one risk is overwhelming and where numerical data is sparse, subjective assessment of the size of the risk will suffice.

Once identified and analysed, risks must be eliminated, reduced or accepted. Risks which result from lack of preparation can be overcome by delaying the start of the project until definition has been improved. It may be possible to eliminate or avoid some especially risky parts of the project. Some of the risks may be transferred to a contractor, but there will of course be a price to be paid whether or not the risk materialises.

Provision must be made in the project estimates for those risks which the employer retains. There must always be contingency—for cost, for time and for technical difficulty. Something will always go wrong and it is necessary for the project to contain some flexibility and some reserve to enable compensating action to be taken.

3.2.8 Conclusion

Many of the matters outlined above cannot be easily quantified, so that some of the most important decisions which will affect the project outcome have to be taken largely on the basis of the experience and judgement of the project manager and his team. The most important influences will vary from project to project. It is the employer's project manager's task to balance often conflicting requirements to develop what is, in his judgement, a well-defined project and the optimum strategy for executing it. Not to do so is to be condemned to be swept along by events, usually to an unwelcome destination.

Chapter 4

Initial Investigations

In the early project stages prior to execution, much effort will have been expended by the employer in matters such as research, development, process improvement, market studies and commercial negotiations. Once the execution stage commences, the project manager will need to commission and manage a number of initial investigations, to underpin the definition of the scope of the project, and to determine the optimum execution strategy for it. The number and extent of these investigations will depend on the degree of novelty in the project, both technically and otherwise. If the employer owns the technology, he is almost certain to wish to investigate potential technical improvements to the plant. Even when using mature technology, few plants are exact repeats of their predecessors. Quite apart from changes forced by differing circumstances, improvements must always be sought simply to maintain competitiveness. It is not proposed to discuss such studies here, partly because this is hardly possible without defining the technology in question and partly because, although the project manager will have a role to play in initiating, managing and guiding these investigations to timely and optimum conclusions, and may also have some technical input, they are principally the concern of the technical specialists.

The execution of any project requires vast amounts of data, much of it of a non-technical nature. It ranges from climatic, soils and seismic data for the site, the availability of services and utilities, the nature and extent of local resources, to the provision of housing and schooling for expatriate staff. For an existing UK site, the vast majority of the information required will already be in the employer's possession. For a new overseas site, most will have to be collected, and many employers and contractors have developed checklists and questionnaires for this purpose. To include such a checklist here would add substantially to the length of this book and it is intended, therefore, merely to discuss in very general terms some aspects that may be of particular concern to the project manager.

4.1 OVERSEAS PROJECTS

The employer's project manager used to working on existing sites in the UK will find a considerable additional project management workload in a foreign project, certainly where the plant is to be built on a new site in a developing country whose physical and administrative infrastructures are in their infancy. Provision will have to be made for this extra work in staffing the project. Not only will there be additional tasks to be performed, of which the collection of data mentioned above is merely the first, but also there will be less support from the employer's organisation. The employer's resources will be less in the foreign country than in the UK: were it otherwise, the investment could be managed from the country concerned. Some matters may require investigation and decision which, in the UK, have long been settled. Other matters which would be handled by other parts of the employer's organisation will fall to the project team; and some that would be handled routinely in the UK will have to be tackled from first principles. Later, during project execution, it may be found that computer systems designed for operation on UK projects and linked to other systems of the employer, for example, those designed to help in cost monitoring, are of no assistance.

Some of the major matters which may have to be investigated in connection with a project to be built in a foreign country are the following, only a few of which are likely to require much attention in the UK:

(1) The establishment of a joint venture company
(2) Project financing, taxation and exchange rates
(3) Statutory obligations—environmental requirements, engineering standards, design approvals, construction permits, operating licences, labour laws
(4) Safety policy
(5) Design, manufacturing and construction resources and costs in the country concerned
(6) Plant location
(7) Import duties
(8) Utilities and feedstocks supplies and transport
(9) Transport of large construction loads.

This has no pretensions, of course, to being an exhaustive list. Project financing, taxation, exchange rates are dealt with in later chapters. The others are discussed briefly below.

4.2 JOINT VENTURES

Most large manufacturing companies would wish to retain full control of their manufacturing facilities, but circumstances sometimes require the establishment of a joint venture company to own and operate a new plant. A common reason for forming a joint venture company is that many developing countries insist upon it, seeing it as a means of transferring technology and increasing the capabilities of their nationals. If a joint venture company is to be formed, the employer's project manager's working relationships will be profoundly affected (we are, of course, considering the case where the employer is taking the lead role in the project). He may play some part in the selection of partners for the joint venture, and will certainly be required to discuss and agree with the partners how the project is to be handled. He may have to include staff from the other partners in the project team. As project manager, he will respond not to his employer, but to the joint venture company, and it will be necessary for him to define his role and responsibilities carefully. He will need to beware of assuming that the ways of working and reporting and requirements for approvals to which he is accustomed will satisfy the joint venture partners, even if they appear to do so on paper. In the developing world, delegation of authority is much less common than in the UK, and uncritical obedience to one's superiors often the rule.

The joint venture project manager must therefore try to establish a project team in which all the members respond not to their employers, but only to the joint venture. This should not be too difficult if all the joint venture partners subscribe to Western ways of doing business. In some countries, however, it is quite unthinkable that an employee should ever put other interests before those of his employer, or do other than his employer tells him. The project manager may thus have to accustom himself to a situation where his team members receive instructions from other sources and make independent reports. Difficulties can arise in the complicated organisational structures that are sometimes established. The interests of the joint venture may not always be identical with those of the individual partners. 'Chinese walls' may be needed but not always achieved, for example, where a joint venture partner has an interest in one of the contractors bidding for a contract, or individually has the right to bid for some of the work. In the first case, knowledge of the competing bids must be denied to the partner. In the second, if the right to bid is to be interpreted as the right to the work at the lowest external bid price, the project manager must understand this and place his enquiries accordingly if he is to keep faith with the other bidders.

If the technology for the project is being provided by the employer under licence to the joint venture, there will be additional contracts that the project manager must help to draft and negotiate. It is probable that he will also have responsibility as the licensor's project manager—to manage the production of the employer's process package for transmission to the joint venture company and to monitor technically the use the contractor makes of it, providing any additional information required and reviewing the contractor's designs. He will thus be serving two masters, and it is very important that he is clear about his responsibilities to each. Considerable thought and effort may have to go into defining the different roles, in making these clear to his supporting staff, and making sure that the rights of all parties are respected.

4.3 STATUTORY REQUIREMENTS

Statutory requirements in an unfamiliar foreign country need to be ascertained. In some newly industrialised countries, it may be found that these requirements are not specified in the detail necessary for their effects on a project to be accurately assessed. A good deal of investigation may be carried out and yet fail to eliminate all uncertainty. Engineering standards and specifications, environmental requirements, design approvals, construction and operating permits, and labour laws are some of the matters that must be investigated. Of course, how far the employer needs to concern himself with these things depends to a large extent on what direct part he is to play in the project, but he cannot be entirely indifferent since many of these rules and regulations will also apply to plant operation. The employer will, in any event, usually be active in the country concerned long before any of the bidders for the main contract, and it would be only common sense for him to make what enquiries he can and to pass this information to the bidders in order to save them time. The employer would, of course, need to make clear to the bidders whether or not he accepted any liability for the accuracy of the information.

Environmental standards are everywhere becoming stricter, and many developing countries choose the toughest rules extant as their model. Although some rules may be obvious nonsense, and spoil the environment they are trying to protect, and others may be ignored with apparent impunity by local manufacturers, a major company has little option but to comply with the letter of the law. Environmental impact assessments are commonly required. The environment prior to the start of construction must then be studied and recorded, so that the changes resulting from the development may be measured. These initial studies may require a year or more, and may need to be commenced as early as possible if they are not to delay the project. They would usually be the subject of a separate contract between the employer and a specialist consultant: in some countries the employment of an approved local consultant is mandatory.

4.4 SAFETY

The project manager is, of course, responsible for providing a plant that can be safely constructed, commissioned and operated, safety being defined to include an acceptable degree of freedom from loss and damage as well as from personal injury. If the plant is to be designed and constructed in the UK, this will not usually present him with any great problems. The legal requirements are well known. Both employer and design contractors will have safety policies and procedures in place which, if operated properly, will provide acceptable standards and more than satisfy the law. A major employer will also employ specialists in the various aspects of technical safety. Construction contractors in the UK will similarly have established safety procedures which the project manager must ensure are checked before contract award and their application monitored. Thus for a plant designed and built in the UK and to be operated by the employer, dealing with safety will be largely a matter of following carefully-drafted and well-established methods and procedures.

Where the plant is to be operated by others, or is to be built and some of it possibly designed outside the UK, these comfortable assumptions cannot always be made. Procedures and specifications drafted for the UK may not be entirely appropriate. In a foreign country the project manager must discover what the law is, how it is applied, and whether the local contractors that are to be employed are accustomed to comply with it. Even then, compliance with the law may not satisfy the employer's own standards. As regards process, or technical safety, although designs may differ to suit particular circumstances, the employer will apply the same standards irrespective of where the plant is to be designed or built. Only fully competent design organisations should be employed and the monitoring and approval necessary to confirm the safety of the design must be undertaken. Construction safety, discussed in Chapter 18, may be a different matter: many construction workers, especially those employed far down a chain of sub-contractors, may be virtually untrained and only briefly on the site. The influence of the standards of the country cannot be escaped entirely. Neither can safe operation and maintenance always be taken for granted where the plant is to be operated by staff not under the control of the employer: this is discussed below. In addition, the project manager must keep a weather eye on prospective neighbours. Many process plants today are built in designated industrial areas, not all to the same standards. The employer's project manager must ensure that, having designed and constructed his plant to a high standard of safety, its operation is not subjected to unacceptable risk of loss, damage and injury from an adjacent plant.

Where the process technology belongs to the employer, and is to be transferred to a third party via a licensing agreement, safety is an important consideration if the process is at all hazardous. The separate responsibilities of the parties must be carefully defined and the licensee must be obligated to do whatever is necessary to design and construct the plant and operate it safely. Between parties of reasonably equal capability and experience, this will not be difficult, but technology transfer often involves inexperienced licensees in less-developed countries where differences in capability, experience and culture are significant and must be taken into account. Guidelines for the transfer of technology have been produced by, among others, the European Chemical Industry Council, CEFIC. Those aspects that particularly concern the employer's project manager are as follows:

(1) The assessment of the capabilities of the potential licensee and the technology which it is consequently considered appropriate to transfer. It is unlikely that the project manager will be responsible for deciding whether and what to license, but he will probably contribute to the assessment.

(2) The provision of the *front end engineering package*, tailored to the particular circumstances.

(3) Approving the engineering contractor who is to perform the detailed engineering for the plant. The employer may restrict the number of contractors who are allowed to engineer the process. The contractors so appointed will enter into agreements precluding them from engineering similar processes based on the technology of others. Sometimes there is pressure from the potential licensee for a different contractor to be used: obviously this would bring disadvantages, even where the proposed contractor was fully competent. Confidentiality will be less secure. The effort necessary to ensure that the contractor fully understands what is required and to review his work would be greater. Few processes are licensed often enough to provide much work for more than a small number of contractors: the appointed contractors may have occasion to reconsider their positions if the work is to be shared more widely.

(4) Carrying out such reviews of the engineering design contractor's work as is considered necessary to ensure that his design faithfully interprets the technology. The extent of this will depend on the general capability of the contractor and his experience with the particular process.

(5) Training the licensee's staff to commission and operate the plant.

(6) Supervising commissioning.

(7) Post-completion activities such as process improvements, approval of plant modifications, exchange of data on safety, health and environmental matters.

The front end engineering package is of crucial importance. It must specify all the process information which the engineering contractor needs to be able to perform the detailed engineering design and construction of the plant, exactly as it would if the plant were to be owned and operated by the employer. In addition, it must explain for the benefit of the licensee the design philosophy of the plant and the operational assumptions on which the design is based. It must draw attention to any aspects where differences in the level of development and in the culture of the licensee might have an influence. Some examples of matters that might need particular mention are as follows:

- The fact that the testing of trips and alarms at the specified intervals is not merely a form of preventive maintenance, but an integral part of the design for safety. A different frequency of testing would require a different design and a different provision of equipment.
- Where flammable inventories are involved, the importance of matters such as the spacing of equipment, drainage from beneath vessels containing flammable liquids, and the maintenance of clear space. Where there is a possibility of a release of toxic gas, or of a vapour cloud explosion, the design will be based on restricting occupation of a defined surrounding area: permitting a shanty town to grow up round the plant may put many at risk.
- The need for the man on the spot to have the power to act in emergency, and for an independent safety function with authority and the power to investigate incidents.
- The need for procedures to ensure that maintenance is carried out safely—the control of maintenance activities by a system of permits to perform work, to enter confined spaces and to control sources of ignition.
- The proper understanding and use of isolation equipment to permit safe working while part of the plant continues to operate.
- The need for a system for the control and proper design of plant modifications, including approval by the licensor of any proposed modification that might affect the process.

The front end engineering package must spell out clearly and in detail the responsibilities of the parties for the various aspects of safety. The employer will not be in control of events once the plant starts to operate. His priorities must be first, to do all he can and should to prevent an accident; second, to be able to demonstrate that he has done so.

4.5 RESOURCES

The engineering resources in the UK will usually be too well known for there to be much need for any investigation. If the plant is to be built in a foreign country, however, it may be a very different matter. A major process plant will employ materials and equipment of such sophistication that a large proportion of it by quantity (and an even larger part by value) can only be supplied by a relatively small number of manufacturers world-wide, and procurement of this will be quite independent of plant location. There will, however, be some low-technology materials and equipment which, if they could be obtained at the right price, delivery and specification, would be purchased in the country in which the plant is to be located. Added to which, in some cases, import duties may be remitted or reduced only where local supply is not possible. Construction will certainly make use of local resources. It may therefore be necessary to survey all possible manufacturers and fabricators to assess their capability. Where there are conditions on the remission of import duty, enquiries for materials and equipment should be issued to local suppliers only where there is no doubt that they can perform satisfactorily. Suppliers are apt to exaggerate their capabilities, resulting in the payment of higher duties when the equipment has later to be imported.

Some countries prohibit the import of labour for construction, often overestimating the technical competence of their own nationals. Particular kinds of skilled labour, not available in the country concerned, then have to be brought in under some other guise—as engineers and supervisors, perhaps. The assessment of construction capability must be done with care. Sub-contractors who can provide little more than labour may claim management and technical skills. Where one major plant is being built, there are usually several, if not many, others and the available resources may be severely overloaded, a fact of which local firms may be aware and which may be reflected in their prices so as to eliminate any expected benefit from cheap labour costs. In some countries the cost of expatriate supervision may be as great as that of the construction labour itself, so it is important to form an accurate view of supervision requirements.

In a developing country, the proposed plant might be just one of a number of projects being encouraged by the government, for example to exploit discoveries of oil or gas. In such circumstances, the employer's project manager would have to investigate whether the demands of the total development for construction resources could be satisfied. If the construction labour appeared inadequate and import was not permitted, satisfactory training arrangements would have to be put in hand. On a major new industrial site, agreements on some common conditions of employment, and to prevent the poaching of labour, would be highly desirable. Some of these matters could be dealt with only by the government, who might need prompting. Others would require co-operation between the investing companies. The contractors who will eventually have the problems at first hand would not be able to contribute at this stage as they would not yet be appointed. The employer's project manager must do his best to see that adequate steps were taken and to make appropriate allowance in his estimates of cost and time for the project.

4.6 PLANT LOCATION

The general location of a process plant, that is to say, the country or area of a country in which it is proposed to be sited, will be chosen primarily on economic and commercial grounds. The desirability of being close to the customers, or to the sources of supply of feedstocks, often dominates the choice for a large-tonnage process plant. There are, for example, good reasons for siting a plant in the country where the largest sales are expected. Even if there were no tariff barriers against imports and transport costs were not prohibitive, few developing countries would be happy to accept large-scale imports for long, if they could see the possibility of local production. This they might soon encourage by investment incentives. Customers also prefer local manufacturers as being a more secure source of supply both in the short term—having a shorter and quicker transport chain, and in the long term—being more committed to business in that country. For a large-tonnage product, the cost of transport is important and the costs of moving feedstocks and product will be key factors in the choice of location. If hazardous chemicals were involved, this would also limit the choice.

Having chosen a general location, the selection of a specific site must take into account additional factors, including several of an engineering nature. In fact, the choice of site for a major process plant is almost certain to be severely restricted:

(1) If the employer has existing similar operations in the country concerned, the advantages of placing the new plant on an existing site, where this is possible, are likely to be so great as to rule out any alternative. The new plant may derive its feedstocks from one or more of the existing units. Whether or not this is so, it will probably be able to make use of existing off-plot facilities such as utilities supply, effluent treatment and disposal, maintenance and administrative facilities, roads and railways, gate houses and fencing, and may be able to share existing personnel.

(2) If a new site is to be selected, environmental requirements, or considerations of visual intrusion and of compatibility with what is already present—what

are in fact, if not in name, zoning restrictions—rule out much of any country. Large demands for water and electricity, questions of transport, and of effluent disposal also restrict plant location, usually to near other industrial development.

(3) The off-plot and infrastructure costs for a stand-alone plant on a new site may be so great as to seriously challenge the viability of the project. Where a new site is being considered, the plant may be merely the first in a series planned for it. The choice of such a site and the development of its infrastructure would then probably form a separate project, which would take into account the other plants in prospect.

(4) A possible alternative is to site the new plant adjacent to another company's plant which is the major supplier or customer, making arrangements with the other company to gain some of the advantages of existing off-plot facilities.

(5) In countries which are attempting to develop their industrial base rapidly, possibly to exploit reserves of oil or gas, a state-supported industrial estate for major industry may be the best, perhaps the only, option.

Once a possible site is identified, a number of purely engineering aspects must be examined. The conclusions from such examinations will affect estimates of cost and possibly programme, and may occasionally rule out a site altogether. Matters which affect the capital cost, but which would be unlikely to lead to the rejection of the site on those grounds alone are the soil conditions, the climate and the risks of earthquakes. The transport of large loads to the site during construction could conceivably be so difficult or so costly as to rule out a site; inadequate water supplies might also do so. The provision of adequate power supplies could require so much to be added to the cost as to render a site uneconomic. Safety considerations—notably those arising from possible release of flammable vapours or toxic gases, from the plant in question or from its neighbours—could make a proposed site unacceptable.

In assessing the suitability of a site, there is no substitute for personal inspection and, however he may have delegated the work of assessment, the project manager should visit the site before a decision is made, especially where the process to be employed contains major hazards. In cases where the project manager's responsibility is limited, for example, to the provision of licensed technology to others, he must be clear whether he has any responsibility to approve the suitability of the chosen site.

4.7 IMPORT DUTIES

Dealing with the import of equipment for a project to be built in a foreign country can be a life-shortening experience. The first requirement is, obviously, to discover the rates of duties that will be payable, so that the appropriate amounts can be included in the sanction estimate. This may prove much more difficult than it sounds. In some countries, knowledge is power, not to be lightly divulged. In others, forward planning is not in vogue and obstacles are surmounted when they appear. In yet others, the rules are so vague, and so capriciously interpreted, that certainty is impossible to achieve. Where there has been relatively little previous importing, expertise will be hard to find. Even where the rules seem clear, traps often lie in wait for the unwary. For example, foreign investment is often encouraged by special treatment, but it may only later be found that the remitting of import duty on some types of equipment does not extend to spares, in which is included installed standby equipment. Written rulings from the highest level may be disregarded, or circumvented, by the customs staff. Where it proves impossible to be sure of the import duties that will prove to be payable, contractors bidding for the project will probably take a pessimistic view. It would then be sensible to require that bidders show their assumptions as to duties separately in their bids, and place the liability on the employer.

Apart from problems with the rates of import duties, there may be problems of delay. Discrepancies in the paperwork can cause inordinate delays, and are to be avoided at all costs. The situation may be exacerbated if the project has been granted import privileges which are being interpreted as strictly as possible. There is no substitute for local knowledge and assistance, especially if unofficial payments have to be made. A good local agent is worth more than rubies, and the employer's project manager may also seek help from any existing operation the employer may have in the country concerned. The direct participation of the plant owner is essential, even if the contractor is contractually responsible for importing.

4.8 UTILITIES AND FEEDSTOCKS' SUPPLY

The availability of utilities and feedstocks supplies may affect both on-plot and off-plot design. Many process plants are large consumers of water. If the plant is to be built in a country where water supply is a problem, the design can often be modified to reduce the water consumption below the level which would be appropriate and economic for a plant to be built, for example, in the UK. Water treatment facilities can be incorporated, usually without crippling expense, to allow poor quality water to be used. When all such measures have been taken, however, substantial requirements may remain and these must be capable of being satisfied if a site is to be acceptable. It can be very difficult, in a country where water supplies are inadequate or non-existent, to obtain credible assurances that they will be available when required. Without these, however, it would not be sensible to proceed.

If the proposed process plant is a large user of electricity, considerable time and effort may have to be spent to establish the nature of the power supplies available. Few countries have an electricity supply system as robust as the UK national grid, and it may be difficult to obtain data on reliability. The employment of specialist consultants, especially if they have previous experience in the country, may be indicated. An inadequate power supply could have serious design implications. Large electrical drives may not be practicable, or may be possible only with some form of soft start. It would seldom be economic for a single process plant to have to generate any large amount of power with the availability and reliability required for key prime movers, so that alternatives to large electrical drives may be necessary. Emergency generation of sufficient power to permit a controlled shut-down of the plant may also be essential.

The availability of feedstocks supplies will affect the storage needed and their quality may call for pre-treatment, or adjustment to the process to allow for impurity. Investigation of the means of moving the feedstocks to site may be required and its reliability assessed. Where transport is by ship, storage capacity is often controlled by the size of the shipload and the need to be able to discharge it, rather than by considerations of a number of days' capacity for plant operation. The requirement for product storage is similarly affected by the means of transport and the distance moved. Consideration has also to be given to the capacity needed to cover a major overhaul.

4.9 OUT-OF-GAUGE TRANSPORT TO SITE

Many large process plants require the transport to site of large and heavy loads for construction. Often, these loads exceed the weights or dimensions permitted on the roads and special arrangements are required for their transport. Loads too large to pass under any bridge, or too heavy to cross one, can clearly be transported only for short distances and with the utmost care. A plant which involves such loads, therefore, must be sited close to the sea or to a navigable waterway of adequate capacity. If not near a port that can handle the necessary loads, a beach over which they can be hauled is a possible alternative. Transport of large loads may be avoided by fabrication or assembly on site and, where appropriate, the costs of this would have to be estimated and compared. However, the site chosen would have to be especially difficult for site fabrication of much equipment to be preferred. Apart from the question of cost, which would be very high if the manufacturing facilities required on site were at all sophisticated, site fabrication would almost certainly add considerably to programme.

Thus, a plant which requires the transport of out-of-gauge construction loads may give rise to an associated project to accomplish it. Special ships will be required, transport by barge may be necessary, and a special route may have to be engineered. The latter could include temporary jetty or harbour facilities, new roads and bridges as well as the widening of existing roads and the temporary removal of street furniture. In some cases, the work necessary will not be sufficiently defined before sanction to allow a lump sum bid, even supposing that the contractors bidding for other parts of the contract are appropriate. The employer's project manager will then have to estimate for the work himself, but will retain the option of how it is to be managed until better definition has been achieved.

Chapter 5

Contractual Relationships

Much of this book is concerned with the contractual relationship between employer and contractor, a matter of overwhelming importance. The relationship is established by a clear understanding of the obligations of the parties and by a firm technical basis for the work. It is sustained by what has been called, in another context, the ethic of mutual obligation: the sense of employer and contractor working together for the advantage of both. If this is lost, then the chances of success are badly damaged. Of course, these remarks imply a direct relationship between employer and contractor, and this is assumed in the following discussion. Were an independent engineer to be engaged and interposed between employer and contractor, as envisaged in many of the model forms of contract and discussed in later chapters, the importance of the relationship would be very substantially reduced.

5.1 COMPETITION

The question of how best to select the contractor, and the implications this has on the ensuing contractual relationship, is of continuing importance. For the past decade and more, fair competition has been the shibboleth of most in the West, but in recent years the continuing industrial success of countries with seemingly different methods has stimulated discussion of possible alternatives. This discussion has, of course, been concerned not only, or even mainly, with the placing of a single order, but with circumstances where there is a continuing need for goods or services of the same kind.

Western methods of dealing with competitors, suppliers and contractors have changed over the years, often encouraged or enforced by legislation. In the 1950s, international competition was much less than today. In some industries, major manufacturers divided the world into spheres of influence. In the UK, boiler manufacturers operated non-competition agreements and electric motor manufacturers operated a ring to fix the prices of their products. Numerous other examples of anti-competitive behaviour could no doubt be quoted. Competition between bidders for a contract, where it existed at all, was less fierce than today, in part reflecting the easier commercial conditions then prevailing. Negotiation to reduce a bid was, if not unthinkable, unlikely to be very productive, though it might succeed in adding some equipment at no extra cost. Specification of the customer's requirements was often rudimentary, as were contract conditions. The contractor was relied upon to supply whatever was necessary to make the plant perform as required, and usually did so without appeal for variations. Since definition and specification were much less, much more depended on the relationship between purchaser and contractor and on their mutual confidence.

In some countries, for example, in parts of the Far East, conditions somewhat similar to these still prevail. There is collusion rather than competition between bidders on price. Differentiation must be on other grounds. Once the rules are understood (and they are not overt as far as the foreigner is concerned), a perfectly satisfactory contract can be let. Prices are not always artificially inflated, the fine print of specification and contract is not over-emphasised, rather is there a Confucian spirit of agreeing to agree. It is all rather reminiscent of the UK in the 1950s and 1960s. Of course, corruption is also endemic in some parts of the Far East, and elsewhere, and this also militates against fair competition.

In the last few decades there has been legislation, especially in the USA, the UK and the EC, to prevent the operation of agreements which reduce competition. In this different climate, industry discovered that a cheaper, if not assuredly a better, deal could generally be obtained by competition and this has since been the watchword of most Western industry, especially in the UK which has probably been more open to foreign competition than most other countries. The accepted best practice in a UK company of any size when placing a contract for services, or an order for goods, has been to invite bids from selected bidders against a detailed specification and to choose the winning bid on clear criteria of value for money—cost, quality, delivery. Public authorities may operate unrestricted bid lists, and may open tenders in public on a prescribed date to try to ensure that the process is completely above-board, but this would be inappropriate where few contractors had the technical and commercial capability that the contract required. Private companies usually operate a more flexible and private system of bid soliciting and evaluation, with internal procedures that try to ensure that all is done as it should be. Even in private industry, however, bid lists are relatively open, in some cases entirely so, but for highly technical contracts, especially those for the provision of services which require the contractor to work alongside the employer, potential bidders must usually pre-qualify. The sensible employer will give proper weight to his previous experience with the potential bidders in question so as to obtain, other things being equal or reasonably so, a list of bidders who for the most part are not new to his requirements and methods of working. He will not too precipitately discard a contractor whose performance on a recent contract might have been below standard, since to do so would be to lose the benefits of hard-won experience. However, admission to the bid list of a company with whom the employer had no previous experience must often be possible if the system is to continue to flourish.

The advantages of competition may be simply stated. Providing his requirements are properly specified, it ensures that the customer gets the best deal possible in all the circumstances. He does not need to worry whether the price is right: it must be or he would have been made a better offer. Competition keeps the contractor on his toes, so that he cannot secure a position as favoured supplier and go to sleep in it. He must continue to seek continual improvement since his position as current supplier gives him only modest advantage over those who would displace him. Fair competition is also the best, perhaps the only real, defence against corruption.

But there are disadvantages to the competitive system. First is the cost of operating it. Time and money are spent by the employer in preparing his enquiry—in defining his requirements to the bidders in complete detail. Time and money are also spent by the bidders in preparing their tenders. Further time and effort is consumed in bid evaluation and negotiation. Then when the order is placed, the chosen contractor may work less efficiently, and satisfy the employer's requirements less completely, than might another whose greater knowledge and experience of those requirements were reflected in his higher price. The competitive system may also encourage an adversarial relationship between employer and contractor, which can consume much time and effort in dispute. At the extreme, and especially if encouraged by the use of inappropriate contract conditions, this adversarial tendency may lead disastrously to litigation, though litigation is not, of course, confined to contracts placed competitively. Conditions of contracts have an important part to play and are dealt with at some length in this book. One might wish the situation were different and long for a return to the situation of the 1950's and 60's, when it was possible, even customary, to place a large contract by no more than a brief letter and to achieve success seemingly equal to today's, with little or no dispute. However, it is useless to hope to turn the clock back. In today's conditions, continuing success will be achieved only by the exercise of considerable contractual skill and care by both parties, and moderate and fair dealing in their relationships.

5.2 PREFERRED CONTRACTORS

Stimulated at least partly by the Japanese example, calls have increasingly been made to replace continual competition by the building of long-term relationships between employer and contractor, in some ways a return to the 1950's situation. Thus in the process plant industry, a major employer might appoint one or two preferred contractors or 'partners', and use them for all, or at least a substantial part, of his design and construction work. The advantages are clear. A continuous, and hence presumably more efficient, working relationship could be established. The objectives of employer and contractor should have more in common as a long-term relationship would be developed which neither would wish to jeopardise. Where the employer was unable to provide much engineering effort, a preferred contractor could more confidently be allowed to work unsupervised. The trend of recent years towards an increasingly confrontational and litigious attitude between contractor and employer should be moderated or reversed. The preferred contractor might also be expected to be more careful of his employer's confidential data and be more readily trusted not to reveal sensitive commercial and technical information. The considerable time and effort spent in the competitive bidding process would be saved. The preferred contractor would become familiar with the employer's requirements, specifications and working methods. A lengthy familiarisation process every time a new contract was awarded would be avoided. Computer systems could be made compatible so that transmission of information was easier.

These advantages, however, will count for little unless the preferred contractor is the equal of his competitors. This may have been true on appointment, but the contractor's continuing efficiency cannot be taken for granted where there is little or no economic pressure upon him to perform. All the evidence shows how difficult it is to remain efficient in these circumstances. The soporific effects of being shielded from competition have been plain to see—in nationalised industries, in public corporations and, indeed, in private companies which have a temporary monopoly. How is the employer, or indeed the contractor himself, to judge whether the contractor remains competitive? It is true that the Japanese seem to have solved the problem, but the Japanese culture is very different from that of the UK and provides a different set of advantages and disadvantages. It is also true that the Japanese example relates mainly to suppliers of small manufactured parts in quantity—to the motor industry, for example—where deviation from requirements may be detected more easily and quickly than in the design and construction of process plants.

It must also be said that, whatever their hopes and intentions, the employer and the process plant contractor do not really have the same objectives. The contractor's objective is a profitable contract, the employer's a successful project. In virtually all cases the contract will be only part of the total project, so that even if the success criteria were the same for contractor and employer, their objectives might still be incompatible. Moreover, both contractor and employer are subject to the tyranny of the bottom line of their respective balance sheets, and circumstances will affect them differently. Organisations and people change over the years, as do capabilities and business objectives, so that those once compatible may be so no longer. Experience leads one to favour repeated assessment and selection of contractors, at least for major projects, simply because of this variability with time.

Contract conditions also need to be considered. An evergreen contract for a continuing, unspecified workload is likely, in the nature of things, to be reimbursable with little incentive for the contractor. Since the intention is for the contractor to become a quasi-extension of the employer's design office, the likelihood is also that he will be charged with liabilities little or no greater than those of the employer's own employees, giving the preferred contractor an increased share of the benefits without a concomitant share of the risks. In these circumstances, the employer would be contractually disadvantaged if he used the preferred contractor arrangement for a project of reasonable size and good initial definition. Contract terms more favourable to the employer could almost certainly be obtained by competitive tendering. Furthermore, unless the preferred contractor is to tie himself entirely to one employer, he will have other contracts which will compete for his resources. He is likely to give a keenly-priced lump sum contract priority over an evergreen reimbursable one. The employer is also denied the opportunity to tap the experience and knowledge of other contractors, which may be of particular advantage on occasions.

The authority of the employer's project manager will inevitably be diminished by a preferred contractor arrangement. Much of the contract for a particular project will be pre-determined by the evergreen contract between employer and contractor, and the project manager will have no influence on it. He will be able to negotiate only those terms which are specific to his own project. In the event of dispute, the contractor has another long-standing and continuous channel of communication to the employer through the managers of the partnership agreement, and no doubt will have little hesitation in using it.

Some contracts would certainly not fit well within a preferred contractor arrangement. A lump sum contract where the risks were allocated to the contractor would be incompatible with it. Where the employer owned and licensed the process technology, he would wish to use those contractors through whom the licensing was done, who might or might not include the preferred contractors. Similarly, for major projects concerned with the manufacture of commodity products, the employer would wish to employ one of the contractors specialising in the particular technology. Where the technology was owned by a contractor there would, of course, be no option but for the employer to use that contractor. The preferred contractor arrangement would thus seem to be more suited to the smaller project, where the technology to be used was either owned by the employer or was not a significant issue. It might also be appropriate where there was to be little or no supervision by the employer, or for projects ill-defined at the outset or which contained a substantial development element—projects which by their nature would require a reimbursable contract to be let.

The best answer, as in much else, lies in moderation. Whatever the contractual form, the relationship between process plant operator and his contractor must have elements of a partnership if it is to be successful. If the choice is for competition for each contract, then care must be taken to consider qualitative factors. Previous dealings between employer and bidders will then influence admission to the list of bidders as well as the assessment of the bids themselves, so helping to provide some continuity of association. If a permanent contractual relationship is chosen, means must be established to expose this to competition at frequent intervals.

5.3 REASONS FOR THE USE OF ENGINEERING CONTRACTORS

Virtually any of the operations of any company can be contracted out. A company may employ toll manufacture, contract research, engineering and construction contractors and many other external agencies. There is, of course, a number of core activities which the company must perform itself if it hopes to obtain an advantage over, or even to continue in the long term to compete with, its competitors. There can be no competitive edge in the use of a contractor in itself, since anyone can do the same. There may, of course, be a competitive disadvantage in not using a contractor where he can perform the work more efficiently than oneself, and a company could prosper by employing contractors more effectively than others.

In the UK, the trend of the last decade or two has been increasingly to contract out activities that can reasonably be performed by specialist providers. As a country develops, so its infrastructure and the provision of services and facilities of all kinds increases. Before the Second World War, a major UK process company was compelled to do many things which would not now be regarded as part of its core business. These might have included the provision of social facilities and services such as housing, sports grounds, recreation clubs and works canteens; ancillary activities like the transport of its products; and much of the engineering support for its own activities—for example, the design and manufacture of specialised engineering equipment required for high pressure chemical processes. In the UK in the present day, there are few goods and services that cannot be purchased, albeit the standard may not always satisfy, and the goods are often imported. In hard times, the advantages of operating with a minimum of permanent facilities and staff loom very large. In boom times, a manufacturer who relies too heavily on outside agencies may well find his development aspirations hampered.

Engineering design and construction are more commonly contracted out than many other activities. The principal reason for this is that, despite what has been said before about the need for continuity of investment in a capital-intensive company, capital expenditure is nevertheless very variable. It may be stopped or started, reduced or increased to suit current circumstances in a way which is not possible with many of the company's other activities. Capital investment is nearly always the first casualty of any recession. Furthermore, a capital project is usually a discrete activity with a defined beginning and end, requiring a temporary increase in resources. It is thus inherently more suitable for the use of an external agency than a continuing activity which employs fairly constant numbers of staff.

Nevertheless, there are good reasons why a process manufacturer should play an active part in the execution of his capital investment programme. Prime among these is that capital investment is a core activity where the direct involvement of a company's staff enables it to achieve better plants than it would otherwise do and, it is hoped, better plants than those of its competitors. There are, nevertheless, manufacturing companies that aim merely to operate the best commercially available processes developed, engineered and constructed by others, and to compete entirely on other grounds, for example, the availability of cheap feedstock, cheap labour, lower transport costs, government subsidies or the protection of tariff barriers. Such companies, which are to be found largely in the developing countries and are themselves of recent origin, will be almost entirely in the hands of contractors from feasibility study to commissioning. They may be successful given their particular circumstances, but will not be able to compete fully on level terms with the world's major manufacturers until they take a more active part in project development and execution.

Whatever the company policy as regards the resources it retains, it is almost certain that the fluctuations of a manufacturer's capital investment programme will require it to make use of contractors on occasion. Despite the frequency with which a large process manufacturer must invest, his capital programme will still exhibit peaks and troughs which can conveniently be smoothed by the employment of contractors, and this must apply even more strongly to a small manufacturer. However, a policy which required contractors to be used only for occasional peak lopping would probably not be the optimum. Its consequence would be that contractors would be engaged only when the employer's resources were at full stretch and least able to tackle the unfamiliar task of managing the external agency.

Typically then, a process plant manufacturer will have some resources, but not enough to execute the whole of his capital programme. He will have a choice of where to deploy his own effort. Virtually all the indicators will point to him preferentially contracting out the larger projects. He may find it difficult to re-deploy resources in the numbers required to execute these himself. Contracting out a large project requires less overhead from the employer than contracting out many small projects. The latter are often modifications to existing plants where detailed knowledge of the plant and close liaison with the operating works is necessary, and which would be difficult for a contractor to achieve. Small projects are also more likely than large ones to be developmental and hence to be relatively ill-defined and to have more pressing secrecy requirements. The employer with resources of his own can aim to use contractors to engineer well-defined parcels of work under adequate supervision, reserving those which are ill-defined at the outset for execution by his own staff. Whatever his contracting policy, the employer would require substantial numbers of staff to specify the optimum plant configuration for projects where circumstances are complicated. A manufacturer without the necessary technical resources even for this would compromise the development of his business. Considerable resources are also needed if the employer is to exert control over the contractor during the life of the project. Without these, the employer would be compelled to use those forms of contract, such as lump sum, which required the minimum of supervision.

There are more positive reasons than the employer's lack of resources why a contractor might be employed to design and construct a new plant. A major manufacturer operates many processes and although his capital investment programme may be large, his investment in a particular process may be relatively infrequent. A contractor may engineer many plants of a given type and be able to offer the manufacturer greater expertise in engineering that type of plant than the latter possesses. Again, the contractor may be the inventor or sole licensee of a process that the manufacturing company wishes to operate, thereby leaving no choice but to employ him. There may be other areas in which the contractor can offer the manufacturer greater experience and expertise. These may include more experience in a relevant foreign country, more expertise in the management of large projects, or greater technological skills in a given field of activity. The contractor can also be expected to do a more professional job in detailed design, routine administration and other areas where his repetition rate is high. Naturally, a company that habitually uses contractors will come to rely upon them. It will not gain experience nor develop skills in those activities that it never performs itself.

As for the reasons which can be advanced in favour of the employer executing his own projects in particular circumstances, some of them are rooted in how the manufacturing company views its business, or at least, particular parts of it. If the company believes its manufacturing facilities are of first importance to its business and a prime source of its competitive edge, it is more likely to carry out its own process and engineering design and, probably, its own construction. Such circumstances may arise where the company has invented or developed a process and believes that it is ahead of its competitors, and hopes to remain so by continued process and engineering development. There can be no doubt that, other things being equal, development can more effectively be done within the company with close co-operation between all the relevant functions.

Confidentiality may be crucially important where the company has developed its own technology, and is likely to be better preserved by doing the work in-house. Contractors vary in the care which they take of employer's information. In the nature of things, they will not be so careful as the employer and this can sometimes be seen in their differing attitudes to the employer's and to their own information. Whereas no reputable Western contractor is likely to pass on a client's confidential information deliberately, he may carelessly and unnecessarily do so, for example, to contractor associates or sub-contractors in foreign countries where the concept of confidentiality of information— particularly if it belongs to a foreign company—has no meaning. In some Far Eastern countries, information disclosed in confidence may very soon reach the public domain—and may even more quickly reach that part of the public with a business interest in it. In any case, there is often an outflow of hard-won technical expertise from the employer to the contractor. This may be not only the fruits of the employer's operating experience, his development of new control systems and miscellaneous hardware improvements, but may extend to improved design methods, notably those having a bearing on safety. Of course, the employer would also hope to gain the benefits of the contractor's learning experiences with other major manufacturers.

It will be more expensive for an employer to use a contractor rather than his own staff. The contractor will seek to make a profit and to be rewarded for any risk he takes, and the employer will incur costs in monitoring and controlling the contractor's work. Compared with executing the work himself, the employer may make few savings at engineer, as distinct from designer, level by using a contractor. Offset against these extra costs will be any savings resulting from the contractor performing the detailed engineering work more efficiently than would the employer.

5.4 DIFFERENCES BETWEEN IN-HOUSE AND CONTRACTOR EXECUTION

There are, of course, differences between the way an employer would execute a project in-house, and the way a contractor would do it. A contractor offers a different selection of strengths and weaknesses and has different objectives. It is important for the employer's project manager to understand these differences and, so far as he can, take them into account in his management of the project. As previously remarked, the objectives of the contractor cannot be identical with those of the employer. The contractor's aim is a successful contract, and will be very much prescribed by the liabilities he has undertaken. A successful contract does not automatically mean a successful project, and in any case is seldom the whole of it. The employer's project manager must endeavour to frame and manage the contract so that success for the contractor means success for the employer. Self-evidently, this means the maintenance of harmonious working relations and the resolution of conflict as soon as it occurs. The long-term employment of a particular contractor, as discussed previously, cannot be a complete answer, since no single contractor would be suitable for all the projects a large company would wish to initiate. To aspire to consistent success in the use of contractors, the employer's project manager must understand the implications of the contract terms on a contractor's behaviour, learn to work to his strengths and compensate for his weaknesses, and develop the necessary skills to manage the relationship between contractor and employer.

Much depends on the contractor's project manager. He may take a narrow, short-term view and manage the project to minimise the contractor's costs, paying little heed to any other consideration. Another and better might consider that the long-term interests of the contractor were best served by giving more weight to achieving the best result for the employer. The best contractor's project manager will give the employer honest appraisals of progress and may occasionally enlist the support of the employer's project manager in obtaining increased resources from the contractor's own organisation. The worst will deny he has any problem until, or even after, it becomes obvious.

A common, though not universal, difference between the contractor's engineer and his counterpart from the employer's organisation is that the former tends to specialise by function and the latter by technology. The consequence of his greater functional specialisation means that the typical contractor's engineer should be capable of a better, more professional job in detailed project execution, especially in the more routine elements, than his counterpart in the employer's organisation. He will be more disciplined and meticulous in the way he operates systems and procedures, but less versatile and flexible. Some employers' engineers, in contrast, may spend much of their careers occupied with a particular process technology which is of great importance to the employer. They may build deep technical expertise in that specific area of technology, but may be employed on any or all of operation, maintenance, design and construction.

An employer's engineer will also usually experience greater variety in his work than his equivalent in the contractor's organisation. There are many different jobs for an engineer in a process manufacturing company, and versatility is sought and encouraged. A period on maintenance or operation is usually regarded by the employer as essential experience for his staff engaged on capital projects, whereas the contractor's engineer might spend the vast majority of his life in the design office with little cause to move outside it. The repetition rate of projects is lower in the employer's organisation than in the contractor's, since the employer's involvement must encompass the full project cycle. The contractor's work, on the other hand, would very seldom commence until the feasibility studies had been done, the major decisions taken and the project defined and packaged for transmission outside the employer's organisation, and then would often concern only engineering design and procurement. The contractor would less frequently be responsible for process design, or for construction and commissioning, and seldom for process development and evaluation. The period of his involvement in what, to the employer, would be a five-year project might not exceed two years. This greater variety of work that is often the lot of the employer's engineer will make him more accustomed to dealing with the novel situation and better able to cope with it.

It is in the nature of things for people to believe that their own organisation can perform better than others. There has probably never been an engineer employed by a major process manufacturer who did not believe that his own company could design and build a plant better than any contractor, given the chance. It is natural to gloss over the errors and omissions of one's own organisation and emphasise those of others. Thus results the oft-expressed opinion that the worst contractor is the one currently employed. But the employer's project manager dissatisfied with a contractor's performance should look first at his own. It is unlikely that a poor performance is entirely the fault of the contractor and, even if it were, the employer's project manager still bears the responsibility for his selection.

Chapter 6

Choice of Type of Contract

6.1 TYPES OF CONTRACT

The feature which most importantly distinguishes the major types of contract one from another is the allocation of risk: which of the parties to the contract is liable for failure to meet expectations in the three areas of cost, time and performance. (In common law, where the contract does not otherwise provide, the contractor has an obligation to do his work to a reasonable standard, at reasonable cost and in a reasonable time, but in what follows, we are concerned with express liabilities.) In theory, there could be eight different types of contract, but half of the mathematically possible combinations of liability would seldom be appropriate to a process plant contract. It would, for example, be an unusual contract which required the contractor to complete a plant to a fixed cost, but which placed on him no express liability either for the timing of its completion, or for its performance. Risk in any of the three areas can, of course, be shared, primarily by setting limits to the liabilities of the contractor.

Measured by the allocation of risk, there are only four fundamentally different types of contract in normal use: lump sum, re-measure and value, schedule of rates, and reimbursable. Lump sum and reimbursable contracts may be used for both design and construction. Measure and value, and schedule of rates contracts are suitable only where the physical output of the contractor can be measured and so, in practice, are limited to construction. The different types of contract may be described briefly as follows:

6.1.1 Lump Sum Contract

In this type of contract, in exchange for a pre-determined lump sum price, the contractor agrees to provide a pre-defined article, which may, for example, be a complete process plant or merely the design for one. The contractor usually carries all, or a major part, of the liabilities for cost, programme and performance. For the design and construction of a complete process plant, the contractor's liabilities would typically include:

- *Cost*: The full liability for cost, except that in some cases the lump sum price may be adjustable for the effects of inflation, in which case this particular risk would remain with the employer.
- *Programme*: Liability for completion on time. The contractor would be liable to pay damages if he was late.
- *Performance*: Liability for the performance of the plant and for making good defects at his own expense.

Of course, any of the risks which the contractor undertakes may be qualified and limited in the contract.

6.1.2 Re-measure and Value Contract

In a re-measure and value construction contract, the contractor tenders a unit rate for each item on the construction bill of quantities, for example, a price per cubic metre of concrete placed. There is no contract price. Instead, there is a tender total, the sum of the products of the unit rates quoted by the bidder and the quantities specified by the employer, which may be used as a guide (and no more than that) to the final cost. The contractor's liabilities will typically be:

- *Cost:* Liability only for his quoted unit rates (which may nevertheless be adjustable for the effects of inflation as well as for some other reasons). Almost all the risk, that is for the estimation of the quantities, remains with the employer.
- *Programme*: Liability for completion on time and for payment of damages in the event of delay.
- *Performance*: Responsibility for the quality of workmanship and of materials supplied.

6.1.3 Schedule of Rates Contract

The schedule of rates construction contract has much in common with a re-measure and value contract. The major difference is that there is no initial bill of quantities, since the schedule of rates contract is placed before the design has an estimated scope of works, and a list of unit operations which the work is expected to require, against which the bidder quotes his unit rates. The contractor's liabilities will be:

- *Cost*: Liability only for his quoted unit rates (which, as in a re-measure and value contract may nevertheless be adjustable for the effects of inflation and for other reasons).
- *Programme*: Given that the scope of works defines the work the contractor has to do only very approximately, the liability of the contractor to complete to programme can hardly be more than the requirement of reasonableness.
- *Performance*: Responsibility for the quality of workmanship and of materials supplied.

6.1.4 Reimbursable Contract

In a reimbursable contract, the contractor is paid his costs of labour, plant and materials plus an element (which may be variously calculated, and is sometimes fixed) for overheads and profit. In design, for example, reimbursement may be based on a series of agreed man-hour rates (which may superficially seem similar to a schedule of rates contract but which is not, in fact, the same since what is being measured is effort—man-hours, and not result, e.g. quantity of concrete) or on salary costs times an agreed multiplier.

There are practical difficulties in the way of assigning liability to the reimbursable contractor, since if he is given any financial liability for programme, or for plant performance, or for the correction of defects, he can spend to excess to try to ensure that he incurs none. If the contractor is to be required to correct his errors (not, logically, his omissions) at his own expense, it may often be difficult to distinguish a design error from the normal process of iteration. Where such an error is identified, there may still be problems in assessing its full consequences and in isolating the cost of correcting these from other expenditure. The contractor's contractual liabilities, therefore, would typically be:

- *Cost*: None, or very little. He would take the risk in any rates which he has quoted (which may be adjustable for the effects of inflation) and for any fixed fee.
- *Programme*: No more than his common law obligation to do the work in a reasonable time.
- *Performance*: Usually no more than responsibility for the exercise of due skill and care in what he does. He may also be responsible for correcting errors in his work at his own expense.

If the contractor purchases materials and equipment as principal, and sells them on to the employer, he will have liabilities for them. These liabilities will, however, usually be matched by those of his suppliers to him, so that he will be at risk only in the event of supplier default.

6.1.5 Relation between Liabilities

It is evident from the above that the liabilities the contractor may shoulder are logically connected. It would be impracticable, in the normal course of business, to have a reimbursable contract which guaranteed an end result, for any restraint from the employer on the contractor's expenditure could release the contractor from his liability. Similarly, a lump sum contract without a defined result would be nonsensical for most process plant contracts. The circumstances of the project dictate the possibilities so far as risk allocation (and hence the incentive for the contractor to perform) is concerned, and the bald choice between lump sum and reimbursable contracts may not always give a result to the employer's liking. Consequently, various hybrids or intermediate types of contract have been used from time to time to try to achieve a more acceptable form. Some of these attempt to obtain the advantages of a lump sum contract without the need for the accurate scope definition which such a contract requires. Others try to give more incentive to the reimbursable contractor. Some of the more fanciful hybrids are characterised more by ingenuity than utility. There is only very limited scope for using the form of contract to correct deficiencies in other aspects of a project.

6.2 PROCESS PLANT CONTRACTS

The main types of contract in use for process plant design, or design and construct, contracts, in order of decreasing fixed price element, are:

- Lump Sum
- Guaranteed Maximum
- Target Cost
- Part Lump Sum, part Reimbursable
- Cost plus Limited Fee
- Fully Reimbursable
- Convertible.

They may be briefly described as follows.

6.2.1 Lump Sum Contract

In exchange for a pre-determined payment, the contractor promises to supply goods or services or both which match a previous definition or which perform to a given specification. Many such contracts include an escalation clause so that the lump sum may be increased to allow for inflation. Also usually included in the contract is provision for varying the lump sum if the scope of work changes.

Much of the advantage of the lump sum contract derives from the fact that it requires good definition of what is to be provided. While this requirement will limit the number of projects in which such a contract can be used, if it can be satisfied one of the major factors contributing to a successful project—good initial definition—will be present. This type of contract ensures that the employer's cost commitment is defined and that clear responsibility for the performance of the contract rests on the contractor. It is possible to obtain full competition between bidders leading to the best available price for the employer.

There are a number of disadvantages to a lump sum contract. These include the different interests of employer and contractor and the possibility that they diverge further during the course of the contract. A long period is required for enquiry, bidding and evaluation. If process design is part of the contractor's responsibilities this crucial phase may be unduly compressed. There will be only very limited flexibility in the scope of the contract. Employer participation in the project will be limited and may prove difficult. The contract price will be increased to include contingency and reward for the contractor's risk, and there may be a danger of the contractor cutting corners to make a larger profit, or a smaller loss.

6.2.2 Guaranteed Maximum Price Contract

In a guaranteed maximum price contract, the contractor bears the whole of any cost over-run but shares the benefits of any under-run with the employer in agreed proportions. This is thus a more onerous proposition for the contractor than a lump sum contract and should result in a higher contract price.

A guaranteed maximum price contract will be based on a rather less complete definition than a lump sum contract. It therefore needs less time to enquire and bid, although evaluation of competing bids is more difficult. It gives the employer the security of knowing the upper limit of cost. The contractor has an incentive to control costs, especially if he shares in any savings. Operation of the contract may prove difficult: the scope of work included in the guaranteed maximum price is less well defined than it would be for a lump sum but the problem of agreeing what constitutes a change or variation (and hence is excluded from considerations of over-run and under-run) remains and is more difficult because of the poorer definition.

6.2.3 Target Price Contract

In the target price contract, both cost under-run and over-run are shared between employer and contractor. Cost savings may be shared differently from cost increases, and the sharing may vary as the over-run or under-run increases. The contractor's share may be significant, but is sometimes quite small—10% is not unusual. Such a contract transfers some of the onus for the cost of the contract to the contractor and requires less previous project development than either a lump sum or a guaranteed maximum type of contract.

Enquiry, bid and evaluation times are less than for a lump sum contract. Bid evaluation may be difficult. The contractor has an incentive to reduce costs, but the price is likely to be higher than the comparable lump sum contract though lower than the equivalent guaranteed maximum price. The contract can be difficult to operate for the same reasons as for the guaranteed maximum contract.

6.2.4 Part Lump Sum, Part Reimbursable Contract

It may often happen that a contractor has sufficient data to cost, say, the design and procurement services element of his bid accurately and so can offer a lump sum for that part of the job, while being willing to offer only a reimbursable price for materials and equipment. Such contracts are common. They need careful management by the employer because the contractor is differently motivated for the different parts of the work. Lump sum design and procurement services allied to reimbursable supply of materials and equipment, for example, may lead to the contractor paying too little attention to the employer's interests in dealing with suppliers. He may not be willing to spend extra man-hours to obtain the best buy, or may fail to deal properly with claims against the employer.

6.2.5 Cost Plus Limited Fee Contract

Since a completely reimbursable contract provides no incentive at all for the contractor to keep his costs down, modifications to this form of contract are frequently sought. By limiting the contractor's fee for his profit and general overhead, while reimbursing his other costs, the contractor can be given a mild incentive to minimise his costs and time. Under this arrangement, his profit and the contribution made to his general overhead reflect the original estimate for the contract, rather than the final total.

There are various ways in which the contractor's fee for his profit and general overhead might be restricted. It could be a fixed lump sum, or it could be a percentage of the reimbursed total with a fixed ceiling. Where there was little confidence in the initial cost estimate for the plant, the fee could vary with the ratio of achieved to estimated reimbursed total, raised to an exponent of less than unity. In other circumstances, the fee could be linked to an incentive clause to provide a sliding scale of payment, increasing as the total cost of the project decreased. Of course, for any of these arrangements to work properly, it is necessary for the profit and overhead element to be removed from the contractor's reimbursable rates.

Only a short enquiry, bid and evaluation time is needed. The employer can participate fully in the project and has (and needs) full control over costs. The employer has no assurance of the final outcome and since the contractor's incentive to control costs is weak, the employer must provide much of the discipline and control if a satisfactory project is to be achieved.

6.2.6 Fully Reimbursable Contract

A fully reimbursable contract may be awarded quickly with little or no preparation, but the employer would be foolish if he then required the contractor to start work immediately. The latter has to be provided with technical information on which to base his work, and has to be told how the employer wants the work to be performed. If the contractor starts before this has been done, there will be some months of wasted effort. The control systems which the employer needs in order to be able to manage the work have to be established: he has to provide much of the management function that in a lump sum contract would be done by the contractor. Hence the employer's supervision costs are greater than for a lump sum contract. A reimbursable contract provides no incentive for the contractor to control his costs so that the employer must monitor the work and the charges carefully if he is to be sure of getting value. The advantage to the employer is that he has full control of what is done.

The employer should also give thought to the matter of providing some incentive to meet programme. Only the very best of contractors will strive equally hard to meet the project programme whether or not he has a contractual obligation to do so. A bonus may be offered, provided the employer can avoid, or is prepared to accept, paying any additional costs incurred by the contractor in his efforts to earn the bonus.

6.2.7 Convertible Contract

The convertible contract provides for commencement on a reimbursable basis with an option for the employer to convert to a lump sum when the work has advanced sufficiently for accurate cost estimates to be made. The advantage for the employer is that he discovers the full extent of his commitment earlier than he would otherwise do, transferring the risk of cost over-run to the contractor at the time of conversion. He pays for this in the margin that the contractor includes in his price—a price that is produced with no competition and with limited room for negotiation. The contractor has no incentive other than to quote a price which he is confident will cover his costs with something to spare, for his alternative is to carry on with the reimbursable contract. However, his price must be based on a cost estimate of which full details are available to the employer, who has the option to convert or not as he wishes. The employer has the advantage, at least, of having a good idea of the margin which the contractor is proposing to include in his price to cover his risk.

6.3 CONTRACTUAL TREATMENT OF DIFFERENT SCOPES OF WORK

The type of contract appropriate is very much dependant on the contractor's scope of work. A reimbursable contract, for example, is more suitable for some activities than for others. A contractor might offer any of the following services:

- Project Management
- Process Development
- Process Evaluation
- Process Design
- Engineering Design and Procurement Services
- Supply of Materials
- Construction Management
- Field Construction
- Pre-commissioning
- Commissioning
- Operator Training

Other, and even finer, divisions in the work of a project could of course be made. These items cannot all stand alone, and although they may be discussed separately below, it must be understood that many could only reasonably be offered in conjunction with others. With this proviso, different items could be subject to different contractual treatments, in many instances in a part lump sum, part reimbursable contract.

The first item—*project management*—is probably best handled reimbursably. It would be difficult to define with any accuracy beforehand exactly what will be required and the costs will not, in any case, constitute a major component of the total project cost. Even if a lump sum were offered, the contractor would not accept liability for more than a professional standard of work. *Process development* is a further item that cannot be reliably estimated in advance and can therefore hardly be contracted on other than a reimbursable basis. *Process evaluation* work is similarly difficult to define and, as a small part of the total project cost, would be another candidate for a reimbursable contract. Since the results of the process development or process evaluation stages define the nature and extent of the subsequent work that has to be done, it would make good sense for a separate contract to be placed for this early work. The contractual arrangements for succeeding stages could then be negotiated, perhaps with competition from other contractors, when more is known about them. As previously discussed, process development and evaluation are unlikely to be contracted out very frequently since this work is the heart of an operating company's business.

The next item listed—*process design*—uses relatively few man-hours compared with detailed design and its cost is a small part of a large contract. Where the employer has made a preliminary design that he wishes a contractor to work up, a reimbursable contract will usually be the best way of proceeding because of the difficulty of estimating accurately the work to be done. However, a process design package purchased from a process licensor will be a different matter. In the nature of things this will be similar to other packages which the licensor has produced. He will have little difficulty in estimating the work required. He will offer guarantees and require payment of a royalty—either as a lump sum or related to production, or both. Such a package, whether produced by the contractor or by a separate, third party licensor, will often be the subject of a lump sum contract.

The cost of *engineering design and procurement services* is fairly easily estimated where the process design has been adequately developed. One might argue that adequate development of the process design before engineering design starts is a necessary ingredient of a successful project and therefore that it should never be necessary to provide detailed design services reimbursably. A lump sum contract should be possible and would be preferred by many. *Materials supply* could only reasonably be undertaken in conjunction with the provision of engineering design and procurement services. To estimate the cost obviously requires a good deal of work and information and manufacturers' quotations must be obtained. It is thus more common for materials to be supplied on a reimbursable basis.

Again, whilst a lump sum bid can be developed for *construction management services* without excessive effort, *field construction* can only be costed on the basis of quite detailed designs—especially if it is the subject of a separate contract. Thus construction management is much more easily bid on a lump sum basis than is field construction, although with the latter, a re-measure and value contract may offer an intermediate option. Consequently, a contract for design and construction may often be split into part reimbursable and part lump sum—the contractor's services being provided on a lump sum basis but materials supply or field construction, or both, being reimbursable. Construction is frequently dealt with through separate re-measure and value or schedule of rates sub-contracts placed at a later stage of project execution.

6.4 FACTORS AFFECTING THE CHOICE OF TYPE OF CONTRACT

In some cases, the employer's project manager will have no choice in the type of contract to be placed. External factors may prescribe what has to be done. Where the project manager has a choice, this must be made early in the project's life because its effects are so far-reaching. In particular, the type of contract to be used has the most profound effect on the amount of work which must be done before contracts can be awarded. There are many factors that can affect the decision. Some may be special to the particular circumstances of a given project and hence can be dealt with only as they arise. The most important matters of general applicability are discussed below.

6.4.1 Finance

If project finance is to be sought, that is to say the capital required to build the plant is to be borrowed and the debt repaid out of the operating profits of the completed plant, the financing institutions will require a guarantee that the project will be completed without further calls on them. This guarantee is unlikely to be provided solely by the employer. Were he ready and able to provide such a guarantee he would probably have other, and cheaper, ways to raise the finance. A completion guarantee must therefore be provided by the contractor. A single-point responsibility lump sum contract is consequently a *sine qua non* for a project financed in this way. The employer's project manager would have little or no control of the type of contract and his project programme would be much affected, not merely because of the work necessary to obtain lump sum bids, but also by the work needed to secure the loans

6.4.2 Allocation of Risk

The employer may, for various reasons, be unable or unwilling to accept the risk of over-expenditure on the project and will therefore insist on a lump sum contract. If, for example, the employer is a new company formed to exploit some natural resource, or is a joint venture established for a particular manufacture, it may well be that it does not have the resources which would enable it to accept the risk of cost over-run. If such a company seeks project finance, a lump sum contract would in any case be required. Many factors can affect the size of the risks which have to be shared. These may be technical, e.g. experience with the type of plant proposed; geographical, e.g. a difficult or little-known location; political or in other categories. A contractor will be reluctant to accept risks over which he has no control, or which are more properly the business risks of the employer.

6.4.3 Cost

The choice of contract will be influenced by what the employer's project manager perceives as the relative cost of the alternatives. His perception will be affected by the experience and culture of the employer's organisation and the relative strengths and weaknesses of employer and contractor.

The employer incurs greater setting-up costs with a lump sum contract. Such a contract will cost more than a reimbursable one, all else being equal, because the contractor will be providing the management of the work and he will also require to be paid for his assumption of risk. Against this, if there is real competition for the contract, keener prices may be submitted. The lump sum contract exerts a disciplining effect on both contractor and employer. The former will work hard not to over-spend because the financial penalty will be his. The latter will strive to avoid expensive variations. If things go wrong, the employer is more cushioned against extra expense if he has a lump sum contract.

With a reimbursable contract, the employer will need to supervise the contract more closely and will incur greater cost in doing so. For his part, the contractor will need to spend less on controlling the costs he incurs: he has no incentive to minimise them. The employer's staff, particularly those who can influence what is done but who bear no responsibility for the outcome, will be less inhibited in their demands for additions and changes. The employer carries all the risk of a cost over-run.

Where the choice between lump sum and reimbursable conditions has to be made only in respect of the contractor's design services, it having already been conceded that the supply of materials must be reimbursable, the cost difference is less of an issue to the employer. To the contractor, however, the lump sum services contract exerts a powerful controlling effect and will almost certainly lead to a lower cost for the services than had they been provided reimbursably. The cost of the reimbursable materials supply is unlikely to be much affected either way.

6.4.4 Definition

The degree of definition of the project is undoubtedly one of the most important internal project factors governing choice of contract, as it is also one of the most important influences on success or failure of the whole venture. Requirements need to be defined very precisely for a complete lump sum contract to be possible. At the other extreme, if what has to be done is still unknown there is no alternative to a reimbursable contract. To define accurately what has to be done is good practice and if the use of a lump sum contract leads the employer to define the project much better than he would otherwise have done both he and the contractor are likely to benefit. It is often possible to define parts of a project before others and this explains the frequency with which part lump sum, part reimbursable contracts are used.

6.4.5 Employer's Policy

The employer may have developed a definite policy, or style, in the way he lets contracts as a result of his experiences over the years. This will owe much to the way in which the employer develops his projects, especially the amount of pre-sanction and pre-contract preparation work that is usually carried out, and to the management capability that he has established and has available for deployment. Some employers, for example, are more comfortable with a reimbursable contract, where they can dictate what is done and can be sure of getting what they want—or at least, face no contractual hurdle in doing so. They may be set up to manage the reimbursable contractor's operations in the necessary depth and detail. Other employers may lean towards the lump sum contract which they may feel gives a tighter, more disciplined job and encourages the contractor to make his maximum contribution. Clearly, there is much to be said for continuing a well-established and successful contract pattern. Equally, it would be foolish of the employer to deny himself the flexibility to suit the contract to the prevailing circumstances.

6.4.6 Project Size

Setting up a lump sum contract requires time and effort and the resulting overhead costs and delay in getting started may not be worth while for a small project.

6.4.7 Competition

Unless there is effective competition between bidders, the employer may find it difficult to know whether the lump sum price he is quoted fairly reflects the going rate. This will not be a problem where the project is a near-repeat of a recent one, since the employer will be able to estimate the cost with reference to the previous plant. In such a case, competition would not be necessary to check prices nor, if the contractor for the earlier plant were involved, would level competition be possible. A reimbursable contract does not require competition between bidders to be assured of fair prices, since a comparison of contractors' man-hour rates can easily be effected. The relative costs of reimbursable bids will be influenced more by man-hours consumed than by the rates at which they are charged, but there is little to guide this comparison.

6.4.8 Inflation

A contractor usually has little difficulty in allowing for inflation if the annual percentage rate is in single figures. Alternatively, this level of inflation can be accommodated by a *contract price adjustment* formula. During periods of higher inflation, however, CPA formulae, which are based on a typical collection of commodities and services, offer only rough justice. More importantly, in such periods, confidence in predicting the future is low. Thus, when there is high inflation a contractor might well be unwilling to offer a lump sum bid, or might require additional margin to cover his risk, even with a CPA formula adjustment for inflation. An employer may well feel better able to take the inflationary risk than the contractor, and periods of high inflation therefore tend to lead to the use of reimbursable contracts.

6.4.9 Timing

Haste alone can seldom, if ever, justify the use of a reimbursable contract, but is not infrequently used to do so. It is true that a reimbursable contract can be placed much earlier than a lump sum contract, but this will be of little benefit if the contractor lacks the information to enable him to perform useful work. Without a proper basis for the work he has to do, the contractor will spend man-hours to no purpose and his appointment and subsequent demands for information will, in many cases, hamper and delay the employer's efforts to define the project's requirements. It is doubtful, therefore, whether much time could ever be gained by placing an early reimbursable contract without adequate preparation. Much of the work necessary to enquire for and prepare a lump sum bid would have to be done whatever the type of contract used, and much of it would be done more quickly during bidding than in the normal course of the project. A lump sum contract will almost certainly give the contractor greater incentive to make progress than would a reimbursable contract.

No doubt the award of contract is an important progress milestone for the employer, which he will be anxious to see achieved. It would be a mistake, however, for him to think that the award of a reimbursable contract would signify the same project progress as would the placing of a lump sum contract.

6.4.10 Resources

If the employer has expert, knowledgeable people available he will wish them to participate in the project, particularly if the contractor is not comparably experienced in the technology in question. In such a case, a reimbursable contract might be indicated, whereas if the bulk of the knowledge and experience is with the contractor a lump sum contract would be more appropriate.

It is obvious that a lump sum contract puts more of the onus on the contractor and makes more calls on his technical and financial resources than would a reimbursable contract. With the latter it is possible to employ a contractor merely on the understanding that he will do his best, and will be bolstered by the employer in areas where he is weak. Not so a lump sum contractor, who must be fully capable of all the work he has contracted to do if the contract is to have a chance of success. Weakness among the potential contractors will incline the employer towards a reimbursable contract.

6.4.11 Industrial Relations

These may dictate how construction is handled. If the plant is to be built on a currently operating site, continued operation of the existing facilities is likely to be given priority over new construction. This may put restraints on the contractor in the way he is able to manage his labour force and may limit contractual possibilities. Indeed, such restraints may lead the employer to prefer to manage construction directly. In any circumstances where the employer has experience of handling the local labour force, but the contractor has none, the possibility of construction management by the employer is one that must usually be considered.

6.4.12 Custom and Practice

All considerations governing the choice of type of contract may give way before the customs and practices of the country concerned. If the contract is to be placed with a local contractor in a foreign country where knowledge and experience of the type of contract proposed is nil, it would be a brave project manager who chose to be a pioneer. In such a country, the extremes are to insist that all is done exactly as it would be in the UK, or to follow the indigenous practices. There may be some intermediate course of action which might be appropriate or which, being familiar to neither side, might give the worst of all worlds.

As an initial starting point, it is generally true that, other things being equal, the more familiar the contractor with the role that he has to play, the better will be his performance. It behoves the employer's project manager, therefore, to consider carefully how things are done in the country concerned and whether such methods could reasonably be used. He must try to understand how business is conducted and so avoid reaching conclusions based on false assumptions. If, for example, there is no price competition between contractors because they collude on price (which was not unknown in the UK in the 1950s and 1960s), there is little point in treating price as the most important determinant of contract type, or indeed, destination of award. Again, a measure and value construction contract, on the lines envisaged in the Institution of Civil Engineers' Model Form, is likely to be less successful in a country where quantity surveyors are unknown.

The decision as to type of contract will depend to a large extent on the confidence the employer's project manager has in the bidders for the contract. If he has sufficient confidence in their capability, he may follow their contractual methods. If, on the other hand, he decides to introduce methods to which he is accustomed but which are novel to the country concerned, it is likely that there will be more than just contractual matters about which he feels uneasy. He will find himself having to make provision for much more training, supervision and management than would otherwise be needed.

6.5 CONCLUSIONS

The choice of type of contract for the major elements of the design and construction of a process plant, and all the concomitants of that choice, goes to the very heart of the nature and timing of the project and the way it must be managed. Of course, this is not simply a choice between one set of contract conditions and another, but between quite distinct ways of establishing and managing the project. The choice is not commonly that, having fully defined what is to be done, the employer's project manager then decides whether to place a reimbursable or a lump sum contract. It is between placing a reimbursable contract quickly on limited definition, or a lump sum contract in six months' or a year's time when the processes of definition, tendering and evaluation have been completed. The differences between projects which utilise reimbursable contracts and those whose contracts are placed on a lump sum basis therefore have two main roots:

(1) The much better definition that a lump sum contract will almost certainly have.
(2) The different pressures and motivations arising from the contract conditions.

As regards the first of these, a high standard of definition is arguably the single most important factor leading to a successful project, so that a contract type that demands this should have a most beneficial influence. Theoretically, of course, there is no reason why a reimbursable contract should not be placed in just as structured a way as a lump sum contract, so that the contractor's work, as opposed to his liability for it, could be founded on the same extent of information and be defined in just the same way as for a lump sum contract. It is doubtful, however, whether this is ever done, and in practice, the balance is entirely in favour of the lump sum contract.

As far as the second item is concerned, both types of contract have their advantages and disadvantages but, so long as the contract does not stray too far from the original expectations of the parties, the balance is strongly in favour of the lump sum. This type of contract exerts pressure on the contractor to reduce costs by improving the efficiency of his operations as well as by economic design and keen purchasing. He also has strict liability for what he produces and so is constrained to maintain quality. Pressure is put on the employer to control his input to the design process carefully to avoid excessive variation costs. The dangers are, of course, that the contractor cuts corners, and that the employer interferes too much.

A reimbursable contract, in contrast, exerts little pressure on either employer or contractor. The latter is paid for all he does and his liabilities are probably no more than to provide his services to a professional standard. All the costs and liabilities remain with the employer, but these are not brought home to his staff in their day-to-day dealings with the contractor. The contractor has no particular incentive to manage his operations efficiently, to put his best men on the contract or to see that surplus staff are moved elsewhere. If he has other lump sum contracts proceeding at the same time, there can be no doubt where his interests, at least in the short term, will lie in the event of competition for resources. The employer must therefore manage both the contractor's operations and his own. He will have control of what is done, but the contract itself will have no restraining influence either on his own staff or those of the contractor.

Thus the employer's project manager must give consideration not only to the situation extant when the contract is awarded, but also to the possible effects of changing circumstances over the contract period. A reimbursable contract offers little resistance to the effects of some changes, such as a developing shortage of effort in the contractor's offices, but is not subject to other pressures, such as the contractor's reducing expectation of profit. A lump sum contract may define the contractor's obligations, but rarely with such force and precision as to ensure that the employer's requirements will be completely satisfied if the contractor is making a substantial loss. In such circumstances, the employer's project manager must endeavour to prevent the lump sum contract turning sour: he may be generous with variations or, in the limit, may convert to a reimbursable contract.

The choice of the type of contract must take account of all the circumstances of the project and the characteristics of the employer's and the contractor's organisations. Most would probably agree that, where circumstances permit, a lump sum contract would offer the best choice, and that this should be the aim. However, there are employer's organisations which as a matter of policy let all major contracts reimbursably, on the grounds that what is required can be got without argument and more cheaply, since there is no contractor's risk to be paid for. Such an employer could develop and put in place the additional management and control of the contractor's operations which reimbursable contracts require. What an employer must not do is to place a reimbursable contract with a management appropriate to a lump sum contract, or to place a lump sum contract with inadequate preparatory work.

Chapter 7

Contract Strategy and Organisation

7.1 MAJOR DETERMINANTS

Once the decision to contract out some of the work of project execution is taken in principle, the employer's project manager has the task of defining the contracts to be placed. This requires, *inter alia*:

(1) Deciding the work to be done by the employer's own staff.
(2) Deciding the contracts to be placed and the scope of each. For example, the employer's project manager might choose to place separate contracts for on-plot, off-plot, effluent treatment, office buildings and so on.
(3) For each contract, defining the functions the contractor is to perform. For example, it might be decided that the on-plot contractor would be asked to provide engineering design and procurement services and to supply materials and equipment, but that construction would be handled separately.
(4) Deciding on the type and the important terms and conditions of each contract.
(5) Deciding on the extent of definition required before contracts are placed. This will obviously depend on the types of contract envisaged and will affect the timing of contract awards.
(6) For an overseas project, predicting the likely effects of financing and taxation and designing the contracts accordingly.

(7) Ensuring that the contracts are compatible and that the liabilities of the parties are fully understood.

(8) Deciding on the organisation and numbers required to supervise and co-ordinate the work of the contractors.

Some of these aspects, primarily those which concern the scope of work to be retained by the employer and the division of the remainder between contractors, are dealt with in this chapter. The choice of type of contract has already been considered in Chapter 6. Chapter 8 considers in more detail the possible effects of financing and taxation on an overseas project. Several later chapters deal with contractual terms and conditions. The organisation of the employer's project team has been discussed in Chapter 2, but it is not possible to discuss the numbers of staff required except by reference to the details of the particular project in question.

It is evident that full definition of the contract strategy and organisation is an iterative process. The answers do not spring fully armed from the project manager's lips. Assumptions must be made and modified and expanded as more information becomes available. Like any design process, the more accurate the initial assumptions, the fewer the subsequent disturbances and changes of course and the more smoothly and efficiently the project will run. The employer's project manager's objective is to develop a strategy in which each part of the project is identified, its basis is well defined, responsibility for its execution is clear and each part is properly co-ordinated with the remainder. The exact timing of events and actions will depend on the particular circumstances of the individual project. The amount of preparatory work done before sanction, and before the award of contracts can vary enormously in practice, and if the employer's project manager values his chances of success he will ensure that it his judgements of what is necessary that carry the day.

For any particular project there may be special circumstances which constrain decisions or point them strongly in particular directions. The important general considerations which affect the allocation of work between employer and contractors are as follows:

(1) The resources which the employer has to devote to the project, their number, capability and experience.

(2) The ownership of the project, i.e. by the employer or a by a joint venture.

(3) The source of the process technology—whether this is to be provided by the employer, the contractor, or a separate process licensor.

(4) The location of the proposed plant—whether it is to be built on one of the employer's existing sites; in the UK or abroad; if the latter, how developed is the country in question.

(5) The state of development of the project at the time when it is proposed to seek bids.

(6) The desired allocation of risk and liability between the employer and the contractors.
(7) The number and complexity of the interfaces: between the various contracts, and between them and the work which the employer reserves to himself, and the ways in which the division of work motivates the contractors.
(8) Finance and taxation.
(9) The capability of potential contractors, and the scope of the services they offer, in the UK and in the country where the plant is to be built.

7.1.1 Employer's Resources

The first consideration underlying the decisions to be taken is the level of resources available within the employer's organisation. If these are negligible, the employer will have no choice but to appoint a managing contractor to perform the work of setting up and supervising the contracts—to act as the employer's project manager in most respects. With more, but still slight, resources the employer could set up the contracts himself providing the work was minimised by the appointment of a main contractor to do all or most of the execution work. If the employer has substantial resources available to manage the project, he could reduce costs significantly (at the price of accepting greater liability) and perhaps save time by placing a number of separate contracts.

Among the contracts that an employer with his own project management resources might place directly are the following:

(1) Contracts for the clearance, grading and fencing of the site. Preliminary work may be necessary, especially if the plant is to be built on a new site, which can be carried out while the main contracts are being enquired for and bid. External factors may influence matters—for example, the employer may have an obligation to fence a new site as soon as possible after it is purchased. It is probable that lump sum contracts can be obtained for these minor works.
(2) Planning permissions, environmental approvals and so on will be needed. In many countries the employment of a local consultant is recommended, or even statutorily required. The required contracts need to be placed at an early date.
(3) Soils investigations will almost certainly be necessary and would often be carried out by specialist consultants. The contract for these investigations may be placed directly by the employer and the information given to the bidders in the enquiry. This will save time and reduce effort, but will make the employer liable for the accuracy of the soils information. (Interpretation of the data may be another matter.)

(4) Where a separate contract for construction is being let, time may sometimes be saved by letting a separate contract for piling work. Again, this alters the balance of liabilities as between employer and contractors.

(5) Investigations may be necessary into electricity and water supplies and the results of these may affect, not merely the engineering but also the process design. In a foreign country, the employment of specialist consultants may be desirable and the employer could let these contracts directly.

(6) Where there are loads to transport to site which exceed the capacity of the existing roads, special provision must be made. The employer may have greater experience of this work than any of the available contractors. In addition, the requirements may not be defined in time to allow the work to be included in the scope of a main lump sum contract. In such a case, the employer may decide to manage the work directly.

(7) Parts of the project may consist entirely of building and civil work with no technical dependence on the rest of the plant. Examples are office buildings, warehouses, workshops and amenities. In most countries these could be designed and built by local contractors. There is little or nothing to be gained by making these sub-contractors of the main process plant contractor and it would increase costs.

(8) Some other parts of the project may be suitable for local or specialist contracts let directly by the employer. Some utilities plants, for example, water treatment plant, boiler plant, effluent treatment plant may be obtainable via lump sum contracts for design, supply and construction. These contracts could be placed directly by the employer at some saving in cost provided that co-ordination problems could be handled satisfactorily.

It will be seen that, even with a main contractor performing what is ostensibly a lump sum turnkey contract for the process plant on-plots and off-plots, there could nevertheless be a number of contracts placed and directly supervised by the employer's staff.

There are other liabilities that the employer with the resources to investigate and assess them might consider it desirable to retain. There may, for example, be uncertainty about the incidence of import duty in a foreign country. The employer may conclude that a contractor is allowing greater contingency to cover this uncertainty than the facts warranted and so decide to relieve him of liability for it. A similar situation might arise in respect of taxation. In such matters, the greater financial strength of an employer might allow him to take a less cautious view of the risk than a contractor.

A major question to be addressed is the possibility of separating on-plot and off-plot contracts. In the UK, the employer with the necessary resources would probably wish to engineer the off-plots himself. On an existing site, they will be intimately connected to the existing facilities and detailed local knowledge would be required to design them, which perhaps only the employer would have. In a foreign country, it would be sensible to employ a local contractor to design the off-plots if companies with satisfactory experience and capability were available. In this case, the question would reduce to whether the local firm should be employed directly as a contractor, or as a sub-contractor to the on-plot contractor. It would be less expensive if the employer placed the contract directly, but he would then retain the liability for the interaction between on-plot and off-plot contracts and would need the staff to co-ordinate the contracts.

If a separate local off-plot contractor were to be used, the case for having separate contracts for some civil and building works outside the main process plant, or for utilities plants, would take on a different complexion. It would probably be sensible to include more of this work in the off-plots contract since fragmentation of a project into separate contracts always increases the employer's workload and liabilities and should be done only where there is believed to be a clear benefit.

7.1.2 Joint Venture Projects

Where the project is to be owned by a joint venture (who, strictly speaking, will become the employer of the contractor, but who will not be referred to in this way here, previous terminology being retained for simplicity), the lines of responsibility, though not necessarily the work, of the employer's project manager may be changed profoundly. This will certainly be the case where the employer, as well as taking the lead role in the project, is also providing the technology to the joint venture under licence. An example of the contracts organisation for a joint venture project is given later in this chapter.

7.1.3 Source of Process Technology

Since the process package is the foundation of all that follows, its source has an important effect on how the contracts are enquired for, bid and placed. At one extreme, bids will be sought on the basis of a definitive process package. At the other, provision of the process package will be part of the contract to be awarded.

If the employer's own technology is to be used, the employer must himself provide the process package. This may be a preliminary version which the appointed detailed design contractor will work up in detail. Alternatively, the employer may produce a final package, leaving little or no process design for the detailed design contractor to do. A third method would be for the employer to use a contractor to help him produce the process package under a separate contract. It would then be possible to arrange matters so that the choice of detailed design contractor is not compromised. In any case, of course, responsibility for the process technology would rest with the employer, who must take care to retain ownership of and copyright in the designs.

If the process is to be licensed from a third party, this may be done directly by the employer or through the contractor. If the former, the employer must place an early contract with the licensor to obtain at least a preliminary process package as a basis for seeking contracts for detailed design. A better arrangement might be for the employer to negotiate the agreement with the licensor almost to completion and to require the detailed design contractor to complete the agreement and take over responsibility for the process package, incorporating it into his bid. This would avoid possible dispute between licensor and contractor about liability for deficiencies in the completed plant and would be especially desirable where the plant included a number of proprietary processes from different licensors, for example, an aromatics plant. At the same time, it would be as well for the employer to arrange to have direct access to the licensors for technical discussion, advice, training and so on.

Where the contractor provides both the process technology and the detailed design, the choice of process and contractor is made simultaneously, which affects the enquiry and bidding processes in ways described in following chapters.

7.1.4 Plant Location

Plant location affects the disposition of contracts primarily because it affects the degree of local knowledge which employer and contractor are likely to have. For a plant to be built in the UK, both employer and main contractor will be 'local' and should possess the relevant experience and information. There may be special considerations where the plant is to be built on an existing operating site owned by the employer. These might restrict the placing of contracts for construction and, in addition, lead to the employer engineering the off-plots himself because of his superior knowledge of the site and of the interactions between the proposed plant and existing facilities.

Where the proposed plant is to be built in a foreign country, the local knowledge of the employer and of the potential main contractors may be small or negligible. If suitable firms are available, the use of local contractors for construction and possibly for off-plot design, even for some of the on-plot detailed design, will be indicated. There will be questions about whether the local companies should be direct contractors to the employer or sub-contractors to the main contractor. Political considerations may obtrude in unexpected ways: for example, there have been instances where it has been considered inadvisable for the bidders for the main contract to be seen to be investigating construction conditions before contract award, thereby requiring the later placing of a separate construction contract.

7.1.5 State of Development of the Project

The precision with which the project can be defined before work starts controls the types of contracts which can be let. An ill-defined project can only be the subject of reimbursable contracts. If the plant is the first of its kind, it is unlikely that, however much effort is expended in trying to define it, anything other than a reimbursable contract would be appropriate. At the other extreme, a repeat plant could fairly easily be defined well enough to allow a lump sum contract to be placed. As has been said before, and will be again, good initial definition is arguably the most important single ingredient in a successful project. The question confronting the employer's project manager, therefore, should be not what contract can be let given the information available, but rather what information is needed to be able to let contracts of the necessary quality.

7.1.6 Allocation of Risk and Responsibility

The way in which the employer wishes to allocate the risks and responsibilities of the project influences fundamentally the number and forms of contract to be used. An employer willing and able to accept risk and responsibility may choose from the full range of contract options. In contrast, one unable or unwilling to accept much risk or responsibility, has only one way to proceed. He must place a single-point responsibility lump sum contract. This requires a properly defined enquiry and, if the project is to have much chance of success, the avoidance of subsequent major change.

If the wish to transfer a major part of the project risk to a contractor arises because of a lack of technical and financial resources on the part of the employer, he will presumably also need to employ a managing contractor to perform much of the work of establishing and supervising the project. This does not much reduce the employer's liability for the design basis, since it is extremely unlikely that the managing contractor would accept strict liability for its correctness. The managing contractor would, however, be much more likely than an inexperienced employer to avoid major error or omission.

7.1.7 Interfaces and Division of Work

The point has already been made that splitting a project into separately executed parts is in itself undesirable and should only be done for good reason. In fact, such reasons are often encountered. Nevertheless, the work should be split reluctantly and only to the minimum extent that the circumstances require. The interfaces between the separate parts of the project should be as simple and straightforward as possible, and it is worth going to some trouble to achieve this. The employer's project manager must recognise that his concern for the overall success of his project will have no real counterpart among the individual contractors. A contractor's prime motivation will be to complete the work for which he is responsible: he will have much less concern for the problems of others. Thus, if he performs design but not construction, he will incline to produce his design information in ways which are most convenient for him. This may not suit construction, who will then have to sort and rearrange it. The design contractor may be less concerned about the control of material, and about the provision of design and materials in a timely manner, if he is not responsible for construction.

The employer must manage all the interfaces between contracts. He must monitor the production of each contractor, must progress and expedite it and seek modification where appropriate. This may require considerable resources. If the split of work and responsibility is very complicated, a successful overall result may require a standard of performance from all concerned higher than is likely to be achieved.

7.1.8 Finance and Taxation

External project finance will usually result in the financing institutions imposing their own requirements on the contracts to be placed. Almost certainly, a single-point responsibility lump sum contract for the complete plant will be required unless the employer guarantees completion.

If the plant is to be built in a foreign country, the taxation regime, especially the possible imposition of withholding tax, may affect contract organisation profoundly. The contracts must be arranged to minimise taxation while forfeiting as few of the employer's contractual rights and benefits as possible. At a more detailed level, business and turnover taxes can affect the way in which contracts are written. These matters are discussed in more detail in Chapter 8.

7.2 CAPABILITY OF POTENTIAL CONTRACTORS

Clearly, the capability of the potential contractors available, both in the UK and, if different, in the country in which the proposed plant is to be built, will affect the contracting strategy. Contractors with the full range of experience and expertise to execute the whole project may not be available. For example, those with the required process engineering capability may not have the necessary experience in the country in which the plant is to be built. The employment of a managing contractor may then be indicated, or the employer may have to take a leading role. It is necessary to take care to organise the contracts to make best use of the skills available.

There are many services that may be obtained from a contractor, including the following:

- Project Management
- Process Development
- Process Evaluation
- Process Design
- Engineering Design and Procurement Services
- Supply of Materials
- Construction Management
- Field Construction
- Pre-commissioning
- Commissioning
- Operator Training.

Not all of these could be obtained from all contractors and not all should be considered as stand-alone items. The provision, for example, of commissioning services or operator training would only be appropriate where the contractor had been responsible for the process design of the plant. Materials supply could hardly be undertaken unless engineering design and procurement services were also being provided. Nor, of course, is it advocated that a project should be split into separate contracts in the way the list might suggest is possible. Fragmentation of a project always introduces additional co-ordination and management requirements and makes the achievement of a successful project more difficult. It also increases the employer's liability because he is responsible for the impingement of one contract on another. The aim of the employer's project manager should be to divide responsibility into as few parts as reasonably possible. This will help to ensure continuity and more comprehensive responsibility and authority, to minimise conflicts of interest and maximise efficiency of communication and execution. Interfaces between different parties to the project must be designed to be as simple as possible. They must be carefully and explicitly designed and continuously monitored throughout. Where, for example, process design, engineering design, and construction are separated, as is frequently done, the employer must provide personnel for co-ordination and technical liaison between them. An employer who habitually uses contractors will probably have systematised many of the methods to be employed.

7.2.1 Project Management

In this context, project management means the employment of a contractor— commonly called a *managing contractor*—to perform many of the duties of the employer's project manager in a project where other contractors are to execute the majority of the work. A managing contractor with the necessary capability could undertake most of the employer's project manager's duties, as described earlier, of project establishment (definition, strategy and contracts) and engineering (design, procurement and construction) but could not wholly replace him. He could perform that part of the work which was external to the employer's organisation—the dealings with contractors—but would be of less assistance during the conceptual stage—in that part of the employer's project manager's role performed internally and which is aimed at helping to crystallise the employer's requirements. This conceptual stage can represent a substantial workload for the employer's project manager, since many projects that a manufacturing company undertakes are inextricably linked with its existing business and require continuous liaison with the operating departments. Except where the project is in a technological field new to the employer and with no more than simple links to his existing business, the employer's project manager will still be needed for this defining role, as well as for liaising between the managing contractor and the employer.

Not all contractors have the capability to act as managing contractor and none of them has the breadth of experience in this role of a major operating company. A contractor might, however, have experience and capability in particular aspects—the management of very large projects, the raising of project finance, operation in a particular country—that the employer did not. New or recently established companies would be the most likely to employ a managing contractor. It would be unusual for an established major operating company to do so.

A managing contractor would be expected to be more expensive than the employer's own staff for a number of reasons, quite apart from questions of relative rates of pay and contractor's profit. His relations with the employer's business team would be more formal. More reports and paperwork would be demanded (because the employer would want to see what he was paying for) and offered (since the managing contractor would use his own more elaborate systems and would wish to document at each stage that he had fulfilled his commitments). A managing contractor would usually call for more extensive reporting from the other contractors employed on project execution and this would probably be anticipated by them and reflected in their prices. It must also not be forgotten that the managing contractor is selling man-hours on a reimbursable basis and so has no incentive to minimise his work, and certainly none to risk providing an inadequate level of supervision.

The quality of the overall management of the project is arguably the most important single factor in its success. If, therefore, the use of a managing contractor is contemplated, the choice of contractor for the role is one which needs very careful consideration. While the quality of the contractor's organisation and management systems is important, and previous experience a key criterion, the crucial factor in the choice is the calibre of the person proposed as project manager. This is not only because of his personal contribution to the project. If the contractor puts forward his best man, it demonstrates a commitment to the project which should result in his also providing a good supporting team. A top project manager would be satisfied with nothing less.

7.2.2 Process Development

Only a company with research facilities of its own is likely to possess the necessary qualifications to undertake process development. Few engineering contractors have such facilities, but there are several companies whose business is the development and licensing of new processes in particular areas of technology. As well as expertise in their own processes, such companies might possess special knowledge in other areas, of which a manufacturer might wish to take advantage. However, most major companies would regard process development, as much as the research which underlies it, as the very heart of their business. The resources they devote to research will far outweigh those that any contractor can show. Nevertheless, however great the resources the manufacturer may command, they are never enough to cover every eventuality and the employment of a contractor to undertake process development may be appropriate in special circumstances. Smaller companies, with fewer resources, are naturally more likely to seek outside help.

Of course, it is impossible to develop a reasonably optimised process without a substantial chemical engineering input nor, indeed, without some mechanical and control engineering contribution. Development must be guided by a knowledge of what is practicable and economic on the full scale, which may require significant process design to evaluate alternative methods of realising the research results, and mechanical and control engineering to establish capital costs and safety. Process development is therefore ineluctably linked with at least the conceptual stages of process design.

7.2.3 Process Evaluation

An established manufacturer is unlikely to employ a contractor for process evaluation, except where he is considering entry to a technological area new to him. In such a case, the manufacturer might employ a contractor to evaluate the processes that are generally available on the market. He would not, however, be likely to want the contractor to go beyond a straightforward technical and, possibly, commercial comparison of the processes on offer. On the other hand, a new venture company in an undeveloped country might have no option but to ask a contractor to carry out full feasibility studies which might extend to recommending the products to be manufactured as well as the processes to be used.

7.2.4 Process Design

The process design capability of contractors varies. Some have very few resources in this area. Others are capable of the later, detailed stages of process design but, as mentioned above, few are expert in process development or in the conceptual stages of the design. Since these last two aspects are closely linked, responsibility for process development should be accompanied by responsibility for the early stages of the design, to the point of flowsheet definition and the production of heat and mass balances. If the manufacturer does this work, it would be possible for him then to employ a contractor to perform the detailed stages of the process design—for example, the production of mechanical and instrument data sheets. If the process is one which is currently in use, so that the manufacturer is developing an improved version based on his existing operation, such a division of work might be convenient and appropriate.

There can be advantages in dividing process design work in this way. The process designer who works closely with research and development to define a process is concerned with the generation of ideas and the solving of problems. Very often he has little appetite for working out these ideas beyond the point at which they are shown to be practicable. His interest is in the development of a process rather than the execution of a project. He is not always the best man to produce a meticulously accurate and consistent set of data sheets to an agreed programme.

If a contractor is used for the detailed working out of a process developed by the employer, it will obviously be necessary to ensure close liaison between the parties. Often, the best way of executing the work is for the employer simply to take process designers on secondment from the contractor to work to the employer's direction and under his supervision. In such a case, the contractor, of course, has no liability for the finished design. This way of proceeding avoids any argument about ownership or copyright in the designs, and makes it easier for the employer to use the ensuing process package to enquire of a number of bidders for the downstream work on the project.

A third party licensor will often provide the detailed process package himself, either to the employer or directly to the contractor. In some cases, however, the contractor is a licensee who is able to tailor the third party's technology to fit the individual circumstances of a particular project.

7.2.5 Engineering Design and Procurement Services

Engineering design and procurement are the services most commonly provided by an engineering contractor. They start from the receipt of the process package, which may be provided by the employer, by a third party licensor or by the contractor himself based on his own or others' processes. The origin of the process package will clearly influence the decision on who is to perform engineering design and procurement. An employer is more likely to perform the detailed engineering himself if he has already produced the process package. If a contractor has done the process design, it is very probable that he will be called upon to carry out the remainder of the engineering. The decision to use a contractor will often be decided simply by the availability of resources to the employer—hundreds of thousands of man-hours are involved in engineering a major process plant project and the employer may not be able to provide these.

Other factors may play an important part in the decision to contract out or not, such as the experience of a contractor in engineering the particular process or ones similar to it, a contractor's knowledge of the country in which the plant is to be built, or his ability to raise finance for the project. The need for secrecy may discourage contracting out, but the data that has to be given to the engineering design contractor is not usually especially sensitive and so can be safeguarded by normal confidentiality agreements. A contractor with no process design capability would be a safer choice as regards confidentiality, although his contribution to the engineering design might be marginally less.

Procurement services are so closely related to engineering that it is not often sensible to separate the two functions if the contractor is capable of both. All purchasing decisions call for a blend of engineering and commercial judgement. Expediting, inspection and progressing are integral parts of project management and the obtaining of vendor data is a vital service to engineering. It is possible to arrange matters so that the contractor handles all procurement except for the placing of purchase orders which is done by the employer, but this usually has little to commend it. Such an arrangement can make it more difficult for the contractor to inspect and expedite and will increase the project paperwork and costs for no benefit. The employer can already control any purchases made in his name, that is to say, where the contractor is purchasing as his agent. If the contractor is to purchase reimbursably as principal, and there are advantages for the employer in his doing this, the employer can still exercise substantial influence by the use of suitable terms in his contract with the contractor. Through the project vendors list he can control recipients of enquiries, he can secure the right to be present at all negotiations, and through the order approval system he can control the final choice of suppliers. His long-term relationships with the latter are little affected by the use of a contractor whether the latter purchases as agent or principal.

It is sometimes desirable to employ more than one contractor for the provision of engineering and procurement services. Probably the most common instance is a foreign project where a UK contractor is desirable for the on-plot process plant because of his experience with the technology, and a local contractor for the off-plot because of his familiarity with local codes and statutory requirements. Co-ordination between the contractors then becomes of first importance. The contractors should be given the clear responsibility for co-ordinating their work and the employer's project manager will need to supervise this closely. Additionally, the UK contractor in such a case may wish to sub-contract part of his work, such as detailed civil and electrical design which is most closely affected by local factors, to a local contractor. This would be acceptable to the employer only if satisfactory co-ordination arrangements were made.

7.2.6 Supply of Materials

Obviously, the supply of materials (meaning here supply on a lump sum basis rather than reimbursably as principal) for a project would always be an adjunct to the provision of design and procurement services. For the employer, the advantage is that the contractor assumes the risks of cost, time and performance but not, of course, without some mark-up to reward him. The contractor will probably consider the risks to be less than those of field construction, unless he has recent experience on the plant site and there is a settled labour situation. It is not uncommon for a contract to be placed for lump sum design, procurement and supply for an overseas plant for which the employer will be responsible for construction.

The definition that is required for the contractor to bid a lump sum for supply is, apart from knowledge of the construction scene, little less than that needed to contract for lump sum design, supply and construction. Careful specification by the employer is in any case required to ensure that equipment and materials supplied are satisfactory.

7.2.7 Construction Management Services

It is possible to separate the management of construction from direct responsibility for its execution. A contractor might provide construction management services on a lump sum or reimbursable basis, but in either case would accept liability only for a professional standard of performance. He would place contracts for the execution work (generally referred to as sub-contracts, though they are in fact direct contracts) as agent for the employer. This can have procedural advantages for the employer. A construction management services contract can be placed with much less information, and hence earlier in the project, than a contract for construction as a whole. Such a contractor can then place 'sub-contracts' for individual parts of the project as the design information becomes available. However, such a method of proceeding does require the availability of sub-contractors who can manage the task, as opposed to those who are simply suppliers of labour. In some less-developed countries, sub-contractors with management capability are rare or non-existent.

There is clearly an advantage in construction being managed by the organisation that is responsible for the engineering design. Communication is easier, design documents more readily understood, responsibility is not divided. Other considerations, however, often dictate a division of responsibility. In the UK in recent years, industrial relations considerations have led manufacturing companies to manage construction themselves on sites where they have existing operations. In foreign countries, the employer may not have the resources or experience to manage construction himself. In that event, it is desirable to employ a contractor with knowledge of the country and a local construction management contractor may be preferred to the use of the UK contractor responsible for the design. If responsibility for design and construction has to be separated, adequate co-ordination and technical liaison has to be provided covering both design information and material supply.

7.2.8 Field Construction

If a main construction contractor is employed, responsible for the whole of construction, he usually has the choice of executing the work through directly hired labour, through the use of sub-contractors, or by a mixture of the two methods. In countries with a developed industrial base, construction is often accomplished through the use of local sub-contractors for the individual trades. Thus there would be a civil sub-contractor, a piping sub-contractor and so on. The advantages of this arrangement are that the sub-contractors can usually offer more settled employment to their workforce and have greater local knowledge. The main contractor could also employ labour-only sub-contractors, which would relieve him of the task of recruiting and hiring labour.

The main contractor using sub-contractors with management capability is acting little differently from the construction management services contractor except that he places the sub-contracts on his own account rather than as the employer's agent, and of course he accepts liability for the whole, especially the interactions between the different sub-contracts. Both types of contractor would prepare and issue enquiries, negotiate and place orders and subsequently manage and co-ordinate the sub-contractors' operations on site. In either case, the supply of design information and materials must be carefully co-ordinated if responsibility for design and construction is separated.

7.2.9 Pre-commissioning

Pre-commissioning, the work of preparing the plant for start-up following its completion, consists of cleaning and checking—work performed under the direction of the commissioning organisation. It is generally done by the construction contractor (or the mechanical erection sub-contractor) supplying labour to work under the control of the commissioning staff. Contractually, it would usually form a reimbursable or day-work element in the contracts of the relevant contractors.

7.2.10 Commissioning

The usual practice is for the employer to provide staff and workers to commission the plant under the supervision of the licensor, if any. Of course, an employer who owned the process technology would require no commissioning assistance, though the engineering design contractor might wish to provide some to give his staff experience. A process licensor, or the engineering design contractor if the technology were provided through him, would supply technical supervision and advice to the employer's plant management but would not usually have executive control of the work, at least in theory. Both licensor and engineering design contractor would have guarantees to meet and would therefore require to participate in the test runs. The agreement for the process licence, and the contract with the engineering design contractor, would have specified the guarantees, test runs and responsibilities for commissioning.

7.2.11 Operator Training

The provider of the process technology will often undertake, as part of the licence agreement, to provide training of the employer's operators at an existing facility which uses the same technology.

7.3   SOME EXAMPLES OF CONTRACTS ORGANISATION

It is evident from the considerations discussed above that a project will seldom be executed entirely through the agency of a single contract, whatever the theoretical advantages of so doing. Even a lump sum turnkey contract for design, supply and construction will seldom encompass more than 80% of the total project. There will always be a substantial amount of work necessary to establish the employer's needs and set up the contract. Even if the employer is totally bereft of resources and engages a managing contractor or consultant at the very beginning of the project, there would be at least two contracts. In practice, the experienced employer will almost always prefer to perform some activities for himself; or will see no advantage in involving the main contractor in the award of some ancillary contracts; or will choose to divide the work by function—design separated from construction, say,—or by area—on-plot treated separately from off-plot—believing that this will produce a better result than using a single contractor.

Division of the project in this way leaves the employer responsible for the interactions between the different contracts. Where the project is split by geographical area and one contractor relies on information from another to carry out his work, it is the employer who will be liable for any shortfall in the timing or quality of that information. Where there is a split by function, the impact of one on the other will be to the employer's account. Thus if design and construction are separated, the effects of design errors and omissions on construction will be borne by the employer, who will then have to seek what recompense he can from the design contractor. There are many external factors—taxation, the timing of events, the knowledge and experience of the potential contractors available—which may influence the contract organisation, quite apart from those which arise from the project itself. Because he is responsible for the interfaces between the contracts and the cross-liabilities which arise, it is crucial that the employer design the contract organisation and the scopes of the individual contracts so that the extent of each contractor's responsibility is clearly defined and easily understood, Simple cut-lines must be the aim. One of the factors considered in plant layout should be the proposed contractual organisation: clear and uncomplicated divisions of responsibility can then be managed with the aid of appropriate cut-line drawings.

There is, of course, a very large number of possible combinations of contracts: probably no two projects will be exactly the same. If the contractual scheme is at all complicated, it is desirable that it is appropriately documented as it develops. A major project in a foreign country may give rise to many contracts, of which few can be considered in isolation. Clearly there are many ways of documenting the situation but the essential requirements are to provide:

- A schedule of the main contracts
- A brief description of the main features of each contract
- A diagram showing the main contracting parties and the contracts between them.

The contract diagram may be found to be the most useful tool for discussion and explanation, and some examples for particular hypothetical circumstances follow.

7.3.1 UK Project Using Directly Licensed Technology

Figure 7.1 illustrates the contracts organisation that might be required for a plant to be built in the UK using process technology licensed directly from a

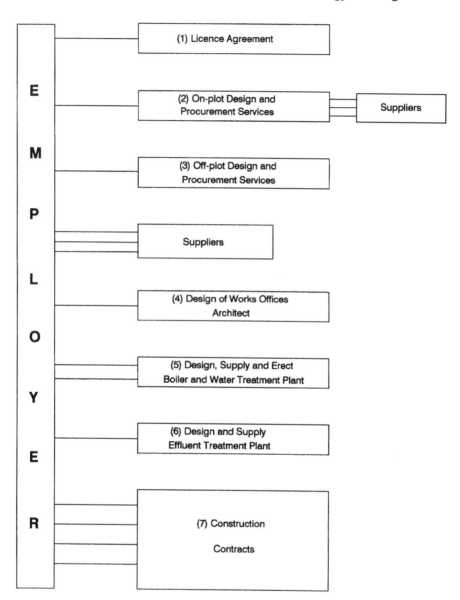

Figure 7.1 Contracts organisation for a UK project

third party. It supposes the plant is to be built on an existing site, and that the employer has substantial design and construction resources. The major contracts are as follows:

(1) An agreement with the licensor for the licensing of the technology and the production of the process package. A common arrangement is for there to be an initial lump sum payment with a running royalty based on tonnage production. The licensor would supervise commissioning and test runs to substantiate his guarantees, and would be reimbursed at quoted rates for this work. Contractually, it is preferable for the licensed technology to be transferred through the engineering design contractor, thus avoiding potential problems in deciding whether any fault lies with the process or the detailed design, but particular circumstances may dictate otherwise.

(2) The main contract for on-plot design and procurement services. Many considerations affect the scope of this contract. If on-plot and off-plot design are to be performed by different contractors, the division of responsibility needs close attention, and is further discussed in a later chapter. The contractor is assumed to be engaged on a lump sum contract for services, being reimbursed for the costs of materials and equipment which he purchases as principal.

(3) General off-plot design and procurement services of a minor nature are assumed to be provided by a small local contractor, chosen because he has considerable experience of similar work on the site, offers lower design rates and can make the many site visits that the work requires inexpensively. This contract is reimbursable and, because of the employer's much greater commercial strength, purchase orders are placed by the employer. The employer may carry out any process engineering required.

(4) A separate contract is placed with an architect for the design of the works office block. The extent of the services to be provided by the architect needs to be considered in relation to responsibilities for the rest of construction.

(5) The steam boiler and water treatment plants required are provided by the respective specialist manufacturers, who carry out design, supply and erection (other than civil work) under lump sum contracts.

(6) The effluent treatment plant is designed by a specialist company, who design and supply equipment against a lump sum contract, but do no construction.

(7) The employer manages the construction himself, placing separate contracts for the different disciplines—piling, civil work, steel erection, mechanical erection, piping, electrics, instruments and so on. More than one contractor in a given discipline may be necessary because of the size of the job, or may be convenient because of the split responsibility for the design work—for example, a separate contractor might be engaged for the works office block, especially if this were to be supervised by the architect. Clearly, construction management has a major task of co-ordination.

This arrangement is by no means untypical, if somewhat simplified. Various other contracts may be placed by the employer: for cost control, planning and quantity surveying services for example. The employer retains a considerable part of the project risk, including the cross-liabilities between contracts i.e. the interaction of one with another. The role of engineer for most of the contracts would normally be filled by the employer's project manager, with the engineering design manager as the engineer's representative in the design office and the construction manager his representative on site.

7.3.2 Overseas Project Using Employer's Technology

Figure 7.2 shows the organisation of major contracts for a hypothetical overseas project using the employer's own technology.

(1) Assistance in producing the detailed design package is provided reimbursably by a UK contractor (who will later be a bidder for the on-plot design and procurement services contract). Contractor's staff are seconded to work in the employer's offices.

(2) There are then a number of small contracts that, for various reasons, the employer has placed directly. Because the plant has a number of large drives, and the reliability and robustness of the electricity grid is questionable, a study of the electrical supply system is commissioned from a consultant with local knowledge. An environmental impact assessment is necessary and use of a government-approved local consultant highly desirable if not quite mandatory. A lump sum contract is placed with a local contractor for the clearing, levelling and fencing of the new site. Soil investigations are commissioned from a specialist consultant.

(3) On-plot design and procurement services are provided on a lump sum basis by a UK contractor, purchasing reimbursably as principal. He sub-contracts detailed civil and electrical design work, which is much affected by local rules and regulations, to a local contractor who purchases as principal.

(4) A local contractor performs design and procurement services for the off-plots on a lump sum basis, purchasing reimbursably as principal.

(5) A separate lump sum contract for piling is placed by the employer, permitting this work to proceed earlier than if it were part of the main construction contract.

(6) A schedule of rates contract is placed with a local contractor for the vast majority of the construction. There are no PC sums or nominated sub-contractors.

(7) Separate lump sum contracts are let for the design, supply and erection (excluding civil work) of the steam boiler and water treatment plants. There may be other contracts which are let similarly.

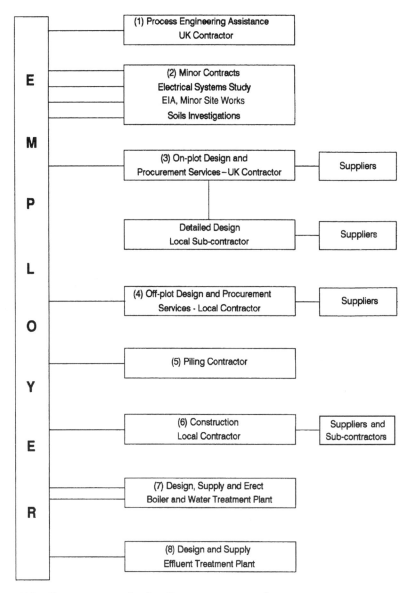

Figure 7.2 Contracts organisation for an overseas project

(8)   A separate lump sum contract is placed for the design and supply, excluding construction, of an effluent treatment plant.

This arrangement of contracts makes no concessions to the effects of financing or taxation, one or both of which is likely to obtrude in an overseas project, and which are considered in Chapter 8. A great deal of the risk remains with the employer. He is, of course, responsible for the process engineering, and for the results of the various initial investigations. The piling work is also outside the scope of the main construction contractor. The employer is liable for the interaction between the various contracts, notably the two main design contracts. As in the example illustrated in Figure 7.1, the major risk area is the liability for over-expenditure on construction caused by faults in the design— inaccurate initial definition of the scope of work, delays caused by late delivery of design information and material, errors and omissions and late changes.

7.3.3 Overseas Project Owned by Joint Venture

Joint ventures add some new ingredients to the contractual situation, because the relationship between employer and the joint venture must be accounted for. They can also cause some simplification if they lead to a lump sum turnkey contract. Figure 7.3 shows a typical contract organisation. (The term 'employer' is retained for the joint venture partner who takes the lead in the project, supplying both the process technology, the project manager and the bulk of his team.)

(1) There is a licence agreement encompassing the supply to the joint venture by the employer of the process package and the necessary technical supervision of the contractor to ensure that his design complies with it. The employer's project manager will be responsible for the execution of this contract on behalf of the employer.

(2) There is a project agreement covering the supply by the employer to the joint venture of project management services. Under this agreement the employer's project manager will become the joint venture project manager and will be responsible, *inter alia*, for securing satisfactory performance of the licence agreement by himself.

(3) There may be, as in the previous example, a number of small contracts that the joint venture will place directly: contracts for environmental impact assessment, for soils investigations, and for preliminary work on site.

(4) It is assumed that project finance is being sought and that the joint venture partners are not providing full guarantees of completion, so that a single-point responsibility contract for design and construction is insisted upon. This will be placed with a UK contractor. He may decide to sub-contract a major part of the work, in which case the sub-contractors would need to be approved; or to form a consortium, in which case joint and several responsibility would be required.

(5) A separate contract, or contracts, is placed with a local contractor for the design and construction of those off-plots which are not related to the process—offices, amenities, workshops and so on.

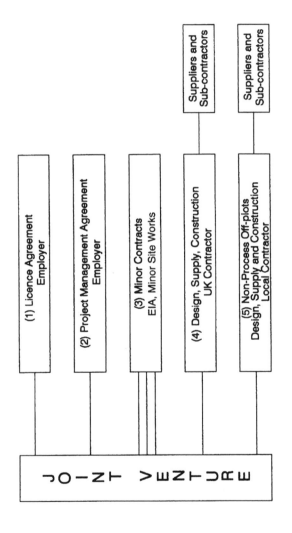

Figure 7.3 Contracts organisation for an overseas joint venture project

This organisation is undoubtedly simpler than would be achieved in practice and ignores the effects of taxation, which are dealt with in Chapter 8. The employer's project manager must think clearly about his role and responsibilities, since he has a dual allegiance—to the joint venture and to his own employer—and to treat them both fairly and equitably, sometimes under pressure from one side or the other, is not always easy. As the joint venture project manager, he is responsible for monitoring the performance of the employer (much of which performance he will be managing on the employer's behalf). He must also monitor the contractor's performance on behalf of the joint venture. Dual responsibilities apply to much of the design: the enquiry produced by the joint venture will contain the process package produced by the employer; the project team in the contractors' offices will ensure, on behalf of the employer as licensor, that the process package is correctly interpreted, and will supervise other aspects on behalf of the joint venture.

Chapter 8

Effects of Taxation and Financing on Overseas Contracts

The effects of taxation and financing must be taken into account in organising the contracts for an overseas project. The taxation to which a UK contractor becomes liable on an overseas project, and which will be taken into consideration in his contract price, may be substantially affected by the way in which the contracts are organised. The taxation of local (i.e. overseas) contractors may also be affected by the way a contract is let. Specific contract requirements may be imposed by financing institutions as a condition of financial support for a project. They will, of course, demand considerable information about the project which will involve the employer's project manager in considerable work and which will need to be allowed for in the project programme. The possible effects of taxation and financing are therefore important matters to consider at an early stage.

8.1 EFFECTS OF TAXATION

Unless foreign taxation can be offset by the contractor against his liability for UK tax, and this is not always possible for a variety of reasons, the contractor will allow for it in his bid, which is thereby increased. As well as avoiding double taxation, it is also desirable to try to ensure that taxes are paid in the most appropriate country. It is therefore in the employer's interest (as well as in that of the bidder wishing to offer the most attractive price) that unnecessary taxation be avoided. The employer's project manager will need to work with each bidder, and subsequently with the successful contractor, to design the most economical contract scheme. Both sides will be guided in this by taxation and legal experts. Bringing to bear the required combination of engineering, contractual and taxation expertise, together with up-to-date knowledge of the possibly uncertain and changing situation in an industrialising country is not, however, always easily achieved. In novel circumstances much work may be required to arrive at firm conclusions about how best to proceed and, long before this, the employer's project manager may have had to make assumptions in his project strategy about the number and nature of the contracts which may prove to be necessary and the time and effort that they will require. He may also have had to commit himself to a cost estimate of the effects of taxation. He therefore needs to have some understanding of the various issues so that his assessments are not too wide of the mark, he can ensure that the right questions are asked of the experts, and the optimum arrangement of contracts is arrived at expeditiously.

The following brief treatment of the subject is intended merely to provide an appreciation of some of the issues involved, based on hypothetical, but not unrealistic circumstances. Expert advice must always be sought but is not always as definitive as might be wished and is sometimes conflicting. Certainty in these matters is often not possible, and some advisers will be more cautious than others. In some Third World countries the laws are vaguely drafted and capriciously applied. They may lack the legal precedents which are necessary to convert the law from a statement of general principles into a set of working rules. It may be difficult to get a ruling from the authorities in advance and even where this is done, it may not always bind the official whose task it is to decide a particular case.

The incidence and rate of taxation may be affected by special privileges for the encouragement of investment that the project may have been granted, and by any double taxation treaty between the UK and the country where the work will be performed. The effects of special privileges granted to a project are sometimes difficult to determine exactly and may eventually prove less attractive than appears at first sight. In general, tax matters often contain much that can only be settled on a case-by-case basis.

A UK contractor will pay UK corporation tax on his world-wide corporate profits, that is to say all his income, both local and overseas, will be consolidated for tax purposes. There are two instances where foreign tax may also be levied on his income or profits arising from overseas work:

(1) The contractor may establish a taxable presence, called a 'permanent establishment', in a foreign country. For example, where a UK contractor sends employees to work on a construction site in the foreign country for twelve months or more, this may cause him to be deemed to have a

permanent establishment in that country. The permanent establishment may be compared to a foreign branch of the company and tax will be levied on the profits deemed by the foreign tax authorities to be associated with the branch. Unsurprisingly, the foreign tax authorities will usually try to attribute as much taxable profit to the branch as possible, including probably all the income associated with the particular project whether it is derived from onshore or offshore work. (Here and in what follows, 'onshore' means within the country in which the plant is to be built, 'offshore' means outside that country.)

(2) Alternatively, the UK contractor may not have a permanent establishment, but a withholding tax will be applied to any income arising from the onshore work he does and, depending on the contractual arrangements, potentially also on income derived from offshore work.

It is this latter case to which the points below refer. Since the rate of withholding tax may in some circumstances be as high as 15% on gross income, this can be an especially severe tax, exceeding the contractor's profit margin. As mentioned above, all profits will fall to be taxed in the UK, so the contractor will seek double taxation relief for any foreign taxes paid against his UK tax liability. This relief is given either under the terms of a double taxation agreement with the country in question, or under unilateral relief where no such agreement is in place, and will allow the contractor to offset the tax he has paid on work performed in the foreign country against his liability for UK tax. However, he may be unable to so offset any foreign tax he has paid on work performed in the UK. Even if the contractor performs only offshore work, withholding tax may still be imposed by the foreign country.

With these points in mind, in place of the single lump sum contract for design services, equipment and material supply and construction that the project manager might wish to negotiate, the mitigation of foreign taxation may, depending on the foreign country's taxation regime, require a more complicated and fragmented contract structure. This will have disadvantages to the employer that will need to be addressed, and in some instances it could be decided to forgo a tax advantage if it has to be bought at too high a price in other directions. In very general terms, if any part of a contract attracts foreign taxation, there may be a danger of the total value of the contact being taxed. The way to minimise the tax liability is therefore to identify those parts of the project which are likely to attract tax and separate them from the remainder. The criteria for such separation vary from one overseas country to another, but some of the main ones are outlined below.

(1) The profit on work onshore in a foreign country is clearly subject to local tax, whereas that on offshore work may not be. It is prudent, therefore, to divide the work into separate contracts for offshore and for onshore work. These contracts may have to be completely separate with no cross-reference

and no interdependence. Payment for and performance of the one must be independent of payment for and performance of the other, as if they were two separate contracts performed by two separate independent contractors. It may help if the contracts are with separate companies—one the UK contractor, the other his wholly owned subsidiary.

(2) An offshore royalty contract, e.g. for a process licence, will usually be subject to withholding tax on the full value of the contract, the whole of the royalty payment being deemed to be profit. Any royalty-bearing part of a project should therefore be isolated in a separate contract.

(3) An offshore design services contract may be subject to withholding tax. The ownership of copyright may influence this. Sometimes, retention of copyright in the design by the designer can lead to the contract being treated as a royalty contract and so liable to withholding tax on the gross value of the contract. Transference of the copyright to the employer may result in withholding tax being avoided or being levied at a lower rate, but this could cause other problems where the process technology does not belong to the employer.

(4) A contract for the supply of materials only, with no services element, is unlikely to attract withholding tax. It may well be desirable, therefore, to split a design and supply contract into two separate contracts. In the limit, contracts for equipment and materials supply could be made directly between employer and suppliers, but this is unlikely to commend itself to the employer.

(5) Withholding tax may be avoidable on the financing interest associated with offshore materials supply if the contract allows for payment by instalments including interest.

(6) In some countries, a business, or sales, tax is levied on every onshore contract. Each layer of sub-contracts then attracts additional tax, making it desirable to minimise the number of sub-contracts, for example in construction.

(7) Business, or sales, tax may be payable on onshore services contracts but not on onshore contracts solely for materials supply. Again, there would be a case to separate services and supply contracts, affecting, for example, contracts placed for civil engineering construction.

Let us look at the possible effects of taxation on the two overseas examples of contracts organisation illustrated in the previous chapter. If for the first example, Figure 7.2, it is assumed that withholding tax is payable merely on any contract with an onshore element, the contract for on-plot design services and materials supply (4) Figure 7.2, will be affected. Although the vast majority of the work of this contract is carried out in the UK, it will contain some onshore element, for example, for site liaison. It will be desirable, therefore, to separate this small onshore element into a separate contract, preferably placed with a wholly owned subsidiary of the contractor, shown as item 4B in Figure 8.1. In addition, the placing of a sub-contract for detailed design with an onshore sub-contractor must be avoided. Either the contractor must do this work himself, or the sub-contract must be changed to a direct contract with the employer, shown as item 4C. The latter course has disadvantages for the employer, and he would probably be willing to accept this arrangement only if he were confident that the contractor would continue to act and accept liability as if the work were still being done under a sub-contract: a side letter to this effect would be appropriate.

The advantages to the employer of the contractor, who is being reimbursed for the cost of materials, purchasing as principal rather than as agent are discussed in a later chapter. In some countries, purchase as principal by the contractor results in the material costs being added to his turnover and becoming liable to local tax. This would very probably rule out the local contractor purchasing as principal in contracts for reimbursable material supply, and would affect contract 4C in Figure 8.1.

If the contract arrangement for a joint venture project, illustrated previously in Figure 7.3 is reconsidered in the light of the assumptions that withholding tax is levied on any contract, onshore or offshore, which contains services, but not on contracts solely for the supply of goods and that sales tax is charged on onshore contracts only if they include services, the arrangement shown in Figure 8.2 might be arrived at. The licence agreement, item 1, is split into two separate contracts, the first for the payment of royalties (the whole of which may be deemed to be profit for withholding tax purposes); the second for licence services—the provision of the front end engineering package, liaison with the design contractor, and the onshore services of commissioning and testing. The single contract for design, supply and construction, item 4, placed with a UK contractor is now split into four separate contracts. The first (4A) is for offshore design and procurement services, which attracts withholding tax. A separate contract (4B) is placed for materials supply. A separate contract (4C) is placed for the services element of construction, which attracts both withholding tax and sales tax. The final contract (4D) is for construction materials. The contract for design, supply and construction of the non-process offplots placed with a local contractor, is split into separate contracts for services (5A) and for supply of materials (5B).

Having separated the project into several contracts, none of which may refer to the others, the employer needs to ensure that he receives the same guarantees from the main contractor as he would otherwise have done. Those guarantees that continue to fall entirely within the purlieu of a single contract will be unaffected, but those which involve cross-liabilities between the newly separated contracts must be re-examined. The example given in Figure 8.1 presents no real difficulty other than with the sub-contracting of part of the on-plot detailed design, previously discussed. In Figure 8.2. the splitting of the

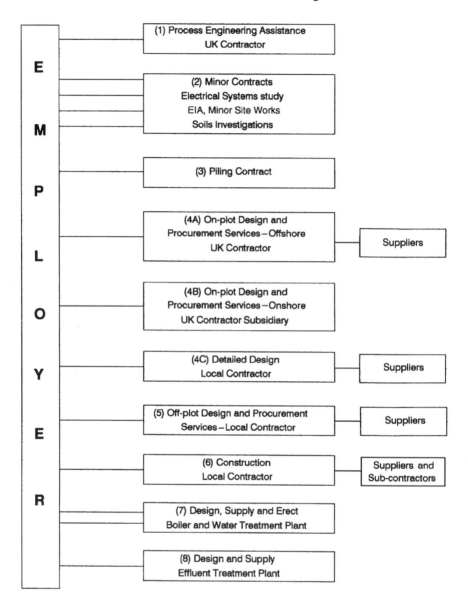

Figure 8.1 Effects of taxation on contracts organisation for an overseas project

single-point responsibility contract for design, supply and construction (4) into four separate contracts raises problems. Let us assume that the offshore contractor for design and procurement services (4A) accepts liability only for the correction of errors and omissions in those services, not for any

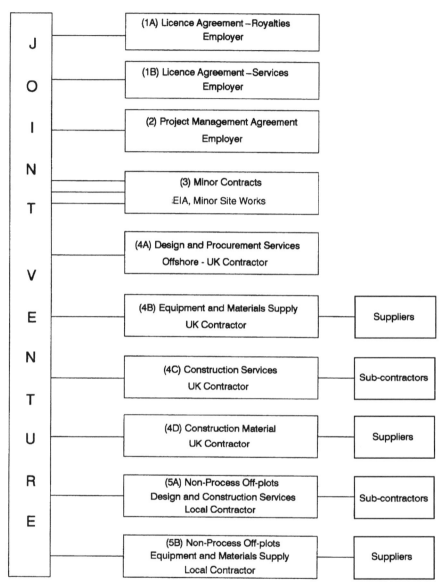

Figure 8.2 Effects of taxation on contracts organisation for an overseas joint venture project

consequences which become evident during the performance of what are now other contracts. It is then necessary, in both contracts for materials and equipment supply, offshore (4B) and onshore (4D), for the contractor to accept liability for correcting all defects, except those which are the fault of the employer or of the licensor. These defects will arise as the faults of the suppliers or from faults in the services provided under (4A) and (4C) respectively. In the onshore construction services contract (4C), the contractor must accept liability for correcting all defects in the plant except those which are the fault of the employer or of the licensor. Defects in the plant resulting from errors in contracts (4A), (4B) and (4D) will thus be covered as well as defects in the construction services themselves. Similar reasoning must be applied to contracts (5A) and (5B) for the non-process off-plots. In both contracts, the contractor must accept liability for all defects except those which are the fault of the employer or of the licensor.

In a single contract for design, supply and construction, the contractor would be expected to accept a total limit of liability covering defects from all causes save those specifically excluded from the limitation, e.g. errors and omissions in design which would have no limit. To divide this total limit of liability among the separate contracts would be to the disadvantage of the employer. In order for the employer's position to be maintained, each of the separate contracts must have the same total limit of liability as would have applied to a single contract. There would then need to be a side letter from the employer to the effect that, notwithstanding the terms of the four contracts, the total limit of liability of the contractor does not exceed the limit specified in any one of the contracts.

There will undoubtedly be other matters which arise and which will need attention as a result of separating the project into several separate contracts. Some may prove intractable, and the disadvantage to the employer may not be worth the tax saved. It is clear that considerable time and effort at a crucial stage in the project development may be required to deal with tax considerations. Further change may be imposed for financing reasons, e.g. separate contracts for ECGD and non-ECGD material supply. The project manager needs to be aware of all of these matters and to make appropriate provision for them in his planning and estimating.

8.2 EFFECTS OF PROJECT FINANCING

Major international companies in the process industries do not usually seek financing for specific projects. If such a company finds it necessary to borrow, it will do so on a corporate basis and the project manager will neither know nor care where the funds for his project originate. There are, however, at least two instances where such a company might wish to seek financing for a specific project and where the work of the employer's project manager will be affected in consequence:

(1) Where the plant is to be built overseas and owned by a foreign subsidiary of the company. In this case, the company may wish to take advantage of the export credit guarantees which are offered by the governments of most developed countries. Export credit finance does not cover the whole cost of a process plant project. It is restricted largely to goods and services exported from the country providing the credit guarantees and to, at most, 85% of their value. This will seldom amount to more than half the total cost of the project.

(2) Where the plant is to be owned by a joint venture company which will seek to finance the project from its future profits. If the plant is to be sited overseas—as is likely, for the most common reason for the establishment of such a joint venture is a foreign country's requirement for local participation—export credit may form part of the financing.

The project manager will usually be no more than a supporting player in the financing process. He needs only a basic appreciation of the ways in which a project might be financed, but this limited knowledge will be useful because the financing may affect the way the contracts are organised and require changes to the contract terms themselves. The project manager with at least a rudimentary understanding of financing will more quickly be able to realise how his project will be affected and to plan accordingly. The following brief account provides an outline of how the work and responsibilities of the employer's project manager may be affected by financing considerations. Financing and its effects can be quite complicated and much of the detail can only be defined with knowledge of the circumstances of a particular project.

8.2.1 Export Credit

The governments of most developed countries assist their exporters of project and capital goods through export credit agencies established for the purpose. Overseas buyers rarely wish to pay in cash for major purchases of capital equipment or for major projects. Few exporters would wish or would be able to undertake the risks of financing. The export credit agencies offer solutions to these problems by providing some or all of the following facilities:

(1) Guarantees to a lending bank of repayment of principal and interest in the event that the borrower—the overseas buyer—defaults on the loan.
(2) Insurance policies in favour of the exporter covering default by the borrower and certain political risks.
(3) Subsidies to allow a fixed rate of interest, which may be below the available commercial rate.
(4) Insurance cover for the exporter against inflation and currency exchange risk.

The majority of export credit agencies, including the UK's Export Credit Guarantee Department (ECGD), act only as insurer, the loans being provided by the commercial banks. Some agencies will lend all or part of the funds themselves, or through an associated institution. An example of the former is the Export–Import Bank (Eximbank) of the USA. An example of the latter is Italy's export credit agency Sezione Speciale per l'Assicurazione del Credito all'Esportazione (SACE) and its associated lender Istituto Centrale per il Credito a Medio Termine (Mediocredito).

The advantages of export credit finance can be considerable. They can include a fixed rate of interest, often subsidised below market levels. They can include long grace periods before repayments start—six months after delivery of equipment or plant commissioning—and repayment periods of five to ten years depending on the country of the borrower. The loans can also be arranged in different currencies to suit the convenience of the borrower. In the case of a major project with large-scale international purchasing of materials and equipment, export credit finance might be sought from several countries from which goods are to be procured. The difference in the costs of credit could then become a factor in subsequent procurement decisions. Some developing countries may offer especially attractive credit terms in order to attract foreign exchange and there may sometimes be a case for procuring less sophisticated materials and equipment from such countries in order to take advantage of these credits. The costs of arrangement and administration are, however, quite considerable and export credit is worth pursuing only where the value of eligible goods or services is substantial.

There are a number of ways in which the lending can be arranged and these are described below.

Supplier credit

As the name suggests, the supplier of the goods takes the leading role and extends credit to the buyer by selling on deferred payment terms. The supplier borrows from a bank to finance the period until payment is received. The export credit agency guarantees repayment of principal and interest to the bank—usually at the 90–95% level—in the event of default by the buyer. The supplier is also insured by the agency against the buyer's default.

Supplier credits are usually offered only in connection with relatively small contracts because of the implications for the supplier's balance sheet of taking the bank loan and passing it on to the buyer. There is an exception, however, in the case of Japan's major trading houses. These group the resources of a number of related, major suppliers together and offer supplier credit for major contracts. Japan's Ministry for International Trade Investments (MITI) furnishes credit insurance and guarantees and the Export–Import Bank of

Japan provides financing directly for 60–70% of the credit, the remainder being provided by commercial banks.

There can be tax advantages with supplier credits. In some overseas countries, withholding tax is assessed on the interest payable on buyer credits but not on that on supplier credits.

Buyer credit

In the case of a buyer credit, the supplier is not directly involved in the financing arrangements. The loan agreement is between the buyer and the lending bank. The supplier is usually paid directly by the bank on presenting evidence of supply. The buyer then repays the bank on the agreed terms. Alternatively, the buyer can pay the supplier directly and seek reimbursement from the lending bank on presenting evidence of payment.

The export credit agency guarantees repayment to the bank if the buyer defaults and also insures the exporter against buyer default and some political risks.

Lines of credit

A project line of credit is similar to a buyer credit but covers a number of contracts instead of just one. It may thus be used when a particular project requires purchases from a number of exporters. It can be arranged before contracts are placed and its subsequent use controlled by the buyer.

The conditions on which export credit from the UK is made available by the ECGD are broadly as follows:

(1) At least 70% of the value of the goods and services must originate in the UK. The remainder, of not more than 30%, may be supplied from other parts of the EC, but may include goods and services from third countries of up to 15% of the value of the UK content. Of the total satisfying these criteria, 80–85%, depending on the country in which the plant is to be built, will be eligible for export credit support.
(2) The buyer must be acceptable (export credit agencies tend to be more flexible in their criteria for acceptability than commercial lenders).
(3) The contractor must be technically and financially capable of executing the project.
(4) The contract must provide for an advance payment to the contractor of at least 5% of the contract value. The buyer must pay at least 15% of the contract value before the credit period (i.e repayment) starts. There are restrictions on draw-down of the loan to ensure stage payments stay in line with the permitted totals of UK, EEC and third country totals.

The credit agency will make it possible for the loan to be offered at a fixed rate of interest, often at less than commercial rates, the difference being borne by the agency. The rates vary from time to time—the offered rates are reviewed at six monthly intervals—and also vary for different borrowing countries. The latter are divided into three categories, rich, intermediate and poor, with the last qualifying for the cheapest rates. To avoid excessive competition, the OECD export credit agencies agree a set of minimum rates which can be offered, which are termed the 'consensus' rates.

The application for export credit must be made before the contract is awarded to the engineering contractor by the employer. Once the application is made, however, the contract may be completed and orders placed with suppliers before the export credit agreement is approved. If the loan is to be on a reimbursement basis, where the buyer pays the contractor and then recovers from the lender, some flexibility of timing in setting up the arrangements is possible. For example, the contract between employer and contractor might include a term giving the employer the right to amend the contract to satisfy the requirements of the export credit agency provided the contractor is reimbursed for any extra cost and indemnified against any obligation which he might incur in consequence. The contract terms will need to provide for the following:

- An advance payment to the contractor of 5% of the contract value. Subsequent payments will need to be reduced by 5% to amortise this advance.
- The payment to the contractor of a further 10% on or before delivery of the goods and services. This and the advance payment must be made by the buyer prior to the start of the credit period.
- Definition of the value of eligible goods and services to be provided under the contract, e.g. for an ECGD-supported loan, separate totals for the value of goods and services from the UK, from the rest of the EEC and from other countries.
- A requirement for the contractor to provide the employer with a supplier's receipt after each payment.
- In some circumstances, it could be desirable to split the contract into two to cover goods and services which are eligible for export credit and those which are not.
- If the ECGD premium payable by the contractor is itself to be financed, its value will have to be included in the totals.

In addition to the contract between employer and contractor referred to above (and which may have to be fragmented for taxation reasons, as previously discussed) there are other agreements—for premium and guarantees, loan and recourse—which will not trouble the project manager. All of this is not done without attracting extra charges—interest, bank fees, premiums—which usually will not be part of the capital cost estimate prepared by the project manager. Obviously, the project manager will wish to know from whose budget these costs are to be paid.

8.2.2 Project Finance

Project finance is the financing of a project on the basis of its future profits. The security for the lender flows entirely from the project and for this reason, if for no other, project financing will always be more expensive for a major established company than corporate borrowing where the assets of the company stand behind the loan. In practice, therefore, a major company will not often seek project financing. Where it does so, it will be for special reasons, such as its participation in a joint venture company where the partners cannot or will not fund their full share of the project from their own resources. It is likely that the project sponsors will provide some of the financing—this will certainly inspire more confidence in the minds of prospective lenders. Although true project financing involves no external guarantees, in practice, few projects are financed without some additional security for the lenders, if only because the provision of some guarantees by the project sponsors will cheapen the loans.

The first step in seeking project finance which concerns the project manager is the production of an *information memorandum* describing the project in detail. This will explain to prospective lenders the nature of the project and the case for the investment. The memorandum is similar in purpose to a company's internal sanction proposal, but the nature of the risk offered to the investor is different. The external lender provides a fixed-interest loan and requires an appropriate level of security; he is not a participant in the risks and rewards of equity investment. Consequently, he requires guarantees of project capital cost and completion which will almost certainly, in the absence of recourse to the project sponsors, require a single-point responsibility lump sum contract for the project to have been negotiated before loans are agreed. Thus the project strategy may be completely different from what it would have been for an internally financed project, and the sequence and planning of pre-sanction work profoundly affected.

The information memorandum will contain full details of the projected economics of the project, with capital costs, production costs and forecast sales volumes and prices. The experience and capabilities of the sponsors and contractors will be described together with the technology to be used. The lenders will require reassurances on matters outside the purview of the engineering project manager. These will include details of the commercial arrangements for the supply of feedstocks and the sale of products. In many cases it will be necessary for these arrangements to be committed before any loan is approved. The information memorandum will contain details of the proposed arrangements.

In cases where it is proposed to use established, bought-in technology for the process plant, responsibility for the technical success of the project may rest almost entirely with the licensors of the technology and the engineering contractor. In such circumstances, the latter would also be responsible for the capital cost estimate and it would be necessary to obtain bids and select both the licensor and the contractor before the information memorandum could be completed. In other cases, one of the project sponsors might provide the process technology and most of the expertise in its application. Much of the responsibility for the technical success of the project would then rest with that company. It could be responsible for the estimates of cost and it would not be necessary, though it might still be desirable, for contractors' bids to have been received before the information memorandum was issued to prospective lenders. Whatever the situation, it will be necessary to describe fully the experience and capability of those carrying the technical responsibility.

Where one of the sponsors has most of the technical expertise and is providing the technology, it is obviously necessary for it to provide the project manager and engineering team. Their contribution to the information memorandum will be to provide the technical details, for example, the description of the process to be used, the estimates of capital cost and time required to complete the project and details of the engineering contract arrangements proposed. The latter will be subject to the requirements of the lenders. To a large extent, these are predictable and need to be understood by the project manager.

The financing for a major project will almost certainly be undertaken by a syndicate comprising a number of banks. External constraints can influence matters, for example, in some countries offshore finance is not allowed to pay for onshore expenditure. It may be necessary to follow up the information memorandum with presentations to and discussions with a large number of prospective lenders, in which the project manager will play a part. These can be quite time-consuming at a stage in the project process when other project management activities are also peaking.

In the absence of recourse to the sponsors (although, as has been indicated, it is unlikely that the financing will be completed without some external guarantees) the lenders will be concerned to see that the project will in all circumstances be successfully completed and so produce revenue to repay the debt. They will look for guarantees of one sort or another and the following are typical requirements for the contract with the main engineering contractor:

(1) A fixed-price, lump sum contract with single-point responsibility.
(2) Any advance payment to the contractor to be secured by an advance payment bond, reducing automatically as stage payments are made.

(3) A contract performance bond of at least 10% of the contract price, reducing to 5% on takeover, 2½% on passing performance tests and zero at the end of the defects period.

(4) A defects liability period of twelve months following takeover, during which the contractor is liable to make good, at his expense, defects arising in the plant which are his fault.

(5) Performance guarantees for those aspects of plant performance for which the contractor can properly be held liable. Assuming that the licensor provides guarantees of the product specification, plant capacity, efficiency and consumption of raw materials and catalysts, the engineering contractor will guarantee the plant's hydraulic performance and its consumption of utilities.

(6) Liquidated damages of appropriate amounts for delay.

(7) An appropriate limit of liability.

(8) Stage payments related to progress, properly certified.

(9) Lenders' rights to have the contract assigned to them if takeover is delayed by more than, say, twelve months.

Very little of this falls outside normal project practice, given the near-absolute requirement for a single-point responsibility lump sum contract. The levels of liability and guarantees may be somewhat higher than might otherwise be required, and the higher these are, the more expensive the contract will be. If the capital cost estimate is to be made before bids are received, the project manager will need to allow for the reward the contractor will require for accepting the risks of a lump sum contract. The contractor may himself require additional guarantees of payment for work done from the sponsors in the event of cancellation of the project.

Taxation considerations may require the single contract to be split, as previously described, in which case it would be necessary to ensure that the employer and lenders were not disadvantaged thereby. Of course, the main engineering contract will not cover the whole of the project expenditure. The costs of the sponsors themselves can be significant if one of them is to manage the project, provide the technology and commission the plant. Numerous other costs may fall outside the main contractor's scope, for example, the cost of land, site investigation work, environmental assessments, site preparation and utilities supplies. The costs of other items that were imperfectly defined—an example might be import duties—could be borne directly by the sponsors if it was thought that doing so would avoid an excessive contingency by the contractor. The project manager might wish to award separate contracts for work which he judges could be more economically placed directly in the country in which the plant is to be built. In this category could be contracts for offices, workshops and amenities, water supply and effluent treatment works where the technical and management skills are available in the country concerned. Little would be gained and extra cost added by employing the companies doing the work as sub-contractors of the main UK contractor.

The lenders will have other requirements. These will include control over contract amendments as well as satisfactory insurance of all work in progress, equipment and materials in transit, erection all risks, consequential loss and third party liability. The lenders will require rights of assignment of all policies and benefits. Project progress reports, some perhaps by an independent engineer, will also have to be provided.

It will be seen that the financing of a project can substantially affect its cost and timing and the way it is handled:

- Considerable time and effort is involved in providing information to, and negotiating with, prospective lenders.
- The requirement for a fixed-price lump sum contract has significant implications on cost and time. The contractor will require rewarding for the risks he accepts: these will include any currency exchange rate risks, where his methods might differ from those which the employer would have used. The time required to prepare the invitation to bid, the bids themselves, and to select the contractor, will be significant.
- The requirements of the lenders must be accommodated in the terms of the engineering contract and subsequently.

The project manager with a reasonable understanding of the financing process and its implications will be able to plan and estimate accordingly. Without such knowledge he may make embarrassing discoveries as the project proceeds.

Chapter 9

Selecting and Assessing the Bidders

9.1 INTRODUCTION

The importance of contractor selection can hardly be overemphasised. The employer's project manager is selecting a partner in a long and complicated future relationship. He is also selecting an agent for whose performance he will be held responsible. Little wonder, then, that the selection of the contractor ranks so highly on the list of his priorities. There are two main stages: first, the selection and assessment of bidders and second, the evaluation of bids. These overlap to some extent and vary in relative importance depending on the nature of the proposed contract. They are described respectively in this and the following chapter.

Before work starts, the project manager will assemble and brief the evaluation team. He will produce a programme and a manpower loading chart for the work. The programme need be no more than a simple bar chart. It cannot be other than approximate because until the bids are received it is not possible to predict exactly what work will need to be done. It will probably have to be revised at this time and again later during the evaluation process. The project manager may provide the team with checklists of the information required and of the important aspects to be examined. Standard reporting formats may also be provided to make it easier to combine individual assessments of bidders and bids into a final report.

The amount of work for the employer's staff can vary enormously from one project to another. For the most onerous of lump sum contracts, the workload (including the preparation of the various documents which the employer has to produce) will be a significant proportion of the employer's total effort on the project. The work of selecting the contractor for a major project, split into the two main stages, is adumbrated below. These are not, of course, all completely separable and discrete activities, nor is their timing as simply sequential as might appear. This can vary substantially and work can be carried over from one stage of the process to another. The preparation of the employer's main enquiry document, for example, may have begun many months before any of the other activities have started, or may follow discussions with potential bidders on the process technology available. Not all the activities listed will be necessary on every project.

The first stage, the assessment of bidders, comprises the following activities:

(1) The preparation and issue of the preliminary enquiry, aimed at establishing the level of interest in the project among potentially eligible contractors.
(2) Consideration of the responses of potential bidders, followed by discussions with them and assessment of the quality of their organisations.
(3) Visits to plants of a similar nature to the one proposed which have been engineered for other employers by the potential bidders.
(4) Drawing up the short list of bidders.
(5) More detailed assessment of the short-listed bidders.

The second stage, the evaluation of bids, comprises the following activities:

(1) The preparation and issue of the main enquiry document (the invitation to bid).
(2) Evaluation of the bids.
(3) Negotiations with the bidders.
(4) Selection of the preferred bid.
(5) Award of contract.

The large variation possible from one project to another in the amount and nature of the work that has to be done by the employer reflects the very wide range of possible circumstances. The type of contract which is envisaged has much the most important effect on what has to be done. If an entirely reimbursable contract is proposed, the work involved in the enquiry documents may be slight, the assessment of bidders will be all-important and evaluation of bids little more than a comparison of man-hour rates and a guess at relative productivities. Some of what follows will not therefore be relevant to a project where a reimbursable contract is to be placed. The second most important determinant will often be the responsibility for the process technology. Other important factors include the experience and prior knowledge of the employer, and the scope of work of the contractor under the proposed contract. No two projects will be the same.

9.2 RESPONSIBILITY FOR THE PROCESS TECHNOLOGY

After the type of contract proposed, the most important of the many factors that affect the work of contractor selection is probably the question of responsibility for the process technology. The three possible situations are as follows:

(1) The process technology is owned by the employer.
(2) The process technology is to be provided by a pre-selected, third-party licensor.
(3) The process technology is the responsibility of the engineering contractor.

In all three categories, of course, it will be necessary to combine assessment of the bidder with evaluation of his bid, but the relative importance of these two aspects varies considerably between the three cases. In the third category, the quality of the process technology offered has also to be assessed.

9.2.1 Process Technology Owned by the Employer

In cases where the process technology is owned by the employer, selection of bidders for the bid list will often be a fairly simple matter. An employer sufficiently experienced to have developed his own technology for a major process plant will almost certainly have wide experience of those engineering contractors likely to be of most service to him. If this is the first application of the technology on a major scale, the employer will be concerned to form a relationship with an engineering contractor that will allow harmonious working throughout a project in which there will ineluctably be considerable development work—in detail, if not in major elements of the technology. Retention of ownership by the employer of any developments will be a major concern, as will the maintenance of confidentiality. Such a contract is likely to be reimbursable. The employer's assessment will be of the bidder rather than the bid—the latter may need to cover little more than man-hour rates and acceptable provisions for confidentiality, copyright and process ownership. The employer will, if he can, choose a contractor with whom he has already developed good working relationships on previous projects. It is unlikely that such a contract would be awarded to a contractor the employer does not know well. In most such cases, therefore, the bid list will be obvious and the employer may allow little or no competition for the contract.

If the employer already operates similar size plants employing the technology in question, then he would naturally look to the contractors whom he has previously employed on the design and construction of those plants to make up his bid list. If the employer's technology had been previously licensed through contractors, he would seek bidders from among their ranks.

Indeed, it is possible that such companies would, pursuant to their licensing agreements, have the right to bid for any new plant employing the technology. The employer would hardly seek to add contractors with no previous experience of his technology to his bid list unless he had specific reason to do so, the most likely being, of course, the need to achieve an adequate number of bidders. There might also be reasons external to the project in question. A new contractor would, in any case, find it hard to compete effectively with those who had previous experience of engineering the process.

Where the process technology had previously been employed on a similar scale, the possibility would arise of a lump sum bid for design and procurement services, for complete turnkey, or for a scope intermediate between these. The employer's main focus of interest would then be the bid—he would, presumably, already have a good knowledge of the capabilities of those contractors with experience although he might need to update his knowledge of their current positions. He would probably have no need for plant visits: the plants that operate his technology would either be his own or be well known to him through his licensing arrangements.

In none of the cases instanced above is the employer likely to issue a fully-developed Pre-Qualification Enquiry as described below. A less formal approach to obtain the information required would usually be appropriate.

9.2.2 Pre-selected Third-Party Licensed Technology

Where the employer pre-selects technology from a third-party licensor, he may have the choice either of taking a direct process licence and seeking a contractor to engineer the plant, or of taking the licence indirectly through the contractor. The latter method has contractual advantages, but whichever way it is done, the employer may not have a free choice of bidders for the engineering design contract because many licensors restrict the number of contractors allowed to engineer plants based on their technology. In any event, the employer will look first (and probably last) among contractors with previous experience of the technology. It is possible that this will produce a sufficiently abbreviated short list and no pruning will be necessary. If there are many contractors with relevant experience, the employer will probably wish to explore their capabilities by visiting them and the plants that they have engineered. In neither case is the experienced employer likely to issue a formal Pre-Qualification Enquiry. The inexperienced employer may well do so.

The balance of interest for the employer between the contractor's capabilities and the bid he puts forward will, as previously mentioned, depend to a large extent on the nature of the contract proposed. Reimbursable contracts will focus interest on the contractor rather than his bid; lump sum contracts will shift the emphasis to the bid, increasingly so as the scope covered by the lump sum increases.

9.2.3 Process Technology Provided by the Contractor

This is much the most complicated and difficult selection process for the employer because, unlike the previous types of project considered, he has not previously selected the process technology. He is thus simultaneously deciding upon the technology to be used, the bidder's experience in its application, the capability of the bidder's organisation and the quality of his bid—the last, perhaps, a difficult comparison between dissimilar offers. The decisions to be made are much more far-reaching than merely the choice of contractor and this would be evidenced by the involvement of senior members of the employer's organisation. Whereas, if the choice of contractor were the only issue, the employer's project manager might have the authority to decide, this would not usually be the case where a decision on the process to be employed had also to be made. This would be a business decision to be taken at very senior level. The project manager would probably do no more than manage the evaluation process and make recommendations.

The number of potential bidders to be considered may be quite large. There may be a range of process technology possibilities making it desirable to spread the net of the initial enquiry fairly widely. In this case, the issue of a formal Pre-Qualification Enquiry would be indicated. This would have to be followed by numerous discussions and plant visits to reduce the potential bidders to a short list. The evaluation of the subsequent tenders from the short-listed bidders is also likely to be a time-consuming task, since the proposals may not be easy to compare.

Clearly, where the contractor provides the process technology, the bids are the most important part of the total evaluation. Where a number of proprietary processes are linked together, as in an aromatics plant, for example, the way in which they are integrated may be just as important as the processes themselves. The difference in value to the employer between different process proposals may be so large as to outweigh all other considerations.

9.3 PRELIMINARY ENQUIRY

It has already been remarked that assessment of bidders is a two-stage process. The employer has first to select a short list of those who will be invited to bid, and then to carry out a comparative assessment of those selected. Production of the short list may require a preliminary evaluation of potential bidders, the level of detail varying from project to project. A major process operating company with many years' continuing experience of the process contracting market will often possess most of the information needed for this purpose. The potential bidders will also be well informed about the employer. In such a case, the preliminary enquiry may be quite brief and informal, aimed merely at updating the employer's knowledge of the contractor's current circumstances and very recent experience. The employer may simply ask to visit the contractor's offices to discuss a possible project, possibly preceded by an agenda for discussion. An employer of less experience, for example a joint venture company newly formed to exploit a particular situation, may issue a formal document—usually referred to as a Pre-Qualification Enquiry—and select bidders for the short list on the basis of the responses received and subsequent discussions. Such a formal approach is especially likely when the employer has devolved the task of project management to another party—a managing contractor or project consultant. The employment of a managing contractor, usually a firm of process engineering contractors, inevitably leads to more formality in the way things are done. The managing contractor may know quite well beforehand who are the most suitable contractors for a project, but he might have difficulty in recommending a choice to his employer without documentary evidence of a fair selection process. In addition to this, the managing contractor will usually be paid on a reimbursable basis, so it is hardly in his interests to strive to minimise his work.

The Pre-Qualification Enquiry establishes the interest of potential bidders in the contract and their suitability for the work. The title of the document is something of a misnomer. Use of the term 'qualification' implies that there is an objective standard which if achieved, will allow a contractor on to the bid list—if twelve contractors reach the standard, all will be allowed to bid. This, of course, is not so as the intention is to select only the required number of bidders. The Pre-Qualification Enquiry must give potential bidders sufficient information about the project for them to be able to decide whether or not they are interested in bidding for the contract. It asks interested companies to submit a proposal containing specified information to enable the employer to assess the contractor's suitability for the bid list. The responses may also confirm or invalidate the employer's strategy for the project. Typical contents of a formal Pre-Qualification Enquiry are given in Appendix 9.1 at the end of this chapter.

9.4 PRELIMINARY ASSESSMENT OF THE BIDDERS

9.4.1 Size of Short List

The employer's primary aim in considering the responses to his preliminary enquiry is to develop a short list of bidders. The ideal number of bidders is three. With only two bidders, the employer is in a weak position—the withdrawal of either would eliminate competition and thus he could hardly disqualify one of them for being late with his bid, for instance. If more than three bidders becomes the rule, then contractors incur unnecessary costs which in the long run can only be recouped from employers. The case for strictly limiting the number of bidders is, of course, not so strong where the bids are for a reimbursable contract or include a lump sum only for design and procurement services. In these cases, where the work involved in bidding is not great, it would not be unreasonable to have four or even five bids if there seemed good reason to do so.

Another reason for limiting the number of bidders is the workload for the employer that results. Selection of the contractor is usually on the critical path of the project and requires the employer (as, indeed, the bidding process requires the contractor) to work at full speed for a considerable period. Each bid solicited must be properly evaluated, as must the capabilities of each bidder. Bids must never be allowed from companies which the employer knows beforehand have no chance of success, except in circumstances where a contractor asks to be allowed to bid purely to bring his capabilities to the employer's attention and in the full knowledge that he has no chance, nor must bids be sought which are not to be properly considered.

At the preliminary evaluation step, probably the most important single factor to be considered is the contractor's experience of engineering similar plants. If there are enough contractors with fully relevant experience, and if plant visits to check the contractors' performances are possible and yield positive results, then to cast the net more widely than this group would require some special justification. If there were no more contractors with fully relevant experience than were required for the bid list, then it might be necessary only to confirm their current capability and capacity. Where there are more than this, means must be found to choose the most suitable.

9.4.2 Timing of Assessment Work

It is a matter for consideration with each individual project how much of the assessment of bidders is done while they are still potential participants and how much after the short list of bidders has been decided. Obviously, the employer wants to spend no more time than is necessary on identifying those who are unsuitable, but time spent in the early stages on those who subsequently qualify for the bid list is not wasted, since this time will in any event have to be spent at some stage. From the beginning, therefore, investigations will be shaped by early views about the relative merits of potential bidders, so that effort may be conserved by concentrating on the more likely prospects. This narrowing of the investigations must not be carried too far, however, for a number of reasons. First, it is essential that each potential bidder is fairly assessed. Second, early conclusions are sometimes wrong and freedom of choice must not be compromised too soon. Third, any focusing of interest should not be apparent to those being assessed.

The employer will try to complete most of the work of assessing bidders, both preliminary and detailed, before bids are received. The way will then be clear for him to concentrate on evaluating the bids, an activity almost certain to be on the critical path and very tightly programmed. Of course, some elements of bidder assessment must wait until bids are received, and some aspects may have to be revisited.

9.4.3 Plant Visits

Were the contractor also to be required to supply the process technology, then investigation of this would probably be the most important task in the preliminary assessment and would have to be pursued until the employer felt himself in a position to make an informed choice. Where there was a wide choice of technology, this could be a major task. An aromatics plant would present a reasonable worst case: a plant that has a number of different process steps, several possible alternative processes, scope for variation in how they are integrated, and a number of contractors with the required experience. In such a case, it might be necessary to visit as many as thirty plants if a reasonably comprehensive assessment were to be done. The assistance of the contractors would be valuable, even essential, in gaining access to some of the plants that the employer would wish to visit. Contractors are always keen to accompany such visits and can perform valuable introductory services. Their presence would, however, be likely to inhibit the exchange of views between the plant owner and the employer and would be best avoided. In any case, it would not necessarily be in the contractor's interest for him to be present because an incomplete assessment may be to his detriment. Of course, the contractors would have information to offer on the plants visited, but this could best be obtained separately.

It is highly desirable that these plant visits do not require the signing of confidentiality agreements. This is simply because, with such a large number of visits, it would be difficult to be certain of the proper observance, over the following ten or more years, of the commitments that would be entered into. The information sought should be pitched at a level that did not require such agreements. The employer's team to make the plant visits—there are obvious advantages in retaining the same personnel throughout—is best composed of the project manager or a senior project engineer, process engineer and plant manager. Preparation is clearly called for, bearing in mind that the receiving company is acting out of goodwill and may not react well to an intensive grilling. A typical list of topics is as follows, though these will clearly vary substantially depending on the nature of the plant to be investigated:

(1) Plant data—size, type, processes, date of commissioning, etc.
(2) Project data—contractors considered, processes vetted, design and construction times, participation by owner in the design and the provision of standards, scope of contract.
(3) General performance of the contractor—general attitude, technical and engineering strengths, post-completion service,
(4) Specific performance of contractor—achievement of programme, capital cost out-turn, variations, guarantees.
(5) Design features—materials of construction, crucial items of equipment, major machinery, etc.
(6) Plant performance—achievement opposite guarantees, capacity, specifications, efficiencies, utilities consumption, ease of start-up, operability, fouling, safety, on-line time achieved.
(7) Plant maintenance—special problems, major shut-down times and required frequency.
(8) Assessment of major design features—critical operating parameters, changes made since start up or contemplated, particular weaknesses, features that would not be repeated in a subsequent plant.
(9) Specific topics relevant to the particular processes used.
(10) From inspection of the plant, the employer would hope to gain a general impression of the standard of layout, design and construction. He would also try to identify trouble spots in operation and maintenance.

Not all plant owners will be willing or even able to provide all the information requested. Much will depend on the relationship between the plant owner and employer company. If plant owner and employer are direct competitors, a visit is in any case unlikely to be possible. If good relations exist between the companies, there may be no need to involve the contractor in setting up a visit, and a fairly open dialogue should be possible. The amount of information gained will depend very much on the skill of the employer's representatives in quickly developing a rapport with the plant owner's personnel: an indirect approach may sometimes prove more fruitful. This series of visits is very likely to be the only chance for the employer to see the plants in question and so he must make the most of the opportunity.

9.4.4 Other Features of the Preliminary Assessment

The employer will have a view on the important characteristics required of a bidder to be selected for the short list, and in his preliminary enquiry will have asked for information on all these aspects of the contractor's capabilities. This would be followed up in discussion. There might be other matters, such as the financial stability of the contractor, that would certainly require discussion if questions were to arise. However, the employer would try to avoid dealing with a contractor of questionable financial strength. Minor doubts might be dealt with by requiring bid or performance bonds. Among other matters for discussion, the calibre of contractor's personnel available for the project would be important as would the standard of his general organisation. The contractor's attitude to certain key aspects of the contract might also come into the reckoning at this stage. A most important factor would be the future workload of the contractor and his keenness to do the job. The amount of work required at this preliminary stage would depend on the nature of the project and the availability of apparently suitable candidates. The employer would be working from the same agenda as described below for the detailed evaluation but, in most cases, pursuing matters only so far as required to decide on the short list.

9.5 DETAILED EVALUATION OF SHORT-LISTED BIDDERS

As described above, the assessment of the contractors' experience, capability and general organisation will have begun during the preliminary evaluation stage, when at least a first assessment must have been carried out in order to determine the short list of bidders. The assessment process will be continued while tenders are being prepared, and will be completed after receipt of the bids. The exact timing will vary with circumstances, but the employer will certainly wish to have done as much of the work as possible before the bids are received, since there will seldom be time to do it all afterwards. If the bids are for design and procurement services only, the evaluation of the contractors' operations becomes perhaps the most important part of the total assessment— certainly this would be the case for a reimbursable contract. For a lump sum turnkey contract on the other hand, the bid itself would be the most important feature in the selection of the contractor.

It is likely that the preliminary evaluation of the contractors before the short list of bidders is established will be carried out mainly by the employer's project management and engineering staff and will involve his functional engineers only in special cases. Detailed examination, if this is required, of the bidders' functional strengths by the employer's functional engineers will usually be carried out only for those bidders selected for the short list. Some of the work that needs to be done, for example, assessment of the proposed project organisation and of the calibre of key project staff put forward by a bidder, will have to await the receipt of bids.

There will be some parts of the assessment work which will be particular to an individual project. Some aspects of the contractor's capability will be of more importance on one project than on another. To take an obvious example, a plant that involved solids handling would require the contractor's strengths in this direction to be assessed. The use of checklists to guide the assessment has much to commend it. While having no pretensions to being exhaustive—there will be many matters on particular projects that are not covered here—the following is an account of the topics that typically will need to be examined.

9.5.1 Experience

Given that the bidder in question is a well-established and reputable process plant contractor, it remains to determine his experience in the general field of the enquiry and with the particular processes in question. Clearly, this is important even where the technology belongs to the employer. Where the contractor is responsible for the process technology, such experience is absolutely essential. An employer would use a contractor who had not previously applied the technology he was to provide only if there were no viable alternative. The employer might wish to assess the innovative contribution that the contractor would be likely to make and, for a major project, would probably look for a judicious blend of forward thinking and conservatism.

The employer would expect the contractor's experience to be demonstrated, where appropriate, by visits to similar plants that he had previously engineered. Of course, if the contractor were to be responsible for supplying the process technology, this aspect would be fully covered in the plant visits made in the course of assessing the technology.

It is important to assess, not only the contractor's experience with the particular process technology, but also his familiarity with other important aspects of the project. This may include, for example, familiarity with the design of ancillary aspects of the plant, experience in the country where the plant is to be built, and his recent construction activity. There is a learning curve in projects as in other activities and, other things being equal, the contractor with relevant experience will perform better than one without. The strengths of the typical contractor do not lie in the effectiveness with which he is able to tackle new tasks, but in the efficiency with which he executes those of which he already has experience. Many projects bear witness to the fact that it is usually the novel aspects that cause problems.

9.5.2 Contractor's Staff and Future Workload

The employer will wish to know the future workload of the contractor and how this compares with his resources. Obviously, the contractor must be able to show that he has the capacity to execute the contract without substantial recruitment, especially for key positions. Extensive use of temporary staff who are inexperienced in the contractor's methods of working is clearly to be avoided. The contractor's circumstances at the time of the enquiry—whether he has spare capacity, how well the project fits into his own business plans—will affect his attitude to the project. The degree of interest and enthusiasm he shows is a key feature. Experience teaches that keenness to win the contract is reflected not only in the quality of the bid but also in the standard of the contractor's subsequent performance. If he is keen to win the contract, the contractor will offer his best men for the job and hence is likely to produce his best work. Two of the most important things which a process plant contractor offers are organised methods of working and experienced staff, and of these the latter is the more important. The same contractor engaged at different times can perform very differently depending on the quality of staff provided for the project. If the contractor is already very busy before taking on the contract in question, the chances are that the staff put forward will not be his best, since those will already be engaged on other projects. The project will suffer accordingly.

The contractor's tender will name the key staff that he intends to employ on the project. The employer will have the opportunity to assess them, to comment upon them and if necessary to request changes. Of course, it is difficult to assess the capability of staff on such slender evidence as the employer will have and his conclusions may well be wrong. Nevertheless, the employer must not hesitate to object to staff whom he considers unsuitable. An incorrect assessment of an individual will not blight a career since the contractor will rightly consider that his own view of his staff is better founded.

The contractor's project manager is, of course, the most important single member of the contractor's team. He cannot single-handedly make up for all deficiencies in the rest of the team, but the project will not be successful if he is not fully capable of the work. The employer should decide who are the other key team members on the project—some functions may be especially important, for instance—and pay special attention to them. The contract should require the contractor not to move nominated key staff off the work without the permission of the employer. On a large project, a contractor may appoint a director to take a personal interest in the project and to be the first port of call for the employer in the event of difficulty. This at least shows some commitment to the project.

9.5.3 Organisation and Systems

Most contractors and employers are organised in much the same way, with project management and functional engineering in different divisions or groups. Some contractors separate engineering from draughting, which may improve efficiency in the more routine activities at the expense of more difficult communication, reduced flexibility and lower tolerance of change. Most contractors have a fully functionalised engineering organisation except for the purchase of complete engineering packages, which are often treated in a rather *ad hoc* manner by the project groups. The employer will probably prefer the contractor to use a task force organisation for his project which relocates all important team members together. This demonstrates the commitment of the contractor to the project, but is only feasible for the occasional major project and then only if the contractor has the necessary accommodation.

It is important for the success of the project that the contractor's organisation is simple and straightforward. Under pressure of circumstances, contractors can propose complicated ways of organising the design which often bring more problems than solutions. For example, the cost of design can sometimes be reduced by sub-contracting detailed engineering to an associate company in a Third World country. This will bring problems of communication. It may succeed if the project is well defined, but there is little doubt that it makes it less tolerant of change. The saving in cost may turn out to be illusory if much expatriate effort has to be employed to co-ordinate and supervise.

The employer needs to be clear who is to perform the work. Some contractors sub-contract more than others. Some have been known to sub-contract the drawing of piping isometrics—though this is unlikely in an age of computer-drawn isometrics. Some use a rating house for the thermal design of heat exchangers, whereas others perform both the thermal and mechanical design of this equipment in-house. Some contractors have their own freight forwarding organisations where most will use an outside agency. Piping procurement may be sub-contracted to a stockist. The employer needs to understand these differences, not only for their effect on performance and liability, but also because they can affect the bid price. They can transfer cost from a main contractor's lump sum services price into a reimbursable sub-contract. The bid prices will need to be adjusted for any such differences in scope, and consideration given to how the method proposed will affect the quality of performance.

9.5.4 Process Design Capability

Major process plant contractors vary considerably in their process design capability. Some contractors are long-established licensees for some processes and have built up considerable knowledge and experience in their application. A few have their own research facilities and have developed their own processes in particular fields. There are others who can offer merely a general chemical engineering capability. No contractor matches a major process plant operating company in the general ability to innovate, to develop a process from scratch and to perform the conceptual stages of design. This is entirely to be expected, for the major operating companies have large research and development departments far beyond the capacity of any contractor. Where contractors can excel is in those more detailed aspects of process design which follow flowsheet definition.

The employer's requirements also vary substantially from project to project. If the plant to be built is based on process technology provided by the contractor, the latter's process design capability will clearly be of first importance. If the technology is to be provided by a third party licensor, the employer with no previous experience of the process would still look for a significant process design capability on the part of the contractor. Where the technology is the employer's, the requirement may be very limited. Of course, other things being equal, the greater the process design expertise of the contractor, the better.

Where the contractor's process design skill is all-important, that is to say, where the contractor is providing the process technology, the assessment of the contractor's capability is subsumed into the assessment of his process design for the plant—it becomes more a part of the bid evaluation than of the bidder assessment. Whatever the nature of the project, the employer will wish his process design specialists to interview and assess their counterparts on the contractor's staff.

9.5.5 Functional Capability and Specifications

Once the short-listed bidders are known, the employer's functional engineers can carry out an evaluation of their opposite numbers in the contractor's organisation. It is unlikely that the employer would wish to undertake this work until the bidders were chosen, because of the amount of time and effort required. The evaluation will cover all the engineering specialisms relevant to the project, with special emphasis on any that were considered more than usually important.

General design methods, use of models, computer-aided design, specifications used, the interfaces with procurement, use of design sub-contractors would be among the topics discussed. For bulk materials it would be important to understand the contractor's methods of material control—take-offs, initial orders, subsequent orders and so on. Examples of the contractor's typical documentation would be examined—engineering line diagrams, electrical one-line diagrams, isometrics, layouts, civil and structural drawings, bills of material, among others. The way in which vendor packages were handled would also be considered.

No employer's functional engineer can be sure that the contractor eventually chosen will be the one which he would prefer, since his assessment is only one part of the whole. It is necessary for him, therefore, not only to rank the contractors in order of merit, but to consider how he would go about doing the job in conjunction with any of the bidders. He will need to define ways in which identified weaknesses in any of them could be bolstered if necessary. In common with all the other employer's personnel engaged in evaluating the bidders, the functional specialists would examine the contractor's experience in the relevant fields, the experience and calibre of the staff proposed for the project, the way in which the contractor proposes to organise his work and the resources he has available.

9.5.6 Planning, Estimating and Cost Monitoring

These are important services to the contractor's project management which merit careful consideration. The employer will wish to know what planning techniques are used, in what level of detail and how frequently the plans are updated. Even more important, but more difficult to ascertain, is how much influence the planning will have on the execution of the project. The way in which the planning service is organised—who is responsible for it and how well it is integrated into the project team—is of relevance here. Methods of evaluating and monitoring progress in design and construction will also be of interest to the employer.

Even if the contractor is not providing the employer with a capital cost estimate for sanction purposes, he will no doubt be obligated to produce control estimates at certain pre-determined stages of the project. The employer will therefore wish to make some assessment of the contractor's experience and skill in this activity, the methods used and the form in which the estimates are produced.

Cost monitoring—the methods used and the frequency of reporting—must be investigated. The employer may wish to define the form and content of the monthly cost report.

9.5.7 Procurement

The interface between design and procurement and the division of responsibility between them are crucial features of the contractor's organisation that the employer will seek to understand. With the sharp distinction between the functions that many contractors maintain, communication can suffer, an important matter when much procurement is a complex blend of the technical and commercial.

The organisation of the procurement process—of the paperwork and activities in the contractor's offices before orders are placed, the assessment of bids and of progressing, expediting and inspection thereafter—should be understood by the employer. Sample documentation should be seen and discussed. Clearly, the employer's interests will vary depending on the nature of the contract—whether procurement by the contractor is to be reimbursable or lump sum and if the former, whether as principal or agent. If the contractor is purchasing on the employer's behalf. the latter will wish to understand the contractor's commercial approach and eventually to agree the conditions of purchase to be used.

The contractor's purchasing experience, of the type of equipment concerned and perhaps in the country in which the plant is to be built, will of course need to be questioned. The contractor will no doubt maintain vendor lists for the relevant material and equipment and the employer will need to discuss these during the assessment process and later, perhaps, to agree them.

9.5.8 Construction

The interface between design and construction will interest the employer irrespective of whether he or the contractor is to construct the plant. The way in which design information is produced for the site, the organisation of construction and how the team fits into the project management organisation, the lines of authority and responsibility, are all matters which the employer will wish to understand. A typical organisation chart for a project of similar size and scope should be requested.

The contractor's experience in the country in which the plant is to be built, and on similar projects should be discussed. The contractor's labour relations expertise, recent track record on industrial relations, experience with open shop or union operations, experience with national agreements and ability to obtain specific project agreements may be relevant in part or in whole. The contractor's proposed labour policy—sub-contracting or direct hire will be of concern.

There may be matters of special technical interest that need to be addressed at this stage. There may, for example, be some especially difficult heavy lifts, or the transport of out-of-gauge equipment may be a necessary feature. The contractor's expertise in such matters should be explored. The contractor's safety procedures and safety record will certainly be of keen interest. Inspection and quality control procedures are further matters to discuss.

9.5.9 Commissioning

If the contractor is to commission the plant, having been responsible for the process engineering of it, then the employer will wish to investigate the contractor's relevant experience, the staff he can put forward and his general methods of doing the job. The interface between construction and commissioning is important, as are the criteria for handover from one to the other, the procedures for safe working and the issue and use of clearance certificates.

9.5.10 Contractual Matters

The employer will need to discuss the contractual scheme that is envisaged and to be assured that this is likely to be generally acceptable to the contractor. If the contractor is to play a part in the financing of the project, he will be asked to recount his relevant experience so that the employer can assess his competence and credibility in this area.

9.5.11 Flexibility and Responsiveness

In all of these discussions, the employer will be trying to assess the flexibility and responsiveness of the contractor. If the contractor is keen to do the job, he will attempt to respond to the client's wishes and to execute the project in a way that the client can wholeheartedly approve. On the other hand, it would be a negative point if the contractor were willing to bend too easily and agree to organisational or locational changes that were likely to impair project execution. On major projects of the kind under discussion, the contractor is expected to have a voice worth listening to and not to allow himself to be overridden too easily by an importunate client. Sensible clients, of course, do not ask the contractor to do things in a way which depart too radically from his standard practice. Any change to established methods should be made only if the benefits are clear-cut.

Whatever the experience and prior knowledge of the employer, he will be searching for the contractor who will engineer the most economically effective plant. The experienced employer will be looking for something more—he will be concerned to assess how effectively he can make his own input to the project. If the plant is to employ the employer's own technology, then clearly the employer will be deeply involved in project execution. Even where the process is to be provided by others and is available to anyone with the money to buy it, the major, experienced company will still wish to inject its own expertise so as to improve, if not the process, then at the very least the reliability, operability and perhaps safety of the projected plant. Not to do so would be to concede that the years of accumulated skill and experience of the employer give him no advantage as regards new capital investment compared to the latest entrant to the business.

9.6 CONCLUSION

Having carried out all the evaluations described, arriving at a conclusion on the preferred bidder may be difficult because quite different aspects have to be balanced—to weigh one bidder's superior project management against the better specialist design capability of another, and so on. Various marking schemes are possible. Marks can be given to each aspect and the results accumulated. This process can be repeated with appropriate weighting factors. Keen golfers who prefer the lowest score to win can rank each bidder in order of preference in each topic and sum the figures. Another approach would be to identify aspects considered unsatisfactory—which might be more significant than mere ranking order. Marking schemes of such complexity can be devised that the result gains a spurious credibility from the sheer elaboration of the calculation. In the end, the result can be no better—it may be worse—than the data collected. Much if not most of the data consists of subjective judgements. The result will carry most conviction if the conclusions from several different ways of analysing the data are the same.

APPENDIX 9.1   PRE-QUALIFICATION ENQUIRY

The contents of a formal Pre-Qualification Enquiry are typically as follows (in many cases, a selection of these topics or a less formal document will be appropriate):

1.   Project Background

It may be desirable for the enquiry to provide background information on the project. If, for example, the project is part of a much larger national effort to establish a petrochemical industry in a newly industrialised country, it would be appropriate to describe briefly the wider situation. The place of the project in the total development and possible interactions with other projects, not least the likely effects on construction labour costs and availability, should sensibly be drawn to the attention of bidders.

2.   Employer

If the employer were not a well-known company it would be necessary to provide information on the company and its major shareholders. The potential bidder needs to have some confidence that the sponsoring company has the financial muscle to proceed with the project.

3.   The Project

A brief description of the proposed project is obviously necessary, and would typically include:

(a) The location of the plant and a description of the site.
(b) The feedstocks to be used and the products to be made.

(c) A brief description of the proposed plant and the processes that will, or might, be used.

(d) The off-plots and utilities that will be required.

(e) Any other site works that the project encompasses that are not part of this contract.

(f) Any technical aspects that it is important to mention at an early stage.

4. Contractual Matters

Information on contractual matters will include some or all of the following:

(a) The scope of work covered by the contract.

(b) The contractual scheme—whether there are other parts of the project to be let as separate contracts to other parties and, if so, how these relate to the contract in question.

(c) A brief outline of the contract conditions proposed—for example, lump sum or reimbursable, currency, taxation, process and mechanical guarantees, requirement for joint and several liability in the case of consortium bids, parent company guarantees and so on.

(d) Whether a bid bond will be required and if so, its terms.

(e) How the project is to be financed and the contractor's part in this, if any.

(f) If a confidentiality agreement will be required before the main enquiry can be issued to a bidder, a draft should be included.

5. Programme

An outline programme for the project.

6. Procedure

Instructions regarding the submission of the contractor's proposal.

7. Pre-Qualification Proposal

This will specify the required content of the contractor's proposal, typically:

(a) Corporate and financial information about the proposed contracting party. If this is to be a consortium, information about each member.

(b) Commitments
Confirmation that no prior commitment will impede the performance of the contract.

(c) Process Technology
The process technology to be used, perhaps with alternatives for some of the steps. The licensing fees, if any, that will be incurred.

(d) Preliminary Execution Strategy

Preliminary proposals outlining how the work would be executed—consortium and major sub-contracting arrangements, location of staff, whether the design work is to be split between offices, outline project organisation, construction organisation and strategy, authority of project manager, reporting structure.

(e) Training and Commissioning

Confirmation that training of the local operating staff can be provided if required and an outline of commissioning assistance that could be provided.

(f) Resources

Numbers of staff in the contractor's employ categorised by discipline, current and expected future workload, career summaries of key personnel who might be proposed for the project. Proportions of temporary staff employed, size of the contractor's organisation one year ago, three years ago. Availability of relevant specialist resources, for example, expertise in noise and vibration, environmental matters, materials, control engineering, safety, equipment inspection.

(g) Experience

Relevant experience of the contractor—with the same processes, with similar projects in the country concerned, retention of staff with the relevant experience.

(h) References

Names of previous clients who may be approached as referees and, if appropriate, for plant visits.

Chapter 10

Evaluating the Bids

10.1 ENQUIRY

The Enquiry, or Invitation to Bid, for a project sets out the technical and commercial basis proposed by the employer for the contract, a basis which may be subject to modification following receipt of the contractors' tenders and subsequent negotiations. The structure of an Enquiry and the terminology used for its various parts are by no means standardised but the following is a description of what, typically, has to be included.

10.1.1 Commercial Basis

This might more accurately be termed the non-technical part of the Enquiry. It deals with the management and co-ordination aspects of the contract as well as the commercial ones. Its contents are as follows:

Bid and Evaluation Procedure

This specifies some of the required contents of the contractor's tender and how the employer wishes the tender to be presented. It may, for example, call for tenders to comprise separate technical and commercial sections. It describes the process of liaison between the employer and the bidders during bid preparation and evaluation. The Bid and Evaluation Procedure will not form part of the contract and will be a dead letter once the contract is awarded. This will be so stated.

The procedure will not set limits to what should be in the tender, but will request the inclusion of items which the employer especially wishes to see. Most of these would probably, in any case, be included by the contractor without prompting. They might include, for example, an outline programme for the work, a more detailed programme for the first three months, particulars of key personnel proposed for the project, comments on the draft Conditions of Contract, rates for variations and details of any sub-contracting proposed.

Scope of work

This sets out briefly the extent of the work which the tender is to cover—the services the contractor is to provide, the materials and equipment he has to supply, what construction he must do and so on. It will probably help to clarify the contractor's scope if the extent of the work to be performed by the employer and other participants in the project is also described. A more detailed account of the contractor's responsibilities should emerge from the Co-ordination Procedure.

Co-ordination Procedure

The Co-ordination Procedure is a most important document which will regulate the dealings of employer and contractor throughout the contract. It defines the employer's requirements for project administration, design, procurement, planning, progressing and expediting, construction and commissioning. Progress and cost reporting requirements are also specified in order to establish the means whereby the employer's monitoring of the contractor's performance can be carried out. Some of these aspects, if dealt with at length, may be more conveniently addressed by separate procedures.

A typical list of contents is given in Appendix 10.1 at the end of this chapter. This is not meant to be exhaustive, since much of the Co-ordination Procedure deals with minutiae. Comprehensive detail is not, however, necessary on all topics. Although the document tells the contractor what the employer requires and how those requirements are to be met, it should be remembered that, based on it, the contractor will produce his own more detailed co-ordination procedure, or job specification, which will form the working instructions to his staff. The employer's aim is to provide the information necessary for the contractor to modify his standard procedures to fit the employer's requirements.

Programme

This is the employer's suggested programme for the whole project to which he wishes the contractor to adhere or, if possible, improve upon.

Contractual matters

If the Enquiry covers only a part of the total project, it would be sensible to begin this section by setting the prospective contract in the context of the whole, explaining how the other parts are to be accomplished and what other contracts are expected. The proposed contract scheme should be explained giving the reasons for the employer's approach, especially if there are special constraints due to financing, say, or taxation. Proposals in respect of payments to the contractor, the liabilities he must assume and the guarantees he must offer should be highlighted. Draft Conditions of Contract should be included.

If the contractor is to have an important part to play in the financing of the contract, the detailed information necessary to provide a basis for his financing proposals must be furnished to him. This may be included in the Enquiry or may constitute a separate document. In either case the lead will be taken by the employer's financial specialists.

10.1.2   Technical Basis

The technical content of the Enquiry will reflect the extent of the employer's involvement in and responsibility for the process technology.

Employer Data

The Employer Data expresses the basic technical requirements of the employer and has to be issued to guide both the production of the on-plot process design package and the subsequent engineering of the project by the contractor. How far the employer wishes to regulate the detailed engineering standards and specifications to be used will vary between employers and from one project to another. Some employers may provide a complete list of standards and specifications; others may limit themselves to providing only those with a direct bearing on the particular process technology and be otherwise content with national, or the contractor's own, standards. Some may limit the specifications to mandatory items, others may include preferences. These are the employer's options which will be influenced by his experience and how far he wishes it to be injected into the project.

The danger for the experienced employer is of over-specification. As experience accumulates, so the tendency is for additions to be made to the specifications in order to prevent recurrence of problems encountered. It is clearly desirable that operating experience should inform the design of subsequent plants, which will be the better for it. However, much of the input from operating staff will increase rather than decrease costs, may tend to over-value operator convenience and to be over-protective towards operator error. If not checked, it may increase the capital cost beyond what business competition will allow. It is no satisfaction to know that a plant would have been the best of its kind had it been affordable. Standardisation necessarily involves over-design, since standards must be set to deal with the worst case among the range they cover. Not all circumstances to which they will come to be applied may be in the contemplation of those originating them. Thus, they may inappropriately transfer requirements from one field to another: a company used to dealing with flammable hydrocarbons will have standards to prevent fire and explosion which will be unnecessary in many other chemical plants. Standards developed for small and medium-sized plants may not be suitable for very large ones: double isolation may be entirely feasible for a four inch diameter pipe line, but not for a forty-two inch one. A design engineer may have little incentive to struggle to reduce what is to be provided, especially where safety is a factor, seeing merely the prospect of extra work and increased personal risk. Standards and specifications are areas where the employer's project manager can with advantage take a direct interest.

If the contractor is responsible for the Process Package then the Enquiry will contain only the Employer Data and the definition of off-plots requirements. A typical list of Employer Data contents is outlined in Appendix 10.2 at the end of this chapter.

Process Package

The second set of data is the Process Package itself. If the employer is responsible for it then he will need to include it in the Enquiry; otherwise it will be for the contractor to produce. In either case, a third party process licensor may be contracted to produce it under a separate agreement with the employer or the contractor. As far as the Enquiry is concerned, such a licensor would be tantamount to a sub-contractor of the employer or contractor and responsibilities would not be affected.

A preliminary version of the Process Package will serve as a bid basis if the Enquiry is for no more than design and procurement services. In such a case, development of the finished Process Package may be done by the employer (or his licensor) in parallel with the bidding process or may be made part of the contractor's responsibilities.

A typical list of the contents of a Process Package is given in Appendix 10.3

Off-plot definition

The terms 'on-plot' and 'off-plot', sometimes called 'inside battery limits' (IBL) and 'outside battery limits' (OBL), need to be clearly defined. Confusion can arise because there are two different distinguishing factors operating. The first is the process technology. By this criterion, the contents of the Process Package define what is on-plot: all else is off-plot. The Process Package defines, in full process engineering detail, the process plant itself and is largely independent of plant location. The off-plots are then those separately defined ancillary services and facilities which are required to fit the plant to its location and satisfy the employer's particular needs. The off-plots will usually be defined only by their performance requirements, leaving the engineering design contractor, his sub-contractors and suppliers to take responsibility for whatever process design is necessary as well as for the engineering. Some of the employer's general engineering specifications may apply. The off-plot will typically include items such as feedstock and product storage and handling, electricity and steam generation and supply, water supply and treatment, cooling water, hydrogen and nitrogen supply and effluent treatment. Gate houses, car parks, roads, offices, canteens, workshops, laboratories, stores and provision for emergency services are other typical inclusions.

The second criterion used to distinguish between on-plot and off-plot is the plant layout. By this criterion, location on the plot plan decides whether an item is on-plot or off-plot. The two definitions often do not give exact agreement. Although in principle, the on-plot and off-plot are separated geographically as well as by process responsibility, this is not always so. Some of what is off-plot as far as the Process Package is concerned may be physically located on the on-plot. An example might be a steam boiler. This is a utility specified to the contractor only by a requirement for a given quality and quantity of steam, but for economy of piping runs might be situated on the on-plot, as close as possible to the user of the steam.

For many plants, and especially for those which are to be built overseas, the preferred way of proceeding may be to engage a separate local contractor for the design of the off-plot. This is likely to be cheaper than employing a single major contractor for the whole of the work because, apart from lower design rates, the local contractor will offer greater familiarity with local circumstances and may have previous experience on the plant site in question. Certainly, he will make site visits more conveniently and cheaply. If the local contractor has limited capability he might take responsibility for less than the whole of the off-plots, performing only that work which is low in technical but high in site liaison content. In any event, it would be highly desirable to have as simple a demarcation as possible between the responsibilities of the two contractors who may be thousands of miles apart. The greater the geographical separation the greater the need for clear and simple cut-lines.

It is evident that, where more than one engineering design contractor is employed, there might well be need to define a third category of plant: facilities which are not part of the process package but which are located on the on-plot. Confusion may then be avoided by referring to this off-plot intrusion into the on-plot by a term such as 'additional on-plot'. The additional on-plot is defined to the contractor in the same way as off-plot, that is to say by performance—what it has to do—rather than by description—how this is to be accomplished.

The contractor would be responsible, together with his sub-contractors and suppliers, for the process as well as for engineering. Some of the employer's general engineering specifications may again apply.

Of course, if the contract is to be split between contractors as discussed above, the information on 'off-plot definition' will form the technical basis of a second contract. With more than one contractor participating in the project, it is obviously important to identify each party's responsibilities clearly. A detailed responsibility chart—sometimes called a 'kissing' chart because it consists of lists of detailed activities with the responsibility for each denoted by an 'x' in one of several columns, one for each participant—is highly desirable.

Sometimes the employer may have taken the design beyond what is necessary for the Process Package and may have explored, in a preliminary way, some more detailed aspects of the design that are to be part of the contractor's responsibility. It might seem sensible to include the results of this work in the Enquiry in order to save the contractor repeating work already done. This temptation should be resisted. If the information is thought likely to be of help to the contractor, it should be given to him separately with a disclaimer to the effect that the contractor may use it at his risk and that the information has no contractual significance. Otherwise, the contractor may base his design on the information and, if it later turns out to be incorrect or inappropriate, may seek additional payment for the changes necessary.

The Enquiry is almost certainly the most important single document that the employer produces. It sets out the initial definition of the project. It is remarked elsewhere that good initial project definition is the most important single contribution that can be made to the success of any project. No pains should therefore be spared to develop as accurate, detailed and comprehensive an Enquiry as possible. This is the basis for all that follows and only if the foundations are properly laid in the Enquiry can the rest of the project be successfully accomplished. Many project disasters could perhaps have been predicted merely from an examination of their Enquiry documents.

10.2   FAIR COMPETITION

The employer who sets up a competitive bidding situation incurs responsibilities:

(1) All bidders must be treated equally. If one of them asks for, and is given, more time to prepare his bid, all must have it. Additional information given to one bidder must be given to all. Such additional information will often be in response to questions by a particular bidder, and the questions may indicate the bid strategy that the bidder is pursuing. If this seems likely

to be significant, the additional information should be passed to the remaining bidders in such a way as not to reveal what prompted it.

(2) Bidders' confidential information must be scrupulously guarded and 'cross-fertilisation' avoided at all costs. The possibility of the latter relates mainly to projects where the contractor is supplying the technology. It may become clear to the employer that a plant combining the best features of the various bids would be superior to any single one of them. Such a plant is, however, unattainable. In this matter, what may seem insignificant to the employer may seem vitally important to the bidder. Only by being scrupulously fair can the employer maintain his reputation over the years and retain good relations with his contractors.

(3) The need to restrict the number of bidders has already been discussed. All the bids must be properly considered, even those which seem to have no chance of success. This does not mean, however, that the employer has to spend equal time on each bid, as discussed below.

(4) It is good practice, though not mandatory, for the employer to explain to the losers why they lost. This may help them submit more appropriate bids in the future. It may also help to convince them that they have been treated fairly, and it is most important that they should believe this.

10.3   EVALUATION OF TENDERS

The first task is to make an initial appreciation of the bids. This should be completed within a few days of their receipt and will give the employer the following options:

(1) To confirm whether any of the bids is likely to yield a proposal which will be technically and commercially acceptable. If this looks unlikely, some hard thinking will have to be done and major repercussions on the project may follow.

(2) To see if any of the bids is sufficiently unattractive compared with the others to warrant less detailed scrutiny. Much earlier, during the process of assessing the potential and actual bidders, some preliminary conclusions will have been drawn, the most obvious being the selection of bidders for the short list. Beyond this, however, a provisional order of preference may have emerged even before the bids are received. If a low preference were to be confirmed by an unattractive bid, the employer would wish to spend less time on considering the latter and to channel his energies in more fruitful directions. The assessment of a bid seen as very unlikely to succeed would be slowed down while more attention was concentrated on bids of greater promise. This is desirable, and sometimes absolutely necessary, in order to

make the most efficient use of stretched resources. There are obvious limits to how far this bias can be carried, however. It must not prevent fair treatment of all bidders. It must not become evident to the bidders, and the possibility that the initial view might prove to be mistaken on fuller consideration must always be allowed for.

(3) To establish the direction in which the ensuing work of evaluation should be guided. The employer will confirm or revise his plan for the evaluation work accordingly.

Following this initial appreciation, it will almost certainly be necessary to hold preliminary discussions with the bidders to clarify doubtful matters, to identify omissions and differences in the bids compared with the Enquiry and generally to confirm the employer's understanding of them. Further discussions will be held as the evaluation work proceeds. These will cover all aspects of the bids, both technical and commercial.

If the contractor is providing the process technology, the discussions may be very protracted. The employer may wish to suggest or encourage alternatives and improvements and to obtain the associated re-costings. At this stage in the project, the employer is in his strongest negotiating position to obtain work and concessions from the contractor.

10.3.1 Process Evaluation

Evaluation of the process technology is required at this stage only if it is being provided by the contractor. The work necessary can vary substantially depending on the nature and extent of the plant. An aromatics plant has previously been suggested as a reasonable worst case example. This is a plant for making aromatic hydrocarbons—benzene, toluene, xylenes, ethyl benzene, cyclohexane—from naphtha and gasoline. It is an assembly of about ten separate processes and since both the feedstock and the desired products vary from one plant to another, no two aromatics plants are identical. The contractor will assemble a group of processes from a number of different process licensors. A lump sum turnkey bid will take him six months or longer to prepare and may take the employer up to three months to evaluate and compare.

Commercial experience with unit processes

The bidder's previous experience in engineering the processes that he is offering will for the most part have been covered during the detailed assessment of the bidders. Assessment requires visits to the plants concerned and discussions with their operators. There may be some particular aspect of the bid that has not been covered and this will need to be taken up at this stage.

Technical assessment of unit processes

Technical review of the processes offered will require discussions with the licensors of the processes as well as with each bidder. Subjects of interest will include the general standard of the chemical engineering design, the calculation methods, design margins and fouling factors used. The neatness and extent of integration of the various units will be of prime interest, as will the energy balance and the consumption of utilities. Relief and blowdown systems will be a major concern.

Comparison of product yields

Product yields are obviously very important. It is necessary to examine how they are to be achieved and what confidence there can be in their continuing achievement over time. Matters such as the severity of treatment, the degree of recycle, the size of equipment, design margins and by-product production need to be assessed. The difference between represented (or expected) and guaranteed yields may cast light on the proposals, as may the tightness of the feedstock specifications. If the employer requires to use different feedstocks, or to vary the product slate, the degree of over-design needed to achieve these will be of interest.

Guarantees

The process guarantees offered by the bidders are clearly crucial factors in the evaluation. Usually, the provider of the process technology will give represented, or expected, figures of product yields and raw material efficiencies which are higher than the figures which he is prepared to guarantee subject to liquidated damages clauses. The difference is usually 5 to 10%, but may be larger if the process is less well proven. To some extent, the margin is a measure of the confidence of the licensor in his process.

In a multi-product plant, the employer will wish to obtain guarantees of individual product yields, so that a surplus of one cannot be offset against a shortfall in another. Good guarantees of by-product yields may be more difficult to obtain. Guarantees of utilities consumptions will be affected by detailed design considerations, so may not be offered by the process licensor. It should be noted that a comprehensive guarantee for a multi-product plant may entail a complex series of acceptance tests, which may become almost impracticable to perform.

Catalyst guarantees can be important where the catalyst cost is a significant part of the operating cost. A guarantee of catalyst life should include replacement on premature failure, and liability for replacement should continue until the guaranteed life is attained.

Economic assessment

The employer will wish to make his own estimate of the capital cost of the proposed plant in as much detail as possible to see whether he is getting value for money and whether all the proposed features are worth the price that has to be paid for them. The employer will need to allow for any changes he thinks will be necessary to improve safety, operability or reliability and also for variations, omissions, start-up modifications and contingency.

Processing costs—feedstocks, catalysts and chemicals, utilities—must be compared as must product and by-product values. These should be calculated on both a guaranteed and a represented basis, modified by any changes made during the evaluation, including any contingencies thought necessary to allow for the bidder's over-optimism. Other costs such as maintenance, spares and royalty fees must be taken into account.

In most cases, the proposals will need to be assessed only for a fixed year at full output in order to identify the best bid. However, if there are large differences in net product values offset by similar differences in investment cost or utilities, it may be prudent to investigate the effects of lower occupacities and of possible changes in prices and costs over time.

Engineering assessment

The employer will wish to examine the detailed engineering aspects of the bidders' proposals—the layout of the plant, the quality and reliability of the equipment proposed and whether it will meet the employer's specifications. If there are differences between the specifications and what is proposed in the bid, these will have to be resolved. The employer has to decide whether to accept the proposals and waive or vary his specifications, or to reject any non-conformance. Possible difficulties in construction will be identified and the design and construction programmes assessed.

Operational assessment

The employer must assess the acceptability of the proposed plant from the point of view of flexibility and continuity of operation, the integrity of the control systems and the extent of inter-dependence between units—too tight an integration and the plant may become very vulnerable to upsets. Start-up and shut-down, ease of access and maintenance, tolerance of abnormal conditions, fouling and catalyst life are among the other factors that should be considered.

Safety review

Of prime importance will be the safety standards of the design. The employer will probably wish to conduct a preliminary hazard and operability study on the bidder's proposals. He will be interested in the methods to be used during the design to ensure a safe plant and will also be concerned about construction safety.

10.3.2 Contract Price

If the contract is to be entirely reimbursable for all goods and services, the comparison of price is simple, if not especially accurate. The bidder will provide details of the man-hour rates he proposes to charge for various categories of staff employed. These rates may be fixed for the duration of the contract or may be subject to quoted escalation. Some reimbursable contracts allow lower rates, excluding profit, for the correction of the contractor's errors (not omissions), although there will obviously be difficulty in identifying the corrective work. Procurement services may be charged at hourly rates or may be a percentage of the value of goods purchased—the employer may specify the method to be used in order to achieve uniformity between bids. For each bid, the employer must try to bring all the quoted charges on to a common basis— for example, the way in which holidays are dealt with. He must then estimate the man-hours that will be consumed in each charging category to arrive at a total estimated cost. In the latter calculation, the employer will have to make some judgement of the relative productivities of the bidders.

A common form of contract is one in which the lump sum bid price covers only for design and procurement services, sometimes with the addition of construction services. All equipment, material and construction costs are then reimbursable where not outside the contract scope. In such a case, the lump sum prices must first be corrected for differences in scope of work. The bids may themselves identify some of these differences as additions or omissions to the scope given in the Enquiry. Others may be a consequence of different treatment of expenses, and ancillary costs such as printing documents. Some will arise from the different methods of working of the contractors, as discussed in the previous chapter, and which the employer will hope to have identified in his assessment of the bidders.

Beyond this, for each lump sum bid, the employer will need to estimate the increase in the design and procurement services cost which will result from variations. In this difficult area, the employer will base his view on his past experience, on his estimate of the man-hours each bidder has allowed, and on his perception of the bidders gained during the assessment processes. A bidder may, for example, give the impression that he expects full and final information from the employer on any topic immediately on request, that approvals must be given quickly and that participation by the employer in the design process will be strictly controlled and curtailed.

The employer's ability to respond to such a regime depends on his circumstances. If his expertise is concentrated in a small number of people, then it is obviously easier to provide rapid response than if the relevant knowledge is widely disseminated among many of the employer's staff so that consultation will often be necessary. The latter case is more likely since the employer's repetition rate of major projects for the production of the same product is usually quite low. The employer's engineering design staff engaged full-time on the project may have little direct experience of the plant in question. They may need to rely heavily on operational staff for specialised technical knowledge of the particular plant and for reviews of operability. Distance between the offices of contractor and employer may also be a factor. Possible mismatching in this way of the intended working regimes of contractor and employer must be thought about carefully; it involves more subtle considerations than can be expressed in Enquiry and bid, and has implications on more than price.

The employer must also add his estimate of his own costs to the bids. These will usually differ from one bid to another. Apart from the considerations discussed above which may affect the employer's costs, transport and accommodation for staff visiting the various contractors' offices may differ substantially. It may well be that the adjustments made by the employer to the bids—for exclusions, variations and employer's costs—will change the order of prices from that of the initial lump sum bids. These adjustments are therefore important and must be made as carefully as possible. Construction management services can in principle be dealt with in the same way as design and procurement services, although the details of the various adjustments will be different.

Obviously, the larger the scope of a lump sum bid, the more important price becomes in the evaluation. Where the lump sum covers design and supply of materials and equipment; or design, supply and construction; price may well be the most important single factor in determining contract award. The employer will need to make careful comparisons of the various bid prices, adjusting them to achieve, as far as possible, equal scope and quality of provision. He will need to make allowances for omissions and for any additional costs that it seems likely will be incurred in order to achieve the required standards of safety, operability and reliability. The employer will almost certainly wish to make his own cost estimates of the bidders' proposals: this will help him to come to a view of the variation costs which may later face him. Claims for such costs will depend on the tightness of the contractor's original estimates as well as on their actual justification. Whereas the bidders put forward their estimates of the scope of the contract as defined in the Enquiry, and can hope to increase their prices during the course of the contract by skilful exploitation of inevitable change and development, the employer's project manager is concerned to identify and minimise the final cost. He must therefore look beyond the bid prices he is given and try to predict, for each bid, the final contract cost that would be incurred if it were accepted. It is on these predictions that the comparison of bids should be made.

10.3.3 Organisation of the Work

The way the contractor proposes to organise and carry out his work under the contract is of prime concern to the employer. If all the design work is to be done in-house by the contractor, then interest would focus on the extent of authority of the project manager, the organisation of his team, whether a task force organisation was to be used and so on. The employer should consider whether the numbers of key staff proposed, of project engineers for example, are in his judgement adequate.

Some of the ancillary activities on the project—inspection, or shipping for example, may well be done by others and the employer's project manager needs to be clear about the nature and extent of such sub-contracting. It has already been remarked in the previous chapter that some contractors habitually sub-contract work that others would regard as a normal part of their in-house operation. If parts of the design itself are to be sub-contracted, the employer should understand why this is being done and what advantages are claimed to accrue. A detailed responsibility chart ('kissing chart'), detailing the split between contractor and sub-contractor, should be included in the bid.

If the contractor is to be responsible for construction, the management organisation he proposes, the methods and extent of sub-contracting, systems of material control on site will all be of interest. Each site has its special demands, whether of access, soil conditions, climate, labour availability or relations or many other possibilities. The employer will wish to discuss the bidders' proposals to deal with these areas. It is up to the contractor to explain and justify the way he proposes to perform the contract. The employer should be aware that the bidders may have their own problems with shortages of resources, both of quality and quantity, and may be offering to the prospective employer arrangements whose only justification is to overcome such problems.

The bidders' design methods will have been reviewed during the bidder assessment stage. Some aspects may be especially important. If the materials which the plant is dealing with are especially hazardous, then the methods the bidder will use to ensure a safe design are of prime importance, and further questioning, to supplement what has already been done during earlier stages of the assessment and evaluation may be necessary.

10.3.4 Contractor Personnel

The key staff for the project will be identified in the bid. Some of these may already be known to the employer's staff through previous projects and some will have been seen during pre-bid discussions. Those with whom the employer has had no previous dealings must now be interviewed, formally or informally, and opinions as to their suitability formed. Although an experienced process plant contractor will have developed systems of working which help to ensure that minimum standards of performance are reached, the quality of staff committed to the project is unarguably a most important factor in deciding the winner of any contract. Certainly, no employer should place a contract with a contractor whose nominated staff are considered inadequate for the task. It can be difficult to assess the capabilities of people with only a very short period of contact, but this is necessary. If some of the staff offered are adjudged unsatisfactory, the bidder should be asked to replace them.

10.3.5 Contractual Matters

Contractual matters are discussed in more detail in later chapters. Suffice it to say here that the employer will need to understand whether the bidder accepts the draft Conditions of Contract included in the Enquiry, what objections he has and how important these are. Any differences will have to be negotiated and acceptable positions reached. The guarantees offered, the licensing terms and the limits of liability which the bidder is prepared to accept are matters which will particularly concern the employer. It is absolutely necessary that all significant points have been settled before work starts on the contract, and highly desirable that the contract itself has been finalised and signed before this happens.

If the contractor is to have a major part in arranging the finance for the contract, there will be a need for extensive discussion. Financing terms can be most important and, in the limit, can decide the destination of the contract award.

10.4 EVALUATION RESULTS

The results of the bid evaluations need to be combined with those of the previous bidder assessments to arrive at a decision on the award of contract. How formally this is done depends on the employer's internal ways of working. It may be affected by the extent of the project manager's authority. If he has the power to decide, he may well consider it unnecessary to spend much time and effort documenting a process with which he has been intimately concerned throughout. On the other hand, if a recommendation has to be made for others to decide, it is unlikely that this can be done without a formal document and presentation. A formal process will almost certainly be required if the project is to be jointly owned or if the project manager is other than a permanent, full-time employee of the employer.

The first requirement is a list of the important decision criteria. Both the list and the relative importance of the items in it will vary from project to project depending on matters such as the ownership and state of development of the technology, the experience of the bidders, the location of the plant and the financing of the project. Given the discussion above in this and the previous chapter, it would be supererogation to attempt to list all the possible decision criteria here. Obviously, some of the criteria—price, cost of finance, programme, guaranteed efficiencies—are objective data, or reasonably so. Others, concerned with the quality of what is offered, are much more subjective. It is not possible to reduce the decision process to mere arithmetic by devising some clever marking scheme embracing all the relevant criteria, both objective and subjective. Such schemes have their place in helping to crystallise thoughts, but should be kept firmly in their place as aid rather than arbiter.

There will, of course, be occasions where the choice is clear cut, usually because the costs—capital, operating or finance—lean so heavily in one direction. It is probably true to say that estimated costs often receive more than their due weight because they are given more credibility than they deserve—the possibilities of shortfalls in performance of the contract leading to cost deviations are not sufficiently considered, particularly by those with little experience.

Having made the decision on contract award, it is important to identify the weaknesses which this brings in its train, and to take steps to counter them. Such steps must be concrete actions, not just vague intentions to watch certain aspects or to exercise more care in some activities.

10.5 NEGOTIATION AND AWARD OF CONTRACT

In some circumstances, especially for contracts let by public bodies, the tendering process may be extremely formal. The bid list may be unrestricted, there will be a precise time by which tenders have to be received, there may be a public opening of bids with the lowest bid automatically winning the contract. The need for justice to be seen to be done takes precedence over all else.

As will be evident from previous discussion, such methods are not appropriate for major process plant contracts in the private sector. The enquiry issued by the employer, however detailed, seldom represents the final word and there is often much to be gained by interaction with the bidders both before and after the tenders have been received. An enquiry for a major process plant project will seldom produce an unqualified bid. These are projects of great complexity and for the bidder to produce a definitive response, even after much pre-bid discussion, will be uncommon. Much may remain that can usefully be discussed and refined and which will lead to adjustment and improvement of the bid.

Negotiation for the award of a major process plant contract can thus be regarded as continuous throughout the period of bidder assessment, selection, bidding and bid evaluation. These are complex and subtle matters. The employer is working hard to communicate his requirements for the project, his preferred balance between cost, time and performance, how he wishes to work with the contractor and what he requires of him. The contractor is trying to sell his methods and capabilities, to adjust his offer to match the employer's idiosyncrasies, to respond to what is wanted and generally to offer the most attractive package.

Far from ceasing when bids are received, the negotiation process increases in intensity. No sensible employer would wish to deny himself the opportunity to obtain the best possible tender, no more than any sensible contractor would wish to proceed with less than his best possible proposal. But post-bid negotiation does place responsibility on the employer, and on his project manager personally, to ensure that all is done fairly. The discussions need to be handled very carefully. Avoiding the transference of technical information between bids—cross-fertilisation—has already been mentioned, as has the need to ensure that all bidders receive the same information. Although discussions with each of the bidders must be kept quite separate, it is entirely possible that information will emerge during discussions with one bidder that needs to passed on to the others, without divulging how the need originated. The same is true of ideas for project improvement, but here one must move very carefully. If the new ideas that emerge are those of the employer, then he will obviously be free to communicate them to the other bidders. If they are those of a particular bidder, he will not. So much is obvious and not difficult to manage. Where problems can occur is when the ideas emerge during discussion and ownership is not clear. The employer will not be free, in many cases, to pass on to the other bidders ideas for improvement that are the product of the employer and a particular bidder acting jointly. In the limit, the employer must seek agreement that such information can be passed on. If he wishes to get the maximum contribution from the bidders, the employer must avoid at all costs the suspicion that anything one bidder says to him may be passed on to the others. The general rule that the employer's project manager must follow is to say nothing (confidentiality apart) to any bidder that he would not wish the others to hear.

Apart from being ethically correct, such behaviour makes sound business sense. The employer is in business for the long term and has everything to gain from a reputation for absolute probity. So has the employer's project manager. The latter needs to recognise his personal responsibility for fair dealing on his project. Pressure to behave unfairly, from whatever source, should be resisted to the point of resignation. Of course, such pressure is not very likely from his employer, but sometimes a keen business manager will push as hard as he can, taking the view that ethical standards of behaviour on the project are the concern of the project manager.

The problem may be more severe in a joint venture with a partner from a country where different methods of doing business apply. If UK standards are to be observed, the project manager may find that he needs to take much greater care of sensitive information and to restrict its circulation severely. Little is kept confidential in some countries, and even-handedness between bidders is uncommon, either because of interests not always disclosed or because of corrupting influences.

The post-tender discussions will also explore the possibilities of price reductions. Much will depend on the employer's project manager's view of the prices quoted—whether he believes they are keen or whether there is much contingency included. Discussions with individual bidders will be coloured by the relative prices of the bids. There is no reason why the high bidder should not be told that his price is high, though such information must stop well short of a Dutch auction—the practice of hawking the current lowest price round the bidders as the one to beat. The project manager will deploy such information as he has. As described in a previous chapter, he will have tried to develop his own estimate for the work. He will have attempted to analyse the bids to discover where the major costs lie and where there may be room for reduction. He will question any part of the price that seems high or any proposal that seems to add unnecessarily to the cost. His approach may have to be different depending on the country of origin of the bidders. In the Far East, for example, bidders from the same country faced with no foreign competition may collude on price so that there may be no prospect of price reduction.

In his price negotiations, the employer's project manager must allow for the fact that the plant which is the object of the contract has yet to be designed and constructed. He is not buying an article of fixed and final characteristics, so that all there is to worry about is the price. Without suggesting that the relationship between price and quality is necessarily linear, or even direct, the contractor who begins a contract in the belief that he is undercharging for his work will naturally seek to recover the position, by minimising what he provides and by the aggressive pursuit of extras. It is unlikely to be to the employer's advantage to achieve a cut-throat price that the contractor either cannot or will not live with. The objective of the employer is not to minimise the engineering contractor's price, nor even the total capital cost of the project of which the former is but a part. It is to achieve the optimum balance of capital cost, operating cost and timing. This will not be achieved by the aggressive pursuit of one aspect to the detriment of all others. There is therefore a limit to how far the employer's project manager will wish to push his negotiations. This will be different in each case, will be only hazily defined, but is none the less important. The successful bidder must believe that he has a reasonable chance of fulfilling his obligations without incurring financial disaster.

Despite all that has been written above, it will sometimes be necessary or expedient to place a major contract by negotiating a single, uncontested bid. Few, in the UK at least, would argue with the proposition that in general the employer is best served by the establishment of competitive tendering on equal terms between a small number of experienced and capable bidders. Free competition on a level playing field is an article of faith in most of the Western world, but it was not always so, and is by no means uncritically accepted in all newly industrialised countries. The effects of the latter are not necessarily entirely adverse as far as the employer is concerned. An arguably higher initial price might be balanced by a reduced appetite for variations.

There can be various reasons, some more respectable than others, why a contract has only a single bidder. The project may be a near repeat of one previously completed. The original contractor may then be considered to have such an advantage because of his previous experience that it would be pointless and time-wasting to seek other bids, as well as unfair to other bidders whose prospects of success are remote—unless, of course, they were to bid with full knowledge of the position. The employer can check the price offered against the cost of the previous contract. A contractor may have such a technical advantage over the rest of the field, either as inventor or sole licensee of the preferred technology, as to have, probably temporarily, no real competition. There may be a requirement for speed which precludes competitive tendering, although the employer's project manager would be well advised to examine such a proposition very carefully.

As far as the employer is concerned, a single, negotiated bid is better than a contest in which there is no real competition. Where there is only a single bidder, the employer can follow a quite different route in negotiating the final price. He will be entitled to seek more information than he would in a contested situation, indeed, he will need more to satisfy himself that he has obtained a fair price since he can no longer rely on the competition to tell him this. He could hardly contemplate awarding an uncontested lump sum contract unless he had from previous experience of similar plants an accurate appreciation of how much this one should cost or unless the bid was on an open-book basis. With less information than this he would be pushed towards a reimbursable contract where he had to consider merely the rates that were to be charged. The issue of the contract cost would thus be postponed to another day.

Simultaneously with negotiations on technical content and price of the bids, the employer's project manager will be negotiating the Conditions of Contract. There will probably have been discussions on these with each of the bidders during bid preparation so that comments set out in each of the bids should be a reasonably considered response to the employer's draft included in the Enquiry. Without giving away any clues as to preference, it should be possible for the employer's project manager to develop matters further with the bidder who is seen to have the best chance of success than with the others whose prospects seem less hopeful. It is highly desirable that the Conditions of Contract be finalised at the same time as all the other matters so that the contract can be formally signed and awarded before work starts. So often, the contractual details are incomplete when it is wished to award the contract and work starts on the basis of a letter of intent. This is entirely unnecessary, may be disadvantageous and is the result of sloppy management. There are not a great many man-hours involved in agreeing the Conditions of Contract, assuming a reasonable first draft as a basis. However, once the contract is awarded and the pressure is off, subsequent progress can be remarkably slow. Many contracts have been completed before the Conditions of Contract were finalised, sometimes to the discomfiture of one or both parties. If it is made clear from the outset that work will not start until the contract is signed, minds are concentrated and there is seldom any difficulty in completing all the contract documentation in a timely manner.

APPENDIX 10.1   CO-ORDINATION PROCEDURE

- *Introduction*—title and purpose of project, scope of work of the contractor, employer's resident staff in the contractor's offices.
- *Communications*—language, meetings, correspondence, document register and distribution.
- *Documentation*—details of all the documentation required by the employer, including specifications, data sheets, engineering units to be used, drawing sheet sizes, drawing numbering, calculations, engineering line diagrams. Numbering of equipment, systems, pipelines and instruments. Requirements for the piping model, critical pipework, cut lines and equipment layout. If the employer is to be responsible for construction, the documents he will require to enable him to let construction contracts, such as scopes of work, must be detailed.
- *Engineering reviews*—details of the design reviews required by the employer, the documents necessary, where the reviews are to be held and the required extent of the contractor's participation. The following is a typical list of reviews for the case where the employer has perhaps maximum involvement, providing the process technology and being responsible for construction and the design of off-plots:
  - Major hazards
  - Explosion pressures and control room design
  - Statutory approvals
  - Flow sheets
  - Mechanical data sheets
  - Layout
  - Engineering line diagrams
  - Electrical distribution
  - Area classification
  - Hazard and operability

- Noise
- Fire fighting and protection
- Means of escape
- Paving and drainage
- Pressure relief and blowdown
- Control philosophy
- Materials of construction
- Cable routing and protection
- Piping model
- Emergency power, utilities and services
- Metering and customs requirements
- Lighting
- Construction access and constructability
- Safety showers
- On-plot/off-plot cut lines
- Service stations
- Heavy lifting study

- *Approvals*—details of the documentation that the employer will require to approve.
- *Procurement*—lists of approved vendors of equipment, enquiries, comparisons of tenders and vendor selection, issue of and amendments to orders, shipping. In some circumstances, a separate procurement procedure may be called for. Much will depend on the terms of the contract. If equipment and materials are to be purchased reimbursably by the contractor, more detail will be required, especially if he is acting as the employer's agent in this regard.
- *Inspection and testing*—specifications and codes, interpretation, reports, test certificates, sub-orders.
  - Progress and expediting.
  - Material control and storage on site.
- *Construction*—the information given under this heading will depend on who is to take responsibility for construction. If the design contractor is to perform the work on site, he must be given the necessary information such as lists of approved sub-contractors, site rules and regulations, safety requirements. If the employer, or a separate contractor, is to be responsible for construction, the design contractor must be obligated to provide the employer with the information he will need to place the construction contract or sub-contracts including, for example, scopes and descriptions of works. He must also provide design liaison with construction.
- *Completion and commissioning*—if the contractor is performing only the detailed design, he may have no involvement on site. If he provides the process technology, his presence during commissioning will be required. If he carries out construction then he will have obligations concerning completion and the provision of assistance during pre-commissioning and commissioning.

- *Cost control and monitoring*—the employer's main requirements must be defined. These should not be very different from the contractor's own procedures, but there may be special requirements, such as periodic control estimates that must be detailed.
- *Programmes and planning*—contractor's programme, vendor's programmes, project progress meetings, material control, project control data.
- *Accounting procedure*—may be necessary where materials are reimbursable and foreign currencies add complications.
- *Spares*—the contractor's responsibility for the ordering and progressing of spares. If the contractor is to produce the spare gear book (or its machine-readable equivalent), this will require detailed description if it is to fit into the employer's existing system and if the contractor is to understand fully what is required and the time and effort involved.
- *Payments to vendors*—a separate payments procedure may be desirable if this is at all complicated.
- *Data books*—content and presentation of the final documentation of the design that the contractor is to produce.

Some of the above contents—procurement, planning, cost monitoring and control, accounting—may be the subjects of separate procedures. This may be because they are standardised, or because they are complicated and lengthy and it is convenient to deal with them separately, or because the full details will be available only after contract award and the matters to be dealt with are non-contentious. The Co-ordination Procedure will, of course, be subject to discussion with the bidders and may be modified in the light of comments made. The employer may develop further co-ordination procedures for other parts of the project undertaken by other contractors, and for his internal administration. Perhaps it is not general practice for employers to produce co-ordination procedures for their own internal work, but this is certainly desirable if the project is complicated or in some respects unfamiliar.

APPENDIX 10.2   EMPLOYER DATA

- *Plant capacity*—annual tonnage required from the plant.
- *Product specification*—this will be based on the sales specification for the product.
- *Feedstock specifications*—availabilities and specifications.
  Site location and preliminary layout
- *Climatic Data*—maximum, average and design parameters for barometric pressure, relative humidity, ambient temperature, wind speed, rainfall.

- *Soils data*—it saves time and money for the employer to provide this if, as would be usual, he has prior access to the site. It is necessary to be clear who is responsible for the data and, separately, for its interpretation.
- *Seismological data*
- *Environmental data*—the local environmental regulations and standards for liquid and gaseous effluents, solid waste disposal, noise levels and permissible worker exposure levels where appropriate. Many countries now require a study of the environment and the effects on it of any development. This will need to be, if not completed, at least well advanced by the time the Enquiry is issued. The employer's own standards will have to be specified if they are higher than those required by law.
- *Utilities and services*—availabilities at the battery limits of the plant.
- *Economic data*—costs of utilities and services and payback times must be specified so that the process can be optimised for the circumstances envisaged.
- *Safety*—the employer's overall safety philosophy for his operations must be defined. Local safety regulations and statutory requirements may be specified by the employer or left for the engineering contractor to discover.
- *Engineering specifications*—the employer's engineering requirements for the project covering design, procurement and, where appropriate, construction. There may be special requirements for the technology concerned and these must obviously be included. General specifications and standards may be provided by the employer or national, or the contractor's own, standards used.
- *Isolation of equipment for maintenance*—the employer's requirements to allow equipment to be safely maintained with the plant on-line.

APPENDIX 10.3   PROCESS PACKAGE

- *Design basis*
- *Plant capacity*—flowsheet rates and occupacity.
- *Feedstocks*—battery limits pressures, temperatures and specifications to meet the design case.
- *Catalysts and chemicals*—specification of requirements.
- *Product specifications*
- *Effluents*—conditions of all effluents at battery limits and noise levels at the plant boundaries.
- *Utilities and services*—specification of requirements at battery limits.
- *Process description*—this describes the operating principles of the plant and defines the main process variables. Outline procedures for start up, normal operation, shut-down and emergencies are included to serve as a basis for the operator's specific, detailed plant operation manuals. Block diagrams of the plant with overall material balances are included.

- *Process flowsheets*—these include all major items of process equipment, all important process and utility pipelines, major control loops and key instruments.
- *Material balances*—the mass flow rate at flowsheet output, composition, physical state, operating temperature and pressure, density and molecular weight for all significant process streams.
- *Equipment list*—details of all main plant items, including proprietary and package units.
- *Materials of construction*—for all main plant items and piping systems.
- *Catalyst and chemicals*—initial charges and estimated consumptions.
- *Utilities and services*—expected consumptions.
- *Process data sheets*—process data for each main plant item to provide a basis for engineering design.
- *Safety*—the design philosophy for safety, a description of the major process hazards and the operational and maintenance principles to be followed to ensure continued safety of the plant. Data sheets for all major protective devices, safety trip systems and alarms. Hazard data sheets for all materials used in the process. If the process package is being produced for licensing purposes, it will be necessary to spell out the safety obligations of the parties, as discussed in Chapter 4.
- *Engineering line diagrams*—these will be provided for all major process systems so as to form the basis of fully detailed line diagrams to be prepared by the contractor. They will show all process equipment, numbered process lines, valves and accessories, heat tracing requirements, instrumentation and any specific process requirements such as layout or pipe routing.
- *Process line list*—a table of all process and utility lines giving data on connectivity, diameter, fluid contents, flow rate, operating pressure and temperature.
- *Process instrument data sheets*—process data relating to all process instruments, including control loops and valves, flowmeters, alarm and trip systems, on-line analysers and other key instruments.
- *Engineering specifications*—specifications dealing with any special features of the process.
- *Plant layout*—preliminary plot plan for the process plant.
- *Effluents and emissions*—details of all process effluents at battery limits conditions.
- *Vendors' lists*—details of approved vendors for special equipment.
- *Laboratory and analytical procedures*—details of special analysis requirements and test procedures.

Where the employer owns the technology and produces the Process Package himself, it will probably be convenient for him to combine the Employer Data and the Process Package. This combination of information—the complete process-related technical information—is sometimes termed the Front End Engineering

Package. A competent process plant contractor, with no prior experience of the process, should be able to engineer the plant successfully from the information contained in the Front End Engineering Package. However, the successful engineering of some processes requires the injection of experience-based 'know-how', difficult to convey properly in advance on paper. For such processes there will need to be an appropriate input from the licensor during the design of the plant.

Chapter 11

Contract Documents

11.1 INTRODUCTION

For the project manager, perhaps the most useful definition of the purpose of the contract is as follows:

'To set down in clear and unambiguous form the nature and scope of the relationship between employer and contractor and the obligations of each, together with the consequences of failing to meet those obligations.'

This is more difficult than it may seem, because contracts for the design and construction of complete process plants are unusually complex. The documents which comprise the contract are voluminous—a requirement for a metre or more of shelf space would not be uncommon. They are produced over a long period of time by many hands and are often the subject of extensive negotiation and amendment. This type of contract fits uncomfortably within the legal framework of offer and acceptance. A valid contract requires a clear offer and an unconditional acceptance of it. In the context of a process plant contract, the employer's Enquiry is an invitation to treat—a mere soliciting of offers. The contractor's Tender, if sufficiently firm, is an offer which the employer may accept. In practice, the process plant contractor's Tender is often qualified, perhaps because of lack of information in the Enquiry, perhaps because of the contractor's inability to define some aspects in the time available. The employer will seldom accept a Tender unconditionally so that his responses will evoke revised offers, or may themselves be counter-offers. At the end of the contract negotiations, spread perhaps over a period of months and involving many people, offer and acceptance will be accomplished at the signing ceremony. It will, it is hoped, be clear to the key participants just what has been agreed, but that understanding will fade rapidly if not properly recorded. Many of the documents that the parties may subsequently seek to rely on may have no contractual significance if they are not formally made part of the contract.

The employer's project manager needs to understand all the various parts of the contract documents, the role each of them plays in defining the bargain, and how they relate to each other. Others will take only a partial view. To the engineers involved, who may have come late, if at all, to contractual matters and who may never acquire the knowledge and experience, nor develop the interest, in this field to match their technical expertise, the project will represent a set of related technical and logistical problems. As regards the legal assistance the project manager may receive, few employers will have specialists in engineering contracts, and even fewer of those will have knowledge and experience of the engineering aspects. To ensure that the technical and legal aspects knit seamlessly together is therefore a most important part of the employer's project manager's job.

Clarity and lack of ambiguity are the essentials, and the project manager must spare no effort to achieve them, but he must also realise that agreement reached at contract award may in part be illusory, or mistaken, or fragile. Even if the contract documents are carefully produced, are clear and are well understood by both parties, it would be too much to hope that, in documents of such length and complexity, there were no errors, omissions, or contradictions. To maintain agreement and good relations between the parties throughout the contract period requires thorough understanding of the contract, its scope and the obligations and liabilities which it imposes, competent administration and reasonable compromise where problems arise. Otherwise the agreement may be found to be insufficiently robust to withstand the stress of events.

It should go without saying that litigation in connection with an engineering contract almost certainly betokens serious failure on the part of the employer's project manager, and can be to no one's advantage but the lawyers'. However, even when a dispute between the parties is settled by agreement between them, the settlement will usually be influenced not only by what they thought the contract meant when they agreed it, but also by what they have been subsequently advised about its legal enforceability. Under commercial pressures, not everyone would honour an agreement where it has subsequently been found that the courts would take a different, and to them a more advantageous, view. Of course, many situations which arise during execution of a contract would not have been specifically considered by the parties at the time the contract was agreed, so that the implications of the contract in those circumstances would not have been thought through. In either event, it is highly desirable that the contract should not only mean the same things to both parties at the outset, but that those understandings should be enforceable at law, even if recourse to litigation is never considered.

11.2 CONTENTS OF CONTRACT DOCUMENTS

In a complicated process plant contract, the precedence of the contract documents does not necessarily follow their chronological order. Events begin with the employer's Enquiry, which is superseded by the contractor's Tender produced in response to it. The Tender may or may not comply with the Enquiry, it is for the employer to examine it to see if it does. If the employer were simply to accept the contractor's Tender, the Enquiry would become a dead letter and the requirements of the employer as defined in it would be incorporated in the contract only to the extent that they were included in the Tender. Of course, a properly developed Tender should itemise all those places where it departs from the Enquiry, but it is for the employer to ensure that he is aware of all such departures. He must then negotiate with the contractor to rectify any errors or omissions, and to accept or reject any changes compared with his Enquiry. This is an onerous task where the Enquiry is a massive document and the Tender equally so. The employer's scrutiny of the Tender may fail to identify some important differences. There may be implicit assumptions in the Tender which contradict the Enquiry and which are not recognised. The answer from the employer's point of view is to retain the Enquiry as a contract document and to give it precedence over the contractor's Tender. This puts the onus on the contractor—who at this point is in no position to argue—to ensure that the Enquiry is amended in line with his Tender.

Together, the contract documents must establish the technical, administrative and commercial basis of the contract and define the responsibilities and obligations of the parties. The documents may be assembled, in order of precedence, as follows:

(1) Memorandum of Contract
(2) Conditions of Contract (Special, then General)
(3) Agreed Changes and Clarifications to the Enquiry
(4) Enquiry
(5) Tender

The Memorandum of Contract, sometimes called a Form of Agreement, is the document to which the parties put their signatures. Since virtually all the matters of substance will have been covered elsewhere, it remains for the Memorandum to cover only those few remaining, typically:

- The effective date of the contract.
- The list of documents comprising the contract and their order of precedence.
- The law that governs the contract. In the case of international contracts it would be desirable to define also the jurisdiction (where any case is to be tried) and the law governing the procedure and administration of any arbitration.
- The appointment of the Engineer to the contract.

It is, in short, not much more than a covering letter.

The Conditions of Contract follow next in precedence. If a standard form is used—of the employer or of an institution or trade association—any special conditions, written to add to or modify the standard conditions, should take precedence. The Conditions of Contract must be drafted with reference to the Enquiry and must dovetail with it.

The Agreed Clarifications and Changes to the Enquiry itemise matters which have been discussed and negotiated between employer and contractor following receipt of the Tender, and which affect the Enquiry or the Tender. This document reconciles the Enquiry with the Tender, altering one or the other or both so that there remain no significant, or at least, unconsidered differences between them. If differences do remain, they are resolved in favour of the Enquiry by virtue of its precedence. It is highly desirable to produce a special document for the purpose of recording these clarifications and changes. If instead, a sheaf of minutes of meetings, letters, telex and facsimile messages are bundled together to serve this purpose, it will almost certainly be found later that these do not give a sufficiently complete story. Communications naturally leave unstated much of the relevant information known to be in the possession of both parties at the time. Several years later, this information will have been forgotten or will be imperfectly remembered and dispute may be engendered. The full and proper recording at the time of what has been agreed has great value. It re-confirms the agreements reached and may obviate much later argument. The Enquiry and Tender are unchanged, since any necessary reconciliation has been taken care of in the preceding Clarification document.

There are, of course, other ways of organising and describing the contract documents: Abstracts of Particulars, Schedules, Scopes of Work are but a few examples of these documents and the terminology that may be used to define them. What is important is that the various documents are listed clearly, that any differences between them are reconciled and that precedence is defined. It is good practice to collect the various documents together for the signing ceremony so that there can be no doubt about what is being agreed. The signing of the Memorandum of Agreement by both parties signifies offer and acceptance.

Having achieved certainty of agreement, the employer's project manager should then communicate the relevant details of the agreement to his team. Any member of the team who has any freedom of action to decide, or who works for long periods unsupervised, should be aware of the general nature of the contract and, where it affects him, of the detail. An employer's engineer who has spent long months developing a particular part of the Enquiry will be confident that he knows what is required of the contractor. Similarly, the contractor's engineer who has developed a part of the Tender will be sure that he knows what is to be provided. However, it is probable that neither was party to the subsequent negotiations at which the Enquiry or the Tender may have been modified. In such a case, it is important that they be brought up-to-date on the agreed situation, otherwise they may both seek to act on the basis of their out-dated knowledge. Again, the contract may be placed on terms which are unusual for the employer, or the contractual relationships between the parties may be novel. If, for example, the employer's project manager is acting as the Engineer to a joint venture company in which the employer has only a minority interest, the obligations of the employer and the responsibilities of his project team may be different and will need explaining to the team.

11.3 CONDITIONS OF CONTRACT

Conditions of Contracts are dealt with at some length in this book because of their importance in projects where contractors are employed to perform most of the work. A UK perspective is taken. In some other countries, notably in the Far East, the written contract may be less important, and relations between employer and contractor more influenced by traditional ways of doing business, a situation which may or may not make things easier. In Western countries, however, the increased competition and keener pricing characteristic of recent years has led to ever more detailed contracts which place a premium on contractual care and skill.

The major requirements for the Conditions of Contract for a major process plant project are as follows:

(1) They must be appropriate to the project. To ensure that this is so, consideration must be given to the work involved, to the knowledge and experience of employer and contractor and, most importantly, to the degree of definition of what is to be done. It will not, in the end, be helpful to seek a lump sum contract price for inadequately defined work, nor to try and invent contract conditions which will make up for deficiencies in definition or in the parties' knowledge. If acceptable contract conditions cannot be agreed, the fault will usually lie in inadequate project definition, and the right course is to do more work to improve definition before

contract award, rather than to try and conjure up some innovative contract scheme to solve the problem.

(2) They must, so far as they can, encourage co-operative working between the parties to the contract and discourage confrontation. The employer must accept that his involvement in the execution work must be controlled and disciplined—especially so in a lump sum contract,

(3) The Conditions of Contract should be confined to matters of principle. They should eschew detail and procedural matters, which are best dealt with by the agreement and issue of separate procedures—co-ordination, payment, accounting, planning, procurement, cost monitoring and so on. These are part of the contract documents, but separate development under the lead of the appropriate specialists will achieve the commitment and understanding necessary for the best results.

(4) The Conditions must satisfy the employer's requirements as regards apportionment of risk and responsibility. These requirements will not necessarily be for the most economic, nor for some mythical 'fair and reasonable', division. The employer may wish to pay a premium to reduce or contain his risk.

(5) They must be clearly understood by both sides, and understood to mean the same things. The employer's project manager must be especially alert to ensure that the contractor has no illusions about his obligations. It will not, in these complicated matters, be to the employer's advantage to have the contractor discover later that he has not fully understood all the implications, even (or perhaps especially) if this has led him to under-estimate his price.

It has already been remarked that the Conditions of Contract should, wherever possible, be confined to matters of principle, with administrative and procedural matters relegated either to the Enquiry, where they will be part of the included Co-ordination Procedure, or to separate procedures. The last are especially relevant where the detail is too extensive to include conveniently in the Co-ordination Procedure, or is non-contentious and not fully defined until after contract award. Among the procedures that might with advantage be produced separately are those which define accounting requirements, those concerned with the details of payment to the contractor for reimbursable materials (especially where multiple currencies are involved), those dealing with the employer's requirements for planning, cost monitoring, procurement, and so on.

Conditions of Contract for the design and construction of process plants must all cover much the same ground and therefore contain a broadly similar list of clauses, or conditions. They will usually be based on, or borrow individual clauses from, previous sets of conditions used by the employer, or else on one or more of the model forms. Of course, it is necessary for the project manager to be closely involved in the drafting of the contract. Typically, the Conditions of Contract will need to deal with the following topics:

- Definitions
- Responsibilities of the contractor
- Responsibilities of the employer
- Duties of the engineer and engineer's representatives
- Contractor's personnel
- Time and delay
- Contract price and method of payment
- Terms of payment
- Variations
- Procurement
- Inspection
- Progress and expediting
- Access and delivery to site
- Site responsibilities
- Care of the works
- Technical support and assistance at site
- Completion and take-over
- Performance tests
- Guarantees
- Defects and defects period
- Property and copyright
- Patent rights
- Secrecy
- *Force majeure*
- Assignment and sub-contracting
- Suspension and termination by the employer
- Contractor's default or insolvency
- Liability for damage and injury
- Limitation of contractor's liability
- Insurance
- Notices
- Arbitration.

There are an infinite number of variations possible in the way the subject matter may be split between clauses, but in practice there is a great deal of borrowing, and hence similarity, between contracts from apparently different sources. The subject matter that is required to be covered in the Conditions of Contract naturally depends on the work the contractor is required to do, but less so than might be supposed. Thus a contract for design and procurement services differs only in a relatively small number of important matters from one for design, supply and construction. The type of contract also affects both the subject matter of the Conditions of Contract and the way in which it is treated, though again, less than might be supposed. Examples of clauses covering the above listed topics, and others, may be found in the various model forms and are not reproduced here. In the following chapters is to be found some discussion on the requirements for and intentions of many of the clauses listed above. This discussion will be based mainly on consideration of lump sum contracts: reimbursable contracts are obviously less demanding in their requirements, but the need for differences in those clauses not concerned with payment and liabilities, where not obvious, may be little or nothing.

There are a number of rules of construction: that a reasonable meaning will be preferred to an unreasonable one, that an error will be corrected where it is obvious what was meant, that the meaning of a doubtful word may be decided by consideration of its context. It is good practice to use the same words where the same meaning is intended: elegant variation has no place in contract conditions. Of more importance in the present context are the rules concerning lists: that where some things are expressly mentioned, others of the same class not mentioned will be excluded, and that if there is a list of things falling into a particular class followed by general words, the general words will be taken to refer to that same class. Finally, and perhaps most importantly in the context of a process plant contract is the *contra proferentem* rule, that where there is ambiguity the words of the contract are construed against the party seeking to rely upon them. For reasons rooted in history, the courts are suspicious of attempts to exclude or limit liabilities and will interpret contract clauses seeking to do this in the strictest and narrowest sense. Such clauses are seen as a defence to a breach of contract rather than as a definition of the obligations which the party agreed to shoulder. This approach may run completely counter to the understanding the parties had of their contract. The courts are similarly suspicious of what they may regard as penal sanctions in the case of non-performance, so that liquidated damages clauses may come under close scrutiny, as may clauses granting extension of time to complete, since these may be seen as means of preserving the employer's right to liquidated damages. These matters are discussed in more detail in later chapters.

11.4 LETTERS OF INTENT

The employer's project manager may come under pressure for an immediate start to be made on the contract as soon as the successful tender has been selected. Sometimes he himself decides that he cannot wait until the contract documents are completed and signed. The finalising of the contract may be seen as mere administrative detail which must not be allowed to delay the project. Details of the contract can be settled while work proceeds, meanwhile a letter of intent will suffice. One of the problems with this is that as soon as work begins, both the contractor's and the employer's project managers are more than fully occupied in running the contract, the legal advisers move on to other work, and finalising the contract becomes a very low priority item. The contractor may be relatively unconcerned, because he will be entitled, at common law, to be paid on a *quantum meruit* (reasonable sum) basis for all the work that he does, and his liabilities can be no more than those originally proposed by the employer for the formal contract and, if these were still the subject of dispute and negotiation, will almost certainly be considerably less. It is not unknown for a project to have been completed before the contract was finalised, much to the disadvantage of the dissatisfied employer who might have wished to enforce what would otherwise have been his contractual rights.

In fact it should seldom, if ever, be necessary to resort to a letter of intent: either the parties are agreed on what they are to contract for, in which case a proper contract can be completed with little further delay (it is notable how quickly matters are progressed if the employer makes it clear from the beginning that work will not start until the contract is finalised), or there is much still to be settled, in which case the employer should not be committing himself blindly—a first stage, or development, contract is a better way of proceeding.

If, despite the above, it is decided that no delay can be brooked, there may be problems in ensuring that both parties understand what they have agreed. There is no special legal significance about a letter of intent *per se*. There is either a contract between the parties or there is not. There is no intermediate stage, no such thing in English law as an agreement to agree (although there is in some other legal systems). A letter of intent is therefore a binding contract or it is nothing, and it needs to be written with care. Its two most necessary characteristics are that its acceptance by the contractor should form a binding contract on clear terms for the preliminary work that is to be done before award of the main contract, and that it should not create any liability in regard to the main contract. Of course, no sensible contractor would proceed unless at least the first of these characteristics was present. As a minimum the letter of intent should contain the following:

(1) A statement that the employer intends to award a contract, subject to the satisfactory conclusion of negotiations (which, being conditional, has no binding force).
(2) Authorisation for the contractor to start work and continue subject to certain limits, of expenditure and perhaps time.
(3) Details of the payment the employer will make for the work authorised.

(4) A statement to the effect that the contract formed by the acceptance of the letter of intent will be subsumed into the main contract if and when the latter is awarded.

(5) Details of any compensation payment to the contractor and of the rights of the employer to the results of work done, in the event that the main contract is not awarded.

Beyond this, the employer may well wish to specify certain conditions which are important to him and which he has already agreed with the contractor. But without importing into the letter the full panoply of Enquiry, Tender and record of subsequent negotiations, the basis of the contract can hardly cover such matters satisfactorily, and the letter can be no more than a stop-gap with very limited shelf-life. It binds both parties to an agreement that is not fully formulated and which may later come to be realised as in some respects ill-considered. For the employer, his negotiating position on any unresolved points is seriously weakened. For the contractor, his work may be terminated at any time, possibly with inadequate compensation. The limit on expenditure authorised under the letter will serve to remind the parties of the need to settle the remaining features of the contract, but all too often delay is allowed to increase until the parties have genuine difficulty in recalling the position they had reached when negotiations were suspended.

Chapter 12

Conditions of Contract

12.1 DEFINITIONS, RESPONSIBILITIES, PERSONNEL

In this chapter, most of the typical clauses required for an engineering contract for a process plant are discussed. No attempt is made to offer standard clauses: this would be supererogation given the numbers of standard or model forms of contract that exist, and would add inordinately to the length of the book. What is attempted is to explain the major implications of the main clauses in a typical process plant contract from the project manager's point of view, so that he may understand more clearly what his contract is trying to accomplish and may in consequence be able to draft, or have drafted, clauses that accurately reflect a clear intention. A process of selection is inevitably involved and the discussion that follows does not represent a comprehensive coverage of the subject: rather have comments been made where it seems the matter is of most interest to the project manager.

12.1.1 Definitions

Clarity of intention and expression is paramount in any contract. If it is clearly understood what it is that the contract should say, and what it should not say, it is relatively easy to find language to express the intention. Plain, direct and precise language should be the aim, avoiding words with a vague penumbra of meaning in favour of those with a sharper and narrower sense. 'When I use a word it means just what I choose it to mean, neither more nor less'—so said Humpty Dumpty in *Through the Looking Glass*, and the prior definition of a number of key words is an important aid to the clarity and conciseness of any Conditions of Contract. Such words should then be used, dignified with a capital letter, in the defined sense only. It is deplorable to state, as do some contracts, that the words defined shall have the meanings assigned to them except where the context otherwise requires.

In a typical contract there might be twenty to thirty terms that can usefully be defined. An illustrative example is the term 'Documentation'. One might begin to draft a contract by making reference to 'drawings', to which the need to add 'calculations' would soon become apparent and then possibly 'all other documents', at which point one might wonder whether models and computer output were included. The advantages of a term such as 'Documentation', which could be defined as 'all drawings, calculations, computer output, data sheets, material lists, specifications, programmes, requisitions, purchase orders, correspondence and all other documents, models and other design aids, including material in machine-readable form, which convey information relevant to the Works' soon becomes obvious. This single portmanteau term may then be used in place of the list, with benefits in comprehensiveness, conciseness and accuracy, since it avoids the possibility of omission in the repetitions that would otherwise be necessary. Documentation is a crucial feature of the contract. The employer will probably require that the Documentation he produces be kept confidential. Documentation produced by the contractor is the main output of his design process and the contractor is responsible for any errors and omissions in it. Property and copyright in it, and the use the employer may make of it, must be defined. The employer (or the Engineer) must have the right of access to it for checking and approval.

12.1.2 Responsibilities of the Contractor

There can hardly be anything more important in the contract than the definition of the contractor's responsibilities, that is to say, of the work he is required to do, the time it must take, and the standard to which he must do it. The vast majority of this definition is provided by the Enquiry, which must, in the specifications it contains, have established the technical standards that are to be adhered to and, in the scope of work which it includes, have set out the extent of the work required. What is needed in the Conditions of Contract is then merely a general statement, in the degree of detail that is appropriate and necessary in view of what is included elsewhere in the contract documents (that is to say, the Enquiry, subsequent Clarifications and Changes, and the Tender, in the order of priority assigned in the Memorandum of Contract), and which makes reference to them. It should be remembered that, as far this contract is concerned, responsibility for the total requirement of the project is simply divided between employer and contractor: whatever is not the responsibility of the contractor is the responsibility of the employer, even though the latter may engage various other contractors to perform the rest of the work.

If there is difficulty in defining the contractor's responsibilities precisely, this is evidence that the contract is being awarded prematurely and that more preparatory work is needed, or that decisions need to be taken by the employer before proceeding further. It is unfortunately true that some employers never come properly to terms with the relationship they require with the contractor and the full implications of it. They are anxious to make progress and keen to engage the contractor as soon as he can begin useful work and contribute to the project's progress, even before some important aspects of the project have been decided, but then expect the same outcome as if the contract had been let on the basis of a fully developed and firm definition.

As well as brief statements defining the scope of the contractor's work with reference to the contract documents, it may be necessary to cover some other aspects of the contractor's responsibilities which are not dealt with elsewhere. An example might be his responsibility to check design by others. Where the process technology was provided by a licensor, or even by the employer himself, a significant factor in the choice of contractor may have been his experience in engineering previous plants based on this technology. The employer would then naturally wish to gain the full advantage of this experience and to require the contractor, within the limits of his knowledge and having regard to any confidentially restrictions, and without his assuming any liability, to review the process package and make any pertinent comments to the employer.

A number of general obligations of the contractor need to be defined. The following list is not exhaustive, nor would all the items listed necessarily be appropriate to a particular contract. Some of them might be found in other parts of the contract:

(1) To satisfy himself as to the completeness and sufficiency of the information provided by the employer.
(2) To work with all reasonable skill, care and diligence in accordance with the contract and applicable statutory regulations, carrying out the work with sound workmanship and materials in conformity with good engineering practice and to the reasonable satisfaction of the Engineer.
(3) To follow the instructions of the Engineer (with appropriate rights of appeal if the contractor considers that any instruction would prejudice the fulfilment of his obligations).
(4) To allow the Engineer access to his activities and the right to inspect all work in progress.
(5) To submit Documentation for approval by the Engineer.

(6) To be responsible for errors and omissions in his design, notwithstanding approval by the Engineer.

(7) To comply with all Works Rules on the site.

(8) To be responsible for the adequacy, stability and safety of all operations on the site, instituting safe systems of working and complying with all applicable safety regulations.

(9) To meet the reasonable requirements of any licensor of process technology, which may be regarded as instructions of the Engineer.

(10) To provide adequate information in a timely manner to any other contractor of the employer whose activities require it.

(11) To provide sufficient personnel of adequate quality to the satisfaction of the Engineer.

(12) To use his best endeavours to retain continuity of personnel.

(13) To keep safe and confidential all Documentation received from the employer.

(14) To perform the design and procurement services in accordance with the contract and make the design available to the employer.

(15) To provide a completed plant suitable for its intended purpose.

It is important to distinguish between the responsibility for performing the work and the liability to pay for it. Otherwise, for example, it might be found that the contractor is not required to correct defects which are not his fault. Generally, the employer would wish the contractor to be obligated to perform all the work necessary under the contract, including any of a remedial nature, howsoever it arose. Who pays is a separate question.

12.1.3 Responsibilities of the Employer

Although everything in the project is, so far as this contract is concerned, the responsibility of either the contractor or the employer, this does not mean that the sum of the responsibilities of both as stated in the contract will equal the total project. The employer's responsibilities that are stated will be only those that he has towards the contractor. They are normally quite simple and straightforward since it is, after all, the contractor and not the employer who is performing the work. These responsibilities are typically as follows:

(1) To provide information on which the contractor will base his work.

(2) To approve documentation produced by the contractor.

(3) To carry out reviews of the design.

(4) To give access to the site on time.

(5) To make payment as specified.

Other employer responsibilities may concern the contractor, where the employer is taking an active part in the project. Examples are the provision of soils data, the transport of out-of-gauge loads from port to site; the storage of plant at site under suitable conditions to prevent deterioration before installation; commissioning, start-up and operation of the plant

Provision of information

Invariably, it will be necessary for the employer to provide information on which the contractor will base his design. Such information might include, in addition to the specification of the process plant in more or less detail, depending on the ownership of the technology; site survey and soils test data; details of any existing installation on the site; details of terminal points and routes for drainage and service pipes and cables; information on the cost of utilities for the contractor to use in choosing sources of energy; and so on. Most of this information will be provided at the bid stage, but some may not be available until after the contract has been awarded. In the latter case the employer would have an obligation to provide the data in a timely manner so that the contractor's work was not impeded. It is unlikely that the timing of the employer's obligations in this respect will be accurately defined in the contract, so that the contractor will improve his prospects of a successful claim against the employer for delay if he gives formal and timely notice should his work be adversely affected.

Approval of documentation

A contract which includes for the design of a process plant will, in most cases, require the contractor to work closely with the employer when carrying out the design. The extent and depth of this collaboration will depend on the source of the technology and on the relative knowledge and experience of the parties. If, for example, the employer has supplied the process technology, or has an expertise in it comparable with or greater than that of the contractor, he will wish to monitor the development of the design very closely and to participate in it. He will wish to feed into the new plant the fruits of his experience in operating and maintaining plants using the same or similar technology. One consequence is that the contract must oblige the contractor to submit Documentation to the employer (or someone identified as acting on his behalf—the Engineer or the Project Manager) for approval. The Conditions of Contract may require the submission of such Documentation for approval as the Engineer considers necessary, with the Co-ordination Procedure defining the requirements more closely, for example, calculations, data sheets, drawings, specifications. As well as approvals of technical matters, key procurement documents and various administrative features of the contract—programmes, order schedules and so on, will also be subject to approval by the employer or his agent. Where the knowledge of the process and the expertise in its application rests wholly or mainly with the contractor, the employer's requirements for approval will be similar in nature but less searching in detail, recognising the reduced scope of the employer's technical contribution—there will be instances where the Engineer is not sufficiently expert or well informed to make any worthwhile technical judgement—and, possibly, the existence of confidentiality restrictions on the technical data.

The process of technical approval by the employer could affect the responsibility of the parties for the design and it is therefore necessary that the Conditions of Contract address this aspect. In the absence of anything in the contract to the contrary, an employer who approved the contractor's designs might, depending on the nature and extent of his approval process, incur some responsibility for them. However, any Conditions of Contract originating in the UK will almost certainly declare that approval by the employer or his agent will not in any way lessen the contractor's responsibility for his designs and that the contractor will retain responsibility for any errors or omissions in them, notwithstanding their approval by the employer. It is clear, therefore, that whatever the meaning of the term 'approval', it is not that which would usually be attributed to it. In normal parlance, approval would imply the assumption by the approver of some responsibility for what he has approved. Here, the word is being used in a special sense, that of reviewing and commenting on the contractor's proposals, possibly requiring modifications to them, while taking no responsibility for their correctness or completeness. It is perhaps the use of the word in this sense, together with a desire on the part of the employer not to weaken his contractual position, that has been responsible for some badly drafted clauses on the subject. Certainly, several of the standard forms in common use, and the behaviour of some employers' personnel, suggest that the aims and implications of the approval process have often not been clearly identified.

The difficulty which some of the drafting committees of model forms seem to have had with the business of approval by the Engineer is exemplified by the relevant clause in the Institution of Mechanical Engineer's Model Form A 1976 Edition (still surviving in many Conditions of Contract which have borrowed from it, although superseded by MF/1 1988 which is a model of clarity on the subject), which contains, in Clause 4, the following:

'Within a reasonable period after receiving such drawings, samples, patterns and models, the Engineer shall signify his approval or otherwise.'

This is grammatically deplorable, and leaves room for doubt, if not more, about what the Engineer must do if he does not approve the items in question, since the word 'otherwise' stands in place of a noun having an opposite or different meaning from approval. One might reasonably argue that if disapproval alone were meant, the draftsman would have used that word. If the Engineer is either to approve or do something else, this covers the field of possible action but gets us no further. What is required of the Engineer if he does not signify his approval is not simply that he pursue some other activity, nor even that he signify his refusal to approve, but that he should reject or disapprove. Further, since the contractor is obligated to modify the design in the case of disapproval, the grounds for rejection must be stated. One can only assume that uncertainty about what was meant by the word approval inhibited the draughtsman from using its antonym, disapproval. The FIDIC standard form for Electrical and Mechanical Works 3rd Edition 1987, based on the Model Form A, avoids this trap and refers, in Clause 6.1, forthrightly to disapproval. However, in the otherwise excellent guide to the use of the FIDIC model form is seen:

> 'The approval of Contractor's Drawings by the Engineer does not imply approval
> of the Contractor's design...'

to which, since the drawings are the manifestation of the design, it is difficult to attribute any very definite meaning.

A clear understanding of what approval means is obviously highly desirable in the interests of efficient contract administration. Both employer and contractor should be clear why the employer wishes to approve the contractor's designs, what he hopes to achieve thereby and what are the contractual implications. At the enquiry stage, the employer provides his technical specifications and scope of work in the degree of detail he thinks appropriate or is able to provide. This, modified as agreed during the run-up to contract award, is the basis of the contractor's design. The purpose of the approval process is for the Engineer to ensure that the design, as so far developed, satisfies the employer's requirements. It would clearly be inefficient, not to say foolish, for the employer, assuming he has some relevant technical expertise to contribute, to refrain from comment until the design, or the plant, was completed. Approval should therefore mean that, insofar as the approval process is reasonably able to determine, the design so far developed:

(1) meets the specification, or
(2) is satisfactory where there is no specification, or
(3) is satisfactory, the specification having been waived.

To maintain that it means less than this is to hold that the employer is unable to recognise his requirements when he sees them. An employer's usual approval process, of course, may be far from a thoroughgoing check of the contractor's work. If, for example, it was required that pressure vessels were to be designed to a particular standard or code of practice, it would not be expected that the employer would often, if ever, check the calculations to see that this had actually been done. He should be able to rely on the contractor's assurance. On the other hand, he would be expected to check a line diagram in some detail and to notice if specified plant items had not been incorporated. Of course, the sensible contractor would bring to the employer's attention any areas where he was proposing to depart from the specification and get specific agreement to them.

Further than this, the approval stage is the last opportunity (other than through a Variation) for the employer to make a major technical input to the design and to give effect to his preferences. Approval, within the limitations of the approval process itself:

(1) confirms the contractor's design, so that he can proceed to the next stage with reasonable confidence that his increasing financial commitment will be made in a way which has the employer's agreement;
(2) signals that the approved design will not be departed from except:
   (a) for the contractor to correct any errors or omissions which might subsequently be found in his work;
   (b) if the design is subsequently found to be unsafe or inoperable;
   (c) by way of a Variation for which any extra time and cost would be to the employer's account.

Thus for the contractor, the approval process is just as important as it is to the employer. A suitable contract condition might read as follows:

'The contractor shall submit to the Engineer for approval such Documentation as the Engineer considers necessary. Within a reasonable period after receiving such Documentation, the Engineer shall approve or reject it stating, where appropriate, the grounds for rejection. Approval by the Engineer shall in no way relieve the contractor of his obligations under the contract and his responsibility for the accuracy, correctness and sufficiency of the Documentation. When approved by the Engineer, Documentation shall be departed from only to correct an error or omission, or where necessary to render the plant safe or operable, or by way of a Variation.'

Some contracts set a time limit for the approval process—the Institution of Chemical Engineers Red Book Clause 20.4, for example, requires the Engineer to approve any drawing within fourteen days after submission. It might be thought that this was entirely reasonable, were it not for the fact that some contractors make a habit of issuing documents for approval in large batches at infrequent intervals, overloading the Engineer and his staff. The Engineer cannot promise to approve quickly unless the submission of documents for approval is also regulated.

In some non-technical areas, the employer's right to approve may be qualified by the requirement that approval should not be unreasonably withheld. The criteria for the employer's approval or disapproval in technical matters are the contract documents, primarily the employer's specification. Sometimes, matters not explicitly covered in the documents are required to be to the satisfaction of the Engineer, and this may be qualified as 'reasonable'. In the Institution of Chemical Engineers Red Book Clause 20.6, the grounds for disapproval are limited to the design not complying with some express provision of the contract or it being contrary to good engineering practice. This is probably as good a definition as can be achieved but will not, of course, help where what is considered good engineering practice by one party is mere personal preference to the other. There is much that an experienced employer might wish to see incorporated into a plant that is not strictly necessary, either for its own sake or to qualify as good engineering practice—some requirements for operational convenience or maintenance access, for example. The employer will include these requirements, as far as he is able, in his Enquiry specification. Thereafter he will endeavour to feed them into the design as it is being developed, in which case the contractor will no doubt do his best to comply if no extra cost is incurred. Otherwise, such requirements will be Variations. Much of the success of the contract will depend on the employer and contractor establishing ways of collaborating which deal with these matters efficiently and with as little disruptive effect as possible.

Design reviews

The procedure for approval of Documentation, as described above, is one that is common to many engineering contracts. It is essentially a passive procedure for the Engineer, who has merely to approve, or reject (preferably with reasons), the Documentation submitted to him. He is under no obligation to make alternative proposals for work rejected, nor would the contractor be obliged to take notice if he did so, though no doubt in practice such proposals are made and accepted. The typical process plant contract, however, requires something more. The extent of collaboration in the design between employer and contractor, though it may vary widely depending on the ownership of the technology and the relative knowledge and expertise of the two parties, will usually be considerable. The employer requires to take a more active part in the design than the approval procedure provides for, and at an earlier stage than the issue of near-final Documentation.

This participation by the employer is commonly accomplished through the medium of design reviews, a feature of the design method which, quite apart from any employer/contractor relationship, has become increasingly necessary in recent years as plants have become more complicated and the potential hazards associated with them have increased. The employer will have listed those reviews which he intends to make, and the extent of involvement in them that he requires of the contractor, in the Co-ordination Procedure. The recommendations and results of the reviews will be positive proposals for incorporation in the design and will be recorded in minutes or action lists. These will have the status of an Engineer's Instruction, so that the contractor will be obligated to comply, subject to a disputes procedure. The contractor would have grounds for dispute if he considered a proposal unworkable or unsafe. He might consider a proposal unnecessary and request a Variation Order. In any event, the contractor would retain responsibility for the completed design. Obviously this is a part of the contract which could cause problems if handled clumsily, but appropriate joint membership of the review panels will avoid much dissension.

The Institution of Chemical Engineers' model forms have nothing to say on the subject of design reviews, but these have become so important in recent years as to warrant reference in the Conditions of Contract. A suitable clause might be as follows:

'The employer shall carry out a number of design reviews, some of which will require the contractor's participation, as specified in the contract documents. Recommendations from the reviews shall be recorded in writing and shall be considered Engineer's Instructions. The contractor shall incorporate such recommendations in his design without detracting from his responsibility for its accuracy, correctness and sufficiency. Where the contractor considers that the incorporation in his design of a such a recommendation would render his design unsafe or inoperable, or would prejudice the performance of any of his contractual obligations, or would justify a Variation, he shall submit his case in writing to the Engineer.'

Site

It is, of course, the employer's responsibility to provide the site. The employer may operate existing facilities on it, but even if he does not, it is very likely that he will have had more time to investigate and familiarise himself with conditions there than the contractor. This greater knowledge may make it sensible for the employer to take responsibility for some matters which in different circumstances would be left to the contractor. Soil conditions are an example. If the employer already has plants on the adjacent area, it is probable that he will already be in possession of much of the necessary data, and will have details of any underground obstructions left from previous plants. Even if the site is a new one, the employer will usually have access to it before the bidders and can save time by commissioning surveys, environmental studies and soils investigations, and will save money by avoiding unnecessary repetition of this work by each bidder. The contract may then provide for the employer to provide and take responsibility for site survey and soils data, and will need to be clear who has responsibility for the interpretation of the latter.

Certainly, the contract will oblige the employer to provide the contractor with timely access to site (assuming that the contractor has responsibilities on it) and to any other land and temporary facilities and services that have been promised. The last may include, for example, the provision of utilities and emergency medical services where the site is adjacent to the employer's existing operations. Details of any such provision should be included in the Co-ordination Procedure. Quality of access is also relevant. If the contractor is required to take full responsibility for operations on the site, he must be given sole possession and control of it.

12.1.4 Duties of the Engineer and Engineer's Representatives

The origins of the custom of appointing an 'Engineer' to the contract are discussed in the later chapters concerning the use of model forms of contract. In the process plant industry, the independent consulting engineer acting in this capacity is not a feature, so that although the term 'Engineer' is often used, and is adhered to for convenience in this discussion, it will usually indicate little more than which of his employees has been charged by the employer with the duties in question, and could be replaced with the term 'employer' with the loss of nothing but this specificity of responsibility. Use of the term 'Engineer' in a process plant contract is likely to be necessary only if a managing contractor is employed, or in the case of a joint venture, where an employee of one of the partners fills the role.

The duties and powers of the Engineer are not collected together in one clause, but are distributed throughout the Conditions of Contract as the arrangement of subject matter dictates. The purpose of the clause under discussion is to establish any limits there may be to the Engineer's authority, to oblige the employer to give notice to the contractor of such limits, and to give the Engineer the power to appoint representatives to whom he may delegate some or all of his duties. This is usually necessary because design and construction for the project as a whole may be carried on in widely dispersed locations, and the Engineer would then not be able to give each the close attention required for efficient administration of the contract. (And some employers may appoint a senior executive to the position of Engineer whose only personal involvement in the contract would be in the event of serious dispute.)

For the employer's project manager, the role of Engineer constitutes only a part of his responsibilities and authority on the project. As Engineer, he is bound strictly by the terms of the contract and must operate in accordance with it, but he may well have greater authority as an employee of the employer. In the various model forms of contract, the Engineer's role varies, as described in later chapters. At its full extent, it encompasses the following:

(1) Acting as the employer's agent to supervise the work of the contractor during the course of the contract, approving design, accepting workmanship

and quality of materials and generally ensuring that the contractor's work is carried out to specification.

(2) Administering the contract by, for example, the agreement of Variations, measurement and valuation of the works, certifying invoices for payment, certifying completion, deciding the contractor's claims for extension to the contract period, for variation of contract rates and for payment of extra costs.

(3) Adjudication in disputes between contractor and employer.

In a process plant contract where the Engineer is an employee of the employer, the third item is unnecessary providing that the contractor does not lack proper opportunity to make representations to the Engineer before decisions are made. There is less need for formality in the second item since the employer's project manager will approve invoices for payment which he has certified in his role as Engineer. If the contract requires the Engineer to act impartially as between contractor and employer in his activities under the second of the items above, then the employer will, with the contractor's agreement, have relinquished control over his employee's actions under this head and will not be responsible for them to the contractor.

12.1.5 Contractor's Personnel

The employer will, of course, have a number of interests concerning the personnel which the contractor intends to employ on the project. In his tender, the contractor will typically have included:

- Curriculum vitae of his staff proposed for the major roles on the project.
- A graph comparing his future expected workload with staff he has available.

The purported availability of capable and experienced staff will have been a major factor in selecting the successful bidder for the contract and the employer will wish to ensure that the promises made by the contractor in this regard are kept. Thus he will wish to secure, so far as he can, the services of certain named persons to fill the roles of contractor's project manager and other senior project positions for the whole period of the project. The names of the people concerned may well be included in the Conditions of Contract and the employer may go so far as to require the contractor to agree special contracts with them to hold them for the required period. Alternatively, the Conditions of Contract may include a provision that the contractor use his best endeavours to retain the services of the particular people in the specified capacities throughout the life of the project, and not to re-assign them to other duties without the consent of the Engineer.

The employer may also wish to minimise the numbers employed on the project who are mere birds of passage—agency personnel who move frequently from one contractor to another as opportunity dictates. Once, this point might have been covered by a condition that the contractor employ no more than a specified percentage of agency personnel on the project, but this has been rather overtaken by the increasing tendency for long-term staff of the contractor to become agency personnel. In fact the contract can have only limited influence in these matters, and difficulty can only be avoided with certainty by the choice of a contractor who continues to have adequate resources available throughout the project period.

The employer will also wish to have the power to require the contractor to remove from the work, and especially from the site, any person whom the Engineer deems unsuitable or who has been seriously in breach of his duties.

12.2   TIME AND COST

12.2.1 Programme

It is usual for the employer to include in his Enquiry the programme to which he wishes the contractor to work. If the contractor is to be responsible for design, supply and construction, this programme would probably be no more than an outline, but more detail would be provided if the employer had done a lot of preliminary work on the project, or was to be responsible for construction or other associated work. The contractor would respond by including his proposed outline programme in his tender. If this was different from that proposed by the employer, it would be necessary in the negotiation to agree, and to define clearly in the contract documents, the project programme which would govern the contractor's liabilities. After award of contract, it is usual for the contractor to produce a three-month look-ahead programme to help manage his activities while he produces a detailed programme compatible with the outline project programme. He would go on to develop schedules for use in managing the procurement of equipment and materials.

The Co-ordination Procedure should specify the requirements of the employer for the way in which the contractor must carry out the planning and progressing function: the form of programmes, the degree of detail, the frequency of reporting and so on. Usually these would not be much different from the contractor's standard procedures—if they were, it would raise questions about the suitability of the contractor—and it would be sensible for the employer to accept the contractor's standard practice where the differences were not important.

The Conditions of Contract would typically require:

(1) The contractor to provide, by a specified date or as soon as practicable, a detailed programme and manning forecasts, compatible with the project programme, and to submit it for the Engineer's approval.
(2) The contractor to notify the Engineer if there was likelihood of delay, and the Engineer to notify the contractor if he considered progress did not match the programme. In either case, the contractor is required to take steps to ensure completion on time, modifying the programme if necessary.
(3) Any additional costs resulting from (2) to be borne by the contractor unless the delay had been caused by the employer.

12.2.2 Extension of Time

Certain dates are contractually important and may require to be specified, for example, the commencement of design work, the date on which the site is to be made available to the contractor, the start of work on site and, most important of all, completion. In most projects, there will be circumstances which, if they occur, will reasonably entitle the contractor to what is usually called an extension of time. This expression is appropriate if the contract specifies a given period for the work to be done. If the contract quotes a calendar completion date, a postponement of the completion date would be more accurate. Circumstances which entitle the contractor to an extension of time must be detailed in the contract, otherwise the Engineer (as distinct from the employer) would be unable to give it. Typically, the Engineer would be empowered to approve extensions of time for completion for delay caused by some of the following, not all of which would necessarily be appropriate to a particular contract:

(1) The issue by the Engineer of an instruction, or variation, or suspension order (in no case required by reason of the contractor's default).
(2) The employer's delay in meeting, or his failure to meet, his contractual obligations.
(3) Any other contractor engaged by the employer.
(4) Increased quantities (in the case of a re-measure and value contract).
(5) Unexpected site conditions not reasonably foreseeable.
(6) Force majeure.
(7) Exceptional adverse weather conditions.
(8) Any cause (not being the fault of the contractor) referred to in the Conditions of Contract.

Although clauses allowing for extensions of time may be regarded as operating to the benefit of the contractor in that they give him the right to a postponement of the completion date in the specified circumstances, they may also protect the employer's interests. This is because, if completion were to be delayed by the employer—for example, by an instruction or variation order issued by the Engineer or a breach of contract by the employer—unless there was provision in the contract for an extension of time to be given, the contract completion date would fall. With it would disappear the employer's right to liquidated damages, which must run from a completion date determined from the contract. The contractor's obligation would then be to complete in a reasonable time and, should he not do so, the employer seeking redress would have to sue for damages at large. Extension of time clauses, where they concern the granting of extra time for delay attributable to the employer, are therefore regarded by the courts as protecting the right to liquidated damages and are construed against an employer seeking to rely on them. They must be considered carefully and cover the reasonable range of possibilities. The use of a catch-all clause allowing the Engineer to give an extension of time in unspecified circumstances as, for example, is done in the Institution of Civil Engineers 6th Edition model form Clause 44(1)(e), will not necessarily preserve the employer's right to liquidated damages.

A difficult matter, which the contract must address clearly and explicitly if it is to operate in the way the employer would wish, is the contractual effect of delays caused during periods of contract over-run, when liquidated damages have become payable, by things which would have entitled the contractor to an extension of time had they occurred during the contract period. These things are of two kinds. There are those which are conditions rather than events, such as the discovery of unexpected site conditions, not reasonably foreseeable. These are independent of date and the delay caused by them would be the same whether they were encountered during the contract period or later. Clearly, the contractor is entitled to more time because of them and, if they are encountered during contract over-run, it would not defy logic to add that time to the contractual completion date, even though this had passed. The second kind are events causing delay which occur during the period of over-run. Some of these may be events which are not the fault of the employer and which affect the contract only because of the contractor's culpable delay. Examples are some instances of industrial action and of force majeure, and should not entitle the contractor to extra time. There should also be no entitlement to extra time as a result of some possible delaying actions of the employer, for example, if having fulfilled his obligations in providing access to the site throughout the contract period, the employer's existing operations adjacent to the site cause him to deny the contractor access for a time during contract over-run. But there can be delaying events during the over-run period which should entitle the contractor to extra time. These cannot, however, be dealt with in the same way as extensions of time during the contract period. If, for example, the Engineer issues a delaying variation during the over-run period, it is logically impossible to add the delay caused by this to the contractual completion date, already some way back in the past. Judged as an extension of time, such a delay period must run from the date the variation was ordered, and the contractual completion date must move to the end of this delay period, cancelling the liquidated damages already payable. This is obviously unsatisfactory for the employer.

It is therefore necessary for the contract to deal separately with those causes of delay which occur before, and those which occur after, the contractual completion date. Not only will the causes of delay which should entitle the contractor to extra time in the two sets of circumstances be different, but the method of providing for that extra time will also be different. Provisions for the granting, during the contract period, of extensions of time and consequent postponement of the contractual completion date should be limited to reasons which arise during the contract period. (The Engineer should, however, be able to grant such extensions of time after the contract period has ended, or after substantial completion has been achieved, this being regarded as no more than an administrative delay in confirming the extension of time to which the contractor became entitled during the contract period.) The contract should then quite separately provide for the Engineer, during contract over-run, to be empowered to grant periods during which the employer's entitlement to liquidated damages is suspended, without affecting the latter's right to the previously accrued damages. Entitlement to liquidated damages would resume once the suspension period had ended. For a process plant contract with the contractor already in culpable delay, the employer's entitlement to liquidated damages might appropriately be suspended for delay caused by the following:

(1) The issue by the Engineer, during contract over-run, of an instruction, or variation, or suspension order (in no case required by reason of the contractor's default).
(2) Provided that the contractor's failure to complete by the contractual completion date played no part:
    (a) the employer's delay in meeting, or his failure to meet, his contractual obligations;
    (b) any other contractor engaged by the employer.
(3) Unexpected site conditions not reasonably foreseeable.

Of the model forms discussed here, only the Institution of Civil Engineers 6th Edition addresses this problem in this way. Clause 44 requires the Engineer to make an interim grant of extension of time within 14 days after the contractual completion date has passed, and to make a final determination of the overall extension of time within 14 days of the issue of the certificate of substantial completion. Clause 47(6) deals with the question of further delay caused after liquidated damages have become payable. It provides for the Engineer to suspend, for various reasons, the employer's entitlement to liquidated damages, without invalidating the right to the damages already accrued. The Institution of Chemical Engineers model forms make no reference to the matter. The Institution of Mechanical Engineers model form

MF/1 in Clause 33.1 provides for the Engineer, prospectively or retrospectively, to grant an extension of time for delay caused by prescribed reasons whether that delay occurs before or after the contractual completion time, and seems to treat the problem in too simple a fashion to achieve certainty of interpretation. The reasons prescribed in MF/1—any act or omission on the part of the employer or the Engineer, any industrial dispute, or reasons beyond the reasonable control of the contractor—are the same whenever the delay occurs and to apply when the contractor is in culpable delay may be over-favourable to him in some circumstances.

12.2.3 Contract Price and Terms of Payment

Reimbursable contracts

Reimbursable contracts are usually paid for on a monthly basis. Payment for the contractor's services may be in arrears, each month the contractor submitting an invoice for his expenditure during the previous month. If agreed, this invoice would be paid via the employer's normal procedures, typically by the end of the month following the month of receipt. Some contracts require the employer to make payment earlier than this. For example, the Institution of Chemical Engineers' model form for reimbursable contracts, Clause 39, requires payment, on fourteen days' notice, about the middle of the month for estimated expenditure during that same month. Correction is applied for previous under- or over-payment. An employer would usually have to make special arrangements to pay the contractor's invoices within fourteen days of receipt, if he agreed to these terms. It is best for the Conditions of Contract to be limited to defining what is to be done, leaving the detail of how matters are to be accomplished to a separate Payment Procedure. It is not unknown for the detail of estimates, validations, reconciliations, audits, invoices and methods of payment so to occupy the draughtsman's attention that the actual requirement for the employer to pay has been omitted from the conditions.

Payment for materials and equipment supplied reimbursably by the contractor is also usually made on a monthly basis, against an estimate of expenditure for the month provided by the contractor. A common procedure is for the employer to deposit the required sum in a bank account on which the contractor draws to pay the suppliers' invoices. Several different currencies are often involved and a major international employer would usually consider that he is in a better position to supply these than the contractor. Again, the detail of such transactions may be considerable and is best left to a separate procedure. The contractor may place his orders on the basis that he pays the supplier when he himself is paid: this will not encourage the supplier to offer the keenest terms. In any event, it is unlikely that the contractor would fund any purchase himself.

Retention money finds no place in a reimbursable contract. In the case of payment for the contractor's services, there is unlikely to be any liability against which retention money could be held by the employer. In the case of materials and equipment, the contractor's estimate of monthly payments due to suppliers already takes account of retentions specified in the contracts with them.

Lump sum contracts

The contractor would not usually be called upon to finance the contract since the employer would expect to be able to do it more cheaply himself. Lump sum contracts are therefore usually paid for in instalments according to an agreed schedule, best contained, together with details of the mechanics of payment, in an appendix to the contract or in a separate Payment Procedure. There are various ways of linking payment to progress, and the employer would propose a method in his Enquiry, or ask the contractor to make proposals. For design and procurement services only, payment may be related to percentage progress on a monthly basis, with power accorded to the Engineer to re-schedule payment if progress was slower than expected. It is important that the Engineer has this power since progress schedules are more often than not optimistic. It also gives him a useful expediting tool. An alternative method is to link payment to the achievement of specified milestones. This appears at first sight to be the better method, but inevitably results in the milestones receiving priority whether or not this is required by events. Clearly, the payment schedule is something that both parties would wish to take into account—the contractor in pricing his bid and the employer in comparing competitive tenders.

Lump sum contracts for design and supply of equipment may require an advanced payment to the contractor—typically of 5 to 10% of the contract price—immediately on contract award. This recognises that the contractor has substantial orders to place early in the life of the project and provides him with the necessary funds. The payment would usually be secured with an advanced payment bond from the contractor. Subsequent stage payments would be discounted by the advanced payment percentage. Retention is also a feature of most lump sum contracts, deducted from each instalment, typically at a rate of 10%. Half of the retention money would normally be paid on completion of the plant and the remainder at the end of the defects or maintenance period, with sometimes an intermediate payment on satisfactory passing of performance tests. The contractor's limit of liability under the contract should normally be a consideration in, but does not have to govern, the fixing of the level of retention money. A common alternative to retention money is a bond valid in the equivalent amount. This would be cheaper for the contractor than the interest on the retained payments and should, other things being equal, result in a lower tender. If conceded in negotiation, a retention bond should therefore result in a reduction in contract price. It is entirely reasonable that a retention bond be unconditional, that is, that it be payable on demand without proof or even declaration of the contractor's default, because the employer is forfeiting the possession of the retention money in agreeing to the bond.

Unless explicitly provided in the contract, delay (within reason) in making payments is not a fundamental breach, that is, it does not entitle the contractor to terminate the contract. Nor would the contractor have a claim for interest on the delayed payments unless this was expressly stated in the contract, although legislation to change this seems likely in the near future. The model forms address these issues, however, and interest on delayed payments is provided for in those of the Institution of Chemical Engineers (both Red Book and Green Book in Clauses 39.5 and 39.4 respectively), the Institution of Mechanical Engineers (MF/1) in Clause 40.2, and the Institution of Civil Engineers (6th Edition) in Clause 60(7). MF/1 and both Institution of Chemical Engineers' model forms also provide for the contractor to be able to stop work if payment is not made within the prescribed period, after giving notice. Any increased costs that might accrue are to the employer's account. The Institution of Chemical Engineers' model forms give the contractor the right to terminate the contract after four months' suspension of work due to non-payment. MF/1 gives the contractor the right, on giving notice, to terminate the contract whether or not he has previously stopped work, but the grounds for termination, somewhat ambiguously, seem to be limited to delay in certification by the Engineer and to exclude delay in payment of a sum that has been certified.

12.2.4 Incentive Bonuses

Probably few would disagree with the proposition that an incentive bonus for the contractor to achieve or better the contract cost, time or plant performance targets, where sensible arrangements can be made, is likely to prove of benefit to a project. A lump sum contract naturally provides the contractor with incentive to achieve his contractual promises, and there is usually little difficulty in providing additional incentive to meet or improve on those promises by a scheme which allows a bonus to be earned. Of course, such arrangements carry the risk that the contractor's pursuit of the bonus may not always turn out to be in the best interests of the project. Careful design of the bonus scheme is necessary.

A reimbursable contract, on the other hand, is not a very suitable vehicle for the application of a bonus scheme of any description. Reimbursable contracts are usual where project definition is lacking, so that realistic estimates of cost and time are not available before contract award nor for some time afterwards. No bonus scheme could therefore be agreed until well after the contractor started work, but this is not in itself an insuperable obstacle, since a bonus is an offer of extra payment which may be made unilaterally by the employer at any time. Any possibility of reduced payment to the contractor would, of course, require his agreement. A bonus for early completion must obviously be arranged while the contractor retains the necessary influence over the completion date, but the problem with offering any bonus to a reimbursable contractor lies in the difficulty of controlling the additional expenditure incurred in his efforts to earn it. However, if early completion were sufficiently important to the employer, he might be prepared to pay not only a bonus but also the extra costs incurred by the contractor in accelerating progress. A bonus scheme for cost reduction would require the reimbursable contract to be converted to some form of target contract.

A bonus scheme that requires merely that contractual promises be achieved suffers the general disadvantage that the contractor is paid a second time for what he has already contracted to do (and possibly a third time in the case of a reimbursable contract where the employer pays the extra costs incurred by the contractor). In the case of a lump sum contract, if such a bonus scheme is a simple one that can be defined before award of contract—for example, a bonus paid on timely completion of the entire plant—the contractor may take it into account in his pricing of the job and so give the scheme something of the same monetary effect as liquidated damages. Even if the bonus scheme were to be based on a detailed programme that would not be available until after award of contract, it is in the employer's interests to explain his intentions to the contractor so that the latter may, if he deems it appropriate, take his chances of earning a bonus into account in pricing his tender.

The employer's project manager should be clear, however, that a bonus scheme cannot have a very great effect on the contract. No incentive bonus will make the contractor's objectives identical with the employer's, though it is intended to bring them closer together, and almost any bonus will tend to distort progress—the contractor will pursue the bonus even though this may, in the event, not be in the best interests of the project. Naturally, the larger the bonus, the greater the risk of such distortion, and the employer's project manager must judge the level of bonus carefully—sufficient to motivate the contractor to earn it, but not enough to swamp all other considerations. A bonus total in the region of 5 to 10% of the contractor's in-house costs might be considered appropriate. Bonus arrangements also operate in a narrow band close to the desired value of their criterion—cost, time or plant performance—and once outside that band, cease to have any effect. Once the possibility of earning bonus is extinguished, the scheme is dead. Thus, while they are a useful adjunct to a project, incentive bonuses cannot make a good contract out of a bad one, nor should they be so large as to have a disproportionate influence on how the work is done.

The essential characteristics of any bonus scheme are that the bonusable event or events should be:

- clearly ascertainable and measurable;
- of real benefit to the employer;
- substantially under the control of the contractor;

Thus a bonus scheme which involved the contractor in the employer's business by, for example, giving him a share of any extra profits earned by early completion, is not recommended. It would not be possible for the contractor to assess either the probability of a profit or its likely level, and his involvement in a business about which he knew nothing and which he could not influence would be entirely inappropriate.

Incentive bonuses aimed at reducing costs, for example shared under-run, have the obvious danger of encouraging under-specification. Bonuses relating to completion may be difficult to arrange except in the simple case of a single bonus on final completion. Where the employer is to commission the plant, such a simple bonus scheme will not serve, since the employer will require completion in differently timed stages and will wish the incentive to apply to all of them. Nor will the opportunity to base a bonus scheme on a single achievement be available if the contractor is responsible only for design and procurement. In this case, the contract again has many end-points—delivery of the materials and equipment to site, completion of the various parts of the design and so on. The employer may arrange to pay bonuses on the completion of a number of key events—chosen for their intrinsic importance or because they signal the completion of a number of significant activities in the network. Such a bonus scheme would have to be based on a detailed planning network that would be completed and agreed only after award of contract, and what could be arranged might be limited if the contractor pushed too hard to agree a plan which made it easy for him to earn bonuses. Of greater difficulty for the employer in a case where there is a number of separate bonuses to be earned, is that he requires all the bonusable activities to be completed on time, yet the whole plant may be delayed by delay to just one of them, in which case he has paid most of the bonuses for no benefit. On the other hand, if all the bonusable events, often referred to as milestones, have to be achieved before any bonus is payable, failure to achieve one milestone would vitiate the whole arrangement.

There is no complete solution to this problem, but a partial answer is for the bonus paid for achievement of a milestone to be related to the total number of milestones so far achieved. Each successive milestone achieved would carry a larger bonus than the previous one. Thus, if there were, say, eight milestones there would also be a table of eight bonuses of increasing value. The first milestone achieved would qualify the contractor for the payment of the smallest bonus in the list, the second achievement for the next smallest and so on. If the contractor achieved, say any six of the eight milestones he would receive the first six bonuses, forfeiting the two largest. This scheme, while it does not entirely meet the point made in the previous paragraph, at least recognises that for the employer there is value in the sheer number of milestones achieved.

It may also sometimes be considered desirable to introduce a bonus scheme specifically to influence delivery of equipment and materials. Such a delivery incentive plan may be aimed at speeding the contractor's performance in specifying, ordering and expediting, or may be aimed at the performance of, and offer bonuses directly to, sub-contractors and suppliers. It would be impracticable, in such an arrangement, to cover more than the most important plant items. The problem for the employer is that such a scheme would hardly be considered necessary except in periods of high industrial activity, when few delivery promises are likely to be met, and it may be difficult to be assured of deriving any benefit from the selection of relatively few items for special treatment.

No bonus scheme will retain its effect if the contract departs substantially from plan, but the effect can be extended if, as well as bonuses for early completion, the contractor is liable for liquidated damages if he is late. However, once the contractor has incurred the maximum liability for delay in completion, he will be guided by other considerations, notably that of minimising his own costs, though he will still have a common law obligation to complete in a reasonable time. If this does not suit the employer, the schemes for bonus payments and liquidated damages might have to be revised and the employer might find himself offering a bonus for late completion.

12.2.5 Liquidated Damages

The parties to a contract can agree beforehand the sums that are to be payable by the offending party in the event of specified breaches of contract. Such sums represent the full liability of the offending party for the breaches in question and are termed liquidated damages. They are held to be especially appropriate where the actual loss would be difficult to assess, or to prove. In the event of one of the specified breaches occurring, the injured party has the right to the appropriate liquidated damages without having to prove, or even suffer, damage. The probability of the offending party having to pay damages following breach is therefore much greater where the damages are liquidated: if they are not, the injured party has to sue to recover damages at large, with the concomitant expense and difficulty of proving the loss he has suffered.

Because liquidated damages clauses can act harshly if the amount to be paid is greatly in excess of the loss suffered, and because, if they are struck down, the employer still has a remedy in an action for general damages, the courts interpret such clauses strictly, construing any ambiguities against the employer. To be enforceable, liquidated damages must be genuine pre-estimates of the likely damage. The courts would rule that such damages were unenforceable because they were a penalty, that is to say, with the purpose not of compensating the innocent party for his loss but of forcing the offending party to perform his obligations, where they were 'extravagant and unconscionable in amount in comparison with the greatest loss that could conceivably have been proved to have followed the breach', although there are no reported UK cases of this happening in building contracts. There would also be a presumption, but capable of rebuttal, that payment of the same amount for a number of different breaches would be penal. Logically, of course, liquidated damages struck down as excessive, and hence forming a penalty, impose an upper limit well above the general damages that may subsequently be recovered.

The exigencies of competition apart, it is difficult to see why any contractor should agree to be liable for liquidated damages as described above, unless he could increase his price. He would be accepting a much higher probability of having to pay damages for no compensating advantage. Certainly, few engineering contracts, and certainly not the typical process plant contract, employ liquidated damages in quite this way. It is not in the interests of business efficiency for the contractor to be liable for the whole of the employer's potential loss, since the premium he would seek to include in his price would almost certainly be higher than the price the employer, with his larger financial base, would be willing to pay. Liquidating the estimated loss would merely increase the risk for the contractor and would demand an even higher premium. The efficient course is for the contractor's liability to be limited to an amount which relates to his beneficial interest in the contract, which would usually be very substantially less than the employer's potential loss. And since it is possible for the largest enterprise to be disrupted by the failure or want of a small component—a kingdom lost for want of a nail— potential sub-contractors and suppliers of equipment and materials would refuse the generally smaller contracts offered them unless their liability was limited.

If the contractor's liability is to be limited to a level much below the employer's potential loss, liquidated damages which are a genuine pre-estimate of the employer's loss can hardly be a contract feature except, perhaps, in the case of damages for delay, by limiting the duration of loss-making for which the contractor would be liable. Common practice in process plant design and construction is to agree liquidated damages at levels related not to the employer's potential loss but to some approximate proportion of the contractor's fees, or expected profits. Limitation of his liability in this way is the contractor's reward for accepting the greater probability of having to pay damages. Both parties understand the liquidated damages to be an incentive for the contractor to meet his obligations rather than an opportunity for the employer to recover his loss, but in all other respects they are intended to operate as liquidated damages.

In the nature of things, a purported liquidated damages clause in which the sums involved are much less than a genuine pre-estimate of the employer's loss will not often be tested in the courts. There are two possible sets of circumstances. The first is where the liquidated damages are much less than a genuine pre-estimate of the employer's loss, and are also much less than his actual loss. The employer might then seek to have the liquidated damages set aside as a penalty and to recover damages at large. The courts have ruled in such a case, however, that the liquidated damages were not a penalty but a limitation of liability, and since the actual loss exceeded the limit of liability, the general damages recoverable would be the same as the originally agreed level of liquidated damages. The second set of circumstances would be where the liquidated damages, though much less than the best estimate of the employer's expected loss would have produced at the time of contract award, were more than the employer's actual loss. In a process plant project, where optimism often rules at the start, such circumstances are not too difficult to envisage—in respect of damages for delay, all it needs is for the expected market for the product not to materialise when expected. In such a case, it would be difficult for the contractor to argue for the liquidated damages to be set aside as not being a genuine pre-estimate. The facts would merely show the difficulty of making an accurate prior assessment, and it seems probable that the liquidated damages would stand.

In process plant contracts, liquidated damages clauses are most often encountered for failure to meet guarantees of plant performance. Liquidated damages for delays in plant completion may be difficult to provide for in a construction contract where, as is common, completion in stages (by systems) is required. The detail of these stages, of which there may be as many as fifty for a major plant, are not usually defined when the contract is awarded, so that the required timings of completion, and any dependent liquidated damages liabilities, can be specified only in outline, leaving the detail to be agreed later. Typically, all the stages would need to be completed for the plant to be of any benefit to the employer, so that individual sums attached to the separate systems, assuming that they were cumulatively less than the estimated cost of delay to the whole plant, would be of the nature of limitations of liability rather than pre-estimates of loss. For such a damages clause to be enforceable the employer might have to be able to show that any deviation from the schedule of staged completion dates would delay the plant as a whole by an equivalent time. Consideration of staged completion will not usually affect liquidated damages clauses in turnkey contracts for design, supply, construction and commissioning, nor in individual supply sub-contracts, and many construction sub-contracts will be affected little, if at all.

As an incentive against delay in completion, liquidated damages clauses operate in much the same way as a bonus for early completion (and where the contract provides for both liquidated damages and bonus, these are sometimes mirror images of each other, though this is entirely a matter for the parties). Limited liquidated damages, like a bonus, have effect only over their operating range. The contractor who has incurred damages up to his contractual limit may well decide that he will henceforward work to complete the contract at minimum cost to himself, although he has still a common law obligation to complete in a reasonable time, and will be liable for unlimited damages if he does not. If this is not to the employer's liking, he will have to offer the contractor new incentives. The Institution of Mechanical Engineers' model form MF/1 provides for a limit on the contractor's liability for damages for any further delay he causes after the liquidated damages have been fully incurred: either a stated sum, or if no sum is specified, that part of the contract price attributable to the uncompleted plant.

Since the courts will interpret a liquidated damages clause strictly against the employer, traps abound for the unwary. The contract must contain a clear mechanism for calculating the damages payable. If the calculation of liquidated damages is not absolutely unambiguous, the courts may void for uncertainty. Care must be taken in defining exactly how the level of damages varies with the period of delay, or with faults in performance, and in a project where sectional completion is possible, with the extent of completion. For example, in a case where the liquidated damages payable varied with the extent of completion, the provision of a minimum level of liquidated damages (and which made it possible for the damages payable to exceed the pre-estimate) was held to make these a penalty. Thus it would be sensible to specify a minimum level only if the contract documents included sufficient detail to show that this was a genuine pre-estimate of the minimum loss the employer would suffer. Based on similar reasoning, liquidated damages which related only to total completion have been held to be penal where the employer was able to take over and make beneficial use of part of the plant.

Liquidated damages for delay must run from a contractually determined date, so that if the contractor were to be given an extension of time for a reason, however justified, that was not provided for in the contract conditions, the damages clause would fail. Where notice is required of the intention to recover liquidated damages for delay, an extension of time given after the notice was issued would require its re-issue. The problems of extensions of time being given after liquidated damages have started to run have been referred to earlier. A contractor who is late in completion and liable to pay liquidated damages may still recover for increases in material and labour costs during the over-run period if the contract has a fluctuation clause allowing this, since the liquidated damages are taken to be an estimate of the employer's total costs and therefore to include such increases. The contractor would not be entitled to recover for such increased costs where the damages were not liquidated. In the case of breach by the contractor allowing the employer to repudiate the contract, the employer would be entitled to recover liquidated damages up to the date of termination and damages at large thereafter, subject to the possible operation of any clause limiting liability.

Care is needed with model forms of contract. The JCT 80 model form contains an appendix to be completed with the agreed amount of liquidated damages. Entering £NIL in the appendix has been held to mean, not that damages were to be at large, which might have been thought the employer's intention, but that no damages, liquidated or not, were payable.

12.3 VARIATIONS

In most reimbursable contracts, there will be little need to address the subject of variations. Such a contract will not usually be based on a well-defined project scope, and where there is no initial definition, a variation from it can hardly be identified. In any event, since the employer is paying for everything that is done (with the possible exception, in theory, of the correction of design errors) the contractor does not have to establish that a variation has been requested in order to be paid for the work it involves. If, however, the reimbursable contractor has obligations to meet programme, or as regards the plant performance, then it will be necessary to identify and deal with any variations which justify an extension of time or a revision to the plant performance criteria. It may also be thought that a system of variation orders might help discipline the process of project execution, but there will usually be little practical difference between a variation order and an Engineer's instruction.

In a lump sum process plant contract, provision for variations is essential because, unless the employer is completely passive, it is most unlikely that any contract could be executed without variations being required. They arise either from changes to the initial project scope on which the contractor tendered, or from changes to previously approved documentation, or possibly from unforeseen conditions or events. Of course, a change is only a variation if the cost incurred by the contractor, or the contract completion date, or the plant performance, varies as a result. It is for the contractor to establish his claim for any extra, and usually for the employer to pursue any saving.

A process plant contract that includes the execution of design must provide for design work to continue while the processes of identification, establishment, estimating, negotiation and agreement of the variation are undertaken. No project can be successfully executed if work has to stop to agree every change. The contract should therefore provide for the following:

(1) Definition of a variation as a change affecting cost, time or plant performance which is approved by the Engineer, who alone has the right to require or approve a variation, with or without first obtaining a quotation for it or agreeing any of its contractual implications.

The contract may also attempt to specify some matters which will not give rise to a variation: defects in the design services or in materials or equipment which are the fault of the contractor or his sub-contractors; the contractor's failure to comply with the Enquiry, the normal process of design development and iteration, correction of the contractor's errors and omissions, notwithstanding that the Engineer's approval may have been given. The contract will not usually specify matters which might give rise to a variation, but clearly, changes to the employer's requirements as set out in the Enquiry are in this category. Approval by the Engineer is a key event: subsequent change initiated by him will be a variation if it results in extra cost, delays the completion date or affects plant performance,.

(2) The contractor's right to propose variations and the Engineer's obligation to consider and respond to such proposals. The Institution of Chemical Engineers' model form for lump sum contracts provides that refusal by the Engineer to agree to a contractor's proposed variation aimed at eliminating a hazard must, if the contractor disputes the refusal, be referred to an Expert whose decision is final. The contractor's right to propose variations is not strictly necessary, since nothing can prevent the contractor making whatever representations he wishes to make. The contractor may indeed propose variations with a view to achieving design improvements, but he will more frequently claim that some part of the work already in progress should be considered a variation. In a contract for a complex process plant, variations often arise, not as the result of deliberate action by the Engineer or the contractor, but as unconsidered consequences of decisions or events.

(3) Provision for the adjustment, by agreement between the Engineer and the contractor, of the contract price, or completion date, or plant performance requirements, as a result of a variation. There is really no sensible way to proceed other than by negotiation and agreement on valuation. In a process plant contract which includes design, the contractor may be required to perform what he considers to be additional work without knowing what, if any, additional payment or time he will receive, and in circumstances when measurement and valuation of the extra work can be very difficult and to some extent subjective. It would be unreasonable to allow the Engineer untrammelled powers to decide the value: this would only lead to later dispute. The Institution of Chemical Engineers' model form for lump sum contracts provides that any dispute on the valuation of variations may be referred to an Expert whose decision would be final.

The contract may well specify those factors which must be taken into consideration in valuing the variation: the work necessary to investigate and estimate for it; the net increase or decrease in the cost of design and procurement services; the change in cost of materials and equipment and in construction costs. It may also require the contractor to use his best endeavours to estimate and agree the value of a variation before work starts, and in any event to produce a quotation within twenty-eight days, say, of the variation being established.

Some model forms of contract impose limits on the variations which the contractor may be required to undertake. While some of these restrictions may be entirely reasonable: that the contractor should not be required to breach any other obligation of his, or to breach any protected right, or to do work of a different kind; few employers would be comfortable with a restriction on the net total value of the variations that he could require—15% or 25% of the original contract price are typical figures. In the case of process plant projects, such figures are often exceeded.

Control and management of variations is a crucial feature in the success or failure of the project. Minimising them is the first essential, managing them efficiently only the second, because however well the variation process is managed, the original objectives of a contract cannot be met if there is gross change during its execution.

12.4 COMPLETION AND TAKEOVER

This will affect only contracts which include construction. The final sequence of events on site varies with the extent of the contractor's responsibilities but is typically as follows:

- Construction
  - Erection completed: completion tests passed.
  - Engineer signs certificate of substantial completion.
  - Conditioning work completed.
  - Contractor provides written undertaking to finish any outstanding work during the defects liability period.
  - Engineer issues takeover certificate: defects liability period begins: half retention money released.
- Commissioning
  - Pre-commissioning: including water trials, trials of rotating equipment.
  - Commissioning: chemicals introduced into the plant.
- Operation:
  - Performance tests passed: possible release of half of remaining retention money.

– Defects liability period ends: release of remaining retention money.

Definition of the end-point of the contractor's work is complicated by the nature of the conditioning and commissioning procedures. Conditioning work consists of operations such as cleaning, flushing, blowing, leak tests, instrument loop checking and calibration, and electrical checks. It must be supervised, or at the very least monitored, by the commissioning team, and will undoubtedly detect errors and omissions which the contractor must correct. The contract must clearly define the contractor's responsibility. In a lump sum construction contract, conditioning could be included in the quoted price; in a re-measure and value, or a schedule of rates, contract it must be done at day-work rates. Not all of the work fits easily into individual sub-contracts for the separate engineering disciplines, since it is of the essence of the conditioning activity that it proves the plant as a whole.

Commissioning of a major process plant is usually done in stages, by systems, of which there may be as many as fifty. The conditioning work must then also be phased. These stages will not often be defined when contracts are let and once commissioning starts, the remaining construction work is likely to be hampered by the safe working procedures required when construction is performed adjacent to live systems. It is evident, therefore, that in many instances it will be difficult to fix liability for the timing of completion on the contractor. At one extreme, the contractor responsible for design, construction and commissioning of the whole plant may reasonably accept liability for the timing of the complete plant. At the other, individual trades sub-contractors may accept liability for mechanical completion of their work, if it is sufficiently defined when contracts are placed, but this will not include the conditioning work which they will perform, if at all, reimbursably. Liquidated damages for delays in plant completion are unlikely to be possible in contracts which fall between these extremes of scope. If the contractor were responsible for design and construction, but the employer for commissioning, the complicated interface represented by a phased commissioning procedure, even assuming it could be defined at contract award, added to the interference with the contractor's work likely to be caused by it, would make liquidated damages liability difficult. A contract for the construction only of a complete plant would be constrained, not only by this interface problem at completion, but by the incomplete state of the design at contract award consequent upon overlapping of design and construction—an invariable feature of process plants.

Whatever the liabilities of the contractor for the timing of completion, the contract must provide for the following:

(1) The contractor to notify the Engineer when the plant, or a specified part of it, is completed and ready for inspection and completion testing, together with a proposed programme.

(2) If the Engineer is satisfied with the inspection and completion testing, for him to sign a certificate of substantial completion, accompanied by a reservation list of minor items on which work remains to be done.

(3) On satisfactory completion of the items on the reservation list, or the receipt of the contractor's written undertaking to complete certain items during the defects liability period, and the completion of the specified conditioning work, the Engineer to sign a takeover certificate.

12.5 CONTRACTOR'S LIABILITIES

12.5.1 Exclusion Clauses

Some mention has already been made of exclusion clauses. All engineering contracts contain such clauses, which limit or exclude the liability of the contractor for certain breaches of the contract. They are as fundamental to process plant contracts as is the limited liability company to trade and industry, for rarely would a contractor be willing to take on an unlimited liability for breach of a major process plant contract. Such liability would normally far exceed his expectation of profit, and the price he would exact if he were to assume it would be correspondingly large, especially given the limited financial resources of the typical engineering contractor. Few employers would consider it economic for the contractor to take all the risk of a major process plant contract. Limitations of the contractor's liability, which define some of the boundaries of the bargain between the parties, are therefore almost always agreed. Just as much as the technical specification, these agreed limits of liability define the contractor's offer: what he is prepared to do for the contract price.

It is, of course, open to the parties to agree whatever allocation of risk best suits them. The contract is a commercial bargain as well as a legal one and the parties will usually choose to allocate the liabilities in the most efficient, that is to say in the cheapest, way. The various model forms of contract allocate risk between the parties in ways which have been found generally acceptable to the majority of employers and contractors, and it is sometimes claimed on behalf of one or other model form, that a major advantage is its fair allocation of risk and responsibilities. This is not, of course, the case. The acceptance of liability is a saleable commodity like any other: it has its price, which is ultimately determined by supply and demand, and no one division of risk is 'fairer' than any other. In general, though, both employer and contractor will believe that a sharing of the risks between them will produce the most efficient bargain.

However, in dividing the risk between them, the parties must have regard to the attitude of the courts to exclusion clauses, and to the statutory control provided by the Unfair Contract Terms Act 1977. Prior to the passing of this

Act, the courts had no power to strike down an exclusion clause on grounds of unreasonableness, and traditionally took a restrictive attitude to such clauses. They were construed *contra proferentem*, that is to say against the party seeking to rely upon them, with the narrowest possible interpretation being placed on the words to make sure that they were effective only if they specifically and unambiguously dealt with the particular breach. An exclusion clause is, to this way of thinking, a defence to an action for breach of contract which would otherwise lie. The implication of this view is that the contractor has an unlimited obligation for the performance of his contract which he has sought to limit by use of the exclusion clause. It need hardly be said that this cannot be so when the limitation of liability was a precondition for the acceptance of any obligation at all by the contractor. It is via the exclusion clause that the contractor has defined his contractual obligations: there can hardly be other and greater obligations unless they exist independently and outside the contract, and this is clearly not the case. In recent years, however, the attitude of the courts has mellowed, and effect will be given to any clause whose meaning is reasonably clear. Part of this relaxation is a tendency to treat clauses which limit liability with less suspicion than those which exclude it altogether; this obviously demands that the courts apply a test of reasonableness in order to classify very low limits of liability as tantamount to exclusion.

There remain the two areas of negligence and fundamental breach where the courts have developed special rules of construction. In the case of negligence, the courts have long considered it unlikely that anyone would agree that liability for this should be excluded or limited. This, one imagines, would be the position of most employers. Broadly, a clause which purports to exclude liability for the contractor's negligence must use that actual word, or an unequivocal synonym of it, if it is to be effective. It is possible for a clause to be drafted widely enough to cover negligence without referring to it specifically: expressions such as 'any act or omission' or 'any damage whatsoever' have been held to be effective, but the courts will look at all the circumstances before construing a phrase in this way.

Fundamental breach is a breach of contract so serious that it denies the injured party substantially the whole of the benefit of it. Until quite recently it was considered that such a breach destroyed the contract and with it any exclusion or limitation clause. The view of the courts has changed in recent years, and it is now clear that, in the event of fundamental breach and termination of the contract by the injured party, the contract continues to govern the offending party's liabilities. Whether liability is excluded or limited depends on the wording of the relevant clause: whether it covers the breach in question.

The Unfair Contract Terms Act 1977 prevents any contracting party from excluding or limiting his liability for death or personal injury resulting from his negligence, and allows liability for loss or damage resulting from negligence to be excluded or limited only in so far as this is reasonable. The Institution of Mechanical Engineers MF/1, which of all model forms is probably the most protective of the contractor's interests, does limit the contractor's liability for loss and damage caused by his negligence: the reasonableness of this would have to be tested on a case-by-case basis. The Unfair Contract Terms Act also requires that, where the contract is on the offending party's standard terms of business, any exclusion or limitation of liability for fundamental breach, or for breach of contract which does not involve negligence, must be reasonable. It seems unlikely that any of the engineering contracting industry's model forms would be regarded as the contractor's standard terms and therefore subject to control in this way. Such a form is the result of negotiation between different sides of industry, and even if the employer could reasonably argue that he was not represented in the negotiations, the contractor could certainly claim that he did not control the drafting of the terms. The model form may well be modified sufficiently for it to be considered non-standard, and in any event, it is usually the employer, perhaps with independent professional advice, who will choose the form of contract, even if this amounts to no more than a choice between different model forms.

12.5.2 Contract Liabilities

In a lump sum contract for a complete process plant, where the contractor is responsible for engineering design, procurement and perhaps for construction, the liabilities that are commonly placed on the contractor can conveniently be considered under six heads reflecting the way in which they are usually grouped:

(1) Errors and omissions in design
(2) Plant defects
(3) Plant performance
(4) Programme
(5) Specific undertakings and indemnities
(6) Loss, damage and injury

The contract will set out to define the contractor's liability separately in each of these areas, In addition, there are terms which may be implied into the contract by law. As has been previously remarked, in drafting a process plant contract, it is important to keep in mind the distinction between the obligation to perform remedial work and the liability to pay for it. Generally speaking, the employer will wish the contractor to be obligated to do everything necessary to complete the plant to specification, including the correction of defects, irrespective of fault. Paying for the cost of correction may be a different matter. Unless this distinction is clearly recognised, it is all too easy inadvertently to omit the requirement for the contractor to correct defects which are not his fault.

Errors and omissions in design

Almost invariably, the design contractor will accept unlimited liability for correcting errors and omissions in his designs, irrespective of whether or not the design has been 'approved' by the Engineer. This is not an especially onerous liability for the contractor, since it requires him merely to provide some extra design man-hours in the event that correction is necessary.

Plant defects

Correction of defects in the plant itself is a much more expensive business than the correction of designs on paper. Plant defects may be categorised as follows:

(1) Those caused directly by faults in the performance of the contractor's own services, for example, equipment wrongly designed by the contractor, or purchased by him against an incorrect specification.
(2) Defects caused consequentially by faults in the contractor's services, for example, the need to modify other parts of the plant as a result of the provision of defective equipment, or its correction.
(3) Defects in materials and equipment which are the faults of their suppliers.
(4) Defects in other parts of the plant caused consequentially by defects in materials and equipment which are their suppliers' faults.

The contractor's liability for correcting these defects will vary with the scope of his contract and the magnitude of his beneficial interest in it. The contractor responsible for design, supply and construction, and who was also a major supplier, for example, a manufacturer of steam-turbines or boilers who acted as the main contractor for a power station, would be expected to carry the maximum liability. Typically, he would remedy defects in all the above categories at his own expense with no, or a very high, limit of liability. His arrangements with his suppliers would be his own affair, but he would be able to seek recompense from them for defects that were directly their fault. It is unlikely that any supplier would accept liability for consequential defects. The contractor with similar responsibilities for design, supply and construction but who was not himself a supplier, would typically undertake similar liabilities but within a lower limit, recognising his much smaller financial stake in the contract.

The contractor responsible only for design and procurement services who purchased as the employer's agent would be liable only for the first two categories of defects, where he himself was at fault. It would be in the interests of business efficiency for him to have a relatively low limit of liability commensurate with his relatively small beneficial interest in the contract. If to his design and procurement services responsibilities were added the supply of materials and equipment as principal, the additional liabilities he could be expected to accept would depend on the nature of the contract. The supply of equipment and material for a lump sum price would typically be accompanied by the acceptance of liability which was unlimited, or subject to a high limit, for the correction of defects in those supplies. He would probably not be expected, however, to carry any liability for the consequences of those defects in other parts of the plant. If the contractor were reimbursed at cost for the purchase as principal of materials and equipment, his liability for correcting defects in those supplies might be limited to whatever he could recover from suppliers, and he would have no liability for the consequences of those defects. As would be the normal practice in cases of reimbursable supply, the employer would wish to retain control over the terms and conditions of the supply sub-contracts.

As well as an upper limit on total liability in any category, the question may arise of a lower limit of value for any one defect, below which the contractor would escape liability. The majority by number, and probably by value, of the errors in the design of a process plant will be minor dimensional errors, mainly in pipework and its supports, which will require site modification. If the contractor is responsible for construction he will obviously correct these as the work proceeds. A contractor providing only design and procurement services and with no site presence may ask to be excused liability for the cost of correcting small defects, below a specified level of cost, on the grounds of inefficient working. It could be argued in support of this, that process plant construction is not often sufficiently well organised for these small errors to be credibly distinguished and costed, and even where this is the case, it may still be necessary to resist counter-claims of inaccurate setting out and location of equipment. On the other hand, if such claims can be made successfully, they may well accumulate to exceed in total the contractor's limit of liability. To agree a lower limit for each defect below which there was no liability could therefore be a significant concession.

The extent of work performed by the process plant contractor as opposed to that done by his sub-contractors can affect the protection enjoyed by the employer. For example, if the process plant contractor with a modest limit of liability carried out both the thermal rating and the mechanical design of heat exchangers (which is sometimes done in order to speed up the provision of drawings for plant layout purposes), the employer's recourse in the event of a mechanical design fault would be against the contractor and limited by the terms of the main contract. If, on the other hand, the supplier of the equipment carried out the mechanical design, then any design fault would be the supplier's who would be carrying the more complete liability appropriate to a supply contract. Sub-contracting can sometimes, depending on the terms of the relevant contracts, provide the employer with greater recourse than if the work had been done by the main contractor.

Plant performance

For the contractor who is also the manufacturer, a deficiency in plant performance is usually treated as a defect which the contractor must correct, as would any other equipment supplier. Where the contractor is providing a complete plant but has manufactured none of it, a different approach is usually appropriate in order to ensure a sensible relationship between his liability and beneficial interest. A further consideration is that the employer may well prefer to keep the plant on line and accept some inefficiency rather than have operation disrupted by what may be lengthy periods of modification and trial. It is usual therefore to agree liquidated damages for defective plant performance but, as previously discussed, at levels that reflect the contractor's stake in the contract rather than the employer's probable loss. Of course, the nature of the contractor's guarantees of performance depends on the extent of his design responsibilities. If the process technology is not provided by contractor, he will be responsible merely for the physical capability of the plant: its hydraulics; perhaps the physical condition of the product, for example the moisture content of a solid product; the plant's consumption of utilities. Process guarantees will then be given by the provider of the process technology and included in the licensing agreement.

Guarantees of performance require that tests be made to prove them, and it would be sensible to provide that, where there is a separate licensor, any performance test may simultaneously prove the guarantees of licensor and contractor. The requirements for the performance tests can conveniently be outlined in an appendix to the contract and any further detail provided in a procedure. It is usual for a process plant guarantee to relate to a period, say seventy-two hours, of continuous full load operation with the specified feedstocks, output and utilities. Provision may need to be made for departures from feedstock specifications, and the method of testing and analysing results must be agreed. It is usual to provide that the tests must be carried out during the defects period, typically within one year of the employer taking over the plant. It may also be provided that the contractor may request a test sixty days after the plant first makes specification product, and that the employer must conduct the test within thirty days thereafter. This should generally satisfy the employer's wish not to carry out tests until the plant has attained a condition of average fouling, while not unduly delaying the test for the contractor. The employer may also have special test requirements, for example, tests of important individual processing units, or plant tests at partial load.

In practice, performance tests on major process plants, although always provided for by the contract, are often waived. They are expensive and disruptive and the design feedstock for the plant may not be available. With modern instrumentation, the employer can obtain a very good assessment of the plant's performance from its day-to-day operation. If business is good, he will not want to disrupt operation by making the test: if it is bad he may have nowhere to store the product that would be made, and no wish to incur the expense of a test. The employer will therefore usually wish operation to take precedence over testing (unlike the provisions of the Institution of Chemical Engineers' model form for lump sum contracts).

Programme

Clearly, delay in plant completion cannot be corrected and damages are the only remedy. These are usually liquidated and again are usually fixed relative to the contractor's hoped-for profit rather than to the employer's loss. The problems of staged completion are addressed in the sections on liquidated damages and completion and takeover.

Specific undertakings and indemnities.

In any contact there will be specific undertakings and indemnities, probably applying to both parties. These will cover such matters as secrecy and confidentiality undertakings and patent indemnities. They will not usually be subject to any limit of liability.

Loss, damage and injury

Considerations of loss and damage to property and personal injury are inseparable from insurance considerations. The contract must allocate the risks and specify who must insure, with the object of dealing with these matters in the most effective and economic way. The subject is discussed in more detail later together with insurance.

Terms implied by law

The courts will assume that the contracting parties intended to operate the contract in accordance with normal usage and custom unless it is otherwise specified and, if necessary for the efficacy of the contract, will imply into it terms such as timely possession of the site and timely transmission of instructions and information. The Sale of Goods Act 1979 provides that goods must correspond to any sample or description, be of merchantable quality, and fit for their intended purpose, provided that the purpose was made known to the seller and his skill and judgement relied upon. The Supply of Goods and Services Act 1982 also provides that services must be carried out with reasonable care and skill, in reasonable time and at reasonable cost unless otherwise stipulated. These implied terms may be negatived by agreement, subject to the Unfair Contract Terms Act 1977.

Overall limit of liability

It is usual for the contract to specify the total liability of the contractor for plant defects, plant performance and delay rather than to provide for separate limits for each. For the same total limit of liability, this is obviously in the employer's interests. An overall limit of liability that is separately stated is also likely to be clearer and to provoke less argument than figures buried at various places in the text. As previously discussed, efficient allocation of risk will usually require that the contractor's liability is limited so that it bears some relation to his hoped-for profit. He will endeavour to reflect his liability in his price, and the extent to which he is able to do this will depend on the strength of the competition for the contract. It hardly needs emphasising that a high limit of liability is not in the employer's interest if the contractor is able simply to add the whole of the relevant amount into his contract price.

Defects period

The usual contractual provision is for the contractor to continue to be responsible, at his own expense, for the correction of defects for a period of twelve months after takeover, and for half of the retention money to be retained for this period. Any defect occurring during this time is subject to a further twelve months' defects period starting from the date of its correction. Similar terms are sought from suppliers, but most will offer only a twelve months' defects period starting from the date of delivery to site. In many cases, this means that the defects period for an item of equipment will expire before it is commissioned. It is sometimes possible to negotiate with a supplier a defects period that begins on takeover, providing that the equipment concerned is stored and serviced in accordance with the manufacturer's recommendations, and is inspected and corrected by the manufacturer at the employer's expense before it is commissioned. In the case of key rotating equipment, this may be well worth while.

12.6 LOSS AND DAMAGE, INJURY AND INSURANCE

A process plant project offers considerable risk of loss, damage and personal injury, and the potential financial consequences are great. The most common risks associated with work on the site may be itemised as follows:

(1) Direct loss and damage to the process plant under construction on the site, including materials and equipment to be incorporated in it.
(2) Direct loss and damage to any other property of the employer, not being part of the plant.
(3) Loss and damage to the property of third parties.
(4) Loss and damage to constructional plant.
(5) Injury to the contractor's employees.
(6) Injury to the employer's employees.
(7) Injury to other people unconnected with the project.

As well as managing his project so as to minimise such occurrences, the employer's project manager must see that insurance is arranged to cover the major part of them. The contract with the process plant contractor must therefore allocate first the risks and then the responsibility of insuring against them. The contract cannot, of course, affect the liability of the contractor or the employer to third parties for loss, damage or personal injury. In the vast majority of circumstances, the employer will not be liable to third parties for the acts or neglects of the contractor.

It is common for the scope of the contractor's liabilities to the employer to be widened beyond those which he would have in common law in order to establish a clear and simple situation. Should this approach be used, the contractor would be made responsible for making good, at his expense, any direct loss or damage to the process plant, howsoever this was caused, up until the time the plant was taken over by the employer. The contractor would also be made responsible for making good, at his expense, any direct loss or damage to the plant occurring during the defects period as a result of the contractor's acts. The contractor would also indemnify the employer against any claim for personal injury, or for direct loss or damage to any property of the employer (including the plant) or of third parties, except and to the extent that these claims arose from acts or neglects of the employer, his servants or agents or of any other contractor employed directly by the employer.

If the contractor is to provide these indemnities, it is necessary that he should be insured appropriately. Everyone has a statutory duty to insure against injury to, or death of, his own employees. It would also be expected that the contractor would insure his own constructional plant. As regards the remainder of the insurances required, it would usually be better for the employer rather than the contractor to be responsible for obtaining insurance, for several reasons. It would be unlikely that any particular contract would constitute the whole of a project, and the above list would not therefore cover all the insurable risks of the project. Other contractors will probably be engaged and the employer may also undertake some work himself. There will also be off-site hazards to insure against. The risks will thus extend beyond the bounds of any particular contract, and it will be easier to be certain that no risk is inadvertently left uninsured if the employer takes responsibility for obtaining insurance for the whole of the project. This will also help to avoid double insurance which, as well as incurring extra expense, could lead to dispute between insurance companies. The employer will probably have existing operations on the site and may have other projects under way there. If so, he would probably be able to extend his existing insurance policies to cover the new contract more cheaply than could otherwise be done. Insurance by the employer also gives greater security of performance: although a contract requiring the contractor to insure should also give the employer the right to inspect the policies and premium receipts, it is doubtful if many employers' project managers exercise this right. To the possibility, admittedly faint, of the contractor's failure to insure should be added that of a breach of condition of the insurance by the contractor. Only at a greenfield site where the employer has no existing installations and the contractor is responsible for all operations would it be appropriate for the contractor to be responsible for insurance of the works.

If, nevertheless, the contractor is to insure, the agreed minimum amounts which the insurance must cover in each of the relevant categories must be stated. Whoever is responsible for insuring, the employer would undertake not to claim against the contractor or his sub-contractors except insofar as the claim is covered by the insurance. Thus, if the employer were to insure, the contractor would have no interest in the extent to which the employer insured his own property and it would be necessary for the contract to state only the insured amounts for loss and damage to third party property and for personal injury. The insurance should always be in the joint names of employer, contractor and sub-contractors since this denies the insurance company the right of subrogation against any of those so insured: if one of the joint names by his negligence causes loss to another of the insureds, the insurance company cannot proceed against the negligent party to recover the payments it has had to make. There would be a number of risks not insured by the employer's insurances. These would be detailed in the contract and would usually include, for example, the cost of rectifying defects (but not the damage they might cause); constructional plant, the property of the contractor and his sub-contractors; liability insurable under employer's liability, motor, marine or aviation policies; the usual exclusions relating to war, government requisition and nuclear activities. It would be for the contractor to consider whether the financial ceiling provided for third party claims and personal injury was adequate, and to insure as appropriate to increase this and to cover other uninsured risks.

There are other project risks of loss and damage that must be insured against:

(1) The employer must insure against his own liability to third parties.

(2) Work in progress in the various manufacturers' works must be insured. Procurement contracts will usually be placed so that the property in the goods passes to the employer or the contractor, depending on who is the principal, as stage payments are made. In the UK, though not necessarily elsewhere, this eases the problems that would occur were the manufacturer to go into liquidation. However, it is usually arranged for risk in the goods to remain with the manufacturer until delivery, so it is for him to insure up to this point.

Particular problems may arise from the use of off-site pre-assembly methods, where materials and equipment are delivered, not to the construction site, but to the pre-assembly points. Where a pre-assembly point is the works of another manufacturer, the latter will usually take the risk in the materials and equipment delivered to him. Piping fabrication, in a major UK project usually divided between several fabricators and carried out in their various works, is a case in point. Where large-scale pre-assembly is undertaken on a site or sites established specially for the purpose, the employer or contractor will need to insure. In some projects a separate entrepôt or staging warehouse may be used to collect and marshal bulk materials prior to their issue for fabrication, and insurance must be considered for this.

Insurance is not, of course, the complete answer to every risk. In the case of piping material, for example, esoteric metallurgical requirements can inordinately extend the time required to replace a relatively inexpensive item by requiring a test history that starts with the ingot. In such a case, money would be better spent on preventing loss and damage rather than on insurance.

(3) Goods must be insured during their transport to site. Many suppliers of materials and equipment will be responsible for delivery to site and will retain the risk in the goods until they are safely off-loaded. The purchase conditions will require them to insure up to that point. Commonly, however, when manufacture is not in the country where construction is to take place, the manufacturer delivers to a specified point, possibly where containers are to be stuffed, or to the docks, and onward transport to site and the appropriate insurance is the responsibility of the contractor or employer. Where the project requires the transport of large and heavy loads, which may involve special ships, transhipment, movement by barge, specialised heavy road transport and the construction of temporary jetties, bridges and roads, the insurance implications must be carefully considered.

(4) The employer may wish to insure against losses incurred by delayed start-up due to accidents off-site, for example, affecting the transport of materials and equipment to the site, and on-site during construction.

(5) The employer must, of course, insure the plant from the date of takeover. This will be part of his normal operating procedures and not a project matter.

12.7 OTHER CONTRACTUAL ISSUES

12.7.1 Assignment and Sub-contracting

Assignment

For a party to a contract to transfer both his rights and his obligations to a third party requires a novation—effectively a new contract agreed by all three parties. Agreement of the parties to the original contract is clearly essential. The employer will have chosen the contractor for his experience and abilities and would not wish to see the contract transferred unilaterally to another who may lack these qualities, nor would the contractor wish to see the contract transferred to one who might lack the employer's financial resources.

However, common law allows a contracting party to transfer his contractual rights, as distinct from his obligations to another by assignment, subject to the provisions of the particular contract. Most contracts, including the model forms referred to in later chapters, restrict the assignment of rights by the contractor, except for money which becomes due to him, by requiring the prior agreement of the employer. Some contracts also similarly restrict assignment by the employer. If the project is externally financed, the financing institutions may well require the right to have the whole contract assigned to them in particular circumstances.

Sub-contracting

Sub-contracting involves no transfer of responsibility, merely vicarious performance of the work. The contractor remains as responsible for the acts and omissions of his sub-contractors as for his own acts and omissions. Even so, there are implicit limitations on how far the contractor can sub-contract. Without the consent of the employer he cannot, in common law, sub-contract the whole of the work, nor any part of it for which the employer has specifically chosen him for his expertise and experience. It seems likely that the latter would include, not only tasks which required highly specialised skills, but also the overall management of the work.

The contract may expressly limit or negate the contractor's right to sub-contract work without the prior agreement of the employer. However, few process plant contractors will directly perform the whole of the work for which they are responsible. The contractor's tender should explain the sub-contracting he intends—both his normal practice and any special arrangements he proposes.

This is necessary not only so that he may be certain that he has the employer's agreement to his proposals, but also because evaluation of the tender could be affected if the sub-contracting proposals were to result in costs being transferred from lump sum services to reimbursable materials.

All or most of the materials and equipment contained in the process plant will be obtained from suppliers or manufacturers, and the obligations of some of them will extend to installation on site including commissioning. This is well understood and the contract will not usually need to sanction this explicitly. The employer may, however, exercise some control over the suppliers to be used through the inclusion in the specifications of a list of approved vendors for important equipment, and may reserve some powers over the terms of such sub-contracts.

The fact that the contractor is responsible for the acts and omissions of his sub-contractors—nominated or not—as if they were his own acts or omissions does not mean that the employer's recourse is always unaffected by sub-contracting. In the design and supply of a heat exchanger, the main contractor may carry out the thermal design and leave it to the supplier to perform the mechanical design. Should the exchanger prove to be defective because of an error in the mechanical design, the terms of the sub-contract with the supplier will almost certainly require him to make it good at his expense and this benefit will be passed through to the employer via the main contract. Some main contractors, however, in order to expedite matters, themselves perform the mechanical design of heat exchangers. In the event of a defect in this design it is likely that the main contract will stop short of requiring the main contractor to do more than correct the design, leaving the employer to foot the bill for a new exchanger. Thus it is seen that the employer's contractual position is not necessarily weakened by sub-contracting—all depends on the terms of the contracts.

Employer selection of sub-contractors

For a number of reasons, the employer may wish to select sub-contractors for parts of the work. Major equipment, such as a large compressor with its drive and power recovery train, can be at the very heart of a process, which may be designed around and in conjunction with it. If the process is owned by the employer he may have carried out months or years of design and development work to integrate a particular configuration of equipment into his process, and in such a case he would wish to specify the supplier or at least to limit the number of potential suppliers. The same might be true of a large and complicated vessel such as a reactor. In other cases, the employer may be influenced by the need to match his existing equipment, so as to simplify operation and reduce the cost of spares. He may have begun to develop an order before contract award in order to save time. He will almost certainly have preferences based on his past experience. In process plant design and construction, the employer's selections will concern both suppliers of equipment and sub-contractors who provide services.

If the employer's selection of sub-contractors and suppliers is done before contract award, the contractor may satisfy himself as to the capability and reliability of those selected. He can obtain quotations from them (sometimes, this may be a matter of taking over a quotation already obtained by the employer) and can include these in his bid. The contractor's responsibility for the selected sub-contractors will be the same as if he had chosen them himself. He has a complete remedy if he objects to any proposed sub-contractor in that he can refuse to tender. It is common practice in process plant design and construction contracts to restrict the contractor to lists, provided in the Enquiry, of employer-approved sub-contractors for various functions and of suppliers for important items or particular types of equipment, any of whom the contractor may employ without question.

'Nomination' of sub-contractors as particularised in the Institution of Civil Engineers' Model Form of Conditions of Contract (ICE6), for example, is a different matter. This procedure is designed to deal with nomination of sub-contractors after contract award. The employer has no implied right to nominate sub-contractors after the contract has been placed, and this must therefore be conferred by express contractual terms. With post-contract nomination, the contractor's bid obviously cannot include the cost of the sub-contract, other than an employer-supplied estimate embodied in a 'Prime Cost Item'. To this the contractor adds the cost of his attendance on the sub-contractor and a percentage figure for his profit.

Broadly under ICE6, the contractor is not obliged to enter into a sub-contract with a nominee to whom he has reasonable objection, or who will not sub-contract on terms which enable the contractor to discharge his obligations to the employer, or who will not indemnify the contractor from claims arising in contract or in tort, or who will not provide security for proper performance or similar conditions on termination to those in the main contract. Once accepted, the contractor is fully responsible for the nominated sub-contractor except in the event of sub-contractor repudiation or default leading to termination. The employer will then be responsible in most cases for any extra cost and delay caused to the main contractor. The Institution of Chemical Engineers' model form for lump sum contracts (the Red Book) is even less favourable to the employer's interests and makes him responsible for extra cost and delay caused by any failure of the nominated sub-contractor to meet his obligations.

Post-contract nomination of sub-contractors seems often to cause difficulties and should be avoided if at all possible. If absolutely necessary, it should be restricted to sub-contractors of whom the employer has prior experience, in whom he has complete confidence, and who will provide a collateral warranty.

In a well-organised process plant contract, nomination should not be necessary. Where it is merely a matter of the employer having a preference for one sub-contractor rather than another to take responsibility for an identifiable part of the contract, this can and should be specified in the Enquiry. Only where part of the contract is undefined at the award stage should it be necessary to think in terms of Provisional Sums, Prime Cost Items and nominated sub-contractors. The employer can hardly expect the contractor to assume full responsibility for matters which are not properly defined, and is unlikely to be successful in any attempt to get him to do so. In many cases where nomination is used, the employer's contractual position may be no better—and may be worse—than if he had contracted directly with the nominee and employed the main contractor merely to co-ordinate the sub-contractor's work with his own.

12.7.2 Agent versus Principal

A common form of contract has the contractor responsible for providing design and procurement services and for supplying equipment and materials. The employer himself then manages the construction or, more especially in a foreign country, engages a local contractor for this. Frequently, the design and procurement services are provided on a lump sum basis with equipment and materials supply reimbursable. In such cases, it is possible for the contractor to purchase the equipment and materials either as agent for the employer, or as principal. Crudely speaking, the difference is that the contractor who acts as principal is liable for defects in equipment and materials supplied irrespective of fault, the contractor acting as agent is liable only where he is at fault. (A contractor providing reimbursable services might also agree to purchase as principal, but this is less common, since it would usually require him to assume a degree of liability for the supply greater than that for his own services.)

The employer needs to retain some influence over what is done. However the purchasing is to be carried out, he is likely to have provided a list of approved vendors for key items of equipment to which the contractor must pay heed. The contractor may add to the list with the employer's approval. (This is less restrictive than it might appear. There are relatively few manufacturers of sophisticated process plant equipment. The experienced contractor and employer are likely to have generated similar lists and the employer will welcome additions of manufacturers with proven capability and experience.) If the contractor purchases as principal, the employer may stipulate some key terms to be included in the conditions of purchase to be used (for example, concerning supplier warranties), and will require the right to participate in technical discussions with suppliers and, should enforcement of supplier warranties and guarantees become necessary, to have the right to have the supply contracts and associated rights of action assigned to him. The employer will, in any event, wish to approve the comparisons of tenders for the supply of materials and equipment, and it will also be to the contractor's advantage that he does this. Major considerations should be set out in the Conditions of Contract; procedural detail should be dealt with in the Co-ordination Procedure or in a Procurement Procedure.

The contractor purchasing as principal will buy the equipment and materials on his own behalf and then sell them on to the employer. Unless explicitly excluded, the Supply of Goods and Services Act 1982 will apply. This will require the contractor to supply goods which satisfy their specifications and which match any samples. It will also require him to supply goods which are fit for purpose if the purpose is made known to him and the employer is relying on his skill and judgement. The contractor will, in any event, be liable (within his contractual limits of liability) to the employer for any faults in the materials and equipment supplied.

Where the contractor purchases as agent, he places orders for and on behalf of the employer. The orders remain the employer's and he may control what is done. The employer will approve the terms and conditions of purchase, which may be the employer's own standard conditions or the contractor's, modified where necessary. The contractor purchasing as agent has no liability for the performance of suppliers except as provided for explicitly in the main contract. He will usually, however, be required to perform a number of actions aimed at getting the suppliers to meet their obligations.

It is necessary to be explicit about the work the contractor purchasing as agent must do. The contractor will ordinarily be responsible for all the work—enquiring for bids, negotiating and placing orders, progressing, inspecting and expediting, verifying and approving invoices—necessary for the equipment and materials to be delivered according to programme. This will form part of his lump sum for procurement services. The employer will also wish the contractor to have an obligation to pursue, short of litigation, any defects with suppliers and to get them rectified, and also to negotiate any claims the employer may have against the suppliers. Without such an explicit obligation, reputable contractors have been known to refuse to act once the plant was completed. Since such work is impossible to estimate accurately for in advance, it is usually considered appropriate for it to be reimbursable, i.e. to be treated as a variation. It should be noted, however, that if the contractor were purchasing as principal in a lump-sum contract for services, the cost of this work would be part of the lump sum, unless explicitly stated otherwise.

In the absence of anything to the contrary in the contract between them, the employer will be liable for any extra costs incurred by the contractor, purchasing as agent, as a result of a breach of contract by a supplier. The scope for breaches causing extra costs to the contractor is large and might include, for example, failure to design in accordance with the required standards, failure to meet programme, and errors and omissions in drawings. These costs are recoverable by the employer from the supplier and the employer would normally instruct the contractor to act on his behalf to recover them. Since there will usually be sums due to the supplier at this stage, and assuming the supplier contract allows for set-off, the employer would have a strong negotiating position. However, the employer would be liable to the contractor for the costs incurred by him in recovering, and would have to make up any shortfall there might be between the contractor's agreed claim and the recovery from the supplier.

Whether purchasing as agent or principal, the contractor must be reimbursed for the costs of materials and equipment. Where the contractor is agent, the employer has the option of paying the suppliers' invoices directly, after they have been verified and approved by the contractor. It is more likely that the contractor will act also as the employer's paying agent, in which case, as with the contractor who purchases reimbursably as principal, arrangements must be made for the money to pass. Where there are large amounts of foreign currencies, it must also be decided who is to obtain these. The aim will be that the contractor should neither gain nor lose through his reimbursable purchasing, and the usual procedure is for the contractor to inform the employer on a monthly basis of the amounts required, which are then paid by the employer into a bank account on which the contractor has drawing rights. The interest on any surplus in the account is the employer's, and the contractor can usually be relied upon not to pay invoices for which the money has not been provided. The detail of this may most conveniently be covered in a separate Accounting Procedure which, because it non-controversial, can be agreed after contract award.

For the employer letting a contract which includes reimbursable materials, there is much to be said for the contractor purchasing as principal. There is single-point responsibility and the employer does not himself have to pursue supplier defects individually. The employer is not liable for any extra costs caused to the contractor by supplier's default. Of course, the contractor's liability is controlled by his contract with the employer and the latter needs to make sure that he does not have lesser remedy than he would otherwise have had against the suppliers directly. In truth, the contractor's liability will not, in many cases, be especially onerous since he may be able to ensure that it is little or no greater than the total liability of his suppliers to him, save for supplier bankruptcy. Where the contractor's liability is no greater than that of his suppliers to him, the employer must understand what the situation will be if, as is likely, some supplier warranties expire before the plant is commissioned.

It is not, however, always possible to negotiate that the contractor purchases as principal. The bidders may refuse, or want to charge too much for assuming the liability. In some countries with a turnover tax, goods which the contractor supplies as principal are considered part of his turnover and hence are subject to tax in a way that his purchases as agent are not. For the major process operating company, the difference between the two arrangements may not be as great as might be at first thought. A major process company has an annual rate of purchasing very much greater than that of most contractors, and has very considerable purchasing power. Suppliers of process equipment are well aware of the influence that the major companies wield over their contractors whether purchasing as agent or principal, and will know that their hopes of repeat orders will depend on satisfying the employer. This is particularly true for major items and sophisticated equipment where the employer's influence may be all-important and where the technical dialogue may well be between the supplier and the process operating company, whatever the contractual situation. A small company with relatively few resources and little purchasing power will be in a different situation and may consider it most important that the contractor act as principal.

12.7.3 Suspension and Termination by the Employer

The employer needs the right to suspend or terminate the contract without cause so that he can respond to the changing commercial situation. During the long gestation period of a major project, demand for its products may change, recede or, in the limit, vanish altogether. A manufacturer cannot sensibly put himself in the position of being contractually bound to complete a plant he has no use for. Of course, the contractor will require payment for all work done and for his unavoidable extra costs resulting from the suspension or termination, and will require to be indemnified against all obligations, commitments and claims. The employer also requires the right to terminate the contract because of the contractor's default. For international contracts where there is risk of violently unsettled conditions affecting the project, both contractor and employer should have the right to terminate in the event of frustration of the contract.

Whatever the reason for termination, the employer must have the right to the work already done and available to the contractor, and the right to complete the plant, with or without the assistance of third parties.

12.7.4 Arbitration

Most of the standard forms of conditions of contract provide for disputes to be referred to arbitration. Some make additional or alternative procedures available such as adjudication (Joint Contracts Tribunal Sub-contract Form DOM/1), conciliation (Institution of Civil Engineers' Conditions of Contract 6th Edition 1988) or the services of an expert (Institution of Chemical Engineers' Red Book 1981). These, and other means of what may be referred to as Alternative Dispute Resolution, have been developed as a result of the failure of arbitration to resolve disputes in ways satisfactory to the parties.

Dissatisfaction with arbitration centres largely on the fact that, although it originated as a cheaper and quicker way of resolving disputes, as now practised it is not always quicker than litigation and may, since it involves paying for the services of an arbitrator and the hire of premises, be even more expensive. What may be considered another disadvantage is that it is possible to appeal the arbitrator's decision to the High Court (on questions of law only, not of fact) and the parties may not (in an English domestic dispute) make a binding agreement to exclude judicial review of the arbitrator's decision until the arbitration proceedings have commenced. There could thus be a risk that arbitration merely adds to an already lengthy settlement time.

The arbitrator should be technically qualified and experienced in the field in dispute, which should serve to expedite the proceedings. However, in legal proceedings, the judge—engineering litigation is tried before an Official Referee who specialises in such cases—is also likely to have considerable relevant experience. Arbitration is private and the arbitrator not bound by precedent. He can therefore be more flexible, but may also be less consistent. Arbitrators also seem more likely to seek compromise between the parties, and less inclined to find a claim entirely justified or completely invalid. Arbitration will seldom be able to deal effectively or conveniently with disputes where more than two parties are involved. There are also pitfalls for the unwary in cases where international contracts are referred to arbitration in a country other than that providing the proper law of the contract.

The privacy of arbitration proceedings will probably be accounted an advantage by the party whose performance is in question—inevitably this will be the contractor. To the employer it will not be an advantage, but since engineering litigation before an official referee is rarely reported to the disadvantage of either party, the point is hardly an important one. It is hard to see what advantage the compulsory reference of contractual disputes to arbitration has to either party. Certainly as far as the employer is concerned, it would be better for the contract to remain silent on the matter, allowing the choice of litigation or arbitration to be made, or agreed, once a dispute has arisen. As a general rule, it might then be expected that disputes with a high technical content involving no significant points of law would best be settled by arbitration: disputes involving difficult questions of law and those where more than two parties were concerned would best be settled in court.

12.7.5 Bonds

A bond is an undertaking by a surety to be answerable for the consequences of failure by the contractor to perform an obligation. It is a secondary liability arising—except in the case of 'on demand' or unconditional bonds—on proof of default by the contractor. The surety or bondsman providing the bond is usually indemnified by the contractor, so that his risk will materialise only if the contractor both defaults and goes bankrupt. A bond is not a contract of insurance so that it does not require full disclosure of all possible risks. It must be in writing and, since there is no consideration from the employer, it must be under seal. Upon the contractor's failure to perform in full, the employer may call upon the surety to make good the loss, up to the full amount of the bond.

Traditionally, perhaps because years ago guarantees were usually furnished by friends and relations rather than on a commercial basis for payment, the courts have tended to interpret matters in the surety's favour. Thus there are a number of ways in which the surety's liability can be discharged unless the guarantee explicitly rules these out. The contract of guarantee therefore needs to provide expressly that the contract will not be voided by:

(1) Alteration to the terms of the contract
(2) Variation in the scope of work
(3) Extensions of time or any other indulgence given to the contractor
(4) Compromise of any contractual dispute
(5) Failure of supervision, or detection or prevention of fault by the employer.

Each of these points has been held by the courts to discharge the liability of the bondsman in cases where there was no express term. In addition the contract should not provide for:

- Notice to be given to the surety of the likelihood of default or of the intention to claim (because this would impose an obligation on the employer which might enable the liability of the surety to be discharged).
- The surety to have the right to carry out the work himself (unless, of course, the employer wishes this to be the case).
- Release of the obligation.

The Institution of Civil Engineers' Model Form of Contract, Sixth Edition, includes a form of bond which satisfies these requirements.

There are, nevertheless, still ways in which the hapless employer can inadvertently void the guarantee. These include:

(1) In the case of a payment guarantee, entering into a binding agreement, supported by consideration, to delay payment.
(2) In the case of a performance guarantee, knowingly overpaying the contractor, or paying too early.

Types of bond

There are essentially two types of guarantee or bond common in process plant contracts. The first guarantees performance—either of a limited obligation, or of the complete performance of the contract. The second guarantees payment or repayment—for example, of advance contract payments or of retention money. The most commonly employed bonds are itemised below.

Bid Bond

A bid bond is an undertaking by the surety to make payment if the bidder is the successful tenderer, yet fails to enter into the contract. It guarantees payment to the employer of losses suffered as a consequence of the bidder's failure. Payment is the lesser of the employer's actual losses or the value of the bond, which avoids the danger of the obligation being considered a penalty which could be relieved against. The bid bond would be payable, for example, where the contractor refused to enter into a contract because of a mistake in his tender.

It is, at the very least, arguable that with proper pre-qualification of the bidders—by selection in a known market where the owner or his professional advisers are sufficiently experienced and knowledgeable, or by a requirement for formal pre-qualification in other circumstances—the incapable and the uncommitted will be weeded out of the bid list. Bid bonds are, it is believed, seldom required by the experienced employer in the UK but are common in North America. In the long run of course, the cost of these bonds is added to the cost of bidding and paid for by employers generally.

Customs Bonds

A customs bond may be required by customs authorities during the process of importing materials and equipment. The requirement usually arises because for one reason or another there is uncertainty about the rate of duty to be paid. This can happen when, for example, the project is entitled to a privileged tariff and there is a dispute about whether this applies to the goods in question, or where the documentation does not meet the requirements of the authorities. A bond would then be required before the goods would be released. In general commerce, customs bonds are often used to defer the payment of VAT and excise duties.

Performance Bond

On proof of the contractor's failure to provide complete performance of his contract, the surety can be called upon to make good the employer's loss, up to the maximum value of the bond. This will often require the employer to engage another contractor to complete the contract and, if so, the bond cannot be called in until the new contract arrangements are ready to be put in place and the additional costs of completing the contract are known.

A performance bond is usually required where there is a significant involvement of the public sector in the project, or where the project is being financed by a banking syndicate with repayment being made from future profits. Private companies financing their own developments in the UK seldom require them, since contracts normally provide for stage payments so that at any given time, the employer will have paid only for the work done and payments to suppliers, less any arrears and retention money. Performance bonds are common in North America where some government agencies are required by law to obtain them, seldom for less than a quarter, and often for the total, contract price. In the UK, such bonds, when required at all, are usually for around 10% of the contract price. In the developing countries, performance bonds are often required but are not usually for more than 10% of the contract price.

Advanced Payment Bond

It is commonplace, in lump sum contracts involving the supply of equipment, for there to be an advance payment on contract award—usually of around 10% of the contract price. This finances the contractor's early work and purchases and enables him to maintain a positive cash flow. The alternative would be for the contractor to finance the work himself, which could be more expensive for the employer since the contractor might well borrow on less favourable terms. Subsequent stage payments on the contract are discounted by the advanced payment percentage (and also by the retention percentage, if any) so that the amount of the advance diminishes steadily over the life of the contract—as does the value of the advanced payment bond taken out to secure the advance against the contractor's default.

Retention Bond

It is normal practice on any process plant contract to retain a proportion—usually 10%—of the payments due to the contractor against the possible costs of correction of any defects. Half of the retention money is usually paid to the contractor on plant completion and the remainder held until the end of the defects or maintenance period. There is sometimes a second reduction on satisfactory completion of performance tests undertaken during the defects period.

A cheaper alternative for the contractor—and therefore presumably for the employer—is for him to provide a retention bond in lieu of retention money. Such a bond will be varied in value throughout the life of the contract to match, usually approximately, the value that retention money would have. This is, of course, itself a kind of performance bond and a single bond can be tailored in value to provide for both performance and retention where both elements are required.

Unconditional bonds

Performance bonds usually require proof of default to be provided before payment is made. It is surely right for this to be so. Indeed, in the case of partial performance, it will be necessary for the employer to engage another contractor and receive his tender for completing the works before a claim can be made. In some cases, however, unconditional or 'on demand' performance bonds have been required which enable the employer to obtain payment on request. These bonds are clearly not appropriate to these circumstances and are open to abuse.

Unconditional bonds are appropriate, however, to advance payment bonds since here the employer is merely recovering that part of his advance that has not already been earned. They are also appropriate to a retention bond, since this is an alternative to the traditional retention money where the employer would have the cash in hand. There can hardly be objection, therefore, to the use of an unconditional bond in these cases.

12.7.6 Copyright

The documentation which the employer provides to the contractor may be extensive. Even if the employer were not the provider of the process technology, he is quite likely to have developed, with the expenditure of much effort, time and cost, detailed functional engineering specifications on which he places considerable value. He would almost certainly wish to retain both property and copyright in this documentation, licensing the contractor to make only such copies as are necessary for the purposes of the contract.

The position is more variable as regards property and copyright in the documentation provided by the contractor. It is necessary to distinguish between documentation provided specially for the contract, and the contractor's standard documentation, computer software and proprietary information which he may use in any of his contracts. Copyright in the latter would always be retained by the contractor, the employer being licensed to make use of it only for the purposes of the project. Considering the documentation specially produced for the contract by the contractor, there are two distinct sets of circumstances:

(1) Where the process technology is provided by the contractor or a third party licensor. In such a case, it would be expected that the contractor would retain copyright in his documentation, licensing the employer to make use of it, free of charge or licence fee, for the purposes of the project. The latter might typically be defined as construction, operation, maintenance, repair, enlargement, modification or reconstruction of the plant, thus restricting the licence to the single plant which was the subject of the contract.

(2) Where the process technology is owned by the employer. Here, the employer would probably wish to acquire the property and copyright in all the documentation specially produced by the contractor for the contract. The owner of a process technology would usually hope to exploit it in a

number of plants, whether these were owned by himself or by others that he licensed. Maintenance of a competitive position would require that each successive plant be a development and improvement on its predecessor. In this development process, it would be helpful if the employer were able to make use of the drawings produced for the previous project—by passing them to the contractor appointed to a new project, for example, and the employer would need to own the copyright in order to be sure that he would be able to do this. If he did not hold the copyright, the employer, as owner of the technology, would be able to give information about the previous plant to the new contractor but not, except by special agreement, by using the drawings produced for the previous plant.

Chapter 13

Model Forms of Contract

13.1 INTRODUCTION

An important feature of engineering construction industry contracts is the use of standard, or model, forms of conditions of contract. The prime movers in the development of these appear to have been the engineering professionals—architects and consulting engineers—who recognised the advantages of the standardisation of contractual as well as of technical matters. This has led to the unusual situation that the major influence on these forms of contract has been exercised by those who are not themselves party to the contracts in question, nor were they acting, in this instance, for either of the parties.

The model forms quite naturally have an influence on engineering construction contract conditions beyond those contracts which make direct use of them. Being widely available, frequently used and, in the case of those applying to the building and civil engineering industries at least, often the subject of litigation, legal commentaries perforce pay them much attention. They offer pervasive examples of particular ways of organising an engineering construction contract and of balancing risk, responsibility and authority under such a contract. They provide repositories of standard clauses for those drafting their own conditions of contract to refer to and perhaps to copy whole or in modified form. Their influence on contracts for engineering design, as distinct from construction, is much slighter since few of the model forms seriously address this issue. Design has traditionally been seen as the preserve of the professionals themselves, but the standard forms for the engagement of an architect or consulting engineer require no more than that the designer exercise due skill, care and diligence.

This widespread influence of the model forms makes consideration of them essential to a proper understanding of engineering construction contracts. This is so even for those who have no intention of using them and, in the present context, despite the fact that few are of much direct relevance to the process plant construction industry. Only the model forms produced under the aegis of the Institution of Chemical Engineers (the Red Book for lump sum contracts, and the Green Book for reimbursable contracts) are intended for use in the design and construction of process plants. Two others—those published by the Institute of Civil Engineers (ICE6) and by the Institution of Mechanical Engineers (MF/1)—are of interest because they may be used for some particular aspects of process plant design and construction. ICE6, or variations of it, may be used for construction contracts. MF/1 may be used as the basis of contract conditions for the purchase of major items of equipment, such as a steam boiler or turbine.

A number of detailed legal commentaries on the various model forms has been published and it is not intended to paraphrase them here. The discussion that follows will deal with model forms only in general terms and from the project manager's point of view, with some more detailed reference in the next chapter to those forms which are relevant to process plant design and construction.

13.2 HISTORY

Standard, or model, forms of conditions of contract have been in use in the engineering construction industries for the best part of a hundred years. The Institution of Electrical Engineers first produced a standard form in 1903 for contracts for the supply of plant and equipment for electricity works, or power stations in more modern parlance. In 1948, a revised version for mechanical and electrical engineering work was issued jointly with the Institute of Mechanical Engineers. In 1951, the Association of Consulting Engineers joined the sponsoring institutions. This standard form in its various versions is usually known as the I Mech E model form. The latest version, Model Form MF/1, for home or overseas contracts with erection, was published in 1988.

The Joint Contracts Tribunal, a body containing representatives from the Royal Institute of British Architects, the Building Employers' Confederation, the Royal Institution of Chartered Surveyors, local authorities and various others, was established for the purpose of producing standard forms for the building industry. Its first version was published in 1909 (although based on a form first produced jointly by the Builders' Society and the RIBA in 1870) and numerous versions and editions have followed. These are known as the JCT, or sometimes inaccurately as the RIBA, forms. Unlike the other model forms, which are sets of contract conditions forming only part of the contract documents, the JCT form is a contract with conditions, that is to say, it needs only the addition of the contract drawings and the contract bills of quantities to constitute the complete contract documentation. This means that the JCT form contains procedural detail which could otherwise have been relegated to separate documents—co-ordination procedure, procurement, payment or accounting procedures and so on.

The Institution of Civil Engineers, together with the Federation of Civil Engineering Contractors, produced its first standard form for civil engineering construction contracts in 1945. Subsequent editions have been sponsored also by the Association of Consulting Engineers. The ICE 6th edition was published in 1991. In the same year, recognising the increasing demands of employers for different types of contract, the Institution of Civil Engineers published as a consultative document the 'New Engineering Contract', a set of six contracts to cover different contract strategies, together with a form for sub-contracts. The stated aim is 'engineering or construction work containing all or any of the traditional disciplines such as civil, electrical, mechanical and building work' but presumably this is to be understood in a predominantly civil engineering context. The New Engineering Contract is very different from earlier standard forms and will probably take some time to gain acceptance. It dispenses with the 'Engineer', distributing his duties among others.

In 1968, the Institute of Chemical Engineers published its first model form of contract for the design and construction of chemical plant. This was the Red Book, intended for lump sum contracts, and was revised in 1981. A version designed for reimbursable contracts—the Green Book—was published in 1976. Notable features of these two model forms were the accompanying guide notes, an indispensable aid to their understanding, but one which not all producers of standard forms have considered necessary. The I Mech E Model Form MF/1 was published with a detailed commentary which serves the same purpose.

There are numerous other standard forms in use. Starting in 1963, the International Federation of Consulting Engineers (FIDIC) has published a variety of standard forms intended for international contracts, which are based on the various UK model forms, covering civil engineering construction, electrical and mechanical works (which also has a detailed guide to its use), design and supervision of construction and project management. The government has its own standard forms for building and civil engineering work—GC/Works 1 for major projects and GC/Works 2 for minor works, generally considered the clearest and best drafted, as befits documents produced by one side, and well known for placing most of the risk with the contractor. Some major UK companies have long had their own standard forms and several trade associations also publish them for use by their members. Standard forms are also produced in some other countries, for example, USA, Australia, New Zealand and Singapore.

13.3 FOR AND AGAINST THE USE OF MODEL FORMS

The arguments commonly put forward in favour of the use of model forms are that many projects are complex, and standardised conditions will deal better with this complexity; that such conditions will ensure a fair and reasonable balance between the parties; that they will lead to lower tender prices; and that they will reduce the work of placing the contract.

13.3.1 Project Complexity

The argument that, because engineering projects are generally complex there is therefore important advantage to be gained if a standard form of conditions of contract is used, hardly bears examination. Projects which are simple, or in large part repetitive, may conveniently use the same or similar contract conditions and, indeed, many engineering contracts may share much the same requirements and be satisfactorily served by standard conditions of contract. Complexity, on the other hand, surely means the probability of novel combinations of technical and administrative requirements, and of complicated divisions of responsibility. In a complex project there will be a wide range of special circumstances to take into account, which could best be dealt with by the use of a specially drafted set of contract conditions.

13.3.2 Fair and Reasonable Balance

The proposition that there is generally to be found a fair and reasonable balance of the requirements and interests of the parties to any engineering contract, and a fair allocation of risks and responsibilities between them, is fallacious. It may also have a pernicious effect, since it can lead to the view among those executing a contract that a given liability has been unfairly placed on them and has therefore no moral, even if it has contractual, force. A fair balance of risk is merely one for which a fair price has been paid, and the latter is determined by the market place. No fair balance exists independent of price. Claiming a fair and reasonable balance of risk for the model forms can only mean that contractors' prices are typically set to reflect fairly the balance of risks found in those model forms. There is usually a most economic way of allocating risk and responsibility, one which will probably result in the lowest overall cost. There may well be a balance of risks and responsibilities that has been preferred in many cases. But none of these is a 'fairer' balance or allocation than any other. Nor is any one of them necessarily what the employer seeks in a particular contract. Different employers, depending on their circumstances, will have different requirements. A government body is likely to be willing to carry more risk than a small private employer, the latter accepting a higher cost as an insurance against unexpected price increases. There is no one single balance of risk and responsibility that is the best, let alone 'fair', for all circumstances, and an employer is entitled to seek and pay for whatever contract conditions best suit him.

What matters, and the only thing that matters in this regard, is that the parties themselves clearly understand their risks and obligations. The acceptance of risk and the provision made to cover it are purely commercial matters. A contractor who dislikes a risk he is asked to assume is at liberty to refuse, or he might emphasise the cost implications. He might offer two prices, with and without the risk in question, but one price would not consequently be 'fairer' than the other. A contractor who accepts a risk which he cannot bear, or for which he is not properly rewarded, may be foolish but he cannot claim unfair treatment.

13.3.3 Lower Tender Prices

It can reasonably be argued that the use of a standard form may result in lower tender prices because tenderers familiar with the contract conditions need make no provision for the unforeseen consequences of unfamiliar contract terms. Of course, this is really arguing the value to the contractor of familiarity with the contract conditions, and the same argument must apply to the employer. It may not be of advantage to the employer to have a contractor expert in conditions of contract with which he himself is unfamiliar. The engagement by the employer of an independent professional engineer to act on his behalf in all matters connected with the contract, which the model forms assume is the case, should solve this problem where there are engineers with the required expertise available. In process plant design and construction, however, independent professional engineers used and accustomed to the management of major projects do not exist.

13.3.4 Reduced Work

It is undeniable that use of a model form of contract will reduce the work of the parties in drafting, understanding and negotiating the contract conditions, certainly if this work would otherwise have to start from scratch. The saving will be little or nothing for the experienced employer who will have, if not his own standard form, at least sets of conditions that can be modified to suit with more or less difficulty. In any case, for a major contract worth many millions of pounds, with much at stake for both parties, this is hardly a compelling argument.

13.3.5 Employer's Experience

Much depends on the experience of the employer, and the quality of the assistance he is able to recruit. For the inexperienced employer, unwilling or unable to obtain for himself expert professional advice, there is much to be said in favour of the use of a model form of contract. An employer embarking on his first capital project needs help with the conditions of contract, and what better guide to what is required than a standard form in general use in circumstances similar to his own? Such an employer would be foolish indeed if he ignored the accumulated experience represented by an appropriate model form in favour of his own first attempt. Provided he is not led to neglect the proper understanding of his contractual position, so that use of a standard form is not made a substitute for the full and proper consideration of the contract, and provided that the circumstances match those for which the model form was intended, it seems unarguable that the inexperienced client managing his own project would derive considerable assistance from the use of an appropriate standard form. Where, as would be sensible, the inexperienced employer engages a consultant to manage the execution of his project, this argument is less strong. The consultant with all-round competence should be capable of providing a set of specially tailored contract conditions though he might, as a matter of professional judgement, consider the standard form the best option for the employer. (But see the comments of the distinguished editor of Hudson's Building and Engineering Contracts, quoted below.)

For the established major process operating company, with the experience and the resources to manage its own affairs, the balance of advantage and disadvantage will be different. Such an employer may reasonably conclude that he has a viable alternative to the use of a model form of contract. Some large companies have their own forms of contract whose origins pre-date the issue of the equivalent model forms. They have the resources and experience to draft their own contracts. However they choose to proceed, they must realise that, because of the way in which the precontract stages are usually handled—the draft conditions of contract being stipulated by the employer in his Enquiry—the courts are likely to regard the conditions as emanating from the employer, and thus to apply the *contra proferentem* rule to construe the conditions against the employer where there is any doubt as to their meaning. Of course, if a model form is used, it really originates not from the employer but from a committee of representatives of professionals and contractors. Thus it is as well for the employer to ensure that the model form conditions are, indeed, those which he desires rather than a less than fully appropriate set that he has reluctantly accepted. It might also be to the employer's advantage to leave it to the contractor to propose the conditions where a model form is to be used.

13.4 THE CHOICE FOR THE EXPERIENCED EMPLOYER

The experienced employer pondering the reasons for and against the use of model forms of contract might reasonably ask the following major questions:

(1) Is the standard form clear in its meaning at all points?
(2) Does it properly reflect the employer's interests?
(3) Does it reflect the organisation and responsibilities required for the contract?
(4) Is it appropriate for the scope of the project?
(5) What is the experience of others, in particular, how much litigation has been engendered?

13.4.1 Clarity

In theory, there should be every reason to expect the model forms of conditions of contract to be clear and unequivocal at every point. They are the product of great experience, produced under the imprimatur of one or more of the appropriate professional institutions and intended to be used widely in industry in both original and modified form. They should be subject to continuous development, and errors and loopholes should gradually be eliminated. They will have been tested in the courts and the meanings of the various clauses should have become well understood. It is disconcerting to discover, therefore, that clarity and certainty of meaning are not their most prominent characteristics. The drafting committees contain representatives of competing interests, none more so perhaps than the Joint Contracts Tribunal, which RIBA-sponsored body produces model forms for the building industry. Here there are nine different organisations represented, and it can only be concluded that the obscure drafting of some clauses has been deliberate, and caused by the inability of the drafting committee to agree. Some of its clauses, like the love of God, pass all understanding, and have endured, unchanged, much judicial censure.

The JCT model form is not one that is likely to concern the process plant construction industry directly, but it is one of the most used model forms and it is salutary to read some of the judicial criticism which it has attracted from the courts over the years. In *Bickerton* v. *N. W. Metropolitan Hospital Board* (1967 1 All ER 977) Lord Justice Sachs remarked:

'The difficulties arise solely because of the unnecessarily amorphous and tortuous provisions of the RIBA contract; those difficulties have for a number of years been known to exist and if, as was stated at the Bar, no relevant amendments have been made in the latest edition of the contract, the position reflects no credit on the RIBA. ... I return to my earlier criticism of the form of the contract and emphasise that it seems lamentable that such a form used to govern so many and such important activities throughout the country, should be so deviously drafted with what in parts can only be a calculated lack of forthright clarity. The time has now come for the whole to be completely redrafted so that laymen—contractors and building owners alike—can understand what are their own duties and obligations and what are those of the architect. At present that is not possible.'

In *Gilbert-Ash (Northern Limited)* v. *Modern Engineering (Bristol) Limited* (1974 AC 689) Lord Reid described the JCT form as 'notorious for its obscurities'. More severe criticism of he drafting of a standard form could hardly be made, unless it is the comments of the Editor, Mr I. N. Duncan Wallace in Hudson's Building and Engineering Contracts 10th Edition 1970, p. 146:

'The time must rapidly be approaching when architects or legal advisers recommending the use without modification of some of the forms of contract in general use at present in the United Kingdom (in particular the RIBA forms) must be in serious danger of action for professional negligence.'

Making allowances for the fact that, among model forms, the drafting of the JCT form seems to achieve an unusual degree of obscurity, it is clear that the user of any model form cannot take for granted the clarity and precision of its conditions.

A specially drafted form may, of course, be worse. However, its draftsman does have a number of important advantages denied those producing model forms. First, he is not a committee and does not have to balance a range of conflicting interests. He is the agent of one employer and there is no organisational reason why he cannot clearly express that employer's requirements, see the government model form GC/Works/1. Secondly, he knows the project for which the contract is required and can pay specific attention to its needs, rather than having to draft for a general case. He is not forced into an unsuitable administrative or organisational pattern for the project, as may be the case with a standard contract. And, of course, he may make use of individual conditions from the model forms as templates where appropriate.

13.4.2 Reflection of the Employer's Interests

In considering whether employers' interests have been properly taken into account in the development of the standard forms of contract, it should be noted that they are produced by committees dominated by 'professionals'—consulting engineers, architects, quantity surveyors and consultants of various kinds. Though never parties to these contracts, the professionals have a powerful role as administrators of them and are well placed to exercise a powerful influence on the drafting of any standard form. Such a form will be of great help to the professional engineer in his business: as the employer's agent he will in many cases be expected to propose the conditions of contract and may not have, within his own organisation, the expertise to prepare such conditions afresh. A familiar form will help his supervision of the contract, whether or not it is the best for the employer's requirements.

Contractors are also a reasonably homogeneous group, as are some employers—government departments and local authorities—and these can achieve proper representation and make their influence felt when standard conditions are being drafted. The vast majority of individual private employers, however, will not—indeed, cannot—be properly represented. Many of them have only occasional need for an engineering contract and their interests are disparate. The latter may be quite different from those of a public authority as regards, for example, the apportionment of risk between employer and contractor in order to avoid, at one extreme, high contingency pricing or, at the other, the possibility of unexpected price increases. In consequence of this lack of representation, first-hand knowledge and experience of the private employers' requirements has contributed less than is desirable to the drafting of the standard forms. These tend to be over-protective of the interests of the professionals and those of the contractors, setting strict limits on the liability of the contractor and, in some cases—re-measure and value contracts for example, requiring labyrinthine and uneconomic procedures.

13.4.3 Contract Organisation and the 'Engineer'

The model forms are based on the assumption that the employer will engage an independent professional engineer to act for him as the 'Engineer' (in building contracts the 'Architect') to the contract. He acts for the employer and simultaneously holds the ring between employer and contractor. Some of the forms, in industries where the independent professional has a strong presence, assume this as the only way of proceeding, others admit the possibility that the Engineer may be a member of the employer's own staff. The implications of this assumption are considerable. It affects the conditions of contract in two main ways:

(1) The Engineer, if he is not to be a member of the employer's staff, must explicitly be given the powers to act on behalf of the employer, as well as any quasi-arbitral powers he is to exercise.

(2) The roles and responsibilities of the parties to the contract will be changed: those of the employer because the Engineer will act for him in most of his responsibilities and may also be given powers to decide disputes, those of the contractor because the presence of an independent professional as the Engineer will reduce the reliance which the employer places on the skill and judgement of the contractor.

The role of the Engineer in civil engineering construction contracts (and, in building contracts, the Architect) follows from the way in which such contracts have traditionally been administered, with design carried out by independent professionals. These traditions were maintained in the early development of public utilities, but have been much less prevalent in private manufacturing, where much of the design and specification of new facilities arises out of, and cannot be dissociated from, existing operations. Consulting engineers with the expertise to design and supervise large projects are therefore largely confined to the civil and some parts of the mechanical and heavy electrical branches of engineering. Elsewhere, for example, in the heavy chemicals and petrochemical industries, where large and continuous programmes of capital investment rooted in the operation and development of existing plants are essential, consulting engineers with the experience and capability to design and supervise the construction of major plants have never been a feature. Despite this, the concept of the Engineer has been imported into some standard forms of contract with no greater justification, so it would seem, than the convenience of copying a tried and tested form, or as Belloc would have it 'Be sure to keep a hold of nurse, For fear of finding something worse'. Thus, for example, the Institution of Chemical Engineers' model forms of contract for the design and construction of process plant feature an Engineer, albeit they concede that he will probably be a member of the employer's staff and adjust his role accordingly. A powerful influence has, of course, been exerted by the professionals themselves, who have a major share in the drafting of the various model forms and are unlikely to be interested in a form of contract which has no role for them.

The need to define the role of the Engineer at all in the contract arises simply because of his traditional independence from either of the parties. Where an independent professional is not appointed, there is no need to define separately the employer and the Engineer, except to indicate to the contractor which of the employer's staff has authority. Sometimes a director or very senior member of the employer's staff may be appointed as the Engineer but will play no part in the contract except as a final court of appeal for the contractor. Sometimes the position is simply left vacant. This is unlikely to cause problems in the event of dispute since it would be found that the employer had held out one of his employees as the Engineer and had thus implicitly given him the authority. The contractor, of course, will know from his general dealings or from the Co-ordination Procedure which of the employer's staff he has to deal with and if he is dissatisfied with his treatment, he has no need of an explicit contractual right in order to appeal to a higher level in the employer's organisation.

The model forms vary in the extent of the role and authority they give to the Engineer. In the extreme, the employer needs bring to the enterprise only the requirement for the project and the money to pay for it, engaging an independent consultant to act on his behalf in all matters concerned with the contract and to provide all the technical expertise it requires. The Institute of Civil Engineers 6th Edition Model Form 1991 (ICE6) demonstrates the role of the Engineer at its apogee. This role can helpfully be divided into four parts:

(1) The work that the Engineer is called upon to do before the contract is awarded. This could include preliminary investigations of various kinds, designing the works, seeking bids for their construction and recommending to the employer the contractor to be appointed.
(2) Acting as the employer's agent to supervise the work of the contractor during the course of the contract including, for example, providing additional design details to the contractor as necessary, approving any design of permanent works by the contractor, reviewing the contractor's programme and proposed methods of construction, accepting workmanship and quality of materials and generally ensuring that the contractor's work is carried out to specification.
(3) Administering the contract by, for example, measurement and valuation of the works and certifying invoices for payment, certifying completion, deciding the contractor's claims for extension to the contract period, for variation of contract rates and for payment of extra costs.
(4) Adjudication in disputes between contractor and employer.

ICE6 does not explicitly require that the Engineer performs all, or indeed any of the prior work defined in the first of these items, but since he has to explain and resolve any ambiguities and to supply any further design that is necessary, this is clearly the expected pattern of events. It would certainly be desirable from the point of view of efficient contract administration for the Engineer to have been responsible at least for soliciting bids and for recommending the contractor to be appointed.

The essential core of the Engineer's role is to act as the employer's project manager, as defined in the second and third of the items above: to supervise the work of the contractor and ensure completion to specification; and to administer the contract by certifying progress and payments and deciding claims. In the case of the former item, the Engineer is acting as the employer's agent and is under his instructions as to the task to be performed, though not as to how it is to be accomplished. In the latter item, when acting as a certifier, there is an implied (and nowadays, in many model forms, an expressed) duty on the Engineer to act fairly and impartially as between the contractor and the employer. However, although he must act impartially as between the parties, he must operate within the terms of the contract—he may think a contract term bears harshly on one or other party but he has no powers to vary it. He cannot substitute his own notions of fairness in contravention of the contract.

The fourth part of the Engineer's role, which differs markedly in extent between model forms, is to adjudicate in disputes between employer and contractor. One may wonder why this should be thought desirable. Most disputes will concern the Engineer's own previous action, decision, or instruction, and reference of such a dispute to him will simply be to ask him to reconsider. However, under ICE6, it is seldom provided that the Engineer must consult with the contractor before making any decision, so that reference of the dispute to the Engineer may be the first opportunity for the contractor to put his case. In former times, Engineers' decisions were often made binding on the parties and, where provision was made in the contract for arbitration, the Engineer was sometimes named as arbitrator, a course of action now effectively precluded by the Arbitration Act 1950 (which permits either party to object to the arbitrator, after the dispute has arisen, on the grounds of partiality, even though it was known when the arbitrator was agreed that his relation to the other party might prevent him from acting impartially). Today, most contracts, and certainly the model forms discussed here, make the Engineer's decisions subject to independent arbitration in the event they are disputed. The question of the Engineer's impartiality is not, therefore, quite so important as once it was. The worst that could happen would probably be the imposition of a few months' delay on the settlement process. In favour of retaining the procedure for first referring disputes to the Engineer for settlement is that, whatever the philosophical doubts, experience with the previous edition of the ICE model form shows that up to 90% of disputes are resolved in this way. Of course, even without a formal requirement, the Engineer would surely reconsider all the circumstances of a dispute before the process of arbitration got under way.

An independent consulting engineer to act as Engineer to the contract would be engaged by the employer on a separate contract which may itself involve the use of a model form, such as one of those produced by the Association of Consulting Engineers (ACE). This contract would define the relationship between the employer and the Engineer, detail the latter's duties and powers and his authority to commit the employer opposite the contractor. It would be a contract for services in which the consulting engineer promised, not a result, but a standard of performance—to exercise all reasonable skill, care and diligence. It would also require the Engineer to exercise any discretion he may have, fairly as between the employer and the contractor.

In general, it is considered that the standard forms produced to regulate the employment of professionals are inimical to the employer's interests. The scales of fees are heavily front-loaded so as to bear no relation to the effort expended and operate very much against the employer in the event of cancellation of the project. There is no obligation on the professional to insure. The liability which he accepts is never more, and may be substantially less, than his common law liability. The one-sided origin of the forms is betrayed by the fact that considerably more space is taken to define the obligations of the employer, who has merely to provide preliminary information and to pay for the services, than those of the consulting engineer who is to perform the work. It will often be better for the employer to engage the professional on the basis of an informal letter.

The model forms of contract do not oblige the employer to engage an independent Engineer. He may use a model form, or conditions of contract based on it, and appoint one of his own staff as Engineer. The employer is then responsible for all the actions of the employee Engineer, including liability for any torts, such as negligence, which the latter might commit (and for which he would not be liable were the Engineer an independent professional). The employer can exercise much greater control over the employee Engineer. He can instruct him what to do and how to do it. However, if the contract expressly requires the Engineer to act fairly and impartially as between employer and contractor in his duties of certification and adjudication, the employer will have agreed to relinquish control of the employee Engineer's actions in these matters, and will not be liable. The standard of impartiality required of the employee Engineer will be no different from that expected of the independent.

The Engineer's duty to act impartially may appear more difficult in theory than it is in practice. In any dispute, the Engineer, independent or not, must still put the employer's side of the matter. He is the employer's sole agent and, if he did not argue the employer's case it would go by default. Even so, the employer will lose the services of the Engineer as his agent during the course of the dispute. The Engineer must then decide impartially between the case he or his representative has just prepared and that of the contractor. True impartiality—coming to the matter with no previous information or preconceptions and with a completely open mind—is obviously impossible. What seems to be achieved more easily than might be expected is fair resolution of the dispute once all the facts are presented.

It might be supposed that the independent Engineer would find it easier than the employee to maintain impartiality in his dealings with employer and contractor. His duty to act impartially is spelt out in his contract with the employer as well as in the main contract and his own organisation should help him to resist any importunate demands. However, he is still subject to the pressures of a business relationship with the employer: the wish to remain in good standing with him and the prospects of future business. The employee Engineer may be correspondingly influenced by his career prospects, but it should not therefore be concluded that he will inevitably be subjected to pressure to behave in particular ways. Major manufacturing companies usually maintain separate engineering departments and sometimes separate construction organisations, some of which are very large. They are as jealous of their professional standards as any engineering consultant and would most strongly resist any pressure to behave in an unprofessional way. Both independent and employee Engineer may have to decide between their own work in design and the contractor's in construction, or be called upon to adjudicate where their own previous decisions are in question. Given that both consultant and employer are well-established, reputable companies, the impartiality of the Engineer will be influenced more by his personal standards of fairness and integrity than by the organisation for which he works.

The employee Engineer will enjoy greater authority than would an independent, not as the Engineer *per se*, but by virtue of his position as the senior member of the employer's engineering staff responsible for the project. If, for example, he is the employer's project manager, has drafted and negotiated the contract and in all matters has spoken for the employer, he will have the authority to decide matters on the employer's behalf and, if he thinks fit, to deal with the contractor more favourably than the contract requires. His decisions will bind the employer.

A contractor might consider the extent of the Engineer's authority as given in some model forms to be inappropriate for a member of the employer's own staff. He could reasonably object to an Engineer who was not independent being given powers to adjudicate disputes, although this is not a vital point where such adjudications are subject to arbitration. He might cavil at the requirement, which many contract conditions include, to work to the satisfaction of the Engineer. However, his concerns might have more to do with the person and the organisation involved than with the question of independence from the employer. Obviously, he might prefer an independent Engineer from a reputable firm of consulting engineers to an employee of a company with which he had not previously dealt. Where the employer was a large and well-established company with a reputation for fair dealing, however, he should have few qualms. Contracts in countries other than the UK might be a different matter. In many foreign countries, the role of the Engineer is not understood and impartiality could not be expected from the independent, much less the employee, Engineer. It would be foolish for any contractor to assume that the use of the term 'Engineer' in a foreign contract denoted anyone other than a fully committed agent of the employer.

13.4.4 Contract Scope

It will be evident from previous chapters that process plant contracts run the whole gamut of possibilities from turnkey contracts with full responsibility taken by the contractor for the entire work, to those where the contractor provides no more than drawing office services under the close supervision of the employer's personnel. There is wide variety of scope of work, of responsibility and liability and of the relative contributions of employer and contractor. The employer contemplating the use of a model form must ensure that it is an appropriate form of contract for the job in hand. Problems can arise from the need to modify a standard form to fit the idiosyncrasies of a particular project. While the use of special conditions to qualify the general conditions of the standard form of contract is commonplace, major change runs the risk of inconsistency and even contradiction between the conditions. The difficulties are not always obvious at first sight, but if the model form is not thoroughly understood in detail as well as in general—the allocation of risk and responsibility, the degree of reliance on the skill of the contractor, the provisions for extensions of time and for liquidated damages, to give but a few examples—the results may be unexpected and unwelcome.

It might therefore be expected that a standard form of contract would have limited value for the experienced process plant operating company, that it would seldom be appropriate to use without modification, and that its main value would be in providing a quarry from which to extract proven examples of individual conditions. It would not be expected that those whose resources and experience allowed would do otherwise than draft their own conditions to meet their own objectives and circumstances, making use of standard clauses as appropriate. The advantages are those of a bespoke-tailored over a ready-made suit. The only question mark is over the skill of the employer's tailor. For the sophisticated employer, who has the resources to draft his own contract properly, this will clearly provide the best fit to his requirements.

13.4.5 Litigation

In considering the possible use of a standard form, the employer must also have regard for the experience of others as measured by the amount of litigation that ensues. Recourse to law seems depressingly frequent where engineering construction contracts are concerned, and especially where the JCT and, to a lesser extent, the ICE model forms of conditions of contract are used. Since any litigation is prima facie evidence of the failure of the project manager, or in the cases of the model forms referred to, of the Architect or Engineer, to manage the contract properly, it is of considerable professional interest to discover its causes. Unfortunately, it seems that no analysis of litigated contracts, to determine the most common reasons for their failure to operate properly, has been done. Such analysis might in any case prove unrewarding, since it is far from certain that the real reasons for the failure of the parties to a contract to manage their bargain satisfactorily will always be deducible from any reporting of the case.

In the absence of such an analysis, one can only speculate. Is building and civil engineering construction inherently more difficult to contract for than other aspects of engineering? The JCT and ICE model forms attract more litigation than those of the Institutions of Mechanical Engineers or Chemical Engineers. No doubt they are much more commonly used than either, but this alone does not seem sufficient to account for the difference. A significant factor must be the division of responsibility for design and for construction. The contractor responsible only for construction must be given vastly more data and information than if he were himself to perform the design, and the complicated interface between designer and constructor provides vastly more scope for error, variation and dispute. The re-measurement and valuation form of contract seems also to establish a regime which encourages dispute and confrontation. It exercises no restraint on change and variation: not only the quantities, but the rates applied to them may be varied. The whole exercise is carried out in fine detail prescribed by a standard method of measurement, the inaccurate application of which is another possible source of change.

The employment of independent consultants—not only the Engineer or Architect, but also the quantity surveyor—must play its part. Whatever the technical advantages of this course, which will be less pronounced outside the building and civil engineering fields where consultants with the necessary skills are less common, it will have the disadvantage that the independent consultant can only apply the contract as it is written—fair or unfair, he cannot depart from it. To him, as to the contractor, the contract will be the total of his responsibilities. Strict adherence to its terms takes precedence over all other things—even the success of the project, with which he is not formally concerned. He may also be more concerned to defend his own performance, conscious that this is being monitored by the employer. His negotiations with the contractor will be conditioned by the knowledge that any admitted error or omission on his part may have to be explained and, in the limit, defended. To the employer's project manager, however, the contract will be but a part of the project for which he is responsible. He will be more relaxed about the fine print and may sometimes act more leniently than the contract requires in the wider interest of his project.

In contrast, where the Institution of Mechanical Engineer's model form is used, the contractor will usually perform design, manufacture and installation. He has total responsibility and a lump sum contract which offers fewer opportunities for claim and dispute. The largest part of his work will be manufactured in his own factory, in conditions which are likely to be much more predictable and controllable than those on a construction site, with a settled and permanent workforce working in familiar circumstances. The contractor's work on site will often be a relatively small part of the total and will usually be in conditions which have themselves been prepared by others— the manufacturer of a steam turbine, for example, will expect to see prepared foundations and a building on site to receive it. The external conditions are therefore much less unpredictable and his work, being based on his own design, relies much less on that of others. The consequences for him of any problems in construction will be less and he will be better placed to absorb them.

The Institution of Chemical Engineers' model forms are used to a much lesser extent and litigation concerning them is seldom reported. Since the contractor is responsible for design, supply of equipment and materials, and construction, his liabilities are comprehensive and hence less open to dispute.

13.5 CONCLUSIONS

In summary, what should the private employer make of the standard conditions of contract available to him? To the small employer, or one who rarely invests in a capital project, if there is a standard form appropriate to his project, this will probably offer the best way forward. Unless he has considerable engineering resources to define exactly how he wishes to have the project administered, and can also deploy the necessary legal and contractual expertise, it is unlikely that any contract that such an employer developed would serve as well. He would, of course, have to suffer the fact that his project might be shaped to fit the standard form rather than for the conditions of contract to be drafted to suit the way he might like the project organised. The inexperienced employer should, of course, be able to rely on his consultant engineer for advice on any modifications that are required to the standard forms.

For the experienced employer able and willing to draft an individual contract, this would normally be his best course of action, given reasonable care and skill.

Chapter 14

Some Relevant Model Forms

Three of the model forms, those sponsored by the Institution of Civil Engineers, the Institute of Mechanical Engineers, and the Institution of Chemical Engineers, are the most relevant to the design and construction of process plant, and have probably exerted most influence on the contract conditions used in process plant design and construction. They are briefly considered below.

14.1 INSTITUTION OF CIVIL ENGINEERS' MODEL FORM 6TH EDITION 1991

The ICE6 model form provides a set of contract conditions for civil engineering construction which is primarily, but not entirely because of the provision for Prime Cost items, a re-measure and value contract. The employer retains most of the cost risk, the contractor being responsible for programme and for the quality of his workmanship and the materials he supplies. Variations of the ICE6 model form are often used for schedule of rates contracts, and for construction in other disciplines, where responsibility for design and construction is separated.

In his tender, the contractor quotes unit, or composite, rates against bills of quantities which have been taken off from the design drawings existing at that stage. From the product of these rates and the billed quantities is obtained a tender total. This is merely an indication of the final contract price, which will eventually be arrived at by re-measurement of the actual quantities as built. There are two possible reasons, other than mistakes in design or in the take-offs, why the final quantities may differ significantly from the initial contract quantities. The first is that unexpected site conditions may be encountered, an effect which should be confined largely to underground works. The second reason, which if it applies to any great extent may, redound to the discomfiture of both parties, is that the contract has been let before the design is sufficiently complete. The re-measurement provisions make it possible to let the contract before the work concerned is adequately defined, leading to the frequent operation of complicated contractual provisions for the revision of costs and time, with consequences that are often undesirable. Not only the quantities but also the unit rates may be varied during re-measurement, depending on the nature and magnitude of any changes. This provides for flexibility, but also requires close and careful measurement and supervision. The measurement process, for example, must be capable of distinguishing defective work which is to be re-done at the contractor's cost. It must be based on the elaborate Standard Method of Measurement and claims are possible if this has been departed from. Successful execution relies very heavily on the skill and integrity of the Engineer and his staff and demands detailed and accurate comparison of the expectation at the tender stage with the final out-turn. It is an expensive system to operate and its loose financial arrangement offers little comfort to the employer, who at the outset may be sure neither of the quantity of work for which he must pay, nor of the rates at which he must pay for it. The detailed involvement of the Engineer or his representatives in all stages of the work may also tend to encourage argument and variations.

14.1.1 Contractor's Liabilities

Reliance is placed on the contractor to manage the works, since he cannot sub-let the whole of them without the employer's consent, and there is no provision for consent not to be unreasonably withheld. The contractor can, however, sub-contract any part of the works at his option (unless otherwise provided) so that his skill and experience in the execution of individual tasks is not usually to be regarded as of special importance to the employer. In this, the 6th Edition of the model form differs from its predecessor, which required that any sub-contract required the Engineer's consent.

The contractor's responsibilities for costs are limited to responsibility for his quoted unit rates. He is responsible for completion to programme, defined as a whole or by individual sections, and liquidated damages for delay are payable. If 'nil', or no figure, is given for liquidated damages, no damages, liquidated or at large, are payable. (This would be appropriate where initial definition was poor, so that the programme could be only approximate, and the contract would be effectively a schedule of rates contract.) The contractor is responsible for the quality of his workmanship and of the materials he supplies and, up to the end of the Defects Correction Period, corrects defects in them at his expense without limit of cost. He is responsible for deciding the construction methods he uses and for the design of any temporary works (although the Engineer may, of course, design specialised temporary works). The Engineer's consent to the construction methods proposed does not affect the contractor's responsibility for them.

14.1.2   Provisional Sums and Prime Cost Items

There are two further provisions of the model form which may complicate the operation of the contract, so much so that the wise employer will avoid them if he can. The first is that the model form departs from the re-measure and value concept by the introduction of the 'provisional sum' and the 'prime cost item', the former a contingency amount for work not specified which may or may not be required, the latter an item of work which contains an employer-defined sum to cover all or part of its cost. The second potentially complicating provision is that ICE6 explicitly allows for the possibility of the contractor performing part of the design of the permanent works, something merely hinted at in the previous edition. It is still implicit, however, that the Engineer performs the majority of the design.

The provisional sum is used, or not, at the Engineer's discretion. It may allow for additional works to be designed by the Engineer and constructed by the contractor in much the same way as the original scope, and this can be accommodated within the re-measure and value provisions, albeit the contractor may need to quote additional unit rates under non-competitive conditions. The provisional sum will probably, however, be used in much the same way as a prime cost item, differing only in being undefined and uncertain at contract award. It seems uncertain whether or not the contractor's programme is to be taken to include the work involved in a provisional sum item.

The total scope of a prime cost item, including design, supply of materials and equipment, and construction, is generally intended to be performed by a specialist sub-contractor or, less usually and subject to his agreement, by the contractor himself. Sub-contractors for prime cost items are usually nominated by the employer. The main contractor may make reasonable objection to a nominated sub-contractor or may object on various specified grounds. These include the refusal of the nominee to undertake obligations and liabilities which would enable the contractor to fulfil his own obligations and liabilities; refusal to indemnify the contractor against claims arising both in contract and in negligence; refusal to provide security for performance of the sub-contract; and refusal to enter into appropriate terms for termination of the sub-contract. If the contractor concurs in the appointment of the nominated sub-contractor, he is fully responsible for the sub-contractor's performance. However, in the event of justified termination of the nominated sub-contract, the employer is responsible for any costs which the contractor fails to recover from the sub-contractor.

Where the contractor carries out the work involved in a prime cost item himself, he is paid either his quoted price, or as if the work were a variation. Where a nominated sub-contractor is used, payment is made on the basis of the cost of the sub-contract, the contractor's costs associated with it plus a percentage for profit. If it proves impossible to nominate a sub-contractor who meets with the contractor's approval, the Engineer may instruct the contractor to choose his own sub-contractor, or invite him to do the work himself, or may vary or omit the work in question. In the last event, the contractor is entitled to his costs and the profit that he would have otherwise made.

14.1.3   Contractor's Design Responsibility

The ICE contracts have traditionally been concerned with construction by the contractor to the designs of the Engineer. For some years the position has not been quite as simple and straightforward as this. Projects have become more complicated and the Engineer's proficiency does not always extend to all aspects of their design. Nominated sub-contractors, responsible for design, supply and erection have come to play a larger part. Many main contractors have also developed substantial design capability. The 5th Edition of the ICE model form hinted at this situation in stating that the contractor had no responsibility for the design and specification of the permanent works except as expressly provided in the contract. The only other reference to the matter was in connection with prime cost items where it was required that any design or specification of the permanent works to be included in a prime cost item must be expressly included in the contract and included in any nominated sub-contract. Such inclusion in the main contract would be necessary if the contractor were to have any responsibility for the design performed by the nominated sub-contractor: it would seem very unlikely that he would be held responsible without this express provision. The reader was given no further clue as to how any other responsibility of the contractor for design might eventuate, or how it would be paid for or what the extent of the contractor's responsibility might be. Essentially, ICE5 merely opened the door to the possibility that the main contractor might perform some of the design, but left it to the parties to deal with it as best they may.

ICE6 takes another step down the road of contractor design. It adds the provisions that the contractor performing the design of part of the permanent works shall submit his design for the Engineer's approval, without affecting the contractor's responsibility, and shall supply operating and maintenance manuals. The Engineer is made responsible for the integration and co-ordination of the contractor's design with the rest of the works. ICE6 also defines the nature of the contractor's responsibility as the exercising of all reasonable skill, care and diligence in carrying out the design. This is comparable with the Engineer's responsibility for his design. It falls short of a fitness for purpose obligation, but it is not clear whether it excludes it. If it does exclude it, is the employer to be denied the benefit of the fitness for purpose obligation which any nominated sub-contractor will in all probability owe to the main contractor for the design as well as all other elements of his sub-contract?

It is doubtful whether ICE6 offers much improvement on its predecessor in the matter of the contractor design of permanent works. Apart from the design element which may be included in any nominated sub-contract, there is still no clue as to how the design obligation of the contractor will arise, of any mechanism for approvals and disapprovals, how design variations will be valued, how the design or the construction that follows will be paid for. It seems clear that, if the main contractor is to undertake the design of a significant part of the permanent works, ICE6 as it stands is inadequate.

Problems may also arise because the borderline between design and construction cannot always be sharply defined and can vary depending on the degree of detail provided by the Engineer. If the contractor is required to decide details which on another contract would be specified by the Engineer, does this work remain design or does it become construction simply because it is performed on site? Certainly, the contractor will often exercise choice—for example in the mix of asphalt or concrete or in the recipe for free-draining material—which is arguably design, whether done in consequence of the Engineer's design activities or the contractor's. With a lesser obligation for design than for construction, the contractor would be encouraged to classify as much of his activity as possible as design. An employer might also suspect that splitting the design between Engineer and contractor, with the former being responsible for integration and co-ordination, might not be the most economic way of proceeding.

14.1.4 Variations

In a re-measure and value contract, change is expected and its management of the first importance. Changes from the initial contract quantities do not themselves call for ordered variations, but may give rise to claims for variations in unit rates or for extensions of time for completion. The Engineer may order any variation which he considers desirable for the completion or improved functioning of the works, and is obligated to order any variation which he considers necessary for completion. It seems that the contractor may therefore have the power to demand a variation where it is necessary for the completion of the works. Certainly, it appears that the Engineer may order and the contractor agree on a variation without the knowledge of the employer who has to pay for it. The variation clauses do not address the questions of variations to the contractor's design or in the construction of that design.

14.1.5 The Engineer

Under the ICE6 model form, the employer relinquishes management of the contract to the Engineer, who is implicitly assumed to be an independent party although this is not absolutely necessary. The employer relies upon the Engineer for the achievement of satisfactory technical standards and gives him extensive powers in the contract to control what is done. The employer may limit the Engineer's authority but any specific requirements for the latter to seek the employer's approval before he can act must be detailed. The contractor is not, however, obliged to check that such approvals have been obtained. Unless expressly stated, the Engineer has no power to amend the construction contract and is expressly required to act impartially as between the employer and the contractor.

The Engineer's duties will typically include all the four items listed in the previous chapter: design of the works before the contract is awarded; supervision of the contractor's operations to ensure that the works are constructed to specification; measurement and valuation and certification of progress and of invoices for payment; and adjudication of disputes. The first item is implied and not essential: the Engineer may provide the designs but is not required to have done them himself. He is, however, responsible for providing them to the contractor. If he did not himself carry out the design, he must obviously have the close support of whoever did, not merely to help with any queries the contractor might have, but also to provide any additional design that may be required. Although provision is made for additional design to be given to the contractor during the course of construction, it is implicit in the conditions that the vast majority of the design will have been done before the contract is awarded, since it is on the design as it exists before contract award that the tender total is based.

The Engineer has powers of approval and acceptance and may instruct the contractor as he thinks fit. The works are required to be constructed and completed to his satisfaction and the methods and speed of construction must be acceptable to him (and there is no test of reasonableness). What makes his influence so powerful is that, at almost every stage, it is his opinion that prevails. He determines any extensions of time to which the contractor may be entitled, though he is enjoined to take delays from various causes into account. He ascertains the value of variations after consultation with the contractor. He decides whether the physical conditions of the site could have been reasonably foreseen by the contractor and determines any extra costs due. At every turn, the Engineer is given explicit powers to decide whether the contractor is entitled to extra cost or time and to quantify the entitlement. Where another contract might allow the contractor the reasonable costs that he incurs, ICE6 allows him the costs that in the Engineer's opinion are reasonable. This is very much a hands-on contract, the hands being those of the Engineer who controls virtually all the levers of power. If any of the Engineer's decisions is contested, it is to the Engineer that the dispute is referred. Any other dispute between employer and contractor is similarly referred. If the Engineer's adjudication is contested it can be overruled only by due process of conciliation or arbitration.

14.1.6 Employer Amendments

The ICE6 model form could be summarised as providing contract conditions for a re-measure and value civil engineering construction contract where flexibility is a paramount requirement. This flexibility is sometimes necessary for underground works where there may be real uncertainty about quantities, and will be required for other types of work where the design is incomplete at contract award. The flexibility is won at the cost of extensive supervision from the Engineer and his staff, including measurement of the work twice, uncertainty as to price, and detailed provisions that provide opportunity for argument and dispute. To this is added arrangements for nominating sub-contractors which disadvantage the employer, together with sketchy provision for design of part of the permanent works by the contractor which, if invoked, seems bound to cause difficulty by its incompleteness.

The employer wishing to use the ICE6 model form as the basis for construction contract conditions would be advised to avoid nominating sub-contractors, or making the contractor responsible for any design of permanent works. He would be likely to require a significant number of amendments to the conditions ranging from the trivial to the important. Some of these changes might reflect a desire to alter the balance of risk and responsibility, others the employer's established procedures, others the particular conditions extant on the employer's site. Different employers will have different requirements, and it is not possible here to do more than give a selection of the possible changes that might be required, in order to give some idea of the size of the task.

The employer might wish the contractor to take some of the risks over which neither party has control, for instance, those of exceptional adverse weather conditions or unforeseen physical conditions on site. Where a process plant is concerned and the employer is at the mercy of volatile market forces, he would require the right to terminate the contract without cause, so that he could not be compelled to complete a contract for which the commercial need had vanished. If an independent Engineer were to be engaged, the prudent employer might require him to obtain approval before ordering variations which would increase the contract price. If an employee were to be appointed as Engineer, it might be appropriate to delete the requirement for all disputes to be first referred to him. Disputes on his own decisions, however, might helpfully continue to be referred first to the Engineer since, depending on the way in which the Engineer exercises his extensive powers, the contractor may have had little previous opportunity for a hearing.

It would certainly be of great help to an employer, both in planning his project and in selecting the best bid, if programmes were required to be submitted with tenders, rather than the successful tenderer submitting his programme 21 days after acceptance. The employer might also wish to use other than the Standard Methods of Measurement. The question of insurances is almost certainly something that the employer would wish to consider: a large employer will probably find it cheaper and more certain to insure the works himself and indemnify the contractor against claims. The employer would probably wish to address the matter of the confidentiality of the information given to the contractor. The replacement of the 'War Clause' by a force majeure clause might well seem sensible.

14.2 INSTITUTE OF MECHANICAL ENGINEERS' MODEL FORM MF/1 1988

The original version of this standard form was developed for use in the electricity supply industry—for example, for the design and supply of a major piece of equipment such as a steam turbine. The characteristics of this sort of project, which are reflected in the model form are:

(1) The contractor carries out the design with little or no input from the employer or Engineer after the initial definition of performance requirements.
(2) The contractor manufactures most of the equipment himself away from the site and this work represents a large proportion of the contract value.
(3) The contractor installs the equipment on site and this work is a relatively small part of the total contract.
(4) The contract will be placed on a lump sum basis with adjustment for inflation.

14.2.1 Contractor's Liabilities

The MF/1 contractor receives the major part of the financial benefits of the contract: he is designer, manufacturer, supplier and erector. Consequently, his liability is essentially one of fitness for purpose. He is liable for the correction of his design and of defects in his plant and that of his sub-contractors and suppliers without limit of cost up to the end of the Defects Liability period. There is also a latent defects period of three years following takeover during which the contractor will make good defects due to 'gross misconduct'—

defined as failure to pay due regard to the serious consequences which a conscientious and responsible contractor would normally foresee as likely to ensue from, or a wilful disregard of any consequences of, an act or omission. Delay in completion is the subject of liquidated damages. Once the maximum liquidated damages are incurred, the employer can set a reasonable time to complete. If the contractor fails to comply, he must additionally pay the employer his loss up to a stated sum, or a sum equal to the cost of that part of the plant that cannot be used. The contractor must modify the plant to meet his performance guarantees. If he fails,the employer can terminate the contract, complete the plant and recover any costs in excess of the contract price from the contractor. The contractor's overall liabilities are limited to such figures as may be agreed between the parties or, if such a limit is not stated, to the contract price for any one act or default. The model form responds to recent developments in common law, which have established that a contractor may be liable to his employer in tort as well as in contract, by specifying that the contract sets out the full extent of the contractor's liabilities in both contract and tort. The consequent exclusion of liability for loss or damage due to negligence would be subject to the Unfair Contract Terms Act 1977 test of reasonableness.

14.2.2 Provisional Sums and Prime Cost Items

Provisional Sums and Prime Cost Items feature in the contract conditions but are given much less prominence and are not described in any detail. Provisional Sums are for undefined requirements which may or may not materialise. The Engineer may seek quotations for the work involved from the contractor or from a sub-contractor, though nominated sub-contractors are not explicitly mentioned. Prime Cost Items are treated similarly, the contractor being entitled to be paid the actual cost plus a percentage for costs and profit which the contractor specifies in his bid. The contractor is relieved of any responsibility for the work or supplies of others unless he has approved the sub-contractor, and has approved any plant that he supplies.

14.2.3 Variations

The Engineer may order any variation provided the contract price remains within a tolerance of plus or minus 15%. Beyond this, the written consent of both employer and contractor is required. The contractor may also propose variations. Variations are valued either by a quotation from the contractor, or in accordance with contract rates where applicable, or as reasonable in the circumstances. Where a variation affects the contractor's ability to fulfil his obligations, after due notice and confirmation of the variation, they will be amended as appropriate.

14.2.4 The Engineer

The role of the Engineer in the Institution of Mechanical Engineers' Model Form MF/1 is a good deal less powerful than the corresponding role in ICE6. His prior design role is insignificant in comparison. Whereas ICE6 is for site construction essentially to the Engineer's design, MF/1 is for the design, manufacture, supply and erection of plant and equipment whose required performance the Engineer has specified. The MF/1 contractor will not usually be responsible for the design of associated civil and building works—these will commonly be designed by the Engineer and constructed by a separate contractor. For everything else, the employer relies mainly on the contractor for the technical input to the project. Many of the Engineer's supervisory duties will consist of inspection of work in progress and monitoring of testing in the contractor's factory. Supervision of erection on site may be a small part of the total. Other factors reduce the Engineer's influence compared with ICE6. Since he is not responsible for the design, there are quite naturally fewer occasions in the contract when the decision of the Engineer is required and his powers of decision are less arbitrary. The Engineer has to grant reasonable extensions of time. He is not given explicit powers to decide changes in the contract price: the contractor is to be paid the costs incurred, or according to his quotation, or according to the schedule of rates, or what is reasonable.

It is recognised that in many cases the Engineer will be a member of the employer's staff rather than an independent professional. Any restrictions on his powers and duties that the employer imposes must be disclosed at the tender stage. The model form expressly imposes a duty upon the Engineer to act fairly within the terms of the contract when exercising his discretion. Nevertheless, it could perhaps be argued that the powers of the Engineer to give instructions and to vary the works will sometimes be out of proportion to his skill and expertise in the work that is being performed.

The Engineer is required to certify claims for payment and to decide on claims for extra time or payment. If any decision, instruction or order of his is disputed, it must be referred back to him, giving him twenty-one days in which to reconsider. This is a narrower reference than that in ICE6 which requires all disputes between employer and contractor to be referred to the Engineer for settlement. If, following the referral, either contractor or employer continues to dispute the matter, it must be referred to arbitration within twenty-one days.

14.2.5 Employer Amendments

There are a number of aspects of model form MF/1 that the experienced employer might wish to consider altering. Some amendments would be directed at changing the balance of risk: for example, deleting the exclusion of contractor's liability in tort already mentioned; making the contractor responsible for the cost of damage to roads and bridges which may be caused during transport of out-of-gauge loads to site. Termination of the contract is another matter where changes would probably be required: the right of the contractor to terminate for late payment might be deleted, and the right of the employer to terminate without cause added. The employer might also wish to see an obligation on the part of the contractor to correct all defects in the works, irrespective of fault, though being paid for the correction of those which were not his fault. The limit of 15% on the total value of variations which the contractor must perform seems unnecessarily restrictive. No employer could sensibly contract on the basis that the contractor could refuse to complete merely because the contract price was altered by more than 15%. The reasonable argument that no contractor would behave in such a way merely supports the case for the requirement to be deleted. The employer might well require the right to use the contractor's drawings to procure spares from others. The clause making all consents subject to the test of reasonableness would be unlikely to be acceptable. Other changes may arise from the particular circumstances of the employer: the insurance provisions will almost certainly be subject to special consideration; there may be site regulations with which the contractor must comply; the confidentiality provisions may need elaboration. If the Engineer is to be an employee of the employer, it might be appropriate to remove his right to adjudicate in disputes.

14.3 INSTITUTION OF CHEMICAL ENGINEERS' MODEL FORM FOR LUMP SUM CONTRACTS 1981—THE RED BOOK

The two Institution of Chemical Engineers' Model Forms of Conditions of Contract for Process Plants are for the design and construction of complete process plant. The first, published in 1968 and revised in 1981, was the Red Book for lump sum contracts. The underlying assumptions in this are as follows:

(1) The design will be performed by the contractor but with a substantial input from the employer.
(2) Materials and equipment will be supplied by sub-contractors and suppliers to the contractor.
(3) Construction management will be carried out by the contractor with substantial use of sub-contractors for the actual construction work.

The typical process plant contract is quite complicated. Design of the plant involves chemical, mechanical, electrical, control as well as civil and structural engineering, and will usually require extensive purchasing of materials and equipment from suppliers world-wide. Construction is similarly multi-disciplined. At the sub-contract level, the contractor may use versions of MF/1 for the purchase of large items of equipment and of ICE6 for construction, and perform the role of Engineer in such sub-contracts.

14.3.1 Contractor's Liabilities

The contractor must complete the work for the contract price. It must be of sound workmanship and materials, be in accordance with good engineering practice, and to the reasonable satisfaction of the Engineer. The plant must be suitable for the purpose for which it is intended. The contractor is responsible for completion on time, and liquidated damages are payable for delay: if none are stated, damages are at large. The contractor is responsible for correcting errors and omissions in design, and must also correct all defects in the plant within the Defects Liability period, both without limit of cost. If the plant fails to pass its performance tests the contractor must modify it at his own expense. Liquidated damages may be provided for delay in completion and for failure of the plant to achieve the specified performance within a given time.

14.3.2 Provisional Sums and Prime Cost Items

The Red Book allows for the inclusion of Provisional Sums, which will be expended, or not, as the Engineer instructs. Prime Cost Items are also allowed for the supply of materials or services by nominated sub-contractors. The contractor may object to a nominee because he would be prevented or prejudiced from fulfilling his own obligations; because the proposed sub-contractor is unwilling to accept contractual terms compatible with the main contract or will not provide adequate indemnities against breach; or because the contractor considers the nominee unreliable or incompetent. In the event of the contractor objecting, the Engineer may re-nominate, or omit the work by way of a variation, or confirm the nomination. If he confirms the nomination, the contractor places the sub-contract on the best terms available and the contract is varied accordingly. The employer indemnifies the contractor against any additional costs he incurs caused by failure of a nominated sub-contractor to perform his obligations, and the contractor is also entitled to extension of time for any delay caused by such failure.

It can thus be seen that the position of a nominated sub-contractor is not much different from that of a direct contractor to the employer, with the contractor providing the employer with management services.

14.3.3 Variations

In this type of contract, with extensive input from the Engineer or employer during the course of the contractor's design, variations may be considerable and the contract has to provide for their efficient management. The Engineer may order a variation and the contractor must perform it—immediately if the Engineer considers that delay would prejudice completion, but otherwise after comment and quotation from the contractor. The contractor may propose a variation and the Engineer may ask the contractor to prepare one. In the latter case the contractor is entitled to be paid for his preparatory work. The contractor may object to a variation on the grounds that the contract price would consequently be increased or decreased by more than 25%; that it would cause the contractor to breach an undertaking to or protected right of a third party: or that it required skills from the contractor that he did not possess (unless a sub-contractor be nominated).

The valuation of a variation may be agreed between Engineer and contractor, or may be a quotation from the contractor, and must be reasonable in all the circumstances. The completion date must be amended as necessary to incorporate the variation, and the contractor may also be entitled to an extension of time if the Engineer delays giving a variation order or approving a contractor's proposed variation.

14.3.4 The Engineer

The Red Book acknowledges the probability that the Engineer will be an employee of the employer, indeed, the employer is made as liable for the actions of an independent Engineer as he would be for his own employee. Thus, whether or not the Engineer is an independent professional, the employer is obligated to ensure that the Engineer carries out his duties, all obligations of the Engineer are deemed to be obligations of the employer, and the employer is responsible for all the Engineer's acts, neglects and omissions. However, the Engineer is required to act impartially between the parties when exercising his discretion or judgement. Thus the employer could not be held responsible when such exercise of discretion was involved since he has relinquished control over his employee in this particular and the contractor has agreed to this. The Engineer has full authority to act for the employer unless it is otherwise stated in the contract.

The Engineer's role is to specify what is required, to monitor and approve the contractor's design (where in practice he will frequently make a considerable contribution), procurement and construction, and to certify progress. The Engineer's power to disapprove drawings is limited to circumstances where they are contrary to an express provision of the contract or to good engineering practice. The Red Book does not give the Engineer explicit power to decide increases in contract price or extensions of time. For some additional requirements imposed on him, the contractor is entitled to the extra cost and expense he incurs. For a variation, he is entitled to additional payment according to his quotation, or what he and the Engineer agree, or what is reasonable. For a variety of delays, the contractor is entitled to extensions of time which are fair and reasonable, rather than decided by the Engineer or wholly dependent on his opinion.

The Engineer has no role in the resolution of disputes. Certain matters—the contractor's objection to a variation and any dispute over the disapproval of drawings—must be referred to an Expert. Other types of dispute may be refereed to arbitration or, by agreement between the parties, to an Expert. There is no appeal from the Expert's decision.

14.3.5 Employer Amendments

There are a number of clauses with which an employer might disagree. Like MF/1, the Red Book provides that no approval or consent required to be obtained under the contract shall be unreasonably withheld. The employer may consider a blanket statement of this kind unacceptable. For some consents, it will be entirely proper that the test of reasonableness be applied but there may well be others where the employer would wish to have unquestioned control. Sub-contracting is too easily allowed, and the contractor has no liability for failure by any nominated sub-contractor. Although the employer is given the right to terminate the contract without cause, the terms, which give the contractor his full profit and any contingency allowances he has included in his contract price, are absurdly generous unless the contract is nearing its end, and would certainly need revision.

Process plant projects are often organised so that the contractor is made responsible only for providing design and procurement services and supplying materials and equipment. The employer then carries out the construction, either directly or by placing one or more contracts for it. The Red Book model form of contract would need considerable modification if the contractor were not to be responsible for construction.

14.4 INSTITUTION OF CHEMICAL ENGINEERS' MODEL FORM FOR REIMBURSABLE CONTRACTS 1976—THE GREEN BOOK

The Institution of Chemical Engineers model form conditions of contract for reimbursable contracts—the Green Book—is quite different from its stable mate in its overall effect, though it shares many of its conditions with the Red Book. The Engineer is much more in control, as befits a reimbursable contract. All sub-contracts require the Engineer's approval and the contractor must comply with all instructions of the Engineer. Liquidated damages may be payable for late completion, but there are obvious difficulties with this in a reimbursable contract. They cannot be set until an adequate programme is available, which in a reimbursable contract is likely to be some time after contract award, and the employer has to be confident of his control of the contractor's operations so as to ensure that the contractor does not avoid damages at the expense of extra reimbursable costs. A bonus scheme for early completion may be easier to manage.

The contractor is liable to make good all defects in design, supply and construction, but at the expense of the employer, except where a sub-contractor or supplier makes good at his own expense or where the defect is the result of the contractor's negligence. The contractor is liable for the care of the works and for making good any loss or damage but his liability for the cost of this is limited to his recovery from insurance. Plant performance may be guaranteed and liquidated damages may be agreed, but this is not easily made compatible with a reimbursable contract and in most cases will probably not apply.

14.5 COMPARISON OF MAJOR ASPECTS

The model forms discussed have obvious differences arising from the use which is intended for them. ICE6 is suitable primarily for construction, MF/1 for design, supply and erection of mechanical or electrical engineering equipment, the Red and Green Books for the design, supply and construction of complete process plant. Some of the differences are the inevitable result of the different circumstances for which the contract conditions are intended. Others arise from the different roles envisaged for employer, Engineer and contractor.

The allocation of design responsibility is one of the most important differences between the model forms. The ICE6 contractor has little or no design responsibility for the permanent works and the model form does little more than allow the possibility. MF/1 is at the other extreme, with the contractor taking full responsibility for the design and the Engineer playing only a small part. The Institution of Chemical Engineers' model forms are devised to deal with a middle situation, where the contractor is responsible for the design but the employer, or Engineer, has a significant input to it. These profound differences echo the different circumstances in which the model forms are expected to be used.

Since he is not responsible for the design, the ICE6 contractor cannot be responsible for the fitness for purpose of the work, but merely for his own workmanship. The re-measurement and value nature of the contract also relieves him of most of the liability for costs, and adds considerable administrative complication. The Red Book and MF/1 model forms allocate liability for cost, time and performance to the contractor, moderated by any limitation of liability that might be agreed between the parties.

Obvious differences are found in the powers and duties of the Engineer to the various contracts. In ICE6, his opinion rules every instance where the

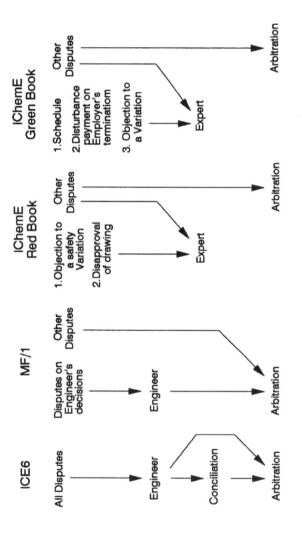

Figure 14.1 Dispute resolution

entitlement of the contractor to extra time or cost is in question and of quantification of that entitlement. He is obliged to consult the contractor in the case of valuation of variations, and in other decisions must take various matters into account, but these are the only conditions on his authority. In neither MF/1 nor the Red Book does the Engineer have such untrammelled power of decision: an award of extra cost or time must in practice usually be agreed with the contractor.

The ICE6 Engineer plays a much more prominent role in the settlement of disputes, as is shown in Figure 14.1. All disputes—those concerning his own previous decisions and any other dispute between employer and contractor— must first be referred to him for decision. In MF/1, only disputes on his previous decisions are first referred to the Engineer. In the Red Book, the Engineer plays no part in the resolution of disputes. To a large extent, this different role in disputes follows from differences in the Engineer's powers of decision. Under ICE6, the Engineer may decide many matters without consulting the contractor, so that the formal dispute may be the first occasion on which the contractor has the opportunity to put his arguments to the Engineer. In other model forms, the process of awarding extra cost or time necessarily involves inter-action between contractor and Engineer, so that the reference of a dispute to the Engineer would be largely superfluous. The model forms also differ in the rest of their procedures. ICE6 provides two further stages—an optional stage of conciliation and a final one of arbitration. MF/1 has a final stage of arbitration to which differences not resolved by the Engineer's adjudication and any other dispute may be referred. The Red Book provides that some types of disputes must be referred to an Expert and all others may be. There is no appeal from an Expert's decision: arbitration is provided for, but only for disputes which have not been referred to an Expert.

Chapter 15

Project Cost Management

15.1 INTRODUCTION

Project cost management is the term which has commonly come to be used to encompass all aspects of project costs—estimating, estimate revision, cost control and cost monitoring. The term cost control is used here in the narrow sense of obtaining early feedback of cost trends and, as a result, modifying the way the project is being executed in order to remain within budget—taking action that would not otherwise be taken. It does not include those important and continual actions to control costs which are part of the normal responsibilities of members of the project team—for example, the evaluation of process alternatives and the choice of the most economic option, keen purchasing, the minimising of change and variation, the placing of sub-contracts on well-defined scopes and specifications, the timely provision of materials and accurate design information to construction—all of which and more should be part of the normal behaviour of any well-managed project team.

Even within this narrow definition of cost control, and hence of project cost management, all members of the project team have a part to play. One or more specialist cost engineers will usually be appointed to a major project, but their role will be largely one of co-ordination, of processing data provided by others. If they are to obtain early cost information it must be from the other project team members. They will often need assistance in order to understand the significance of new data and to predict its effect on the project total cost. Any inclination on the part of members of the project team to behave as if responsibility for costs has been delegated and may safely be left to the cost engineer must be resisted.

The main objectives of project cost management may usefully be defined as follows:

(1) To establish a sound and accurate sanction estimate of the eventual project cost.
(2) To control (in the narrow sense defined above) the costs of the project throughout its design, construction and commissioning.
(3) To maintain an up-to-date estimate of project cost throughout the life of the project.
(4) To manage the cash flow of the project within any constraints which have been imposed.
(5) To account for the money spent and produce a coherent set of capital accounts.

These are listed in order of importance. Clearly, if the initial estimate is correct, all but the last item can be forgotten, though few would be so confident as to act on such a premiss. If the initial estimate is badly wrong, nothing will repair the damage. Cost control, though clearly next in importance, is very much secondary to a sound estimate since the power to control costs is necessarily limited once the scope of the project has been defined and rapidly diminishes as the project proceeds. The third item in the list, the maintenance of an up-to-date estimate, is essential to ensure that any tendency to exceed the sanctioned cost is recognised in advance. Cash flow management is unlikely to be a burden where a major company is the employer, except where forward currency contracts are entered into, or where the project is externally financed. The last item in the list, though necessary, is merely bean-counting and could be done, admittedly at greater cost and inconvenience, after the project is completed.

What seems often to be insufficiently appreciated is that satisfactory project cost management cannot be achieved through the agency of a single system. A formal cost management system can, and should, be established which, taking the sanction estimate as a basis, tracks the actual expenditure, revises the estimate on a continuous basis and produces at the end of the project a coherent set of capital accounts. Unfortunately, this system will be quite inadequate as a source of information for control purposes, since the cost data will be produced too late for effective action to be taken. It is therefore necessary to have other means of providing information on which action can be based—early enough so that corrective action may still be possible.

15.2 ESTIMATING

15.2.1 Sanction Estimate

In the vast majority of cases, the employer will sanction a major project only against what he believes is a firm estimate of capital cost. He will almost always have more investment opportunities than he can afford to pursue, and will rarely incline towards the large-scale funding of a mere speculation. Unlike a contractor, therefore, the employer's project manager must always provide a firm capital cost estimate which he believes has the required accuracy and reliability. He cannot refuse to offer a firm price because the project is inadequately defined. He does not have the contractor's alternative of offering to do the job reimbursably. He must provide an estimate, not of the cost of implementing a specified flowsheet, against which variations can be claimed if changes occur, but of the final project cost, including the cost of any changes that might be made during project execution.

The employer's project manager's first task must therefore be to work with the business promoting the project to define what is required. This will be a specification of plant performance rather than a detailing of project scope. The latter is then developed in conjunction with the other interested parties in the employer's organisation—the business, research and technical departments, production—in the most appropriate way. Exactly how this is done will depend on a number of factors. The employer's organisation and methods of working, the nature of the particular project, the breadth of the project manager's remit and his relationship with the other parties, and the importance or contentiousness of particular issues, will be major determinants. Definition of the project scope in process and engineering terms, however, will usually remain the final responsibility of the employer's project manager and, for the most part, the details of what is to be provided will not be approved by others in such a way as to diminish the project manager's responsibility for them.

To achieve adequate definition may require delaying the start of the project beyond the date hoped for by the business sponsor. It is in the nature of things that the moving spirit in a business is often a manager impatient of constraint, who has previously succeeded against the odds and intends to keep on doing so. The more successful he has been, the faster his rise in the organisation and the less his experience of trouble. To him, the project manager may appear to be delaying matters unnecessarily and to lack the drive that a successful project requires. The project manager may be put under intense pressure to act earlier than he considers prudent, but must not allow himself to be persuaded, against his better judgement, to proceed with inadequate definition or with an unsatisfactory estimate unless the situation is clearly understood and accepted by the sanctioning authority. Much depends on the project manager's personal standing and credibility. In the end, he is responsible, as will be made abundantly clear in the event of over-expenditure. He can be overruled only by his own departmental superiors, who would thereby take the responsibility. An experienced senior project manager could hardly be overruled on these matters without being replaced.

In many cases, the employer's staff will prepare the sanction estimate, without help from any contractor. This is especially likely if the employer is providing the technology. The processes of seeking authorisation for the capital expenditure and of enquiring for and evaluating bids may then be undertaken simultaneously, so reducing the gestation period of the project by several months. The employer's project manager must decide when the project has been adequately defined, so that the estimate basis has the required degree of certainty, and must decide to what extent firm prices must be sought from suppliers and sub-contractors. He must make appropriate allowance for rewarding design and construction contractors' risks where lump sum contracts are expected. He must decide the level of contingency required. He will look primarily to the project cost engineers to perform, with assistance from himself and other members of the project team the actual work of estimating. It is, of course, essential that the key members of the project team fully understand the basis of the sanction estimate, so that they can quickly identify and react to any changes from it that occur during project execution.

In other cases, and certainly where the employer has no prior knowledge or experience of the technology to be used in the proposed plant, the contractor must be relied upon to provide the sanction cost estimate, at least for the on-plot part of the project. If the employer has no design resources at all, he must also look to the contractor for the cost estimate for the off-plots. In such cases, the employer must solicit and receive bids before he is able to quantify the necessary capital expenditure and seek authorisation for it. If such an employer wished the work to start earlier, he would necessarily have to place a reimbursable contract. This should desirably be a preliminary contract to cover only the work of project definition and the development of a reliable estimate, or at least must give the employer the option to cancel if the first reliable cost estimate proves not to be to his liking. If long-delivery items were to be ordered as part of this first stage contract, the cost of cancellation would, of course, be substantially increased. A two-stage sanctioning process would in any case be necessary.

15.2.2 Estimating Methods

There are two fundamentally different types of estimate which may be used to estimate the capital cost of a new plant. The first of these is the synthetic or 'shopping list' estimate where the plant is specified in considerable detail and the costs of all its elements assessed and summated. This requires considerable effort in both design and estimating. Whatever the precision that theoretically can be achieved, in practice the method is prone to error and inaccuracy. The reason that shopping list estimates for process plants are used where the most accurate costing is required is that, by seeking and including firm prices from suppliers and sub-contractors for all major parts of the project, the proportion of the plant that has actually to be estimated by the project cost engineer can be reduced substantially. This remaining proportion will then often be estimated by methods which are essentially factorial, that is to say, by using analytically-derived data about common operations to provide composite costs, or unit rates, at the detailed level. The synthetic estimate can thus achieve an acceptable standard of accuracy, essentially by relying on others and their willingness to accept the risks of cost over-runs. Even so, great care must be taken to include everything necessary, since anything which is not specifically included will be omitted.

Analytical, or factorial estimates are based on the analysis of the achieved costs of previous projects. The relative ease of use of factorial methods—especially the comparatively small amount of plant-specific data that they require—makes them particularly valuable to the employer since he has need to make many estimates. These range from quick costings for the evaluation of research ideas and of competing processes to fairly accurate estimates for sanction purposes. Only a very small proportion of the projects which an employer initiates is successfully progressed into actual plant, yet most will require a number of cost estimates of varying accuracy to be made.

The simplest factorial estimate is one based on the achieved cost of a similar plant, the main adjustment being to allow for a difference in plant capacity. The cost/size relationship is well known: the ratio of the costs of two similar plants is proportional to the ratio of their sizes raised to an exponent. The value of this exponent varies with the type of plant and has been the subject of much study and published data. The exponent approaches 1.0 if extra plant capacity can be obtained only by the addition of more process streams in parallel. It can be as low as 0.4 if the change in capacity can be achieved entirely by the use of different sizes of equipment. The most common range of exponent for a complete process plant is from 0.6 to 0.85. Adjustments to the estimated cost so derived will, of course, have to be made for inflation and for off-plots which, being particular to the individual site, always have to be considered afresh. This method can be used only with successive plants employing the same process and is therefore of limited application.

Since one of the main advantages sought from a general factorial method of estimating is a reduction in the effort needed in estimate preparation, it follows that it must be based on information which emerges early in the design process. For process plants, the obvious candidate to provide such a basis is the cost of the equipment, or main plant items, which the plant contains. These can be defined, and costs obtained, with the expenditure of only a modest amount of detailed design effort. If the other plant costs—civil and structural work, bulk items such as piping, electrics and instruments, and the costs of erection, can be related to main plant item cost a useful estimating system can be achieved.

At least two such methods have been developed. The first has its origins in work by H. J. Lang (first reported in *Chemical Engineer* September 1947), who related the total cost of a process plant to the total cost of the main plant items included in it. The simple ratio of one to the other gives the Lang factor. Factors for various types of plants have been published, but a good deal of further development is required to obtain the accuracy usually required for sanction purposes.

For a process plant of a given type, the Lang factor can be shown to be related to the average main plant item cost, and allowing for this relationship enables greater estimating accuracy to be achieved. Further detailed analysis of achieved costs makes it possible to split the factor into separate overall factors for the cost of each of the functional elements of a plant, for example, the cost of piping, of instruments or of construction. Given copious amounts of achieved cost data to analyse, and the effort to match, it is possible to arrive at a series of individual factors which may be applied to the cost of each main plant item to give the associated cost of each functional element. Thus, for example, for the cost of the piping associated with a given main plant item, the system would offer a number of curves of factor value against main plant item cost. Each curve would relate to a given type of piping installation, for example, traced and lagged carbon steel piping in a structure, and the estimator would choose the most appropriate. The advantage of so doing is not that an individual cost, for example, of the piping associated with a given heat exchanger, is accurately estimated, but that by selecting in this way all the factors to be used, the estimator defines the character of the plant. He is thus able to arrive at a composite, overall factor with a precision that could not be achieved by other means. Two further adjustments need to be included in such a system. The first is a correction for the higher costs of special materials, which will affect the cost of the main plant item but not that of, for example, its associated foundations. The second is to compensate for the effects of inflation on main plant item cost when determining factor value. An estimate produced by such a factorial method is not, of course, suitable as a basis for much subsequent cost monitoring, since the only itemised costs it contains are those of the main plant items.

A second factorial estimating method is based on the use of a series of notional models of small sections of plant, each of which defines in physical detail the functional elements associated with a given main plant item. Choosing a model type for each main plant item defines not a cost factor but the physical details of that section of the plant. The total costs of this are then automatically computed using standard data in the computer program. This is a far more elaborate method than the first and is much more powerful. It can be used to produce both physical quantities and cost data in detail for the whole plant, most of this data being internally generated in the computer program which has of necessity to be used. It is possible to adjust the data to allow for the changing costs of labour and raw materials. Such a method provides a reasonable basis for cost monitoring during early project execution—until a more detailed estimate is prepared—since all the quantities on which the estimate is based are defined.

Factorial methods have the great advantage that they will include all the usual requirements for a process plant without the need for everything to be specified. In experienced hands, they can provide an accuracy of about plus or minus 10% on the total—equivalent to that usually required for sanction purposes—provided the main plant item costs are correct. Since there will inevitably be inaccuracies in the main plant item costs, such accuracy will not be achieved. The gap may be bridged in three ways, separately or in combination. The first method, as mentioned above, is to seek firm prices for a major part of the project cost. This allows a lower standard of accuracy on the remainder of the estimate, but may require substantial pre-sanction work. The employer's project manager may have difficulty in getting agreement to delay the start of the project in order that this can be done. Second, if the new plant is a near repeat of one recently built, then enough credible cost data of direct relevance may be available to upgrade the estimate accuracy to the required standard. Third, an estimate judged to have an accuracy, for example, of plus or minus 15% can be increased by 5% to alter the range to plus 10%, minus 20%. Further than that, but not to be relied upon too heavily, if the need for economy is appreciated by all the parties concerned at the outset and is accepted as having overwhelming priority—a far from common occurrence—strong cost control during project execution can help to cut the project coat according to the cloth available. With these steps for assistance in greater or lesser degree, factorial estimating methods will serve to provide a sanction quality estimate. Of course, the prudent estimator will make use of all methods and all sources of data available to him, checking his conclusions in as many different ways as possible.

The development of any factorial method of estimating to the stage at which it can be used with confidence requires much effort and very large quantities of achieved cost data. Systems can be purchased, but there is still considerable work to be done by the intending user to validate a system for his own circumstances. It will be evident that factorial systems, being the result of analysis of previous plants, have built into them the engineering standards used in those plants. There are many aspects of a plant which are undefined on a process flowsheet and which have a major effect on costs—safety in design, productivity in construction, standards of access and isolation for maintenance, layout, weather protection, to give just a few examples. The standards implicit in an externally developed factorial estimating system may not match the user's which, in any event, will change over time. Adjustment will have to be made, by trial and error, for any differences. Factorial estimating methods are not, of course, to be recommended where comparative estimates of small sections of a plant are called for. In such cases, where the small difference between large quantities has to be determined, the safest method is to identify the hardware differences and cost these in detail.

15.3   COST MONITORING

Over-expenditure may sometimes be justified. It is much more difficult to explain away why it was not predicted, or was incurred unknowingly. Of course, the project manager's prediction of the final cost will be less precise at some times than others. He will have the results of the last formal cost estimate. For what has happened since he will, once orders begin to be placed and new cost data begins to flow in quantity, look to the Monthly Cost Report. This is the main output of the cost monitoring system, and will typically contain the following information for each cost code:

(1) Cost code
(2) Description of item
(3) Cumulative expenditure
(4) Cumulative commitments
(5) Cost required to complete
(6) Expected final cost
    (a) Target ($=4+5$)
    (b) Development allowance or contingency
    (c) Total ($=6a+6b$)
(7) Latest control estimate
(8) Sanction estimate
(9) Variance this month
(10) Total variance ($6c-7$)

There will also be comment on and explanation of changes, and statements of any assumptions which have been made. The Report should be accompanied by the Cost Diary, as described later, or its equivalent, and should include curves comparing actual and predicted expenditure and commitments. It will also be necessary for it to give the latest position on exchange rate effects if extensive use of foreign currency is a feature of the project. The problems of dealing with multiple foreign currencies are discussed later.

The Monthly Cost Report requires considerable effort to produce, and usually forms the basis of a monthly cost review meeting. It is important that its weaknesses are understood, and that excessive reliance is not placed on it. It is usually far from being an accurate monthly re-estimate of the cost of the project, and will provide an increasingly unreliable update of expected final cost as the previous formal estimate recedes into history. Consequently, the project manager must judge the desirable timing of the next formal estimate, basing his decision on the magnitude of the changes which have taken place in the project since the last estimate was made and on his view of the efficacy of the cost monitoring system. He will usually be permitted a tolerance of plus or minus 10% on the sanctioned total for the project, and in theory at least, work should stop as soon as it is apparent that this tolerance is likely to be exceeded, and remain suspended until approval for the forecast extra expenditure is obtained. The project manager must not, therefore, allow significant uncertainty to develop between formal estimates.

15.3.1 Expenditure and Commitment Curves

Before sanction, it is necessary to predict the timing of expenditure and commitments to help estimate the impact of inflation, and to predict cash flow requirements. It might be thought that, on a well-defined project, if sufficient time and effort were devoted to listing all the proposed orders and sub-contracts, the order values and the predicted timing of payments to be made, together with expected construction payments and internal expenditure, a reasonably accurate forecast of the timing of expenditure and commitments for the project could be developed. In fact, this is not the case. For a number of reasons, which include the inevitable optimism of the project plan, the dilatoriness of suppliers in submitting invoices, and delays in approval and payment (it is in the nature of things that any unexpected event will delay payment), the forecast by such methods of expenditure and commitments for a complete process plant is always far too early. Experience shows that the most accurate prediction is obtained by rule of thumb methods, and most employers will have developed their own empirical method of forecasting which amounts simply to applying the relevant project parameters to a particular shape of S-curve.

It is usual to produce, as part of the Monthly Cost Report, a graph comparing the timing of actual and predicted cumulative expenditure and commitments for the whole project. This will be examined with some care but little profit. The empirical nature of the predicted curve gives no great confidence in its accuracy and this apart, any deviation of actual figures from the prediction may be the result of variations in costs or timing, or both. Not only is there no way of distinguishing, but some effects, for example, those of delay and of over-spending, act in opposing directions. Of course, gross deviations will be recognised, but in such circumstances other alarm bells would surely have rung long before. For a project where costs are reasonably on target, scrutiny of these curves will tell nothing about the final cost.

For individual phases of the project, where expenditure and progress are more directly linked—such as construction, where expenditure is mainly the result of the consumption of man-hours on site, and physical progress can be more easily measured—the comparison of actual and predicted expenditure will provide more of an insight into progress and costs. But even here, much the same information will have been available earlier from comparisons of actual and predicted man-hour usage.

15.3.2   Cost Required to Complete

Since expenditure and commitments *per se* are of little use in cost forecasting, most of the value of the Monthly Cost Report lies in how the 'cost required to complete' is arrived at. On a major project, so much effort may be expended in collecting and sorting information on expenditure and commitments and in dealing with inflation and currency effects, that it is entirely possible that no more than a monthly record of expenditure and commitments will be presented, together with a repetition of the current estimate figures. The cost required to complete would then be no more than the difference between the accumulated commitment and the previous estimate of expected final cost, from which nothing could be learnt.

The minimum that should be done for the Cost Report in the early stages of the project is that order values for equipment replace estimated values in the project estimate, so that over-commitment on any item is immediately reflected in an increase in the project total (or, at least, in a reduction in the unallocated contingency). There may be more to be learnt from early main plant item orders than merely that those particular items are over-spent or not, but it is very possible that time and effort will not permit many of these conclusions, for which the cost engineer will usually require the considerable contributions of other project team members, to be drawn. Increased main plant item costs may presage a general finding of under-estimation, so that estimates of other main plant item costs should be increased accordingly. Other deductions of significance may be possible from such early figures, for example, that the cost of a special material employed in the project has increased, and estimates of other items making use of it should therefore be revised. If the current project estimate is factorial, then logic demands that the other parts of the estimate which are factored on main plant item costs be altered. Later, expenditure must be related to work done in order to revise estimated item totals. A great deal of effort is necessary to determine the cost required to complete for a major project. It is unlikely that the monthly attempt at it will be very reliable during a period of significant change.

15.3.3 Timing of Information

One of the major drawbacks of the Monthly Cost Report is that it is out of date before it appears. From the cut-off date for information into the project's costs section, anything from three to six weeks will elapse before the report is issued. There are additional, previous delays. Information of necessity flows down routine channels into the cost section, and will often arrive a considerable time after the first intimation of a cost increase has been received in the project team. For example, the cost of a piece of equipment will be reported formally to cost section at the earliest when the order is placed, but it may by then have been evident for some months that a significant increase was inevitable, even if this could not be precisely quantified. In the case of orders placed by the employer's own organisation, the reporting route may well be from the Purchasing Department to Accounts Department and from there to costs section, adding yet more delay and risk of error.

In fact, the cost information processing systems of a large employer, unlike those of the process plant contractor, are not usually designed with the interests of an individual project in mind. They are main frame systems designed to deal with all the transactions that the employer undertakes. An individual project will form a small part of the total information flow and its interests will be subordinate to those of the company as a whole. Information will be designed to flow from one data processing system to another without human intervention. Frequently such systems lack the flexibility that project systems need. They may deal only with orders which are placed, and accounts which are paid, from the home country of the employer. They may be unable to handle foreign orders or currencies, or single orders of large enough magnitude. They may not be able to sort information in the necessary ways, or will produce reports in which the project data is submerged in masses of other information. A major foreign project will have a number of separate cost centres, perhaps in several countries, each of which will require a formal cost monitoring system to be established and operated and whose individual reports must be brought together into the Monthly Cost Report for the project.

Thus the formal cost monitoring system for a project is not well designed as a spur to action. Rather is it a record of what has been committed and spent. By and large it receives, and can process, only firm information, not preliminary guesses. Because it is an attempt to report comprehensively, accurately and in detail, and may later be expected to provide the capital records for the project, it requires much time and effort to sort and process the data. This is doubly so if inflation and exchange rates, discussed later, are significant factors. At best it will be possible in the Monthly Cost Report to take partial account of the implications of the new data that it has received. It is too much to expect that the cost engineer, not being party to the design, nor perhaps even to the production of the estimate if the functions of cost estimating and monitoring are separated, will be able to explore fully the implications of all cost changes on a monthly basis. In a properly managed project, the cost report will seldom offer the project manager much new information, merely greater accuracy about some of the things he already knows.

These strictures apply to any formal cost monitoring system for a large project, although with the advent of desk-top computers able to handle the necessary volumes of information, a somewhat more rapid response can be achieved. A project-centred cost monitoring system—contractors' systems are necessarily so designed—can be better tailored to project requirements.

15.4 COST CONTROL

The limitations to what can be accomplished by cost control, that is to say, through action being taken when costs are seen to be increasing beyond what was expected at sanction, have already been alluded to above. To be at all effective, action to control costs must be early action. It cannot wait upon the slow grinding of some massive bureaucratic system of reporting what happened the month before last, and which in any case, does not begin to operate until the most important formative stages of project execution are over. It is the action that is about to incur the excessive cost that must be modified if any influence is to be exerted. At all stages of the project, in matters both great and small, the control that can be exercised diminishes with time. Influence is obviously greatest when the scope of the project is being decided. What you do not have costs nothing (and needs no maintenance). To revise the scope definition at a later stage of the project in an attempt to reduce costs may do quite the opposite and incur extra time as well. Only if part of the original scope can be cleanly and easily deleted is significant cost reduction likely to be achieved in this way. Lesser opportunities for control become available as successive design, purchasing and construction decisions are taken. The most effective way of controlling costs once the project scope has been defined does not wait upon the receipt of cost data presaging over-expenditure, but lies in the careful provision of correct information on which to base the succeeding stages of the design, the placing of orders and sub-contracts and the performance of construction—in short, the avoidance of change and variation.

Most of the important decisions, in any branch of management, have to be taken before very much data is available. This is as true of cost control as of any other management activity and by the time the formal monitoring system has got into its stride, the opportunity for more than minor control action has largely passed. The realisation that this is so can easily be obscured by the vast quantity of cost monitoring work done, and the large number of voluminous reports, tables and graphs produced, when it is generally too late to do much more than watch events as they unfold. It should be clear from the discussion in the previous section that the formal Monthly Cost Report has little to do with cost control, and everything to do with the detailed and accurate recording of costs. It does not begin to be issued until orders for equipment are being placed, by which time all or most of the major aspects of the project are fixed, and even then will always be several weeks behind events. For information on which to base his cost control actions the project manager must look elsewhere. He requires an informal, simple system, involving the minimum number of key staff, which will give him early warning of potential cost increases. He does not require accurate or comprehensive figures of such increases, nor could such a system provide them.

Thus there are two cost systems that the project manager must establish and use. In addition to the formal system epitomised by the Monthly Cost Report, there must be an informal system which responds more rapidly to events. The two systems are not, of course, completely separate and information flows from one to the other. The informal system can take one of several forms. Perhaps the simplest is the Cost Diary, or Cost Trend. This is simply a list of possible significant changes to the project, together with some estimate, however conjectural, of their associated costs. The employer's project manager and all key members of his team must contribute to the Cost Diary. These are the people familiar with the basis of the estimate, who know best which areas of cost are most uncertain and what has been allowed for, who can identify changes and can sense when things are not turning out as expected. The Cost Diary should be maintained throughout the project and can later form an appendix to the Monthly Cost Report, items being deleted from it as they are assimilated into the cost report proper.

Another, more developed, method is the Key Item Cost Report, which begins by listing those items most likely to cause over-spending. This may be because of the very high cost of an item, or the unreliability of the estimate for it, or its technical uncertainty and the likelihood of changes to it or any combination of these and other reasons. The sanction estimate for each key item is included, together with its key parameters—parameters which can be checked at an early stage of project development and which will give an indication of cost trends. The list of key items will change as the project progresses. It is of little use including items for which no further information will be available for a year.

To go much further than the Key Item Cost Report is to risk making the system bureaucratic and unable to respond as rapidly as required. The purpose of the informal system is merely to identify a potentially serious cost increase, not to quantify it accurately. Once identified, a decision can be taken whether further work is appropriate to assess the potential cost increase more closely, or whether action should be taken immediately to avoid it, or both. It would, however, be optimistic to suppose that either of these methods will result in all significant changes being identified. Changes in those aspects of the project which are the responsibility of the process and project engineers, such as engineering line diagram changes and additional items of equipment, will probably be detected, but there will be less success in functional areas, for example, the late discovery of the need to pile a foundation. In such a case, it is more than likely that the civil designer will not be familiar with the estimate basis and so will not recognise a change, nor report it. Of course, the project manager will endeavour to see that changes to functional elements of the project are quickly reported, but should not rely on it.

To ensure that all, or at least the vast majority, of changes are detected and quantified with all their ramifications and with reasonable accuracy, there is no substitute for a formal revision of the estimate. This takes considerable time and effort, and good reasons will always be advanced why next month would be a better time, either because more data would then be available or to avoid delay to some critical activity. It is the project manager's task to decide when the time is appropriate for a re-estimate and to insist upon it.

15.5   THE PROJECT COST MANAGEMENT SYSTEM

In establishing the total cost management system for his project, the employer's project manager must be conscious of a number of general difficulties that any large project faces. Important among these are communication problems. The need, which such projects have to process and transfer large quantities of information accurately, militates against dealing quickly with any individual item of information. The project systems grind small, but very slowly, exchanging speed for certainty, and cannot be relied upon to provide information for control purposes. There may be hundreds of people engaged on the design and the project manager must appreciate that not all of them will pay much attention to the cost implications of what they do, regarding these often as unwelcome intrusions into the much more interesting technical tasks which are their real concern. Engineers' lack of interest in considerations of cost is encouraged by the trend to increasing specialisation. No longer, it seems, is an engineer one who can make for 50p what anyone could make for a pound. The employment of quantity surveyors grows apace, cost engineering is increasingly a recognised speciality and estimating is often divorced even from cost monitoring. This specialisation has no doubt led to greater expertise in the performance of the separate tasks, but at the expense of widening the divisions between those who incur costs and those who monitor and report them. It adds to the communications problems on a large project and often results in the cost implications of design developments being overlooked until a formal revised estimate is made.

The project manager must have regard for a number of other matters specific to the particular project. He must consider the completeness and certainty with which the project scope is defined, and the nature and expected accuracy of the sanction estimate. He must give thought to particular areas of uncertainty or of external threat. He must also consider the quality of his own organisation, the pressures upon it and the strengths and weaknesses of his project team. He must assess the cost management capabilities of the various contractors to be employed. With all these considerations in mind, he will have directed the development of a Cost Management Procedure, as part of or separately from the Co-ordination Procedure, which sets out what is required by way of cost management for the project as a whole and details the obligations of the main contractors engaged. This will have formed part of the employer's Enquiry, and hence will be part of the contract documents.

The following is a model for a cost management system for a typical process plant project, which may be modified to take account of the circumstances of a particular project. The project manager must identify those aspects of his project which are likely to be the causes of over-spending and monitor those in such a way that any tendency to over-spend is noticed immediately:

(1) *Sanction estimate*. It cannot be said too often that this is the most important single element. The employer's project manager must decide when the scope of the project is sufficiently firm to allow the sanction estimate to be prepared. He must decide what, if any, firm prices are required from suppliers and sub-contractors. He must have regard to all the circumstances of the project. If project finance is being raised, the lending institutions will have a powerful voice and will probably require that much of the total cost of the project is covered by lump sum bids from contractors. Only an urgent need for project completion coupled with a forecast high rate of return justifies less than usual accuracy, which can and must then be allowed for by increased contingency.

It is essential that the sanction estimate be properly detailed and documented so that it may sensibly be used as a basis for cost monitoring during the period until the first control estimate is produced.

(2) *Scope monitoring*. The scope of the project always needs the most careful monitoring. The months immediately following the production of the sanction estimate are the most important in this respect. This period will include the several months, between completion of the estimate and the obtaining of sanction, that are necessary to allow the financial case for the project to be finalised and for authorisation to be sought and given. If the sanction estimate is based on less than final flowsheets, data sheets and equipment lists, this first monitoring stage is all the more vital. But

whatever the supposed certainty of the process design, detailed design usually gives rise to some changes, even for a repeat project.

Process plant projects are seldom disastrously over-spent solely because the cost of the scope as initially defined is more than was expected. Where this is the case, the cause will almost certainly be unexpected inflation or currency movement, for which the project manager would probably feel he had some tenable excuse. Inadequate definition is nearly always the cause of gross over-spending. The key to the whole matter of cost management, therefore, lies in making sure that the project scope does not exceed what was sanctioned or, if it must, to see that this is quickly understood and the appropriate action taken. If the project emerges unscathed from the period of finalising its scope and process design, it will augur well for the eventual outcome.

The main feature of the cost management system at this time is the Cost Diary, or the Key Item Cost Report, as described above, or some similar informal procedure. It is too early for the Monthly Cost Report to be produced. The volume of project information being worked on is manageable, but a high proportion of it will have significant influence on the project cost.

(3) *First control estimate.* Experience shows that even the best cost monitoring systems fail to pick up all the changes that occur, much less allow accurately for them, and that a complete re-estimate is required at intervals throughout the project. A key decision of the project manager is when to order the first control estimate. If there has been much development of the sanction flowsheets, an appropriate time will be as soon as firm flowsheeets, data sheets and equipment lists are available. An estimate based on a firm scope at the first available opportunity is something that no sensible project manager would forgo. If producing the estimate requires that other work be delayed, as those concerned will often claim, then this is a price that should willingly be paid.

(4) *Equipment order monitoring.* As soon as the first control estimate is produced, it is used as the basis of the next stage of cost monitoring (although, of course, external reports must continue to compare the expected out-turn against the sanction total). This stage of monitoring is concerned mainly with the cost of orders for main plant items. The Monthly Cost Report will now be started and, as discussed above, must include as good an estimate as possible of the cost to complete. The Cost Diary will be continued and, dealing with preliminary cost information, will be a month or more in advance of the monthly report. The project manager will now be calling for other data, such as a comparison of the estimated and actual cost of equipment ordered so far. Any over-spending on equipment can be multiplied by the project 'Lang' factor to get a first idea of total cost effect.

(5) *Second control estimate.* When the majority of the main plant item prices are to hand, a further control estimate should be prepared. At this stage, preliminary bulk take-offs from engineering line diagrams will be available and will be taken into account. This may be the first non-factorial project estimate.

(6) *Monitoring of bulks and sub-contracts.* Subsequent monitoring following production of the second control estimate will be concerned above all with the monitoring of bulk materials, sub-contracts and construction sub-contracts.

   The Monthly Cost Report will now be well into its stride, but the Cost Diary should be continued. The project manager will take particular note of important cost items—he should now have a clear idea of where costs are likely to exceed the original expectation. He will also be watching for the cost effects of the design reviews by his production colleagues, who may need their enthusiasm for the best of everything restrained.

(7) *Third control estimate.* When final take-offs of bulk materials have been made, another control estimate is desirable. Subsequent monitoring will be mainly concerned with construction. This alone is hardly likely to overspend the project since it is usually only about one-third of the total cost. By this stage, only fine tuning of costs is possible. Unless the expected final cost already exceeds the sanction total, or is near to doing so, costs begin to occupy less of the project manager's time and attention. On the other hand, the processing of costs for the Monthly Cost Report will be at its peak. There is unlikely to be need for a further control estimate unless something dramatic and unexpected occurs.

15.6   THE EFFECTS OF INFLATION AND EXCHANGE RATE MOVEMENTS

15.6.1   Inflation

The usual method of estimating the capital cost of a project is to start by costing at current prices. To the total is then added a percentage to cover the forecast rate of inflation. A single percentage figure which is a weighted average for the whole project will probably be used. The typical expenditure and commitments curve for a project has a centre of area two-thirds of the way through the project period and the forecast inflationary increase to this point in time is used to increase the expected final cost. If there is substantial foreign currency expenditure, it will be necessary to consider the forecast rate of inflation separately for each currency. It is, of course, possible to make these calculations in more detail by splitting the project into shorter periods, but given the limitations in predicting the timing of expenditure and commitments already referred to, and the uncertainty of inflation forecasts, this may not always be worth the effort. It is hardly practicable to construct the estimate from the beginning using inflation-adjusted figures for each item of expenditure nor, for reasons discussed below, would this be likely to give greater accuracy.

In calculating the increase in total project cost due to inflation, the prediction of the rate of inflation is itself the most obvious source of error. In many countries, the only forecast available is of the retail price index. This represents the average housewife's basket of groceries, with the addition of one or two other household expenses such as (in the UK) mortgage repayments. This will not correspond very closely to inflation in the cost of chemical plant, even of those costs which arise in their home country. Some of the content of plant ostensibly originating in one country may come from another where different inflationary conditions apply. A country's retail price index may have some influence on its construction wage rates, but will have little effect on the cost of stainless steel plate and none at all on the cost of imported materials. Thus, even if the prediction of change in the retail price index is accurate, the relevance of the forecast to process plant design and construction is limited. In the UK, data on wage rates and material prices for different industries are published regularly and a specially tailored index may be constructed.

Forecasts of any sort contain a strong element of extrapolation. Major disturbance is seldom anticipated. In February 1974, for example, the best prediction of the inflation of process plant costs for the twelve months of 1974 was 18%. By June 1974, this forecast had increased to 30%, much to the discomfiture of those responsible for projects sanctioned in the interim. A further feature of process plant equipment costs, not reflected in any published index, is their response to the cyclical nature of the activity level in the industry. When things are slack, prices may remain unchanged for several years or even be reduced. As soon as activity increases, prices will rise substantially—perhaps by as much as 30%—to recover losses in previous years and restore profitability. Construction costs are similarly affected, by changes in productivity as well as by wage rates. The effects can be seen in analyses of project cost performance over the years. In slack periods, projects are on average under-spent; in boom years over-spent. The effects of the industrial cycle on prices must be taken into account on any large project. An educated guess would need data on prices of comparable equipment and construction costs in sufficient quantity over an adequate period.

A second source of error is in the forecast of timing of the expenditure, limitations on the accuracy of which have already been discussed above. A third factor affecting the accuracy of forecasts is the view on price that each supplier takes, which will depend on his own view of inflation, whether the materials he requires are to hand or have to be specially ordered, the timing of the next wage rise for his workforce, the strength of the competition for the order and various other factors. It is clear, therefore, that in periods of high inflation, the accuracy of any capital estimate may be seriously compromised by inevitable inaccuracy in estimating the inflation effect, even if the estimate is otherwise accurate. Process plant contractors can avoid this problem by refusing to quote fixed prices in such circumstances, but no such escape route is available to the employer. In periods of high inflation, his estimate may contain as much as half the total cost of the project in a single inflation figure, derived by the inaccurate methods adumbrated above.

In view of the magnitude of the inflation allowance which has to be included in periods of high inflation, attempts have been made to monitor its consumption separately. These are misconceived. The idea of generalised inflation is a rough and ready concept and inflation allowances are not susceptible to analysis. Before cost monitoring begins, it is necessary to distribute the inflation allowance over the itemised costs of the project, having regard to the expected timing of expenditure on each. This, of course, cannot give results of great accuracy: the calculation of inflation on individual items has already been dismissed as a method of determining inflation for the project as a whole. The actual escalation of prices for individual items occurs in steps, not continuously as an inflation index would suppose. This may lead to apparent under-spending on early orders, followed by over-spending on later ones.

Inflation indices are lagging indicators. Long before an index has been published, the prices of equipment and of sub-contracts will have increased. Any over-expenditure may first and for some time appear as simple underestimating. It is not until later that the actual inflation index can, perhaps, be used to explain the increased costs. With a major employer, it is not often that there will be restrictions on the timing of expenditure, but if there is a pattern of expenditure that has to be followed, this is an additional complication. Nor is it usual for considerations of interest on capital employed to be taken into account. The employer's project manager may buy early to avoid price escalation and will not usually be penalised by higher interest payments.

15.6.2 Exchange Rates

It is necessary to monitor and control all costs in the currency of sanction, and this requirement is not affected by loans for the project being raised in other currencies. The sanction currency will usually be the currency of the country where the plant is to be built. All other currencies, including sterling where appropriate, are foreign currencies and it causes nothing but confusion if cost data is repeatedly expressed in sterling simply because sterling numbers can most easily be understood. Because of the vagaries of exchange rates, the project manager may, for example, find his project over-spent in the currency of sanction, but not in sterling. This may be interesting but is ultimately irrelevant.

It is often possible largely to eliminate the risk of exchange rate movement by entering into a forward contract for the purchase of foreign currency (foreign in the sense of being other than the currency of sanction). The forward rate is the price agreed now for payment at the agreed date when the foreign currency is delivered. The uninitiated might suppose that the risk of exchange rate movement is thereby transferred to the seller, who forecasts the future exchange rate and gambles on his prediction. In fact, the forward purchase of a currency involves no risk on the part of the seller. The purchase price is determined by the current exchange rate and the difference in interest rates obtainable on the currencies concerned in the transaction. The seller secures the foreign currency now at the current spot rate. He then adds or subtracts the difference in the interest that will be earned on the currency he is now holding compared with that which the purchase currency would have earned. Thus, a higher interest currency will be cheaper on the forward market than the spot rate and is said to be at a discount to a currency with a lower interest rate. The latter is said to be at a premium.

All contractors will wish to eliminate the exchange rate risks of a project by buying forward. To a contractor, each project is a separate venture and must stand or fall on its own. To the large employer, other considerations will obtrude. A large company with income and expenditure arising from numerous ventures in different parts of the world will wish to combine the cash flows arising from its various activities and if it is to buy forward at all, to buy for the net result of the combination. Decisions to hedge or not will be taken by a separate dealing department. This makes it impossible to isolate the effects on one particular project. It is, of course, possible for the employer to buy forward notionally for a particular project—to arrange an internal 'contract' between the project and the employer's finance department—so as to allow the exchange gains or losses on the project to be properly attributed. If this is not done, the project will be apparently exposed to exchange rate risks. The sanction estimate will have to include forecasts of exchange rate movements and the project manager will have to account for performance in this respect.

The project manager should, therefore, have at least some elementary understanding of the interactions between inflation, interest and exchange rates. In a perfect market, and assuming that economic conditions are in equilibrium, there are a number of equivalences which hold in theory. These may be briefly described as follows:

(1) *Purchasing power parity.* This is based on the premiss that internationally-traded commodities must cost the same, wherever they are purchased. Were it possible to buy such a commodity in one country cheaper than in another, a profit opportunity would exist to buy in one country and sell in the other. The activities of arbitrageurs doing this would result in the narrowing of real price until the profit potential was extinguished: thus, if

inflation rises in one country more than that in another, the exchange rate will fall in order to compensate for the difference. It is, of course, a long step to extend this argument to general price changes. Many of the goods making up a retail price index either cannot be or are not traded internationally, so that rise or fall in exchange rates to compensate for differential rates of inflation does not obviously follow. At best, one would suppose, there must be a considerable time lag. And of course, the activities of arbitrageurs are not the only influence. Producers themselves may take advantage of the situation to increase their profit levels, and government action may have a major effect. Nevertheless, it is evident that inflation and exchange rate movements will act in opposing directions so that their combined effect will be moderated and, so far as an individual project is concerned, the inflation it suffers will tend towards the home country rate of inflation. If purchasing power parity exactly obtained in practice, then the home currency rate of inflation would apply to the total costs of a project, irrespective of where those costs originated.

(2) *Interest rate parity.* This concept states that the difference in interest rates available in two internationally-traded currencies must be balanced by the difference between the spot and forward rates of one currency in terms of the other. Were this not so there would be opportunities for risk-free profitable covered interest arbitrage. The arbitrageur could borrow for a specified period at fixed interest in one country, convert this loan into the currency of a second and invest in the second country at a higher fixed interest rate. The proceeds to be received from this investment could then be used to buy forward in the first country for delivery when the original loan was due, producing more than sufficient to repay the initial loan and interest. The exploiting of these opportunities would soon result in the balancing of the exchange and interest rates.

(3) *Real interest rates.* A third hypothesis, sometimes known as the Fisher effect, requires that real interest rates, i.e. actual interest rates adjusted by the expected inflation rate—should tend toward the same in each country. Where investment is internationally mobile, any other situation would result in the flight of investment to wherever the returns were highest. This, of course, assumes that the investment opportunities and risks in the various countries were perceived as identical, and ignores the effects of governmental restrictions on the investment of capital.

Additionally, in an ideal world, it would logically be the case that the forward rate for a currency for delivery at a specified time should equal the predicted future spot rate at that time. Any difference would result in trading which would correct the imbalance. On the other hand, if this relationship were certain there would be no point in buying forward. In practice, the difference between forward and expected future spot rates will reflect the uncertainty in the latter.

Finally, the so-called International Fisher Effect suggests that differences in interest rates will equal the expected change in the spot rate of exchange over a period.

Of course, the real world is rather different from the model which these relationships outline. The model is based on the assumption that the economic world is in equilibrium, which must seldom be the case. Purchasing power parity assumes that all goods are internationally traded—or that prices behave as if they were. Many powerful influences on the situation are neglected. The interventions of government, the actions of manufacturers to improve profit margins, barriers to the mobility of capital and many other factors which may have an important effect are ignored. When the model is compared with reality it is found that interest rate parity holds pretty well, but that the other relationships are mere trends—in the long term they are useful guides but in the short term are far from an accurate description of events.

Estimates

Problems of currency exchange first affect the work of the project manager in drawing up the sanction estimate. This must initially be produced in the currencies that are expected to be used. This estimate, using perhaps as many as a dozen different currencies, has then to be converted into the currency of sanction. There are two ways in which this might be done, depending on the way in which the employer intends to deal with the problems of currency exchange:

(1) The employer may decide to accept the risk of future exchange rate variation himself or, at least, will not buy forward for the individual project. In this case, the necessary conversion of the multi-currency estimate into a single currency is similar to that which must be made to allow for inflation. The timing of expenditure in each currency must be predicted—annually or quarter by quarter—and the exchange rate for each currency must be similarly forecast. The expenditure in each currency in each period must then be converted to the sanction currency. Usually, the calculations to account for predicted rates of inflation and fluctuations in exchange rates will be performed together by the multiplication of the three matrices.
(2) The employer may decide to buy forward. In this case the timing of expenditure must be forecast and arrangements made for the necessary forward purchase. There are clearly problems of timing here opposite sanction, since no commitment to buy forward can be entered into until the project is authorised, yet the cost of currency purchase must be assumed in the sanction estimate. It may, however, be possible to take options to buy forward.

If it is the intention that major parts of the project should be the subject of lump sum contracts, and the employer's estimate is prepared before receipt of bids, the estimate must reflect the fact that the contractors will buy forward, whether or not the employer does so. Of course, if the difference between forward and current spot rates equalled the forecast change in the spot rate, the result of both ways of calculating the exchange rates effect would be the same. In the real world the difference may be significant.

The question of exchange rates will also complicate consideration of contractors' lump sum tenders. Unless the employer has agreed that the bidders take options on forward purchases of currencies which, even if they are available, is unlikely because of their cost, the bidders have no choice but to bid either in a basket of currencies or in the sanction currency converted at current spot rates. The firm price at forward rates would be provided immediately before the contract was awarded. The incidence of projected expenditure in the various currencies will not be the same for each of the bidders and it will be more difficult for the employer to compare the bids with each other and with his own estimate.

Forward purchase of some currencies is not possible. In the case of others, only short term contracts are available. In such cases, however, the risks may be substantially reduced by forward purchase of an associated currency. In Europe, the Exchange Rate Mechanism ties many currencies to the Deutschmark, and many South East Asian currencies voluntarily track the US dollar. The UK project manager generally finds himself dealing with three independent groups of currencies—US dollar related, European and Japanese. His project will be sanctioned in one, and subject to exchange rate fluctuations with the other two.

Cost monitoring

Dealing with fluctuations in exchange rates, where currency has not been bought forward, can add very significantly to the time and effort required to monitor project costs. For a new plant to be built in a Third World country and sanctioned in the currency of that country, the estimate will have been made in perhaps as many as a dozen different currencies at current prices. The effects of inflation and exchange rates will have been calculated by predicting the timing of the expenditure of each currency, the forward rates of inflation and the future spot rates of exchange. This will provide a total cost in the sanction currency but the detail of the estimate will remain in its original form. For the purposes of cost monitoring, each individual item in the original estimate has to be adjusted for the effects of inflation and currency exchange before it can be compared with its corresponding expenditure and commitment.

The budget for a particular item is, initially, a figure in the currency of purchase, excluding inflation allowance. To obtain the required figure for cost monitoring purposes, it is necessary to add a suitable inflation allowance and to convert to the sanction currency. If there are expected to be stage payments, these must be taken into account, perhaps by converting each stage payment at a different exchange rate. When the order for the item is placed, the price has again to be converted to the home currency at the exchange rates now forecast for the agreed times of stage payment in order to determine the commitment. When the first stage payment is made, it must be converted at the then current exchange rate. If this is different from that previously assumed, the expected final cost of the item in the sanction currency will change, and future stage payments will be altered by any revised forecast of exchange rates. There may be hundreds of such calculations to be made each month. Almost certainly the calculations will have to be done manually. On a major project, serried ranks of cost engineers will be needed and it must be questioned whether all this effort is worth while. Many project managers will look for short cuts. It may be appropriate to perform all cost monitoring in the exchange rates predicted at the time of sanction and to maintain a separate calculation of the effect of changes in exchange rates for the project as a whole.

Such a short-cut system would operate as follows. The weighted average exchange rate for each currency used on the project would be calculated from the predicted timing of expenditure and the forecasts of exchange rates. These rates—let us call them the project rates—would be used to convert both the detail of the sanction estimate and all expenditure and commitments into the sanction currency. (Of course, the detail of the sanction estimate would have to be revised from time to time as some orders were placed in countries other than those originally predicted.) This would enable actual expenditure and commitments to be compared in detail with budget, to a reasonably close approximation. It would then be necessary separately to estimate the error caused by using the project rates of exchange. This would be done by maintaining a separate parallel summary estimate which listed the expected monthly or quarterly expenditure in each currency. The total of each month's or quarter's actual expenditure in each currency would be converted to the sanction currency using the actual average exchange rate for that month or quarter. Predicted future expenditure in each currency would be revised to take account of the actual expenditure so far and would continue to be converted at the project rates. This, of course, would still fail to give absolute accuracy, but would very probably be good enough for all practical purposes.

Purchasing

Any major process plant project, wherever it is to be built, involves international purchasing since, with the possible exception of the US, no country has so many manufacturers of large or specialised process plant equipment that foreign vendors may reasonably be ignored. The sanction estimate will have been based on assumptions about the origin of the equipment; assumptions which will range from an informed judgement or even certain knowledge in the case of a particular item, to a mere guess at the proportion of equipment which may be purchased in a particular country. In the case of a plant to be built in a foreign country without a developed process industry, the country of origin of the eventual construction contractor may be far from certain at sanction. It follows, therefore, that adjustment will be necessary to the estimates of foreign currency requirements which were made in the sanction estimate.

Of course, these sanction estimates of currency requirements cannot be allowed to dictate the placing of orders. The competing bids must be compared using the best information available on exchange rates. Major vendors may be prepared to accept payment in the sanction currency. As a general rule, however, where government-supported export credit finance is not involved, the employer will obtain a better deal by paying in the vendor's own currency.

Chapter 16

Planning

16.1 INTRODUCTION

Time was when the main planning tool was the bar chart. This was, and remains, an excellent method of displaying time-related information, but does little more than that. In particular, it does nothing to help understand or define the logical connection between activities: the logic that underlies the bar chart for the most part remains hidden. In the late 1950s, several independent teams developed new planning techniques which allowed explicit consideration to be given to the sequencing and inter-dependence of separate activities. In the USA, the chemical company Dupont, together with the Rand Corporation, developed the Critical Path Method for planning the design and construction of chemical plant. The US Navy, assisted by Booz, Allen and Hamilton, developed the Program Evaluation and Review Technique (PERT). In France, Professor Roy developed Graphes et Ordonnacements (Networks and Scheduling). In the UK the Central Electricity Generating Board developed a planning system primarily for use in maintenance overhauls. All the systems were essentially the same, with but minor differences. Two different methods of notation were developed: activity-on-arrow and activity-on-node, and both continue to be used. A unique feature of the PERT system was that it required three estimates to be made for the duration of each activity. Collectively, they are now commonly referred to in the UK as Critical Path Scheduling (CPS) and the techniques are much too well known to need description here.

The advantages of the network method were clear to see, and in the process plant field it was quickly adopted, first by the major operating companies and later by the contractors. Although benefits were gained immediately, the best way of applying the technique to capital projects took a decade or more to establish. With planners seduced by the idea of a comprehensive document which could contain all the planning information for a project, and which could be more or less easily manipulated by the use of computers, networks burgeoned and blossomed until the time needed for preparation was comparable with or even greater than that for the project itself: networks of 10,000 activities and more were not unknown. It was all too easy, when during the course of a project the answer to a question was not instantly available by consulting the network, to resolve to plan in more detail next time. This was analogous to preparing a street map for the whole country because, having navigated to the desired town by using a small-scale road map, this was found inadequate to direct one to the required address.

There is little doubt that the use of computers to process CPS networks added substantially to the over-valuation of the technique which, in some minds, came to be almost synonymous with project management. Whole new professions were established, keen to sell hardware and software to the credulous. Systems succeeded one another with bewildering rapidity, with development seemingly more important than application. Heaven was always just around the corner in the shape of increased capacity, improved flexibility and greater speed. If networks took too long to develop, help was at hand in the promised development of systems for the speedy assembly of very large networks from standard sub-networks. Resource aggregation, and even resource allocation were vigourously canvassed. The original PERT requirement of three estimates of duration for each activity, not something which had caught on much in practice, was overtaken by suggestions for multiple durations and elaborate ways to deal with uncertainty.

In overestimating the contribution that network techniques could make to a capital project, the staff of a typical process manufacturer might well have been influenced by the fact that CPS could, with advantage, be applied quite rigorously and in great detail to the planning of overhauls of large process plant. Here, all the necessary conditions are satisfied. The time available for planning is large in comparison to the total duration of the work being planned—perhaps a whole year compared with a few weeks. The work itself is very well defined in detail and consists of many simple activities, of a fairly similar kind, that can be sequenced, timed and resourced fairly accurately. Materials and equipment can be assembled beforehand so that virtually all activities during the shut-down are under direct control. Moreover, the economic value of minimising the length of shut-down is so great as to justify almost any efforts in that direction.

The design and construction of a chemical plant is very different. There is usually less time to plan the work than to perform it. It would be a brave man indeed who claimed detailed knowledge of every activity and its inter-dependence with others, especially in the design process. The project manager would do well to remember von Hayek's characterisation of planning, albeit in another context, as the 'replacement of accident by error'. In any case it is clear that, at the detailed level, there are many possible ways in which activities may be ordered and sequenced, and indeed that even the most detailed network will contain only a small and fairly arbitrary selection of the activities that are necessary to the project and will not do justice to the iterative nature of much of the work. Many design activities are discontinuous, stopping and starting as resources permit or as external influences dictate: their durations are inherently uncertain and depend on circumstances outside the control of project management. Only a few of those engaged in the design and construction of a major chemical plant are under direct control. An example of the uncertainty of the duration of an activity is the time required to enquire, evaluate bids, negotiate price and place the order for a complex proprietary item of equipment such as a large process gas compressor—very probably an activity on the critical path. Unless repetition of an existing unit had already been decided upon, it would be advisable to allow the potential vendors latitude to propose alternative solutions. All would then depend on their responses: not simply the time taken to bid, but also the nature of their proposals. Significant technical differences would require considerable, and unpredictable, time and effort to evaluate.

Resources are not commonly included in a network for the design and construction of a process plant. To do so would require a massive increase in elaboration of the network because of the intermittent and fluctuating nature of the resources applied to many activities, especially in design. And given that most of the resources are employed by sub-contractors and suppliers, it is doubtful whether much would be achieved. Consequently, the durations of most design activities are based on average elapsed times achieved in the past rather than calculated from work content and resources available. Some design activities which are important as regards time may make no significant use of any resources that can be planned for.

Increasing experience in the use of CPS techniques has seen a welcome return to the old ideas of different levels of planning, in different degrees of detail for different aspects of the project—something which had always been inseparable, because unavoidable, from the use of bar charts. These ideas had never really been abandoned by the process plant contractor, who had been saved from the worst excesses, had he been disposed towards them, by being given no time to over-elaborate his planning, either during bid preparation or between contract award and the commencement of design work.

In general, planning in UK process plant design and construction has seemed to be carried out in more detail, and with more sophistication, than in other developed countries. This is perhaps especially so among employers' organisations. To some extent this may be a consequence of the labour difficulties of past years: it was always easier to plan than to execute. Despite this extensive planning effort, project managers have seemed all too ready to abandon the plan as soon as any problem has arisen, as instanced below in considering the all-important question of the starting date for construction. The too-facile way in which planning engineers seem sometimes able to plan their way out of difficulty, absorbing late deliveries, for example, can also sap confidence, raising the question of why this better way of organising the work was not proposed in the first place.

16.2   OBJECTIVES AND ORGANISATION

The objectives of planning may be defined as follows:

(1) *To define the actions necessary.* In the broadest sense, this is quite simply the marshalling of thoughts before taking action. Its value depends on the familiarity of the employer's project manager with the work in question. At the minimum, for the experienced project manager faced with a sequence of activities with which he has long been familiar it provides a valuable check-list. Where the project manager is not certain what has to be done, either through inexperience or because of the unusual nature of the project, it is essential. The early work of investigation required to establish the viability of the project, define its scope, decide the way it may best be organised and financed, and obtain authorisation, will certainly have unique features. For a major project, this phase will be of the utmost importance to the employer's project manager. Its planning, which will never attain great sophistication and which will probably be subject to continuous change over a long period, has its greatest value in the help it provides in defining and clarifying what needs to be done. The time-critical activities must be identified but, at this broad scale, are usually fairly obvious.

(2) *To establish the project timing.* Except in circumstances where there is time to do extensive detailed planning before any work starts—a state of affairs which sometimes results from protracted delay in authorising the project— the completion date will usually be fixed from a bare outline plan. It will thus depend upon the broad-scale judgements of the project manager and the experienced members of the project team rather than on the processing of masses of data, and will usually be none the worse for that. A frequent dilemma of the project manager in setting the completion date is that this should simultaneously provide a difficult target to stimulate progress, and a date on which to base business planning. A common solution is to have

different target and forecast completion dates: the project team works to the former, business planning assumes the latter.

(3) *To assess the workload and resources required.* The employer's project manager needs to assess the magnitude and timing of the resources needed to manage the project on behalf of the employer and to perform the project work which is to be undertaken directly. Most organisations are subject to resource constraints, and the way the project is to be executed may have to be altered to reduce requirements.

(4) *To monitor and report progress.* Planning must provide a baseline against which performance is measured and controlled. This is a feature of the execution phases of the project and performance is measured and controlled against the much more detailed plans and schedules which are developed at that time.

A crucial task of the project manager is to keep the forecast completion date under review. Most project managers will be reluctant to alter this, since they will believe, probably quite correctly, that once slippage has been officially acknowledged and reported, all hope of recovery is lost. On the other hand, to stick to a forecast completion date that all the project team knows is unrealistic deprives the programme of credibility.

It is important that the planning function responds directly to the project manager. Like estimating and cost control, planning is a project control function, but properly used, it is more than this. It affects all parts of the project, and responsibility for all of these comes together only at the project manager's level. Planning is useful only insofar as it influences action: it will do this properly only if it is seen that it has the authority and support of the project manager and that he uses the plan to drive the project forward. The usual practice on a large project is to have a senior planning engineer reporting to the project manager, to whom the other planning engineers—for design, construction, off-plots and so on, respond.

It is also important that the project manager, no less than the engineering design manager, construction manager, and other senior engineers, plays a direct role in the planning process. Too much emphasis on the techniques to be used can obscure the fact that the planning of process plant design and construction is not exclusively, or even mainly, concerned with the manipulation of hard data. For example, it is necessary to take into consideration the state of the world-wide process plant construction industry—the workload of design contractors and of fabricators in all the countries that are likely to provide vendors. The state of the construction industry in the country in which the plant is to be built must be considered. During boom times, major projects proliferate, not only in the process plant industry, but in most others. The cycle of boom and slump seems unavoidable since it is only at times when industrial economies are prospering that demand increases and there is the need for new plants. The planning response to this cycle should not be merely to feed into the programme the longer delivery dates of fabricators. This is only the tip of the iceberg and, in any case, these times are likely to prove optimistic. What must also be allowed for is that, when activity is at a high level, management is stretched, workforces are diluted by the recruitment of people with less experience and capability and therefore of lower quality, and few, if any, contractors, sub-contractors or suppliers will meet their obligations. Labour will become more expensive, less available, less reliable and of lower capability. The accompanying inflation adds additional pressures: when quoted prices are higher than expected, more time will be spent to try to stay within budget. Progress that was easily achieved in slack times may be quite out of reach when order books are full. To allow properly for these external pressures requires the experienced judgement of the project manager and the senior members of his team.

The experience of the project manager may also be required to ensure realistic planning. It is possible to plan so to overlap activities as to remove all tolerance of mishap: the slightest delay can then cause major upset. It is also possible to carry too far the generally sensible practice of developing the plan backwards from the completion date. One may see it argued that a plant should be designed in the order it will be commissioned: if it is to be commissioned by systems, this should dictate the design sequence. In fact, of course, each stage of the project process has its own imperatives—the order in which things must be designed, or constructed, or commissioned—for the work to be possible at all, or to minimise cost and time. Planning may sometimes be carried out in intricate detail quite incompatible with the accuracy of its component information: however sophisticated the manipulation of the data, it is the accuracy of the information that determines that of the plan. Even for the most experienced, there will be many details of the design process that are fundamentally unpredictable. These include the durations of many design activities—much may depend on the answers to problems that have yet to be identified, let alone solved, and on circumstances beyond the designer's control, such as the responses of vendors. Activities are not undertaken in isolation: those responsible will be subject to other demands and the durations included in any plan can only be averages based on past experience. Allowance must therefore be made for these uncertainties. Too complicated a meshing of activities, too much overlapping will cause more than delay. It will cause error and confusion.

16.3 PRE-CONTRACT PLANNING

Defining the project strategy, as previously discussed in some detail in Chapter 3, is usually the most important project planning activity for the employer's project manager. It makes few demands on any specialised planning technique. Bar charts are often adequate, though a simple network may prove useful. At the inception of the project, when all that is known is the broad intention of the business management, the employer's project manager must hurry to develop an approximate idea of what the project involves, identifying its various major components and producing rough estimates of the time required for each. At this stage, the major uncertainties are not usually about how the engineering design, procurement and construction may be accomplished, nor how long each will take—experience will probably give the project manager the ability to estimate the time required to a first approximation without too much difficulty—but with the earlier activities of technical definition, plant location, feedstock and utilities supplies, finance, the process of obtaining project sanction and other hurdles that have to be successfully negotiated before execution can commence. Many of these activities are under the control not of the project manager but of other members of the business team. Nevertheless, the project manager must incorporate them in his plan and set targets for them. This will give rise to the overall project plan. which will endure, in many succeeding versions, for the life of the project.

The pre-sanction activities with which the project manager is first concerned proceed, in many cases, simultaneously and to a large extent independently. There is little interaction, for example, between the execution of the process design and the acquisition of finance—the project manager has merely to make sure that the necessary process data is made available to include in the information given to potential financing institutions. Clearly, it makes sense to plan these disparate activities separately, providing that the necessary limited interaction is allowed for.

At this stage, and indeed throughout the project, the most effective way of planning will be to develop an overall plan in modest detail and then to prepare more detailed plans, keyed to the overall plan, for closer assessment of specific aspects. Thus, in his pre-contract planning, the employer's project manager might develop plans as follows:

(1) *Overall plan*. This would set the project in its commercial context. It would treat the main parts of the project as single bars or activities, for example, obtaining sanction, design, construction. It would be the master plan for the project and from this would be derived the forecast completion date.
(2) *Research and development*. If there were a significant process research and development effort involved in the project, network planning might be helpful. While it may not often be possible to plan research activities at all accurately, since what has to be done may depend on how things turn out, the identification of the critical project path can be helpful in injecting urgency into the proceedings and emphasising the necessity for the work to converge on decisions, rather than diverge in search of knowledge.

(3) *Local investigation.* If the plant were to be built in a country of which there was no previous knowledge, a separate plan covering the necessary investigatory activities might well be appropriate.

(4) *Finance.* If the project were to be financed externally, it might be helpful to develop a programme for the various activities required.

(5) *Sanction.* The process of obtaining sanction can be a long and complicated one for a major project and a plan of the activities required may be helpful.

(6) *Contracts.* Contracts planning must start with defining the various major contracts to be placed. For each, the selection of bidders, the issue of enquiries to contractors, the evaluation of bids and subsequent negotiations leading to award of contract may usefully be analysed in one or more separate sub-plans.

16.4   EXECUTION PLANNING

Following contract award, the main burden of the detailed planning falls upon the contractor, the role of the employer's staff being largely to monitor his efforts. Circumstances—a protracted run-up to sanction, or unique experience by the employer of the particular plant—may, however, lead the employer to develop preliminary programmes for design and construction which he would provide to the contractors as a basis for their own planning. The employer might also have listed, in his Enquiry, critical items which the contractor must tackle immediately, for example, the procurement of crucial equipment on long delivery. The employer may have done preliminary work on specifying and enquiring for these items. He will, of course, have to plan any parts of the project, for example, the transport of out-of-gauge loads, the design and construction of off-plot facilities, for which he is to be directly responsible.

16.4.1   Design

The Enquiry will have included an outline overall plan for the project which described to the contractor what is expected of him. In his bid, the contractor will have responded with his own outline plan, which may have differed from that proposed by the employer. The employer's project manager will have been concerned to identify any differences, to analyse their effects and to assess their credibility. Consideration of the contractor's planning organisation will have been an important aspect of the bid evaluation. The employer's project manager will have tried to assess, not only the capability of the contractor's planning function, but also its integration into the project organisation. Unless the planning engineers are fully part of the project team responding to and receiving support from the contractor's project manager, planning may be remote and ineffective with little or no influence on action.

The employer's Enquiry may describe in some detail the planning which he requires the contractor to do. It is doubtful, however, whether this is a particularly useful thing to do since the contractor either has acceptable procedures for planning and control, in which case the Enquiry is mere supererogation; or his planning procedures are inadequate in which case his bid is unlikely to be successful. Typically, the contractor would be expected to plan as indicated below

Initial schedules

Since the contractor will usually be required to start work immediately upon contract award, he will need to do some planning to carry him over the first few weeks of execution. This will usually take the form of:

- A three-month *launch programme* in bar-chart form, which identifies the activities which must be commenced in the first three months, together with departmental responsibilities.
- A *critical procurement plan*, again in bar-chart form, setting down the early procurement actions required for long-delivery items of equipment. These items may have been identified in the employer's Enquiry, or in the contractor's tender.
- A *sub-contract plan* in bar-chart form identifying time critical sub-contracts and the actions necessary during the first three months of the contract to allow early placement.

Overall plan

Immediately after contract award, the contractor would commence the preparation of the overall project plan. This would be based on the agreed contract programme, as included in the Enquiry with any amendments agreed as a result of the contractor's tender. It would identify all the important project milestones, the interfaces between design and procurement and construction, and the critical paths. Following review and agreement in the contractor's organisation and with the employer, this would be developed in further detail. For the design phase, a CPS network of around five hundred activities might serve for a major project, and a similar number for the construction phase.

In procurement planning, it is necessary to identify each item of equipment, as well as each order for bulk material, and to monitor progress from the issue of each requisition to delivery to site. This is a vast amount of detail which would overwhelm the network if it were to be included in it. The solution is to prepare separate material and equipment schedules in tabular form to provide the basis for monitoring and control.

Monitoring and reporting

The contractor will monitor progress against plan on a continuous basis and take action accordingly. This information will form the basis of monthly reports to the employer which will be discussed at a monthly progress meeting. The importance of this meeting will depend on relations between employer and contractor and their working relationship. At one extreme, contact between meetings may be limited, so that the monthly progress meetings become the forum for the ventilation of all concerns and complaints, for the sudden appearance of claims for variations and for the springing of surprises and reporting of bad news. A more successful project will usually be achieved if relations between employer and contractor enable problems to be dealt with as they appear, so that the monthly progress meeting is an opportunity for a general appraisal of progress rather than the occasion to deal with individual problems.

Naturally, contractors have standard formats for their monthly reports. The employer will have considered these during the tender stage and put forward any special requirements he might have. It is not, of course, likely to improve the contractor's efficiency if unusual reporting demands are made on him. Some employers may find the contractor's reports too prolix and elaborate, but may find it difficult to get their bulk reduced. Producing formal reports can occupy a significant part of the contractor's total design effort and it is important that they are kept to the minimum necessary.

16.4.2 Construction

The design and construction of a process plant are always overlapped, for obvious reasons of speed, as well as for others which have previously been discussed. The availability of design information and material is therefore phased, and there is an intricate interface between the design and construction plans. The construction plan is based on forecasts of the release of design approved for construction, and of material and equipment delivery dates. If the design contractor is responsible for construction, this interface should be easier to manage than if the employer, or a third party, is to take over. A separate construction organisation can be expected to be less tolerant of the failings of design, and less willing to undertake extra work to make up for them. Where there is separate responsibility for design and construction, management of the interface between them is a crucial part of the employer's project manager's responsibility, often made more difficult by too early a start on site.

It might seem unnecessary to remark that all concerned with the project should work to the same plan. However, experience shows that it is not unusual for the construction manager to have a view of the programme and completion date quite different from that shown in the overall project plan. This failure of project management commonly follows from mismanagement of the interface between design and construction. When the project plan is developed, the date for the start of construction is determined on the basis of an estimate of when sufficient design information and material will be available. It is usual, it would hardly be exaggerating to say inevitable, for some aspects of the design to be late. No effort will be spared to try to ensure that items on the critical path, commencing with the design of piling and civil foundations, are on time. Often however, when the due date for the start of construction arrives, the design is behind programme. Unless the situation is obviously beyond redemption, the design organisation will usually argue that the deficiencies are not sufficient to justify delaying the start of construction: enough is available to permit work to begin. If the construction manager bows to this pressure, work starts on site on the planned date, and the project is reported as being on time. What has actually happened is that the delay arising from late design has been transferred without public acknowledgement to construction, whose task has thereby been made more difficult. From this point on, the construction manager has reservations about the project programme and may develop his own plan. If the initial plan was valid, the correct course of action in such circumstances would be to wait until the specified design information and material were available. This is the proper trigger for a construction start, not calendar date. As discussed in a later chapter, too precipitate a start condemns the construction management to act as expeditors of design and procurement for much of the time rather than as managers of construction.

If the design contractor is responsible for construction, he should begin to plan construction four to six months before the expected start of civil work on site. If he is to carry out the work by direct hire, his planning will need to go into more detail than if construction is to be done through sub-contractors. If a separate construction contractor is to be employed, or if the employer is to manage construction himself using sub-contractors, it is necessary for the design contract to require the contractor to provide planning information at an early stage. Even so, it is obvious that the lead time available for construction planning will be limited, and it will be difficult to place construction contracts on other than a re-measure and value, or a schedule of rates, basis.

16.4.3 Commissioning

If commissioning is to be in stages—by process systems—as would be usual for a major project, the interface between commissioning and construction planning will be quite complicated, and the commissioning and construction planners must work closely together to co-ordinate the two plans. There is also much else to be done, before the actual work of commissioning begins. The transfer and recruitment of staff, the training of operators and maintenance personnel, the production of operating manuals and, on a greenfield site, the establishment of a whole new works organisation, are some of the tasks that will be necessary. All of this preliminary work must be planned, though little of it connects in detail with design and construction.

Chapter 17

Design

17.1 PRE-SANCTION DESIGN

The project must be defined well enough before sanction to allow a capital cost estimate and a schedule with the required accuracies to be developed. In a relatively small number of cases, where the employer is inexperienced and commercially available processes are to be used, the employer may depend upon the contractor to perform all the necessary work of project definition and cost estimating, and will then sanction the project on the basis of a lump sum bid. In many cases, however, the employer will develop his own capital estimate for sanction purposes: he may wish to speed progress by seeking sanction at the same time as he enquires for and negotiates bids from contractors; he may have more knowledge and experience than any contractor of the type of plant which is to be built; the project may not be defined well enough for a contractor to provide a dependable estimate.

Where the employer does develop his own estimate, the amount of pre-sanction work required if the project is to have reasonable prospect of success may be considerable. The minimum requirement will be for a new plant which is a near-repeat of a previous one, where as little as 5% of the total design work performed before sanction may be sufficient. At the other extreme, the requirement might increase to as much as 25% where the plant is the first of its kind. In the latter case, a two-stage sanctioning procedure would usually be indicated. The first stage of sanction would cover merely the expenditure necessary to develop the project to full definition. At the second stage, the viability of the project would be reconsidered against the more accurate cost estimate that would then be available.

The importance of definition to the success of any project has been amply emphasised in earlier chapters. This definition can be achieved only by design work performed before the irrevocable step of full sanction is taken. (In theory, a company may cancel a sanctioned project at any stage. In practice, it usually needs a catastrophe for this to be done, and the more common process of the slow accretion of evidence that the original project basis was misconceived, which few will wish to believe, will seldom qualify.) Pre-sanction design work by the employer should include considering and deciding on any process and major engineering improvements he hopes to make. Evaluation techniques such as Value Analysis should be employed at this stage. The experienced project manager will regard the amount of pre-sanction design performed as a crucial criterion of his project's chances of success, and will strenuously endeavour to ensure that it fits the circumstances.

17.2   CONTRACTOR DESIGN

17.2.1   Employer Participation

The extent of participation of the employer's staff in the design performed by the contractor varies with the scope and type of the contract, with the approaches of both employer and contractor, and with the technical knowledge and experience that the employer has to contribute. At one extreme is the reimbursable design and procurement contract based on the employer's technology, where the employer carries out construction. Here the employer's involvement in the contract can be expected to be at a maximum. At the other extreme lies the lump sum turnkey contract where the contractor provides the process technology and is responsible for design, supply and construction. Even in this case, however, the process plant contractor may not be expert in all that he provides, in the sense that a major manufacturer, say of a boiler or turbine, is expert in the equipment that he offers. In many aspects of a process plant project, even one provided via a lump sum contract, an experienced employer may have expertise that exceeds that of the contractor and will wish to see it utilised.

For an experienced employer, there will be parts of the design, where operating and maintenance experience impinge most strongly, in which no contractor will be considered sufficiently expert, since none has this experience to a significant extent. The employer will wish to specify in detail what is done in these areas. Hazard and operability studies will cover many of the topics, but there are others such as maintenance access, and the provision of equipment isolation to allow safe maintenance while the plant is on line. Where the new plant is based on the employer's own technology, there will be much up-to-date technical detail that only the employer's operating staff can provide. Even where the technology to be used is commercially available and widely offered, it is only by incorporating into the design the fruits of his previous operating experience that the employer can differentiate it from that available to the merest tiro in the business. In all of this, it must be remembered that the more experienced the employer, the greater the risk of over-specification in operational, just as much as in engineering, matters. The employer's project manager must be careful to see that the plant is not made unduly expensive either by over-engineering or by excessive attention to operator convenience.

During execution of the design by the contractor, the duties of the employer's project team include the following:

(1) The contractor's work must be monitored to ensure that it meets specification and is otherwise satisfactory. The religious temperament—faith without scrutiny—will not profit the employer's project manager. The contract will specify the contractor's obligations. As well as complying with the specifications included and referred to in the contract documents, the contractor may have explicit obligations to satisfy the reasonable requirements of the employer (or 'Engineer'), to conform to good engineering practice and to provide sound workmanship and materials.

(2) The employer's project manager must manage the employer's technical input to the project. This will include explaining, and perhaps reconciling and expanding on, the employer's specifications; arranging for attendance of specialists at technical meetings and at design and model reviews; approving drawings and other contractor documentation. The employer's staff will need to review all flowsheets, line diagrams and other schematics, equipment designs and the piping model. If the employer owns the technology he will initiate and lead many of the reviews. In any event he will be vitally concerned with the safety of operation. Plant maintenance will be another feature which will draw the employer's attention: he will agree the spares requirements for the plant and may be responsible for producing the spares catalogue.

(3) The employer's staff must monitor the work of procurement, the extent depending on the terms of the main contract. This may include confirming the qualifications of proposed vendors, participating in technical discussions and negotiations with vendors of equipment and materials, reviewing quotations and bid comparisons, and approving the placing of orders.

(4) If the employer, or another contractor, is to manage the construction, the necessary construction input must be made to the design. This should include scrutiny of the way the design information is to be provided to construction, considerations of constructability and construction access,

the heavy lift programme, proposals for off-site fabrication. Design information is frequently presented in the way most convenient for the designer, and is then sorted and re-arranged on site to make it convenient for use by construction. Overall, it would save both cost and time if the information were presented in the required form in the first place, and this might require a variation for the design services contractor.

(5) Progress and costs must be monitored and, so far as possible, influenced in the desired way. A monitoring system based on physical work completion is to be preferred: the weighted average of data sheets, calculations, drawings, specifications and so on. The system will be optimistic because of the unknown effect of revisions and modifications. In a reimbursable contract, comparison of physical progress with man-hour usage will give an indication of the accuracy of man-hour budgets.

(6) If the contract is reimbursable, the employer's project manager must ensure that payments to the contractor match the man-hours of staff employed on the project and, if the contractor has no liability for the time of completion, he must see that adequate numbers of staff are employed. Whatever the form of contract, he must certify invoices for payment in accordance with the contract terms.

It is important that the activities of the employer's project team should be managed so as to try to help rather than hinder the contractor. This might be thought so obvious as not to require remark, did not experience show otherwise.

17.2.2 Employer's Resident Team

The organisation and remits of the employer's team resident in the contractor's office have already been considered in an earlier chapter. On a major project, the team will be led by the project engineering manager, and the full-time members will be project engineers, and as appropriate and timely, process engineers and operations staff. Functional specialist engineers will not usually be permanently resident in the contractor's office. They and other members of the employer's project team—planning and cost engineers, procurement staff—will visit as appropriate. The project engineering manager will need the clearest of instructions as to the extent of his authority. The contractor must also be clearly informed on this score: the typical contract would require that notice of the project engineering manager's appointment and the extent of his powers be given in writing—in the terminology of many standard forms of contract he would be the Engineer's Representative. The extent of authority that will be delegated to him will depend mainly on the workload of the project manager, in particular the physical dispersion of the project, and the experience and ability of the project engineering manager. At one extreme, with an experienced project engineering manager and a project of wide geographical dispersion, the project manager might delegate almost full powers to the project engineering manager, reserving to himself only matters which would cause the budget to be exceeded, and the approval of variations.

A major responsibility for the project engineering manager will be to control the employer's technical input to the project, much of which will be made through technical discussions, initiated by either party. Many of the discussions which the employer initiates will already have been foreshadowed in the Co-ordination Procedure, for example, the formal technical reviews. Appropriate members of the employer's team will wish to be present at important technical discussions with vendors and, where equipment and materials are being supplied on a reimbursable basis, at key commercial meetings also. No meeting between the staff of employer and contractor should take place without the knowledge and authority of the project engineering manager, who will initiate and arrange most of the meetings. Many will concern functional specialists and the project engineering manager will decide whether a project engineer needs to be present for co-ordination purposes.

It is customary for the design contractor to produce a monthly report which forms the basis of the monthly project meeting. This is attended by both employer's and contractor's project managers and project engineering managers, and other members of the employer's project team, as appropriate.

17.2.3 Co-ordination Procedure and Job Specification

Relations between the employer and contractor during the course of the project will be regulated primarily by the standard procedures of the contractor, modified as necessary by the employer's requirements specified in his Co-ordination Procedure. The latter gives details of the project, the administrative and personnel details that are necessary, the employer's requirements for how the design is to be carried out, including piping model, design reviews and so on, procedures for planning, cost control, procurement, progress and expediting. A more extensive list of contents is given in Chapter 10 on bid evaluation.

Immediately after award of contract, the contractor will produce his own co-ordination procedure, sometimes called the job specification. This describes, for the benefit of his own team, the nature of the project, the scope of the contractor's work, and the methods and procedures to be used. It assimilates and gives detailed effect to the employer's Co-ordination Procedure and is submitted to the employer's project manager for approval.

17.2.4 Contractor's Approach to Design

The employer's project team will be better able to manage the project, and to assist the contractor, if they understand and allow for the way in which his approach to design is likely to differ from their own. From the point of view of project management, the most crucial considerations in the design of a process plant are:

(1) that the completed design should offer the best possible compromise between cost and performance;
(2) that the design should be as free as possible from error;
(3) that the design process should be efficient in its use of man-hours and completed in a timely manner.

The contractor will not place quite the same relative values on these aspects as will the employer. The latter will be more concerned with the first of these considerations—the quality of the completed design—since the capital and operating costs of the plant will be major factors in determining the profit which it will earn for him over the life of the plant. Both employer and contractor will be anxious to avoid error and to keep to programme, though motivated by different considerations. The contractor, however, will be more concerned with design productivity, since it is by selling design man-hours that he earns his living. This would not be so important to an employer performing his own design, since the cost of design accounts for only a small part of the total for the plant. The contractor would therefore be expected to be more efficient in his use of design man-hours, and to have more highly developed systems than would the employer. Not only is the contractor doing more of this work, which is the heart of his business, but he has to cater for a rise or fall in numbers as the workload varies. Until recently at least, numbers of staff employed by the typical contractor have varied more widely than those of the typical major manufacturer. Thus, the contractor's systems have to be good enough to allow fast assimilation of new staff. They need also to provide a record which will withstand scrutiny by the employer and demonstrate that the work has been properly done and, in the case of reimbursable items, will account for the money spent. All of this means that a contractor's design methods will tend to be more formal and bureaucratic than those of an employer, and the recent introduction of Quality Assurance has reinforced this, seeming often merely to improve the audit trail rather than the standard of the work done, and at the expense of extra time and effort. Except for field purchase, the contractor will have few, if any, short cuts for use in emergencies, simply because, unlike an employer who has frequently to deal with the shut-down of operating plants, he has little or no requirement for them. It follows from these considerations that the contractor's systems will be less tolerant of change than those of the employer, a consideration which should not be lost sight of by the employer's staff.

It would, of course, be foolish to characterise all contractors as the same. There are profound differences. At one extreme is the contractor who offers little more than drawing office services, who aims to provide only a general engineering capability and looks to the employer for all process input and much else besides. Small firms of contractors usually fall into this category, but even some large firms may not be too far removed from it and be only too eager to court the employer's decisions on technical matters, so saving man-hours and reducing their liabilities. At the other extreme are contractors who can see little place for any contribution from the employer, being quite confident of their ability to perform without it. Employers too, vary. Some prefer the contractor who merely does as he is told. Some may have little to contribute to project execution. Others, and this is surely the best way, seek to obtain the best possible result by combining the strengths of both parties. There are contractors also who take this approach and they should be cherished.

The contractor's approach in carrying out the design is, of course, conditioned by the terms of his contract. He will often contract for a lump sum for design and procurement services, with reimbursable supply of materials. In such circumstances, it is clear that his short-term interests, at least, are skewed towards the efficient operation of his design process—he will be encouraged to minimise his man-hour costs. In procurement, this may be reflected in the pursuit of the easiest deal rather than of the most competitive price. This may be evidenced in various ways. Items may be grouped into bulk orders, often an economic way to proceed, but sometimes not. Where the plant is to be built in a foreign country, local purchase may be the cheapest and be technically satisfactory, but may require additional work for the contractor in enquiring and specifying, in subsequent checking and in inspection. The contractor may be reluctant to provide this extra effort even though this may be part of the contract and to the advantage of the employer. Where the contractor is acting as agent for the supply of materials and equipment, he has no liability for the performance of the equipment and so may be less than keen to go the extra mile to ensure satisfactory performance. He may also be inclined to place orders before definition is sufficiently firm in order to demonstrate progress, leading to claims on the employer for both extension of time and increased cost.

In any contract limited to services, the contractor's concern with the capital cost of the completed plant is at best indirect. This is not to suggest that he will ignore plant cost, or that he will have no interest in plant performance beyond his explicit obligations: merely that he may have more powerful competing interests. Other types of contract will exert different influences on the contractor's behaviour. A lump sum turnkey contract, for example, will give the contractor strong concern for the capital cost, but his interest in the eventual operation of the plant will be focused on his explicit contractual obligations. A fully reimbursable contract would, in contrast, exert little influence, but might not fare well against competition for resources from other, more pressing, contracts that the contractor might have.

This different balance of interests of the contractor is an important factor in the rather different nature of the contractor's design process compared with the employer's own in-house operation. Most projects executed in-house by employers are small or medium-sized, often have a significant development element, and may be embarked upon without too much certainty as to how things will turn out, at least at the detailed engineering level. This approach—which without too much exaggeration might be characterised as a voyage of discovery—is not one that would commend itself to a contractor even if he were contracted on a reimbursable basis. For lump sum contracts, design must be a more convergent process, directed along a more certain course of fleshing-out and detailing a given outline requirement. The lump sum contractor will assume that what has been outlined in the Enquiry is what the employer wants, that it will work, is not experimental, needs no development other than of a secondary nature necessarily involved in detailed design, and that proven equipment exists to perform the necessary unit operations. Only if these requirements are fulfilled is it possible for him to produce an estimate of man-hours of sufficient accuracy to provide a lump sum bid for design and procurement services. If his lump sum bid were to extend to cover the supply of equipment or the carrying out of construction, he would require much additional data from a previous similar completed project.

Failure by the employer's project manager to come to terms with the differences between the employer's and contractor's approaches to design and with the consequences of contractual pressures on the contractor's behaviour may have serious effects on the project. To the inexperienced employer, it may seem that the lump sum turnkey contract offers the most difficult challenge, since the contractor has clear objectives which, at least under stress, are not fully compatible with those of the employer. He may contrast this with the reimbursable contract, where the contractor has no incentive to do other than what he is instructed. But the lump sum turnkey contract must have been properly defined before the contract was awarded, and much prior thought, by both employer and contractor, will have gone into its establishment. The contractor has an incentive to complete and will do so with or without the assistance of the employer. The employer's problem is mainly to ensure satisfactory quality. The reimbursable contract on the other hand may often be poorly defined when it is awarded. All the initial lack of definition, both technical and administrative, must be made good during the execution of the project. In many cases, the reimbursable contractor's position may be not so far from that of a labour-only sub-contractor, the provision of a workforce to work to the instructions of the employer.

Whatever the form of contract, the employer's project manager exerts an important influence. He must endeavour to operate so as to assist rather than disrupt the contractor's design process, and must try to ensure that the disparity between the objectives of contractor and employer never becomes too large. There are many elements in this. The establishment of the project on a firm and accurate definition is crucial, the careful management of the employer's input into the design is very important, and some flexibility in the interpretation of the contract may be necessary. On the other hand, the employer's project manager must be alert to those situations where the contractor may incline to do less than justice to the employer's interests, and be ready to apply corrective pressure.

17.2.5 Orderly Design

In a large project, technical uncertainty is usually eschewed from the outset, at least in private manufacturing industry. The rewards of major new projects are seldom so large as to justify inviting more than the absolute minimum of risk and uncertainty, of which there will inevitably be quite enough, compounded of optimistic initial assessments and ineluctable vicissitudes of execution, to make life interesting. Minor technical risks must, of course, often be undertaken. To use only methods and equipment that are fully proven for the required duties would be to stagnate and to lose competitiveness. But the employer's project manager must balance the risks and corresponding benefits carefully and be prepared for problems. Most of the expertise in such technical matters will be provided by the functional specialists, with the project manager being concerned mainly to set the ground rules and to be involved in the most important decisions.

Thus it is that major projects fail for reasons of administrative inadequacy much more often than for technical reasons. Errors in design are most frequently caused by the lack of an orderly design process, the importance of which can hardly be overstated, especially when materials' suppliers, equipment manufacturers and the construction industry are overloaded. This may not easily be appreciated by the project manager whose previous experience has been with smaller projects where he can carry in his head sufficient detail to allow him to control events, and where he can personally ensure that all the members of the design team are working along the correct lines. The ramifications of a large project make this impossible. Success is crucially dependent on the existence and use of clear, formal communication channels, on the avoidance of confusing messages, and the minimising of change. Mussolini is reputed to have said that when he heard the word 'culture', he reached for his revolver. For a project manager, the equivalent word would be 'change'. The employer's project manager, no less than his opposite number in the contractor's organisation, must never lose sight of the effects of any proposed change on the progress of the design, as well as of its benefits in plant improvement. Some otherwise beneficial proposals may have to be rejected because of the disruption their implementation would cause.

If the objectives of time, cost and performance are to be achieved, a major project has little tolerance of uncertainty and change. Many project failures have their roots in lack of discipline in design. The problems result not simply from externally imposed changes, but often also from over-ambitious compression of the design process. Too relaxed a programme leads to delay, too precipitate a style to mistakes and confusion. Design is not, of course, a straightforward sequence of activities undertaken one after the other, one task being completed before the next is begun. Many inter-dependent activities must be carried on simultaneously. Many of these are iterative, not only in themselves but also in their interaction with others. They require to be started on preliminary data and revised, sometimes much more often than once, as more accurate information becomes available. Feedback from other and later stages is frequently required in order to confirm or invalidate a proposal. Design activities are commonly overlapped so that one is started before its logical predecessor is completed and, provided information comes forward at the necessary rate, the second activity may progress unhindered and time saved.

The design process is thus a fairly delicate mechanism, with a definite limit to how far the compression process—the overlapping of activities and their commencement on preliminary data—can be taken without jeopardising the work. If activities are commonly started too early, based on preliminary information, the consequence may not be simply one of abortive design work, though that will be important to the contractor. It may be difficult to ensure that all the early design that has been based on preliminary information is properly revised when firm data is available. Such revisions are changes which are built into the project by the way it is organised. They are no more welcome than any other changes and have similar consequences. The integrity of the design may be compromised. A further effect is that designers who are repeatedly required to work on data which are subsequently changed, perhaps several times, will react adversely. It is difficult to maintain enthusiasm when experience suggests that much of today's work will have to be done again tomorrow. Excessive overlapping of activities seems characteristic of projects undertaken in the UK. Where detailed comparisons can be made with similar projects in the US, these often show that in the US, each phase of a project is started later and takes less time.

Of equal importance is the response to the inevitable delays and failures to achieve targets which will occur. Too much overlapping of activities and complication in the initial plan will leave no scope for recovery. Any attempt at recovery of time lost must rely on one or more of the following:

(1) The taking-up of slack in the original programme.
(2) Improving on the initial programme by finding a cleverer way of doing things which reduces the time needed. Such improvements are frequently

delusory, requiring more compression and overlapping of design activities and more work based on preliminary information. The result may be more abortive work and, at worst, loss of control of the design process.

(3) The employment of more resources—often not the answer to design delays where the problem may be one of shortage of information, perhaps to be provided by others, on which to work.

(4) The taking of design decisions based on less than full information. This may allow work to proceed more quickly and, from a procedural point of view, is satisfactory provided the decisions can be adhered too.

The contractor's and employer's project managers must always have as a primary concern the maintenance of orderly design and construction processes which are efficient and timely and minimise abortive effort but, above all, retain secure control of data and information flows. Contractors' personnel, who make a living selling design man-hours, are usually more conscious of this than are the staff of the employer.

The importance of an orderly and disciplined design process is greatly increased in times of high industrial activity. Many factors then come together to make design and construction difficult. Design, material supply, fabrication and construction become overloaded and the management and labour involved in each are stretched and diluted to a lower quality. Both quality and timing suffer. Few, if any, contractual promises are met and these only with continuous monitoring and expediting. The 1970s were times of rapid expansion and offer many examples of projects failing which in less frenetic times would have been satisfactorily completed. In such circumstances, frequent failure to meet time targets requires frequent adjustments to programmes and activity sequences. It many instances, these adjustments merely make matters worse. It is not too often that time can be made up without sacrificing something, and it is as well to recognise this at an early stage rather than to push ahead with programme changes that will only hinder.

Examples of the problems met in the 1970s are easier to describe where they cross the interface between design and construction, referred to in the next chapter, and between design and supply. During this period, because of the long order books of equipment manufacturers, it often became necessary to reserve capacity for the fabrication of major equipment items before full details of requirements were available. This was obviously not done without some commercial penalty, but the advantages to programme were often considered to justify the extra cost. Capacity would be reserved as required by the project programme, usually not, in the event, achieved. The project manager's options were then either to delay the start of fabrication and meet the fabricator's extra costs (which the latter would be legally bound to mitigate), or to give the fabricator preliminary data on which to proceed. The latter course of action is only sensible if it is accepted that the preliminary data must be accepted as the final design and is not to be changed when further detail emerges from the design process. Similar action may be taken to reserve forward capacity with piping fabricators. If the design is not ready when fabrication is due to start, there is no sensible alternative to waiting until the design is available. Attempts have been made in such circumstances to make progress by fabricating spool-pieces—common shapes of piping—in the hope that these can be found a place once the piping design is complete. Such attempts have usually failed.

Orderly design as described above may seem to be the very antithesis of what has in recent years come to be known as the 'fast-track' project. However, this term seems to mean different things to different people: all depends on one's starting point. In civil engineering, for example, fast-track may mean little more than the mere overlapping of design and construction, something which in a process plant project has always generally been considered necessary, because of the need to order equipment at an early stage to obtain certified vendors' drawings, without which the design cannot proceed to the detailed stage. This necessarily entails that construction should not then be long delayed, not only because of the cost and difficulty of storing uninstalled equipment, but also because of the cash flow implications for the employer who, having expended the major part of the project cost, will be keen to see his assets set to work.

In the process plant industry, a fast-track project is one which borrows more extensively than usual from previous similar projects. There are few projects of any size which owe nothing to previous designs; few in which every design problem is considered anew. A fast-track project is one in which previous designs are made use of in some detail; where the advantages of speed outweigh any benefits that could possibly be obtained from a re-design. Fast-track is therefore appropriate only for projects where the process concerned is reasonably mature and improvements are not sought, and where capital cost is not of primary importance. If fast-track could have any meaning in a project with few antecedents, which posed fresh design problems and where capital cost was of crucial importance, it would be a brave, not to say foolish, project manager who attempted it.

17.2.6 Freezing of Design

A related subject to orderly design, indeed, a necessary component of it, is that of the freezing of design. The project manager freezes the design when he issues instructions that no further changes are to be made without his specific approval. Any design is capable of improvement, no matter how much time has been spent on it and how much expertise and experience have gone into its development, but as time goes on, the incremental benefit of additional effort becomes smaller. In the case of some of the employer's operating staff, it is particularly important that their enthusiasm for continual refinement be curbed since to those whose job it will be to operate the plant, questions of design efficiency, time and budget may not loom very large.

In theory, the design should be frozen when safety is assured, and the risks of having an inoperable or significantly inferior plant are less than the risks of wasting money or delaying completion. In practice, the general rule is to freeze the design in stages, as soon as the project manager believes that he will not be forced to backtrack on his decision. Of course, it may be necessary occasionally to unfreeze parts of the design. Considerations of safety, operability or overwhelming advantage may force the issue. There is, however, an obvious need to maintain the credibility of the freezing process. Some points at which the design is frozen follow naturally from the design process: the carrying out of each of the reviews listed later in this chapter, the process of approval by the Engineer. These are stages in the design when a fair amount of detail has been developed. There is also a need to freeze more general aspects of the design at earlier stages.

17.2.7 Design Reviews

An increasing feature of the design of process plants in recent years has been the proliferation of reviews to check, as appropriate, that the project and process requirements have been properly interpreted, that the materials of construction have been properly selected, that the plant can be efficiently constructed and that it will be safe and operable. However much one might deprecate the trend to design by review which appears to elevate the critic at the expense of the author, the increasing complexity of modern plants, and the numbers of people involved in their design, make it inevitable. Quite apart from their overt purpose of introducing a wider spectrum of knowledge and experience to check what is proposed, technical reviews can provide an important subsidiary benefit: they can communicate what is being done to operating and maintenance staff and secure their commitment to it.

In the Co-ordination Procedure, the employer should have specified the formal reviews that he wished to hold. He should also have defined where the reviews were to be held, which of them the contractor was required to attend and, preferably in the case of a lump sum bid, the number of man-days which the contractor should allow for attendance. The employer's review requirements will vary from project to project, in accordance with the contribution which he wished and is qualified to make to the design. Where the employer owned the technology and so was fully involved in the design, he would wish to carry out reviews of the following, probably in his own offices because of the large numbers of his staff who will be involved, with the contractor's design team represented:

- Engineering line diagrams (process lines)
- Area classification

- Electrical distribution
- Steam and condensate
- Relief and blowdown
- Materials of construction.

The employer owning the technology would probably hold the following reviews without contractor attendance:

- Hazard and operability
- Plant operational control
- Engineering line diagrams (service lines)
- Voltage dip and automatic start of electrical gear.

The following joint reviews would be held in the contractor's offices, centred largely on the piping model:

- Block layout
- Constructability
- Paving and drainage
- Switch house location
- Safety shower location
- Service station location
- Piping routing
- Cable routing and protection
- Fire prevention, protection and means of escape
- Control room and panel layout
- Maintenance access
- Noise sources and acoustic treatment.

17.2.8 Technical Safety

Sophisticated process plants are not inherently safe, in the sense that they cannot usually be designed so as always to fail to a safe situation without any imposed control. Although inherent safety is striven for, process safety is to a large extent dependent on the use of instruments, trips and alarms. For those safety aspects of the design that can be assessed quantitatively, the plant is designed to particular safety criteria. One such is the Fatal Accident Rate: the number of fatal accidents expected in a group of one thousand men in a working lifetime (one hundred million man-hours of exposure). An FAR of 0.4 for any single risk is a design criterion often used. The average FAR for the UK chemical industry is 4, of which half is due to ordinary industrial risks such as being run over. An FAR criterion of 0.4 therefore assumes that the typical plant has no more than five significant risks if the industry average is not to be exceeded.

If the plant is to use the employer's own technology, the employer will take the lead in reviewing the design to make certain it is adequately safe. Even with technology supplied by others, however, the employer will wish to be fully involved. The major stages in the work to ensure that the technical safety of the plant will be adequate, much of which forms part of the major reviews of design listed previously, are as given below:

Major hazard identification

Based on preliminary process design information, the potential for major hazard—fire, explosion, and release of toxic materials—will be identified, and if possible, designed out. Of course, for an existing process this will all have been done before and it will be necessary only to consider anything that is new, or to explore the potential for improvement.

Mechanical design standards

Equipment data sheets and engineering line diagrams will be reviewed to confirm that satisfactory design conditions and suitable materials of construction have been selected. The pressure relief and blowdown review provides further confirmation of design conditions and ensures that equipment cannot be over-pressured.

Plant layout

Many of the reviews affect, or are affected by, the plant layout. Where appropriate, the review of vapour cloud explosion pressures may influence the siting of the plant in relation to external installations, its general layout and the location of the control room and other occupied buildings. The plant layout may also be affected by the reviews of fire fighting and protection, means of escape, electrical area classification, cable routing and protection, and paving and drainage.

Operability and maintenance

When firm engineering line diagrams, draft operating instructions and maintenance methods are available, a detailed critical examination of the operation of the plant will be carried out to confirm that the plant can be operated and maintained safely and effectively. This is the detailed Hazard and Operability Study, a technique invented in ICI in the 1960s and now widely practised in the process industries. Similar studies, of a more preliminary nature and in less detail, will have been performed earlier on the basis of the process flowsheets.

Confirmatory reviews

Part of the commissioning team's remit should be to check that the plant has been built to design, and that actions from earlier safety reviews have all been taken. The team should also review the specific question of the personal safety of those working on the plant.

There are, of course, numerous statutory requirements in the field of safety that must be complied with, and the employer's project manager must be responsible for ensuring that all the necessary statutory approvals have been obtained. In particular, for those plants to which it applies, compliance with the Control of Industrial Major Accident Hazards Regulations 1984 may call for substantial effort from the project and commissioning teams.

17.2.9 Piping Model

Time was when the detailed layout, including piping, of a process plant was designed and documented chiefly by means of general arrangement drawings—plans and elevations. A large number of these would be prepared for a major plant, sectioned by horizontal planes. Such drawings have not been common in the last two or three decades, being superseded, so far as piping is concerned, by isometric drawings of individual pipelines. There is then no drawing of the plant which depicts everything which is to be installed, and consequently none which can be relied upon to detect interference between different items. In the absence of a general arrangement drawing, the task of checking for interference is assumed by the piping model. A preliminary sketch of each pipeline is prepared, the line is run on the piping model, and the final isometric then drawn. The model also fulfils several other important functions. Being three-dimensional, it is much more easily followed by operating staff seconded to the design team, who will be less accustomed than the regular design staff to visualising the plant from drawings. The model becomes the central feature of the layout review and is used in the checking and approval, as well as in the initial layout, of the piping. It is also a very useful aid on site, to such an extent that it is not unknown, where a model has not been used in design, for a post-design model to be built simply for use during construction.

The advent of computer-aided design has provided an alternative way of detecting interference but has not, in the view of most engineers, yet eliminated the need for a three-dimensional model. It is still common practice to run the piping on the model before input to the computer. And probably few employers' project staff would concede that computer-aided design has yet provided an equivalent review tool. A detailed piping model is expensive, costing between 5 and 10% of the total design cost, so that it is not something to embark upon unnecessarily. It would usually be dispensed with where the plant was a near repeat of an earlier one on the same site. In such a case the benefit to be gained from it, in design or construction, would hardly justify the cost.

The required scale for the model would be specified in the Co-ordination Procedure. This is usually 1/33 for a large plant. A smaller plant, or an especially difficult section of one, or individual models of pre-assembled units, might be produced to the larger scale of 1/25. The Co-ordination Procedure would outline the extent of equipment to be shown on the model—instrument and cable runs, instrument housings, junction boxes and so on—and more detail would be found in the piping specification.

17.3 VARIATIONS

Although lump sum contracts should be based on good initial definition of what the contractor has to provide, unless the employer takes no part in the design process, some changes attributable to him during execution are inevitable. These will give rise to claims by the contractor for increases in the contract price, or for extra time, or for changes to his obligations for plant performance. If he agrees, the Engineer will authorise these claims as variations to the contract. Variations are concerned with matters for which the contract provides and which can therefore be settled by the Engineer appointed under the contract, and whose authority flows entirely from it. Claims for breach of contract which may justify damages are outside the purview of the Engineer, though not necessarily outside that of the employer's project manager. (There may be contractual claims other than variations which the contractor is entitled to make, where there is specific provision in the contract giving entitlement. Examples might be a claim for indemnity against patent infringement, or for extension of time for completion in certain circumstances.)

Careful control and management of variations is a crucial factor in the success or failure of a project. The disruptive effect on the design of a large number of variations will be substantial, as may the extra cost and time incurred. The relationships between employer's and contractor's personnel may be adversely affected by an excessive number of variations, and a good deal of emotion generated if matters are not carefully handled. It is sometimes said (not entirely in jest and not, of course, by a contractor) that, on average, contractors' claims are one-third fraudulent, one-third speculative and one-third justified. If this is in truth the belief of the employer's personnel, it is no help to the achievement of a successful outcome for the contract. The employer's project manager's first priority should be to minimise the number and value of variations, the second to deal with them as quickly and efficiently as possible.

While variations can hardly ever be entirely avoided, they can be minimised by good initial project definition, careful contract documentation and a determination to resist design changes. If not rigorously controlled by the employer's project manager, some changes may be merely manifestations of the preferences of various members of the employer's staff, not necessarily members of the project team. Among these will usually be some who claim the right to influence what is done without accepting any responsibility for the outcome and, indeed, in many cases with no conception of the baleful effects of their actions. In most large projects, there will be more than enough variations arising from errors in the initial definition, from justified improvements to the design, from errors and omissions and from delays in the passage of information, without adding unnecessarily to them. For those variations which are considered essential, an effective and systematic procedure for their processing is required.

Most contractors will profess to prefer a contract with no variations, and will claim to lose money on them. Many employers' project managers, faced with what can seem to be inordinate claims for relatively trivial changes, will find this hard to believe. But in truth, while contractors may do their best to exaggerate the effects of any change, the employer's staff will usually significantly underestimate them. Since the total value of variations on a contract can easily exceed the contractor's expected profit, it is not hard to see why the contractor is keen to pursue them. And although the employer's project manager may consider that the charges for variations which he has to accept are excessive, he should be able to console himself with the thought that a lump sum contract with a reasonable level of variations will probably provide a better outcome than would have resulted from a reimbursable contract.

In reimbursable contracts, there will be no requirements for variations, unless the contractor has obligations to meet programme, in which case it will be necessary to provide for the possibility of variations which require extra time. It may also be desirable to operate a system of variations merely to assist in the orderly execution of the project.

17.3.1 Origins of Variations

Variations may arise from conflicts in the initial contract documents. These documents may be extremely voluminous and the work of many hands over a prolonged period, so that inconsistencies are almost inevitable. They must be construed as they stand—not what they ought to say, or what they were intended to say. The Engineer has no power to amend them, however much they may need it. An express order of precedence will help to resolve conflicts but is unlikely to cover all eventualities, for example:

- Memorandum of contract
- Special conditions of contract
- General conditions of contract

- Agreed changes to the employer's enquiry
- Employer's enquiry
- Contractor's tender.

The Engineer must endeavour to resolve any differences. Whether the contractor has consequent rights to variations will depend on the circumstances. The contractor has no claim merely because he has misunderstood the employer's Enquiry. Nor, with the order of precedence given above, has he a valid claim because his tender did not include for all the employer's requirements (unless there was a subsequent modification documented in the Agreed Changes).

Variations arising during execution of an initially well-defined contract will not usually all, or even mainly, result from deliberate initiatives or changes of mind by the employer's staff. More often, they will arise as a consequence of developing definition and design. No Enquiry specification can cover everything, and some of the employer's input to the design as it progresses may well require the contractor to perform work additional to or different from what he may have reasonably assumed in his tender. The employer's preferred solutions to problems which arise may be different from those the contractor would reasonably employ, left to himself. Whether an employer's requirement gives rise to a justifiable claim by the contractor sometimes depends on its timing: if made late, it may involve change to work already performed. Conversely, the employer may precipitate a variation, and incur liability, by rushing in too quickly with solutions to problems. The employer's input would not occasion a variation where it is:

(1) given via the original Enquiry specification;
(2) directed to ensuring that the contractor complies with the Enquiry specification;
(3) additional to the Enquiry specification if the contractor is put to no greater expense of time or money;
(4) a result of demonstrating that the contractor's design is unworkable or unsafe.

A variation would be justified if the employer's input:

(1) countermanded the original specification giving rise to greater expense or time;
(2) affected design already performed and approved (except where identification of a contractor's error was the cause) and gave rise to extra time or expense;
(3) increased or decreased the scope of the contract.

If the employer was responsible for delaying the work, the contractor would be entitled to any extra cost he incurred as a consequence, and would be entitled to extra time, that is to say, a postponement of the completion date, if this were affected. It is, of course, often difficult to identify the delay to completion resulting from a particular action or omission, or to distinguish between the effects of overlapping delays. If the work delayed is not on the critical path and remains so, then the contractor will not be entitled to any extension of time but he will nevertheless be entitled to be reimbursed for any extra cost incurred. Where the employer is not responsible for the delay, the contractor will not in general be entitled to compensation, but may be entitled to extra time, for example, in the case of force majeure. This term has no precise legal meaning, but the contract will usually provide a non-exclusive list of examples of circumstances which would be considered force majeure. Most contracts allow the contractor to claim for an extension of time where force majeure circumstances cause delay—but only for the delay caused, not necessarily for the whole period during which the circumstances exist. Extra costs due to force majeure usually lie where they fall.

Claims involving delay can arise in a number of ways. Delay in provision of information, or in approval, by the employer could, if it affects the contractor's work, justify a claim though it might be difficult to make the case. In this regard the contractor will be better placed if the contract is explicit about the timing of information passing and approval. Prolongation of the work by the employer—where the start is not delayed but progress is hampered and the duration of the work prolonged—may also justify a claim but may often be difficult to demonstrate convincingly. The same difficulty of proof will attach to a contractual claim for low productivity, more common in construction than design. Again the contractor will need to show that this is the fault of the employer.

17.3.2 Procedure

If the contract is to keep to programme, it is essential that claims for variations are not allowed to hold up the work. The contractor may therefore be required to perform work for which he has claimed additional payment and time, before he knows the results of his claim. It is clearly important for the success of the contract that the contractor has confidence in the employer to treat his claims fairly. The contractor needs an effective method of identifying changes and an efficient procedure for processing variation orders. For the employer, any system must have certain essential features if it is to deal with variations successfully.

Timing

Variations must be dealt with expeditiously as they arise. The contractor owes it to the employer to provide him always with an up-to-date picture of his commitments. Early notification will help:

(1) The employer to try to mitigate the extra cost. He may have the option not to proceed with the variation.

(2) The employer to find the money, or at least to give his project manager the opportunity to budget for it. A contractor who fails to submit his claims until the employer's budget is fully committed does his chances of a satisfactory settlement serious harm.

(3) To maintain the contractor's negotiating position. Whatever the strict contractual situation, during the life of the contract the employer depends on the goodwill and motivation of the contractor.

(4) To give the contractor early indication of the employer's attitude to claims, enabling him to adjust his own behaviour accordingly.

(5) To avoid arguments about the sequence of events, which is often of crucial importance to whether a claim is justified.

(6) Both parties to estimate the effects of the variation while events are fresh in the mind.

It is natural that the employer's first reaction on being presented with a claim may be to look for arguments to refute it. The sensible contractor will avoid providing the employer with arguments based on the timing of notification and presentation which have little to do with the merits of the claim itself. The employer who, at a late stage in the project, is presented with a large additional bill about which he had no previous knowledge has a justified grievance.

Entitlement

The contractor has to state the reasons he considers himself entitled to extra time or payment. A variation proposal should therefore begin by citing the relevant Engineer's instruction or other matter giving rise to it. This is often enough, but some claims may require a narrative justification.

Quantification

It is usual (except, perhaps, in some cases where the contractor himself suggests the work giving rise to the proposed variation) for the contractor to be paid for the cost of preparing the estimate of cost and time, whether or not the variation is accepted. Following negotiation and agreement, the contract price, programme and any other of the contractor's obligations are adjusted as appropriate.

The prices of variations arising during the design phase are agreed on the basis of estimated rather than achieved costs. This must be so, since a design variation will seldom be amenable to measurement on site even if the delay in payment that this would cause were tolerable. Variations, unlike claims for damages, are estimated on the basis of price rather than cost, that is to say, the contractor's costs and expenses, overheads and profit are all included. Design man-hour rates, including overheads and profit, to be used in the estimation of variations will have been specified in the contractor's tender. Of course, an increase in time-related overheads is only strictly chargeable where the extra work of the variation extends the period required for the design. The same is true of project management: while it is usual for a contractor to attribute some man-hours by his project manager to each variation, where a full-time project manager is employed these can only be justified if the design period is extended. However, underestimation of the design period is common and the last 10% of the work, not on the critical path, almost always drags on beyond what was promised. The contractor has usually therefore no difficulty in demonstrating increased consumption of overheads, whether or not this was all the result of variations.

17.4 PROCUREMENT

Close co-ordination of procurement with design is absolutely necessary and, to ensure this for their in-house design projects, some employers incorporate procurement into each functional design section. Each specialist design engineer is then responsible for all aspects, both technical and commercial, of the materials and equipment in his speciality. This method of working has much to commend it but few, if any, contractors organise their affairs in this way. The usual practice is to have a separate procurement department working from requisitions provided by engineering. This may sharpen commercial skills but will produce a satisfactory overall result only if there is close co-operation between engineering and procurement. Especially with sophisticated technical equipment, the purchasing process is a combined technical and commercial one, and difficulties will result from trying to deal separately with each in sequence. Some contractors' procurement departments have been known to seek to maximise their own control of events: they exclude engineers from vendor negotiations if they possibly can and adopt administrative practices— such as the passing on of bids for technical consideration only when all have been assembled—which hinder progress. The way the contractor handles these matters should have an important bearing on contract award. It helps if engineering and procurement, as well as construction, form a single department in the contractor's organisation.

The task of the employer's project manager is to combine the purchasing strengths of contractor and employer in the most effective way. A major international process operating company will, for the majority of its projects, have a good deal to offer. The value of engineering purchases that it makes annually will far exceed that of most process plant contractors but will, of course, contain a high proportion of purchasing for maintenance which has only limited relevance to the procurement of major capital equipment. Nevertheless, such an employer's commercial clout will be formidable, not least because of the continuing nature of his capital investment. His international purchasing knowledge and experience will undoubtedly be patchy, good in some areas and non-existent in others, but so indeed will be that of the contractor. Where the employer has experience of the process technology in previous similar plants, his knowledge and experience of potential suppliers will be especially valuable, even more so if the process is one he himself developed. In any case, potential suppliers can be expected to understand the influence that an experienced employer will have on vendor selection, and will respond best to the combined influence of contractor and employer.

For a plant built overseas in a developing country, the employer's contribution may be particularly valuable if he already has employees in the country who can help. For such a plant, use of local manufacturing resources may, for some items, save cost without compromising technical standards. A contractor with no previous experience of the country may, left to his own devices, fail to take full advantage of this. A contractor's procurement organisation is often rather office-bound with the issue of formal enquiries, often of formidable bulk, to potential suppliers the only way of proceeding. For their part, potential suppliers are expected to respond in a formalised manner and to travel to the contractor's offices to discuss their bids. While satisfactory for dealings with experienced vendors, this may not meet the needs where suppliers local to the site, perhaps with an inadequate command of English and a lack of familiarity with the specifications, are concerned. If such suppliers are to be encouraged to bid, greater flexibility and special effort will be necessary. The common form of contract for lump sum design and procurement services with reimbursable materials and equipment, however, provides no incentive for the contractor to expend extra, unbudgeted procurement effort in order to obtain lower prices, especially if one consequence is the need for additional design effort to explain requirements. The employer will need to take a direct interest if he is to achieve the best results in such circumstances.

A perennial problem with the procurement of equipment for major process plant is that, given the length of the construction period, the conventional one year's warranty offered by most suppliers is likely to expire before the plant is commissioned. This will leave either the contractor or the employer, depending on the terms of the main contract, with no contractual remedy should the equipment fail to perform when it is started up. It is sometimes possible to extend the warranty on pain of storing the equipment on site in controlled conditions and paying for the supplier to inspect the equipment immediately before it is put into service. For important machinery, this is well worth doing. Late delivery of vendor design information is also a frequent problem: as bad if not worse than late delivery of the corresponding equipment. It is usual, where stage payments are to be made, to make these conditional on the receipt of certified vendor drawings. This may not be enough to avoid the need for much expediting.

17.4.1 Lump Sum Contracts for Supply

The form of contract obviously influences the role of the employer, who will have relatively little involvement in procurement where the contract provides for the supply of materials and equipment as part of a lump sum price. The employer's requirements should have been adequately specified in the Co-ordination Procedure. The experienced employer will have provided a list of approved vendors of equipment (and, if the contract includes construction, a list of approved construction sub-contractors). These will be companies with whom the employer has had previous satisfactory dealings, or which he has inspected, and who can be employed without further reference. The contractor may propose new names for inclusion in the lists and these are likely to be accepted by the employer, subject to inspection, since there is often a shortage of suppliers and sub-contractors of proven capability and experience. The approved vendors' list usually covers only key items of equipment. For the rest, the employer will usually make no conditions.

The employer will almost certainly wish to have the right to attend technical meetings with potential suppliers of important equipment items and will have specified this in his Enquiry since, despite the lump sum nature of the contract, the employer will still wish to ensure that his knowledge and experience is brought to bear. He may have much greater technical expertise than the contractor in some of the equipment to be purchased. The terms and conditions of sub-contracts and orders will not concern the employer, since his interests will have been secured in the main contract. It is for the contractor to obtain from his sub-contractors and suppliers terms and conditions which will enable him to meet his obligations to the employer.

Whatever the type of contract, the employer will be concerned about the ordering of spares and will detail his requirements in the Co-ordination Procedure. It is absolutely necessary that this should be done because few contractors have much conception of what a workable spares system involves since they have no experience of the long-term operation and maintenance of plants. The cost of spares is usually much less if ordered with the equipment, so that vendors must be required to include a priced list of recommended spares in their bids. If the contractor is to produce the spare gear book, an allocation of responsibility that would be sensible only if the employer had no existing operation on the site and lacked the resources to do it himself, it would be desirable to detail requirements with some precision or, alternatively, to specify the man-months of effort that the contractor must include in his bid for this task.

17.4.2 Reimbursable Supply

Where materials and equipment are to be supplied reimbursably, the employer will be significantly involved in the procurement process, and the Co-ordination Procedure will contain a good deal more about procurement than in the case of a lump sum contract. Very possibly a separate Procurement Procedure will be developed. As well as the lists of approved vendors and sub-contractors, this will contain the employer's requirements for the ordering and progressing of spares, for producing the spare gear book and for approving comparisons of vendors' bids. Both parties will wish to see bid comparisons approved, the employer to retain control of expenditure, the contractor to protect himself against any future liability. The employer may stipulate a minimum order value below which orders may be placed without his approval, but the contractor may not wish to take advantage of this. The form of the bid comparison, especially the way in which the various cost elements are taken into account, among them first cost, currency, transport costs, maintenance and operating costs, needs to be agreed but can be done after contract award. Decisions on the supply of major equipment often require the balancing of technical and commercial aspects. The problems may be particularly complex where proprietary equipment is concerned and where alternative solutions may be proposed by potential suppliers. The employer may need to define various utility and opportunity costs if correct decisions are to be arrived at. All the interested parties will need to work closely together.

There are numerous other matters which must be discussed and agreed between employer and contractor, among them the number of bidders to be sought in the typical situation, shipping details, insurance considerations, payment terms and document distribution. It is vital that the employer's staff understand that all dealings with potential and actual suppliers and sub-contractors are co-ordinated by the contractor, and that there must be no unilateral dealings or negotiations, however close a prior relationship may have been between vendor and employer's functional engineer.

If the contractor is to purchase equipment and materials as principal, and sell them on to the employer, the latter may have no interest in the terms and conditions of the sub-contracts and orders, since his contractual concerns will be covered in the main contract. This will not be so, however, if the contractor's limit of liability depends on the liabilities accepted by his sub-contractors and suppliers, in which case the employer might wish to lay down, in the main contract, minimum acceptable liabilities for sub-contractors and suppliers. The employer will probably require the right to be present at both commercial and technical meetings between the contractor and his suppliers and sub-contractors. If the contractor is purchasing as the employer's agent, then the orders are the employer's own. He will probably have specified the main terms and conditions for these orders in the Co-ordination Procedure, and will have reserved the right to approve them. He will, of course, have the right to attend both commercial and technical meetings. Whatever the terms of the main contract, however, the employer will probably wish to attend only those meetings which are concerned with reasonably important orders.

Procurement arrangements can differ importantly from one contractor to another. Some will provide freight forwarding services themselves, others will use agents. Some will make extensive use of stockists for bulk materials such as piping. Such differences have a bearing on the contract price, which the employer's project manager should have understood when bids were being considered. They can also have implications on project control: for example, it will be more difficult to assess the position on piping materials orders when a stockist is being used. The grouping of equipment orders is also common practice with some contractors. This will be to the employer's advantage if cheaper prices can be obtained than by placing many smaller orders. The employer should beware, however, of the grouping of orders merely to save procurement effort.

It will be necessary to devise arrangements to transfer to the contractor the money he needs to pay suppliers' invoices. The general rule is that this process should be financially neutral; that the contractor should neither gain nor lose. Various arrangements are possible but the essence is that the contractor produces a monthly list of invoices which are to be paid; the employer then pays the required sum into a bank account on which the contractor is able to draw but on which interest accrues to the employer. With a large project, there is likely to be a variety of foreign orders and, where government-supported finance is not involved, it is usually cheaper for invoices to be paid in the vendor's own currency which is provided by the employer, making the transaction rather more complicated. Where the contractor purchases as the employer's agent, it is possible for the employer to pay suppliers' invoices directly. This is an inefficient way of organising matters and is not to be recommended. Unsuspected difficulties may arise where computerised systems are in use: such a system may not allow for the payment of invoices for orders placed by others, in which case dummy orders will have to be raised and a good deal of extra work done to no benefit. Cost monitoring will be complicated by the establishment of another cost centre.

17.4.3 Expediting and Inspection

Expediting is carried out by the contractor's procurement team, but too often relies overmuch on the telephone. There is no substitute for expediting visits for important orders. These can sometimes be combined with technical discussions, and progress will also be reported in inspection reports. Some large employers have their own inspection service and may take responsibility for inspection. Most large contractors also have an inspection department, and there are a number of independent inspection agencies of good reputation. The degree of inspection required will vary greatly depending on the material and equipment concerned, from minimal inspection for standard items to an inspector resident in the shop throughout manufacture for important items such as a large compressor. The employer will require to see all inspection reports.

Some less-developed countries require major equipment to be inspected and tested under the supervision of an approved inspection service. Inspection by an agency, however eminent, not on the approved list will not suffice. Substantial delay in completion will be caused if all equipment has to be inspected and tested again after delivery to site, so it is essential that an approved agency be used. The obvious solution would seem to be to seek approval for the inspection agency that it is intended to use. For UK companies, however, there may be a hidden snag. Although the country concerned may profess, quite sincerely, that any inspection agency of the necessary experience and competence may gain approval, this may be predicated on the assumption that such an agency has government approval in its own country, an assumption so obvious as not to be worth mentioning. The fact that the UK government does not approve inspection agencies, when discovered later, may prove an insurmountable barrier.

17.4.4 Material Control

Many hands are involved in getting materials and equipment to site. Design is responsible for the technical and procurement department for the commercial aspects. Inspectors seek to ensure that materials and equipment conform with specification, expeditors to ensure that delivery is to programme. Shipping department arranges transport. External services: stockists, inspection agencies, freight forwarding agencies, may also be involved. The process does not end even when the materials and equipment are received on site, for they must be sorted and stored there and issued as required to the construction workforce. Procurement department will normally have the responsibility for getting the materials and equipment to the site on time. On a major project, a daunting mass of detail is generated and the wise employer will demand the appointment of one or more dedicated material controllers to co-ordinate all the necessary activities and collate all the information. Without such an appointment, it will be difficult to maintain adequate surveillance of all that is going on so as to trigger corrective action when necessary.

Careful control of material is especially important where off-site fabrication is contemplated, as described below, and where responsibility for design and construction is separated. In the latter case, it is worth considering whether the design and procurement contractor should not be made responsible for the receipt, storage and issue of materials on site.

17.5   OFF-SITE FABRICATION

As standards of living rise and the cost of labour increases, so it is necessary to use labour ever more efficiently. In general, this can more readily be done, and with less risk of disruption, in the settled and controlled environment of the factory than on the construction site. Thus there is a continuing trend to perform more of the work of construction off-site, a trend which is naturally more pronounced in the developed countries. Progress in this direction is accelerated from time to time by the examples set by construction projects in hostile environments, such as the Alaskan North Slope and the North Sea, where construction is so difficult that the economics are heavily in favour of as much off-site fabrication as practicable. The methods and techniques developed in response to these extreme conditions then find application, in modified and diluted form, to plants constructed in less difficult locations. In the case of a major process plant, the techniques must be applied partially and piecemeal, since there can seldom be any question of the whole plant being constructed in this way.

Off-site fabrication can have profound effects on the design process and must be decided upon, and its extent defined, well before detailed design commences. It requires increased management effort in design and procurement. It incurs other additional costs in the supervision of the fabricators, the sorting and shipping of materials, transport of the fabricated units and any necessary rectification work on site. Special lifting gear—frames and spreader beams— will be particularly expensive because of its requirements for testing, and the need for it should if possible be avoided by designing the units for the lift conditions. For off-site fabrication to be economic, these increased costs must be more than offset by the higher productivity of the off-site work, added to the savings achieved on site in any or all of time, reduced site congestion, scaffolding, storage and supervision. In many cases, it will not be possible to estimate the costs and savings with any great accuracy but typically, a difference in productivity of off-site working compared with work on-site of about 5% should balance the extra costs of design and procurement. This should not be difficult to achieve in UK circumstances and, together with the possibilities for saving time, leads to the conclusion that any work that can be transferred off-site without special difficulty should be.

17.5.1 Piping Fabrication

The fabrication and erection of pipework is the Achilles heel of most petrochemical plant construction, and a major plant may contain some hundreds of kilometres of piping. In the UK, though not in less-developed countries, it has long been customary to carry out fabrication off-site. Since the UK is badly served by contractors in this field, those available being too small to do all the work required for a major plant and, for the most part, devoid of any great management competence, major projects are complicated by the need to employ and supervise several piping fabricators, as well as several erection contractors. Some design organisations pay little more attention to an order for piping fabrication than to the procurement of a pressure vessel, but the problem needs a good deal more attention than this.

Piping materials and valves are procured by placing a large number of orders on a large number of suppliers. This material must then be sorted into erection material—mainly flanged items which will be installed on site—and fabrication material. The latter must be sorted and dispatched to the various fabricators together with the appropriate piping isometric drawings. Where different materials which cannot readily be identified—for example, different grades of stainless steel—are to be used, steps must be taken to control their use, possibly by limiting each fabricator to one type of material. It is difficult to see how all this can be accomplished satisfactorily without the use of an entrepôt, or staging warehouse. This may be located on the construction site, or possibly elsewhere. At the warehouse, all materials and drawings will be received, sorted and dispatched to the various fabricators and the site. The regular, periodic dispatch of drawings together with the materials for which they call will enable strong control to be exerted on the fabricators' operations.

The typical piping fabricator fabricates pipework as material and design information comes to hand in the most convenient order for himself, and dipatches it to the site as it is completed. This is highly unsatisfactory for the erection contractor: much time is wasted in trying to find material when it is required for erection and inevitably, some pipework is fabricated a second time. If piping erection is to be carried out efficiently, it is highly desirable that fabricated pipework be delivered to site in an orderly way, that is to say, each consignment should relate to only one construction area and should consist of complete pipelines together with their associated pipe hangers. The fabricated pipework can then be stored on site in a way which allows swift and efficient retrieval for erection. Needless to say, close supervision of the piping fabricator, based on appropriate conditions in his contract, will be required for this to be achieved.

The cost of the staging warehouse and of close supervision of the fabricators is, of course, considerable, and it is necessary to make sure that it is included in the project estimate. Compared with the unmanaged alternative, however, there is little doubt that the consequent reduction in construction costs will result in a net saving.

17.5.2 Vendor-packaged Units

A vendor-packaged unit is a pre-assembly produced by the vendor of the principal equipment items which the unit contains. There are some long-established examples—oil-fuel pumping and heating units, refrigerator units—and it is becoming increasingly common for vendors of other types of equipment to be asked to extend the scope of their supply. Vendor-packaged units can offer considerable advantages because the vendor can be made responsible for the procurement, and possibly some of the detailed design, of the additional materials which he incorporates in his unit, so reducing the work of the design contractor. An increasingly common example of the vendor-packaged unit is the fully trayed and dressed distillation column. Large savings in time as well as cost may be achieved in this instance because the work of traying and dressing can be done at ground level with the column in a horizontal position, something often not practicable on site.

17.5.3 Pre-assembled Units

A pre-assembled unit is a complete, small section of plant put together off-site by an assembler who has no responsibility for design, and none for procurement except possibly for the supply of fabricated steel and pipework. A large process plant may contain a number of these units, assembled by several different contractors at different locations. Partial pre-assembly in this way presents quite difficult problems for the design organisation. Design has to be frozen earlier, and subsequent changes will cause greater problems. Design and procurement are complicated by the necessity to split out each pre-assembly as a separate mini-project with its own package of design information and materials. Piping isometrics will be increased in number because cut-lines need to correspond with the pre-assembled unit boundaries. Extra design effort may be required on steel framing and site connections. Some of the design information may have to be provided in more detail if the assembler lacks familiarity with some part of the work. Logistical problems will certainly be increased, as will the requirements for supervision and inspection.

The use of partial pre-assembly therefore puts additional burdens on project control and organisation. Given that the project is sufficiently well organised to cope properly with these additional strains, it does allow savings to be made in construction cost and time. Obviously, the magnitude of the savings will depend on the nature and size of the pre-assembly programme.

Chapter 18

Construction and Takeover

18.1 INTRODUCTION

In recent decades, it has been common for employers in the process manufacturing industries to manage their own construction in the UK, even where contractors have been employed to perform the design. The reasons for this are rooted in recent history. The rapid development of the petrochemical and chemical industries in the 1950s and 1960s included a number of major projects completed under turnkey contracts for design, supply and construction. Few of these were wholly successful, the shortcomings being attributed largely to poor construction performance. Direct hire of construction workers by the contractor was the norm, and if not directly the cause of the poor industrial relations which were seen as a dominant factor in the problems, the short-term nature of such employment certainly did not help. As a consequence, employers were led to manage construction themselves, using their own permanent labour force, or local sub-contractors with a large proportion of permanent employees. Taking direct control of construction was hardly breaking new ground for the employers, since most found it necessary to maintain a construction management organisation to manage the work of modification to existing plants, intimately connected with operation and maintenance. There seemed every incentive for the employer to retain direct control of construction throughout the 1970s. Industrial relations deteriorated nationally and the employers' stakes were steadily raised as the sites on which new plants were built continued to be developed and the potential cost of the transfer of industrial relations problems from construction to existing operations increased accordingly. Industrial relations much improved in the 1980s, many employers reduced their engineering staffs, and it is to be expected that contractors will manage UK process plant construction more often in the future.

Whether employers were correct in thinking that the problems of the 1960s were primarily the fault of the contractors' construction managements is open to doubt. Certainly, it can be argued that the employers did no better in the 1970s, when virtually without exception, all major projects in the UK were late and over-spent, some quite extravagantly so. Much of the blame was fairly placed on the workforce, but objective assessment of process plant construction during that time tended to produce the conclusion that some of what was thought wrong with construction was actually the fault of earlier design and procurement. On many large projects, inadequacies in the provision of design information and materials to construction was such that there was never any realistic prospect of the construction management meeting its objectives. The degree of success that would have been achieved had design and procurement performed properly can never properly be assessed.

During the 1970's, all aspects of project execution were made much more difficult by an overloaded industry. It was evident that many project managers, although alive to most of the factors affecting their projects, did not adequately appreciate the effects of boom conditions. It is, of course, during such times that large projects are often sanctioned—they are, after all, at once the consequence of the increase in demand for their products and the cause of similar over-heating in the process plant design, supply and construction industries. This over-heating affects all facets of a project. The staffs of all the parties concerned—employer, design contractors, suppliers, construction contractors, sub-contractors—are diluted by expansion and reduced in knowledge and experience. Project execution becomes much harder since understanding of the work is less; communications are more difficult; more mistakes are made; few, if any, of the parties meet their commitments despite much increased progressing and expediting effort. The work is performed under intense pressure for early completion in order to catch the market for the product. The difference between a project carried out at a time when industry's capacity is less than fully utilised, and one executed during boom conditions is, to use a military analogy, something like the difference between a battle against a much weaker enemy and one against the fiercest resistance from an equal or superior force. Success in the first offers no guarantee of success in the second.

Whether or not he manages construction directly, the employer exerts a powerful influence on construction and cannot escape all responsibility for what is done, although his may not be the prime responsibility for all, or indeed any, of its aspects. The employer's influence and responsibility are least where a lump sum design, supply and construction contract has been placed. Even in a turnkey project, however, the employer's influence remains considerable if he cares to exert it and can be exercised for good or ill. His influence is felt first, through the conditions he specifies in his Enquiry and subsequently includes in the contract, and second, through the pressures he exerts on the contractor during execution. These pressures, for example to maintain or vary the construction start date in response to events, are not always explicitly sanctioned by the contract, but can nevertheless be influential. It is for the employer's project manager, in construction as in all other matters, to make sure that the employer's influence is exercised in ways that will benefit the project.

Where the employer manages construction directly, placing separate contracts for different aspects of the work, he controls two of the three main factors in the construction process, and has a powerful influence on the third. Even where a construction management services contractor is appointed, the employer may still exert this control and influence at one remove. Firstly and most importantly, he controls the availability of design information and material. Secondly, he controls the types of contracts that are awarded: the relationships between the parties, the responsibilities each takes and their incentives to perform. The third factor, the actual execution of the work, is the responsibility of the various contractors. However, the employer can exert considerable influence on this through the exercise of his rights, including those of approval, under the contracts.

18.2 ORDERLY CONSTRUCTION

Reference has been made in the previous chapter to the importance of an orderly design process and the perils of too much overlapping of design activities. An orderly construction process is equally desirable. Construction is much more costly than design, and correction of error vastly more expensive in metal and concrete than on paper. Quality is as important in construction as in design, but the efficiency with which resources are utilised is of even greater concern. There is thus everything to be said for not commencing the major expenditure of site work until properly prepared. This may seem a blinding glimpse of the obvious, but it is a more than common failing for the project manager to yield to temptation, or to pressure, and to start construction before everything is properly to hand. This will not usually be before design is at least half-way through—in the US, some companies will claim not to start construction until design is virtually completed (though not everything will then have been delivered). In Chapter 16 on planning, the point was made that the planned date for the start of construction will be derived from an assessment of when adequate design and materials will be available but that, when the time arrives, the logic of this is usually ignored. All too often it is then the calendar date that influences the start of construction rather than the availability of data and materials.

Where design and construction are separated, the placing of construction contracts or sub-contracts heralds the commitment of major construction resources. It is important that these contracts are placed on the basis of reasonably accurate data. Premature placing—sometimes by the contractor in order to demonstrate progress—leads to claims for extra costs and extensions of time. If the size of the job is underestimated at contract award, the wrong contractor may be chosen, or the contractor may provide an inadequate management team which he is unable or unwilling to augment when the actual size of the job becomes apparent. The timing of the start of construction must be based not on the forecast date given in the plan but on the availability of design and materials. The project manager, in conjunction with his construction manager, must decide, not on the first possible date on which there is something which can be done on site, but when work can start and continue uninterruptedly, making efficient use of the resources employed.

From previous remarks it will be evident that more liberties can be taken with the availability of design information and materials during slack periods in the industry than during periods of over-heating. Unfortunately, this will run counter to the demands of the business, which will be most eager for completion in boom periods when demand for the product is out-running supply. Resisting pressure to make the earliest possible start, from those who will later accept no responsibility for the painful consequences, is a key task of the project and construction managers. If the criteria for the commencement of the various aspects of construction are clearly defined in advance, it will be much easier to resist this pressure and to follow the original intent. The following are examples of criteria that might be agreed for a major process plant:

(1) *Piling*—to commence when full information on half the total number of piles has been received on site, and when information on the remainder can be guaranteed to be available before the piling programme is one-quarter complete.

(2) *Civil work*—to commence when half of all civil drawings have been received on site, and when all underground design has been received for the particular construction area in which work is to start.

(3) *Steelwork erection*—to commence when 70% of all steelwork (including handrails, stairways, etc.) has been fabricated and, for the particular construction area where work is to start, when all steelwork has been fabricated and all underground civil work and paving completed.

(4) *Piping erection*—to commence when, for the plant as a whole, 70% of the main plant items have been installed, 70% of the steelwork erected and 70% of fabricated pipework delivered; for the particular construction area

where work is to start, all plant items have been installed, all steelwork has been erected and all fabricated pipework delivered.

Since design programmes are almost invariably optimistic, strict adherence to these criteria will usually mean postponing the start of construction compared with the plan. There is no magic formula which will secure design and materials early. The greatest scope for improvement in the flow of design information and materials is from prompt decisions and early freezing of design, but this is a hard lesson which seems to be learnt only from experience. Of course, the initial delay waiting for civil design to be sufficiently well advanced allows all other aspects of the design to proceed nearer to completion, so that there will probably be no need for further delays before the start of other disciplines. The criteria for the commencement of civil work are therefore most important and need careful consideration. In fixing them it should be borne in mind that they are based on estimates of the number of drawings that will be produced, and that such estimates are likely to be exceeded, even before changes are allowed for, so that the actual percentage design completion will be less than appears.

It is, of course, easy to agree to such obviously sensible proposals at the outset, especially in the aftermath of some project disaster. Those without much project experience may be persuaded that nothing will go wrong this time: that mere good intentions will be enough to secure good performance. Relatively few will have the steadfastness to stick to their principles under pressure, to delay the start of construction when all around are shouting 'Forward'. If, however, the criteria are strictly observed, quite startling improvements in productivity and speed of construction may be achieved compared with the common method of starting on site as soon as there is anything at all that can be done. There are several reasons for this improved performance. All design is an iterative process which is often based on assumptions about the results of work still to be done. To press for early issue is to risk many subsequent changes. Civil design, being the first to be required on site, is usually issued for construction before all its underlying assumptions can be verified. Inevitably, some of these assumptions will prove to be wrong and it is commonplace for approved civil drawings to be revised several times in the course of early site work. A later start means that these revisions will be made, for the most part, before work commences, so that construction changes will be very much reduced. Other parts of the design will benefit similarly. This, and the accompanying improved availability of materials will result in a significant increase in productivity. In addition, construction management, relieved of the necessity to spend much of its time expediting design and materials, and having a firmer grasp of what is to be done, will be able to plan the work better and manage it more effectively. The workforce will not be demoralised by frequent changes and by continually having to rip out today what was installed yesterday, nor by the belief that the management has no idea what it is doing.

While the actual improvement that may be achieved by timing the start of construction properly must depend on individual circumstances, savings of 20% in construction cost, compared with sanction estimates based on experience with more conventional starting times, have been achieved. For piping erection, always a key measure of construction performance, the savings can be much greater. Comparing piping erection productivity for two major UK projects on the same site, completed two years apart but both in a boom period, the first constructed to a conventional programme and started with woefully inadequate design information and materials, the second in which the start of construction was delayed by six months to assure an adequate supply of design and materials, piping productivity in terms of metres per man week was nearly 250% greater on the second project. Of course, there are many factors that can affect such a crude comparison, among them average pipe bore size, wall thickness, type of material, and complexity of the pipework, but the best estimate of the effect of all these factors in this case is that their net effect was small.

There still remains the question of whether the initial delay to the start of construction caused by sticking to the start criteria, which might be as much as six months compared with the original plan, can be recovered. This is not, however, the correct question. The original plan would not have been achievable because adequate supplies of design information and materials were not available on the programmed start date. The true question is which procedure would have produced the earlier completion—an early start with inadequate design and materials, or a later start with everything properly to hand. The comparison of piping erection productivity given above certainly leaves no doubt that as between those two projects, a later start resulted in quicker completion. In the second project, 100,000 metres of piping were erected in twelve months. If productivity had been merely one-third of this, in line with achievement on the first project, it would certainly not have been possible, for reasons of space and manpower availability, not to mention management capability, to have tripled the workforce to maintain the same piping erection programme.

The shapes of construction progress curves for the various functions give a good qualitative indication of efficiency. These curves commonly exhibit a lengthy initial period during which progress is slow. For some functions, something of a gradual start is perhaps inevitable, but this is often unduly prolonged by inadequate supplies of design and materials. This slow initial progress is not, of course, matched by the graph of labour usage, consideration of which will demonstrate the inefficiency of construction during this early period. It is this unproductive initial period that is reduced or eliminated by delaying the commencement of construction until information and material is adequately available, enabling the ideal construction progress curve—a straight line from start to finish—to be more closely approached. Few would quarrel with the proposition that there is an optimum time for starting construction which will produce the lowest cost consistent with no time penalty. What experience teaches is that the common error is to start too early. Experience also indicates that the quality of the start seems to set the pattern for construction to a much greater extent than can perhaps be logically explained. A project that begins with efficient and productive working seems able to sustain this: one that starts off badly finds it difficult to improve.

Of course, the type of contract used will have a strong bearing on how construction is executed. If a single contractor is responsible for design, supply and construction, it will be for him to decide when construction begins, though the employer may still influence him. If separate construction contracts are to be let, these will prevent too precipitate a start if they are placed on a lump sum basis or something approximating to it. Whatever the contractual organisation, the employer's project manager should endeavour to prevent construction beginning until adequate design and materials are available on site.

These remarks are made primarily from a UK perspective. They apply to construction in other countries, but perhaps with not quite the same force and with different emphases. In continental Europe and the US, there is evidence to suggest that delays in design and procurement can more easily be recovered during construction (despite the greater effort expended in the UK on planning). In underdeveloped countries, labour costs may be so much lower that construction productivity is of little concern, although low labour costs are not always mirrored in sub-contractors' prices. Generally, however, such low-cost labour requires much expatriate supervision, the cost of which may be greater than the labour that is being supervised, so that the length of the construction period is still most important from the point of view of costs.

18.3 TYPES OF CONTRACT

18.3.1 Lump Sum Design, Supply and Construction

There can be no doubt that, given a competent contractor, it is to the employer's advantage to place a single lump sum contract for process plant design, supply and construction. Responsibility is placed clearly and unequivocally on the contractor. Interface and communications problems between design and construction are confined to the contractor's own organisation. Of course, such a contract would require a definitive basis at the time of the Enquiry. Whatever information the employer provided must be firm: not perhaps a great problem if the contractor or a third party licensor provides the technology, but becoming increasingly onerous the greater the employer's part in the project.

The contractor quoting for lump sum design, supply and construction bases his estimate of the cost of construction on far less detailed and definitive information than he would require if he were to quote for construction only. There are several reasons why he is prepared to do this. Construction will represent only about one-third of the total cost of the contract and his risk on it is therefore less in the context of the total contract. He will expect a bigger margin to cover the risk he does take. He is much more in control of what is to be provided, and the employer's influence is much reduced. Furthermore, and most importantly, it is unlikely that the contractor would quote in this way unless he had previous experience of the design and construction of similar plants. A lump sum design, supply and construction contract will therefore be possible only in particular circumstances.

In addition to the main contract for the process plant, large projects often call for subsidiary contracts. For some of these it may be appropriate for a contractor to take responsibility for design, supply and construction. A common example is the provision of a cooling tower.

18.3.2 Separate Construction Contracts

It is common for separate contracts to be placed for design and supply, and for construction. There are several reasons for this. There will generally be no great advantage to the employer in placing a single contract for design, supply and construction unless it is on lump sum terms, and as described above, this is achievable only in certain circumstances. For many projects, the early information available is sufficient to allow a lump sum contract for design (perhaps with reimbursable supply) to be placed, but not to allow detailed consideration of the contracting arrangements for construction. If separated from design and supply, the award of a contract for the whole of construction, or for construction management services, may be postponed for several months, at which time there would be a better basis for it. By placing separate contracts for early work—for site clearing and levelling, for piling—the employer can, if he wishes, postpone the award of the main construction contract still further. There may be reasons why the employer does not wish the design and supply contractor to manage the construction—the contractor may lack the necessary capability or resources, or the required experience in the country concerned, or the employer may wish to manage construction himself.

Where construction is to separated from design and supply, the options for the employer are as follows:

(1) *Single contract for the total construction.* In the UK, this would not be a common way of proceeding for a process plant, and such a contract would probably be a second one awarded to the design and supply contractor.

Only process plant contractors would have the necessary experience for the task and the contractor responsible for design and supply would have a marked advantage over others, so that it is difficult to envisage the contract being placed elsewhere. In some other countries, where local knowledge might outweigh the advantages of having carried out the design, and where there was more of a lump sum tradition and a less-developed sub-contracting industry, a single contract for the total construction would be more likely. In any event, since complete design information on which to base tenders would not be available, a different construction contractor could hardly contract on other than a re-measure and value, or a reimbursable basis.

(2) *Contract for construction management services*. The contractor would provide construction management services, probably on a lump sum basis, and would place 'sub-contracts' (these are actually direct contracts with the employer covering the work in individual disciplines, but are conventionally referred to as sub-contracts) as agent for the employer. This method of proceeding requires a developed sub-contracting industry. It is not a practicable method in countries where sub-contractors are mere suppliers of labour.

(3) *Employer provides construction management services*. This has been commonplace in the UK during the last few decades. If the employer has the necessary resources and experience, it has much to commend it, since it avoids the complication of bringing in another contractor, but again requires a developed sub-contracting industry. The employer places the 'sub-contracts' directly, and remains in full control of the site.

Whatever the contract arrangements, the use of separate contractors for design and for construction places a greater responsibility for the satisfactory completion of the project on the employer, since the cross-liabilities between design and construction fall to him. It is the employer, not the design contractor, who will be responsible to the construction contractors for the adequacy of design information and materials and who must manage the interfaces between the design and construction contractors. The design contractor, having no responsibility for construction, may be less concerned than he would otherwise be about the constructability of the plant. He will produce his design in a way convenient for his design office. The employer's project manager must ensure that any consequent deficiencies are made good. He must ensure that there is an adequate construction input into the design— either from the construction contractors or from his own construction engineers. He must make sure that the design provided is adequate for efficient construction and may perhaps require more, or differently organised, information to be produced, possibly at extra cost. The employer must ensure that the construction contractors understand in detail the form in which the design information is to be produced, and arrange for them to spend time in the design contractor's offices if this is considered necessary. The design contractor must of course be obligated to provide the necessary information at the appropriate time to allow the employer to enquire for and place the necessary construction contracts. This information will include construction specifications; standard details; scopes and descriptions of work; quantities, either detailed bills or more approximate estimates; and programmes. The design contractor may also be required to provide design liaison on site. All of this must be covered by the appropriate provisions in the design contractor's contract.

Where multiple separate construction contracts are to be placed, the alternatives are fully reimbursable, re-measure and value, schedule of rates, or lump sum contracts.

Reimbursable contracts

Enough has been written earlier about reimbursable contracts to make it clear that they are often the last refuge of the ill-prepared and the disorganised. This form of contract can be used, however, not as the unfortunate consequences of inadequate preparation, but as a deliberate policy adopted in order to ensure that the contractor works exactly to the detailed instructions of the employer. This requires detailed management and supervision by the employer, recognising that the form of contract itself provides no discipline or incentive, either for the employer to define properly the basis of the contract, or for the contractor to execute it. The employer's workload will be greater than for a lump sum contract and much more of it will follow contract award. The contractor may be remunerated on the basis of a fixed management fee plus daywork rates or, less desirably, on daywork rates which include an element for the cost of management. A fixed management fee reduces the incentive for the contractor to expend as much effort as possible on the contract.

Of course, reimbursable contracts have their place where the job is desperately urgent, or is truly impossible to define. Such work is, however, much more often associated with existing operations than with major new capital investment.

Re-measure and value contracts

Again, much has been written earlier about this type of contract. The fundamental difference between it and a reimbursable contract is that in a re-measure and value contract the contractor is paid at quoted rates for his output—the materials and equipment that he installs on site; in a reimbursable contract he is paid the costs he incurs for his input—the resources he uses and materials he supplies. The re-measure and value contractor also accepts programme liabilities. He quotes 'preliminaries' for his fixed and time-related costs and unit rates for such items as cubic metres of concrete and metres of pipe erected: there is an initial bill of quantities but the work is re-measured as it is completed. In the UK, the quoted rates are finely detailed; in other countries, often much less so. One of the major features of the re-measure and value contract is its flexibility, at once a strength and a weakness. This flexibility is a necessity where the contractor has to perform work which, of its very nature, cannot be accurately defined in advance. The obvious example is work below ground. Such work apart, it is desirable (and presumably the way that this form of contract was originally intended to be used in the civil engineering industry) to complete the design, measure the drawings and produce a firm bill of quantities as a basis for the contract. Minor changes resulting from circumstances encountered during execution can then easily be dealt with by re-measurement.

In principle, the re-measure and value contract can deal with substantial change and variation, and its flexibility in this respect leads to it often being placed on less than adequate design information. Depending on how it is used, it may range from being almost a lump sum contract with pre-defined quantities that are departed from hardly at all, to something much nearer a schedule of rates contract. It is not, of course, merely cost which is affected if the quantities vary and changes are made, but time as well. The re-measure and value contractor is responsible for programme, and may incur liquidated damages if he is late. There are naturally provisions in the contract for the completion time to be varied if the quantities change, or if the employer causes delay. The flexibility of the contract is obtained at the expense of a considerable administrative burden on the Engineer. Where in this range, from near lump sum to approaching schedule of rates, a particular contract lies depends on the employer. The contract conditions will generally disadvantage the employer if change is extensive.

Schedule of rates contracts

Taking the flexibility of the re-measure and value contract to its extreme results in the schedule of rates contract, probably the most commonly used form. Like the re-measure and value contract, the contractor quotes 'preliminaries' and unit rates. However, less information is provided at the bid stage. There are no drawings or bills of quantities, the job being defined merely by the scope and description of works. The list of rates which the contractor has to price is longer, since everything that might be found to be required once the design is completed is included. The contractor has to take something of a gamble on which rates are likely to be most important. Sometimes, an employer will price the schedules from his own experience and ask the bidders to specify any adjustments they would require.

Of course, if no quantities are given, the contractor cannot accept liquidated damages for delays to programme. In fact, his incentive is not to complete the work to programme and in the order required by the employer, but in the way which maximises his productivity.

Lump sum contracts

If the initial bill of quantities is firm, it is possible for the contractor to quote a lump sum price, together with unit rates for any changes or variations. This might be little different from a re-measure and value contract awarded in the same circumstances. Alternatively, and less desirably, changes and variations could be dealt with on a daywork basis, the contractor providing a schedule of daywork rates for this purpose in his bid.

It is not possible to place a contract for the whole of a process plant's construction against other than estimated quantities. The nature of the project, as has been discussed elsewhere, makes it impracticable to complete the whole of the design before construction starts. On the other hand, for 'sub-contracts' for individual disciplines, it is possible to take the design nearer to completion before contracts are placed and so get nearer to a lump sum. Further progress towards defining accurately the work to be undertaken in a contract can be made by splitting the work in each discipline into defined parcels and enquiring for and letting separate contracts for each. Clearly, this involves additional effort to let the contracts, and may increase the number of contractors on site and the risk of interference one with another. Properly managed, however, better initial definition will give better results.

18.4 SELECTION OF CONSTRUCTION CONTRACTORS

The general policy as regards the contracting of construction will be determined in the early stages of the project, before the design contracts are let. If a lump sum contract for design, supply and construction is to be placed, the question of construction will be addressed in the original Enquiry, to which the designated construction manager should have contributed. The employer's requirements for how the work should be organised on site and possibly sub-let should be specified, although his consideration of these matters may not be well developed, something he may later regret. Construction specifications should have been defined. The employer may wish to impose conditions, for example, that the work be done by the use of local sub-contractors rather than by the direct hire of labour by the main contractor, on working hours and on the co-ordination of terms and conditions of employment used by sub-contractors. On an existing site, the main contractor will need to be informed of the site rules and regulations and any special conditions that must be complied with. The construction manager designate should be responsible for assessing the construction experience and capability of the bidders.

In a single contract for design supply and construction, the employer involvement in the detail will obviously be at a minimum. Where construction is to be contractually separate from design and supply, enquiries must be issued to potential contractors for each contract which is to be let. Some of what has been written in previous chapters on contractor selection will apply. The construction enquiries will be based on information from the design contractor and from the employer. The responsibility for assembling and issuing the enquiries may, of course, be given to the design contractor or may be retained by the employer. They will typically include the following:

(1) *Scope of works.* Details of the scope of works for each of the contracts to be placed will be produced by the design contractor, in accordance with his contract. If the construction contracts are not to be awarded on the basis of detailed drawings and measured bills of quantities, it is crucially important that estimated quantities are reasonably accurate. On them is decided the number of contracts to be placed to deal with the work in each discipline and the identity of the bidders on the short lists. For the bidders, the scope and description of work is an important element of their tender basis including, most importantly, their management proposals. Unfortunately, it is common for the scope of works to be grossly underestimated. Contractors may then be appointed who are incapable of managing a job of the actual size they will be eventually called upon to do. Even if the contractor is capable, recognition that the extent of the work is much greater than expected may dawn slowly, and the contractor's management organisation never augmented adequately to come to terms with it. Consequently, the employer's project manager would do well to check the design contractor's estimates of scopes of work, especially against any other similar projects of which he has knowledge.

Following completion tests, and prior to the introduction of feedstocks into the plant, the commissioning team will require considerable pre-commissioning work, primarily the blowing, flushing, cleaning and drying of all pipelines and equipment. It can be an advantage as regards flexibility of labour if this work is made part of the mechanical erection contract, on a daywork basis.

(2) *Drawings and bills of quantities.* If a lump sum, or something approximating to it, is required, the enquiry must include the detailed drawings. It is possible to issue these in two stages—the major part with the

initial enquiry and the remainder a short while before tenders are due for submission. Measured bills of quantities may be included in the enquiry, or these may be left for the contractor to develop. The first course saves time and effort in total, and goes further to ensure a common bid basis.

If the design on which bills of quantities may be based is not available, the alternatives are the reimbursable and the schedule of rates contracts. In the latter case, it will be necessary to list the unit operations which are expected to be required, for the contractor to quote his unit prices.

(3) *Programme.* The required programme of the work must be specified. For a lump sum or a re-measure and value contract, the contractor will usually be made liable for failure to meet the agreed programme.

(4) *Construction specifications.* These will be produced by the design contractor but the employer will probably have some input, either directly or by including his construction specifications in his original Enquiry on the design contractor. They will include all reference drawings and standard details.

(5) *Site rules and regulations.* If the plant is to be built on an existing site, the employer will have rules and regulations which apply and with which he will require the contractors to comply.

(6) *Safety.* Especially if the plant is to be built on an existing site, the employer will have safety standards and rules that apply. The bidders will need to be informed of any known process hazards, statutory requirements, special working conditions. and emergency procedures. The bidders will be asked to provide information on their safety policies, procedures and records, and to include in their bids their proposals for ensuring the safety of their operations, probably in the form of method statements. Responsibility for the provision of first aid, medical and ambulance facilities must be clarified: on an existing site the employer may provide these.

(7) *Labour agreements.* There may be site, or national agreements, which control payments to the workforce. The employer will probably wish to ensure co-ordination of the terms and conditions of employment of all the workforce on the project, and possibly with others elsewhere on the site, and may have requirements regarding schemes for performance-related pay.

(8) *Conditions of contract.* The proposed conditions of contract must be included in the enquiries.

In assessing the bids, experience and demonstrated capability will be a major factor. Process plant construction is unusually complicated and experience in other fields is of limited value: erecting the steelwork for a football stand does not adequately prepare a contractor for the much greater complication and more restricted access of a process plant. The contractor's management capability, in general and as manifested in the staff he proposes for the contract, is of supreme importance. The contractor's existing workload must be examined and judged against his resources. The bidders' organisations and procedures, including their systems of dealing with materials should be examined. Bidders' safety policies, procedures and records will be scrutinised. If the contract is of the re-measure and value type, there will be no contract price, but the tender total will be calculated by applying the unit rates quoted to the quantities specified in the enquiry. It would be undesirable to accept, without further work, the tender totals as representing the relative costs of the bids. A view of how the quantities might vary should be taken and the tender totals re-calculated to assess the effects of this. The bids should also be examined to see whether the tender totals are especially sensitive to a few particular rates and what consequences might follow.

18.5 CONSTRUCTION PRODUCTIVITY

The attention paid by the employer's project manager to the subject of construction productivity is usually too little, too late. Since in the UK, the cost of process plant construction is about one-third of the total project cost, and the majority of this is for labour, it is clear that productivity on site is very important. It is also clear that a productive site will be an efficient one. This is not a subject to be left entirely to the construction manager to deal with, or worse, individual sub-contractors, since some of the most important pre-conditions for a productive site must be established before work starts. Some of the key features are as follows:

(1) *Availability of design information and materials.* This has been discussed above under the headings of orderly design and construction, but is of such prime importance that no apologies are offered for referring to it again. Only if there is an adequate supply of information and materials, and a low level of change, can construction management plan and organise the work properly. If these conditions are not met, the productivity of the workforce will be affected, not only by interruptions caused by lack of materials and information, and by the time spent ripping out and repeating work, but also by the demoralising perception of management as incompetent and disorganised. In contrast, the impact of a well-managed site must surely be one of the most important of all motivating factors for the workforce. And as previously remarked, there is also little doubt that the way work starts on a particular contract or sub-contract tends to set a pattern for the remainder of it. Recovery from a poor start is difficult: a good start sets standards which can be maintained.

It is also important that construction understand the ways in which the design information is presented. The construction manager should have been consulted on this score during the design process. If not entirely satisfied, he may have secured changes, or at least had notice of the need to make good any deficiencies on site.

(2) *Storage and retrieval of bulk materials on site.* This is a matter of some importance on a major project and has already been referred to in previous discussion of off-site piping fabrication. Much working time can be lost searching for material and efficient storage arrangements will pay dividends: for example, piping erection materials could be pre-sorted and bagged for each pipeline. Material control is one of many areas where close attention to interface problems between design and construction—for example, the former may control materials by requisition, the latter by order—is indicated.

(3) *Access and working conditions.* Some employers let a scaffolding contract directly and provide temporary access as free issue to sub-contractors. This is done primarily on safety grounds, to make sure that the provision of proper access is not skimped in order to economise, but also to help productivity. It will need to be carefully managed, since only the employer will have an interest in the efficient use of scaffolding and its removal when no longer required. Working conditions have an important influence on productivity and experience suggests that the provision of the best conditions that are reasonably practicable influences behaviour generally, beyond the immediate application. For example, the site could be paved before steelwork erection starts (this will require the connections of steelwork to foundations to be above grade, and hence must be considered at the design stage). Temporary weather protection should be provided wherever reasonably practicable—structures sheeted in, movable canopies provided.

(4) *Productive time.* A relatively low proportion of the time of construction workers is spent actually on construction work and there is great scope for improvement by increasing this. Both the topics mentioned immediately above—storage and retrieval of materials, and access and working conditions, bear on this question. Layout of the site, organisation of the work and the supply of design information and materials are obviously important.

(5) *Overtime.* Many UK sites routinely work overtime, but except where there is some special factor, such as the remoteness of the site, this is to be deprecated. Regular overtime usually results in the same amount of work being distributed over the longer hours. Occasional overtime may be worth while, but if progress must be generally accelerated, other approaches, such as double day-shift working, will be more fruitful.

(6) *Training and communications.* Site induction and safety training are essential. Good communications are important in developing a sense of participation and many different forms have been developed, ranging from

problem-solving teams and quality circles to site newspapers and open days.

(7) *Performance-related pay.* This can provide valuable incentive provided the scheme is carefully designed to take account of the variability of the construction environment and the difficulty of measuring performance. Group bonus schemes would seem generally to be preferred, preferably with independent auditing.

18.6 SAFETY

Construction is a dangerous business. In the UK, the Fatal Accident Rate in the construction industry is over 60, so it is about fifteen times more dangerous to work on the construction of a plant than on its operation. Strenuous efforts have been and are being made to improve the situation but it is obvious that construction is inherently more dangerous than routine work in a settled situation. Of course, construction safety is legally the responsibility of the contractors and sub-contractors who employ the construction workers. On a greenfield site, it might be appropriate to give the main contractor complete control of the site, so that the employer had no responsibility for it, but on an existing site the employer would almost certainly retain some responsibilities that bore on safety—to provide safe access, perhaps, or to provide training in specific site-related matters. Either way, in most cases employers would accept some moral responsibility for the safety of the construction workers on their sites. They would certainly take all reasonable steps to appoint contractors with good safety records and procedures and to monitor their performance.

As a general rule, the construction contractor is responsible for the safety of construction, for the methods used and for the design of any temporary works required. The plant designer is responsible only for the safety of the plant after it has been completed and is not obligated to consider the safety of the construction process in his design. Occasionally, the method of construction is a key feature of the design, and the designer would then design the temporary works and be responsible for their safety. But however the contracts may split responsibility between design and construction, the employer has an overall interest and will endeavour to ensure that safety and ease of construction receive due consideration in the design. A major part of his efforts in this direction will be the reviews, with the design contractor, pertaining to construction access, constructability, and the heavy lift programme.

As described above, assessment of safety policy and record will form part of the process of selection of potential construction contractors. The employer's Enquiry may specify construction methods which are considered to provide safer working conditions, such as the use of large mobile cranes. Construction tenders will be required to include method statements, especially for hazardous work, and details of safety personnel and procedures. On an existing site the contractor will be required to adhere to the employer's Works Rules and various guides and specifications on construction safety topics. The employer should also provide induction training for the contractor's employees covering any aspects of safety specific to the particular site. Safety will be a permanent agenda item at monthly progress meetings, and safety incentive schemes may be appropriate.

In the UK, safety procedures and working practices are established which, if they have not yet produced the desired levels of safety performance, are resulting in steady improvement. The position will be much less satisfactory in the case of an unindustrialised country, where construction poses safety problems quite different from those facing plant operation. The latter offers a structured and controlled environment, where less depends on the attitude of the individual. Plant operators are long-term permanent employees of the employer and may be trained, and their attitudes conditioned, over a long period. In much less controlled conditions, construction safety depends crucially on the attitude of individuals. These may hold life cheaply by Western standards and many may be completely unskilled, having never seen industry before, much less process plant construction. Far from being long-term employees of the employer, many will be transient employees of a sub-sub-contractor. Working methods may be primitive, less safe than their modern equivalents, but socially desirable in order to maximise employment. Only the most rudimentary training may be possible. To insist on UK construction safety standards in such circumstances might be to deny much of the local population employment on the project, would cause inordinate delay in completion and significantly increase costs. It would certainly make investment in the country concerned less attractive and possibly lead to it being reduced. In such circumstances, the best approach to construction safety would probably be to improve working practices and carry out training to the extent that is reasonably practicable, aiming for a significant improvement over local standards.

18.7 TAKEOVER

It is usual for commissioning to be carried out under the supervision of the owner of the technology: the contractor, a third party licensor, or the employer himself. If the employer is responsible for commissioning, then this may be managed by the receiving works, rather than by the employer's project manager. In any case, the bulk of the staff concerned in the commissioning will be provided by the employer, and will be composed of experienced operating staff who must work closely with design, construction and the works, and many of them will go on to operate and maintain the plant on a permanent basis. As discussed in Chapter 17 on design, the first members of the commissioning team to be appointed will be the works representatives on the employer's project team. The assembly and necessary training of the rest of the team will need to commence some months before the first part of the completed plant is to be handed over. Plant operating instructions and emergency procedures must be produced. At the same time the commissioning plan must be developed to dovetail with that of construction, fleshing out the bare outlines that were included in the project programme at the sanction stage.

The construction management will be concerned to agree the timing of takeover and the required condition of the plant at that time. Both the size of the commissioning task and its nature require that it be carried out in a phased way: it is not practicable to start up everything at once even if resources permitted. The possibility of overlapping construction and commissioning therefore arises, and this is commonly done. However, the way in which the construction of a process plant is most efficiently organised does not match the requirements of a phased commissioning programme. Construction is usually and most conveniently organised by geographical area. Completion and handover by geographical sections may be entirely suitable for some civil engineering works, and may also be appropriate for some of the off-plot parts of a process plant which can be completed and handed over separately: associated plants such as water treatment and steam raising, facilities such as amenities, stores, workshops, and perhaps storage. The main process plant, however, cannot usually be started up by geographical section: it must be commissioned by systems. Each such system: utilities such as water, steam, cooling water, and the various different process streams, must be commissioned in total or something approaching it. There will be some tens of systems on a major process plant and they will cut across most, if not all, of the geographical construction areas.

The consequence is that, at an appropriate, fairly late stage, there must be a shift from construction by area to completion of outstanding work by systems. This introduces inefficiencies into the construction process which, if the change is timed correctly, will cost less in time and money than the savings that are achieved in commissioning. Clearly, the timing of this change is one that requires close and expert attention if the best result is to be achieved, and the optimum will vary from one project to another. The nature of the plant will affect matters. The more closely integrated it is, both physically and from the process point of view, the smaller the scope for phased commissioning. Safety is a prime determinant of how far construction and commissioning can be overlapped. Systems which are commissioned and made live will run through areas where construction is still proceeding. These will be mainly services such as water, steam, compressed air and electricity: hazardous chemicals would certainly not be introduced at this stage. High safety standards, and rigorous clearance and permit to work procedures will be required. Both construction and commissioning labour forces will need to be experienced, well trained and disciplined. Where this is not the case, the extent of overlap must be reduced accordingly. It would be prudent, for example, to avoid much overlap between the construction and commissioning of a greenfield plant in a developing country, where the construction staff lack experience and perforce most of the operating staff are newly recruited.

The takeover of a major process plant from construction to the commissioning team is a complicated business. The work that follows erection—cleaning, inspection, testing and generally confirming that the plant is in a fit state to start up—is extensive. If not properly managed there can be a good deal of duplication of effort by the construction and commissioning teams. It is therefore important that both should be clear about what is required and who is responsible. Proper budgeting and allocation of costs is also desirable. The various responsibilities might be defined as follows:

- *Construction*
  - *Erection*: complete to design and specification. Defects rectified, cleaning, flushing and pressure testing completed. Construction equipment, rubbish and debris removed.
  - *Conditioning*: including air and steam blowing of lines, leak tests, any further water flushing required, service tests and acid washing. Oil changed in gear boxes, motors run to confirm direction of rotation. Instruments loop checked and calibrated, checked.
  - *Takeover*.
- *Commissioning*
  - *Pre-commissioning*: including water trials, trials of rotating equipment.
  - *Commissioning*: chemicals introduced into the plant.

Although the conditioning work is the responsibility of construction, the definition of what needs to be done and the final standards of acceptance would be laid down by the commissioning team, who must monitor what is done. The nature of the conditioning work is such that an individual trade sub-contractor is unlikely to agree to its inclusion in the programme for which he accepts liability. His liability would be for mechanical completion, conditioning being done reimbursably on daywork to the direction of the main construction management.

A lump sum design, supply and construction contractor would be responsible for all this work. Where construction is separated from design and supply, care is needed to define the exact limits of responsibility, especially where liquidated damages for delay are provided for. Mechanical completion and takeover by the commissioning team may be separate stages separated by the conditioning stage. In a re-measure and value, or a schedule of rates, contract conditioning would usually be done by the mechanical erection sub-contractor on daywork, provision for which should have been included in the contract.

18.8 MODIFICATIONS

Once the plant begins to take shape on the ground it will attract the attention of operating staff and requests for modifications will be made. In the early stages of construction, the employer's project manager's main concern will be to refuse these on grounds of their disruptive effect and consequent increased cost and time. He will argue that the project team contains representatives of the production function who have agreed the design and will maintain that changes will be admitted only if they are needed to make the plant safe or operable. He will not be unduly concerned that a modification will render the plant unsafe. At this stage, with the design still in progress, any modification that is allowed will go through the normal design procedure and will be subject to the full panoply of technical and safety checks.

In the later stages of construction, and during pre-commissioning and commissioning, the situation will change. The commissioning team will not have the skill and resources to design and implement modifications themselves and, unless strict control is exerted, safety may be compromised. Examples abound of seemingly harmless modifications causing major problems: a valve inserted to isolate two sections of a plant temporarily so as to facilitate start-up; a temporary start-up filter being inserted on the wrong side of a pressure trip. Short cuts may seem desirable in the hectic circumstances of pre-commissioning and commissioning, so much so that modifications probably represent the greatest potential source of hazard. At no time—during design, construction, commissioning or subsequent operation—should any modification to the plant be made without being subject to the full design treatment. A strict system for the approval of all modifications that affect the process, however trivial, is required.

Index